The Poisoning of the American Mind

The Poisoning of the American Mind

Edited by
Lawrence M. Eppard,
Jacob L. Mackey,
& Lee Jussim

GEORGE
MASON
UNIVERSITY.

George Mason
University Press

George Mason University Press
Fairfax, Virginia

Copyright © 2024 by George Mason University Press

ISBN: 978-1-942695-39-4

Cover & book design by Hannah W. McLaughlin

Cover image adapted from "Man Reading Newspaper" by Danya Gutan from pexels.com

First edition.
Library of Congress Cataloging-in-Publication
Data forthcoming.

Printed in the United States of America

For our children. We tried.

Acknowledgements

Thank you to our wonderful significant others, families, friends, and colleagues for the substantial amount of support and feedback that you gave to us as we prepared this book—it is deeply appreciated. We would also like to thank all of those people of all political stripes committed to consistently speaking the truth even when it is difficult to do so—our society cannot heal without you, and we have been profoundly inspired by so many of you. And thank you to all of those organizations and institutions that helped us bring this book to fruition, including George Mason University Press, The Connors Institute, Shippensburg University, *The Bulwark*, *Skeptic Magazine*, *The Conversation*, the Heterodox Academy, NewsGuard, Ad Fontes Media, the *Journal of Controversial Ideas*, *Issues in Science and Technology*, Free Black Thought, *Unsafe Science*, the Australian Academy of Science, *Harper's Magazine*, *National Affairs*, *Arc Digital*, and *The Lorem Ipsum*.

CONTENTS

PART III: PROBLEMS IN LEFT-WING SILOS

PART IV: I DON'T KNOW—THEREFORE, ALIENS

PART V: PARTING THOUGHTS

OVERVIEW

CHAPTER 1
Golden Age of Information[1]

By Lawrence M. Eppard

These are dangerous times. Never have so many people had so much access to so much knowledge and yet have been so resistant to learn anything. In the United States and other developed nations, otherwise intelligent people denigrate intellectual achievement and reject the advice of experts. Not only do increasing numbers of laypeople lack basic knowledge, they reject fundamental rules of evidence and refuse to learn how to make a logical argument. In doing so, they risk throwing away centuries of accumulated knowledge and undermining the practices and habits that allow us to develop new knowledge.

—Tom Nichols, author of *The Death of Expertise*[2]

Someday, historians will look back at this moment and tell one of two stories: The first is a story of how democracy and reason prevailed. The second is a story of how minds grew fevered and blood was spilled in the twilight of a great experiment that did not have to end the way it did.

—Adrienne LaFrance, executive editor of *The Atlantic*[3]

In the 20th century, America built the most capable knowledge-producing institutions in human history. In the past decade, they got stupider en masse.

—Jonathan Haidt, coauthor of
The Coddling of the American Mind[4]

False, partisan, and often deliberately misleading narratives now spread in digital wildfires, cascades of falsehood that move too fast for fact checkers to keep up. And even if they could, it no longer matters: a part of the public will never read or see fact-checking websites, and if they do they won't believe them.

—Anne Applebaum, author of *Twilight of
Democracy*[5]

The most obvious explanation for American political life since the end of the Cold War is that we have become an unserious country populated by an unserious people.

—Jonathan V. Last, editor of *The Bulwark*[6]

The unbundling of truth makes the business of democracy ever more difficult to conduct. As we fly ever farther apart, we can only hear each other when we scream.

—Martin Gurri, author of *The Revolt of the Public*[7]

With the rise of radio, television, and now the Internet, it sometimes seems that anyone can have their opinion heard, quoted, and repeated, whether it is true or false, sensible or ridiculous, fair-minded or malicious. The Internet has created an information hall of mirrors, where any claim, no matter how preposterous, can be multiplied indefinitely. And on the Internet, disinformation never dies. 'Electronic barbarism' one commentator has called it—an environment that is all sail and no anchor. Pluralism run amok. . . [M]any of the important issues of our day are reduced to he said/she said/ who knows? Any person could be forgiven for being confused. This cacophony of conflicting claims is particularly unhelpful when it comes to sorting out matters related to science, because science depends on evidence, and not all positions are equally grounded in it.

—Naomi Oreskes and Erik M. Conway,
authors of *Merchants of Doubt*[8]

In the U.S. today, both liberals and conservatives are regularly bombarded with misleading information as well as flat lies by people they believe to be trustworthy and authoritative sources of information. As a result, we are faced with an epistemic crisis that is poisoning American culture. As Brookings Institution senior fellow Jonathan Rauch argues: "[T]his is the first time we have seen a national-level *epistemic* attack: a systematic attack, emanating from the very highest reaches of power, on our collective ability to distinguish truth from falsehood."[9] Unfortunately, I do not see an obvious way out of this mess.

As one example, even years after it took place, most Republicans believed the 2020 presidential election was stolen[10]—despite not only a lack of evidence[11] but also the fact that the author of this "Big Lie" (Donald Trump) telegraphed that he would make such a preposterous claim *before the election even took place.*[12]

As another example, this time from the left, one risks serious damage to their reputation[13] in some progressive circles by simply acknowledging biological differences between men and women[14] and the impact of those differences on people's lives.

Misleading information comes in a variety of forms, including ideology presented as fact, malinformation (true information used in a misleading manner), misinformation (false information), and disinformation (intentionally false information).[15]

While there are several factors one could plausibly blame for our current predicament and I do not pretend to know all of the causes, I believe that the sources of information that the right and left rely on—and how some of those sources have declined in quality over the last few decades—play a primary role.

We Live in a Golden Age of Information

I make a strong claim when I write that American culture is being poisoned, so I realize the whiplash this must cause the reader when I simultaneously argue that we live in a golden age of information. Let me explain.

Imagine for a moment that you were to travel in a time machine back a century or more into America's past. You greet somebody you encounter there and ask to be taken to their most impressive library. This person honors your request, and upon arrival he/she brags to you about the immense knowledge contained within the library's walls. You then retrieve your smartphone from your pocket (with a noticeable smirk on your face) and explain to your host that this small device in your hand gives you access to exponentially more information than their library could ever hope to. Your new acquaintance would be left speechless (if he/she believed you).[16]

You then hop back into your time machine, blast some Huey Lewis, and get up to 88 mph as fast as possible, leaving him/her bewildered as you disappear back to the future—all without kissing your mother!

It might seem odd to say this, but I nonetheless contend it is true: Americans have easier access to high-quality factual information, and more of it, than ever before.[17] As *The Atlantic's* David Frum quipped: "I was promised flying cars, and instead all I got was all the world's libraries in my pocket and the ability to videochat 24-hours a day for free with my grandchildren on the other side of the world."[18] This should in fact be a golden age of information.

The scale and quality of knowledge production that occurs in the modern world is a marvel and a historical breakthrough. As social psychologist Jonathan Haidt explains, our modern epistemic system is:

> a set of institutions for generating knowledge from the interactions of biased and cognitively flawed individuals. English law developed the adversarial system so that biased advocates could present both sides of a case to an impartial jury. Newspapers full of lies evolved into professional journalistic enterprises, with norms that required seeking out multiple sides of a story, followed by editorial review, followed by fact-checking. Universities evolved from cloistered medieval institutions into research powerhouses, creating a structure in which scholars put forth evidence-backed claims with the knowledge that other scholars around the world would be motivated to gain prestige by finding contrary evidence. Part of America's greatness in the 20th century came from having developed the most capable, vibrant, and productive network of knowledge-producing institutions in all of human history, linking together the world's best universities, private companies that turned scientific advances into life-changing consumer products, and government agencies that supported scientific research and led the collaboration that put people on the moon.[19]

Jonathan Rauch has written extensively about our modern epistemic system. In this system, he notes that there are a variety of important rules[20] that have led to its success, including:

- Any hypothesis can be floated.
- A proposition qualifies as knowledge only if the larger epistemic community agrees that it has withstood vigorous questioning and criticism: "You can believe and say whatever you want. But if your beliefs don't check out, or if you don't submit them for checking, you can't expect anyone else to publish, care about, or even notice what you think."[21]
- Validated propositions are provisional—they qualify as knowledge only until they are debunked.
- The epistemic system is defined by its values and practices, not by its borders. It includes all evidence-based professions that require competing hypotheses to be tested and justified and that hold each other accountable for errors.
- There is no authoritarian oversight—the epistemic system relies on a decentralized,[22] non-coercive process that forces participants to convince each other with evidence and argument.[23]

Regarding the "truth" that this system produces, Rauch argues:

> In everyday vernacular, *reality* often refers to the world out there: things as they really are, independent of human perception and error. Reality also often describes those things that we feel certain about, things that we believe no amount of wishful thinking could change. . . [Objective reality] is a set of *propositions*: propositions that have been validated in some way, and have thereby been shown to be at least conditionally true—true, that is, unless debunked.[24]

This epistemic system includes many intelligent and hardworking people working across interconnected and often overlapping fields, including journalists, scientists, researchers, scholars, government workers, judges, lawyers, and social/political commentators, among others. The "body of validated propositions"[25] this community collectively produces is greater than the knowledge any one contributor could personally possess or understand. Participants work in places like news organizations, universities, government agencies, courts, law offices, think tanks, nonprofits, and corporations.

Within these organizations, there are a variety of important built-in guardrails and quality controls:

> The distinguishing characteristic of journalism is professional editing, and its institutional home is the newsroom, which curates and checks stories, trains reporters, organizes complex investigations, inculcates professional ethics, and more. The distinguishing characteristic of academic research is professional review: a sophisticated, multilayered project distributed among university faculties,

journals, credentialing organizations, scholarly conferences, and so on. Modern jurisprudence, policy development, and intelligence collection would be unthinkable without institutions like the courts, law schools, and think tanks, as well as agencies like the Congressional Budget Office, Bureau of Labor Statistics, Central Intelligence Agency, and many others—all staffed and run by elaborately trained people who exchange detailed knowledge across specialized channels, using protocols developed over decades and centuries. To be an accomplished scholar or journalist requires years of training and acculturation, which only institutions can provide.[26]

As cognitive scientists Steven Sloman and Philip Fernbach explain in *The Knowledge Illusion*,[27] human beings live within a community of knowledge. The entirety of human knowledge exists in the larger community, with only a tiny fraction contained within individual people's minds. Most of us do not know much about how even basic everyday things like toilets or zippers truly work,[28] despite how vitally important they are in the modern world. But does this lack of knowledge about myriad aspects of our daily lives hold us back? Not necessarily. In fact, it can be seen as an advantage:

> A modern society cannot function without a social division of labor and a reliance on experts, professionals, and intellectuals. . . No one is an expert in everything. No matter what our aspirations, we are bound by the reality of time and the undeniable limits of our talent. We prosper because we specialize, and because we develop both formal and informal mechanisms and practices that allow us to trust each other in those specializations.[29]

If each of us had to master everything we rely upon in order to function, it would be necessary for our world to be extremely limited and technologically basic. We are able to excel in the modern world not because of our incredibly complex understanding of it, but because of the *community's* collective understanding of it and our reliance on the expertise of others within that community to sustain it.[30]

Our ever-evolving and ever-improving understanding of reality is produced by "error-seeking inquirers"[31] working within an impressive structured epistemic system of institutions, resources, rules, values, and norms involving "impersonal critical exchange to seek truth and hold each other accountable for accuracy":[32]

> Although the network is a human creation and all its participants are people, it far exceeds the comprehension of its creators, and it undergoes a version of natural selection, driven by its own dynam-

ics. The reality-based network behaves like an ecosystem, producing a body of validated propositions whose composition humans can influence but not control. That is objective reality, insofar as we can know reality. The totality of those propositions is as close as we come to objective truth.[33]

Members of this system have agreed to a social compact[34] assuring they "follow certain rules and forgo certain claims because other group members will do the same."[35]

The "error seeking" part of this is key. In a court of law, you are innocent until proven guilty. But in our epistemic system, it is useful to think about claims as being wrong (or at the very least, their veracity unknown) until shown to have significant empirical support. This is the only way it can be. The reverse—that all claims are true until proven false—would be epistemic chaos, as philosopher Guy Elgat points out in discussing whether we are all just brains in vats in some *Matrix*-style dystopia:

> Should we then suspend our judgment and neither affirm nor deny the belief that we are brains in vats? Is it the most that we can hope for? It is easy to see that this way madness lies, for then we will also have to suspend judgment over an infinite number of equal or worse absurdities. We would thus have to admit that we can't really say whether unicorns are real or not, whether there is or there is not a troupe of invisible leprechauns dancing the hora behind our backs, or whether or not we are professional assassins whose incriminating memories are erased by our employers, the undetectable aliens from planet Xanadu. This would be utter epistemological bankruptcy.[36]

As Elgat argues, this would be epistemic anarchy: to assume a claim is true until proven false is to assume *all* possible alternative claims are true until proven false. The opposite is the only way the epistemic system can work: the veracity of claims is unknown until significant empirical support is demonstrated.

All knowledge claims must be (a) testable and falsifiable,[37] (b) offered up for rigorous critique by the larger community, and (c) able to withstand attempts at falsification in perpetuity:

> For Popper, science proceeds by means of what he calls 'conjectures and refutations.' Scientists are confronted with some question and offer a possible answer. . . Popper says scientists then do their best to refute this conjecture or prove it wrong. Typically, it is refuted, rejected, and replaced by a better one. This too will then be tested, and eventually replaced by an even better one. In this way science

progresses. . . For Popper, at the core of the scientific method is the attempt to refute or disprove theories, which is called the 'falsification principle.' If scientists have not been able to refute a theory over a long period of time, despite their best efforts, then in Popper's terminology the theory has been 'corroborated.' This suggests a possible answer to the question of why we ought to trust what scientists tell us. It is because, despite their best efforts, they have not been able to disprove the idea they are telling us is true.[38]

And as geophysicist Dorian Abbot and his colleagues write:

> [R]ealitybased scientific communities must be open to conceding and correcting errors. The ability of science to selfcorrect—one reason that scientific truth claims are uniquely credible—can be epistemically contrasted with conformity to religious and political dogmas, which are disturbingly closed to selfcorrection. Selfcorrection is facilitated by pluralism to maintain intellectual diversity and maximize the chances of uncovering provisional truths. Intellectual diversity ensures vigorous skeptical vetting of scientific claims by a critical mass of doubters who ultimately accept being bound by objective truths once they have been rigorously determined by extensive evidence.[39]

Within the epistemic system, there are countless people with countless points of view and interests who are busy at work every day attempting to disprove the ideas that are published in academic journals, newspapers, and other major outlets of information:

> What makes science so powerful is that it's intensely self-critical. In order for a hypothesis to pass muster and enter a textbook, it must survive a battery of tests designed specifically to show that it could be wrong. If it passes, it has cleared a high bar.[40]

Ideas are constantly tested against new pieces of evidence and our collective assumptions are adjusted according to how these challenges play out. As Mercatus Center visiting research fellow Martin Gurri notes, "We can never know with certainty that any proposition is right. We can only try to show that so far, it hasn't been proven wrong."[41]

Participants in the epistemic system have voluntarily plugged themselves into a decentralized yet organized network of (largely professional, trained/credentialed, experienced, specialized, and expert)[42] colleagues with diverse viewpoints[43] who read the work of others and then build upon it using acceptable, rigorous, and reproduceable methods. Participants share their methods and results with, and justify their interpretations of their findings to, the larger epistemic community so that it may critically evaluate their work. Findings are checked against existing information and alternative explanations in an objective and dispassionate manner[44]—while many participants are decidedly *not* objective and dispassionate, these are attributes of the *system as a whole* (when it is working properly) despite the failings of individuals within it. Outside evaluators act as devil's advocates who attempt to find shortcomings in the findings. System incentives tend to operate in such a manner that competing researchers or journalists are promised career gains when they show that a prevailing claim is wrong and that *their* work is actually more accurate. Others will try to replicate findings which challenge major pre-existing understandings—bias may crop up in one person's work, but subjecting the findings to scrutiny by several other qualified people with varying viewpoints and interests (who are incentivized to prove the claims wrong) should reduce the impact of any one individual's biases on the overall process:

> One way to look at science is as a system that corrects for people's natural inclinations. In a well-run laboratory, there's no room for myside bias; the results have to be reproducible in other laboratories, by researchers who have no motive to confirm them. And this, it could be argued, is why the system has proved so successful. At any given moment, a field may be dominated by squabbles, but, in the end, the methodology prevails. Science moves forward.[45]

As Greg Lukianoff and Jonathan Haidt explain:

> Each scholar suffers from confirmation bias—the tendency to search vigorously for evidence that confirms what one already believes. One of the most brilliant features of universities is that, when they are working properly, they are communities of scholars who cancel out one another's confirmation biases. Even if professors often cannot see the flaws in their own arguments, other professors and students do them the favor of finding such flaws. The community of scholars then judges which ideas survive the debate. We can call this process *institutionalized disconfirmation*. The institution (the academy as a whole, or a discipline, such as political science) guarantees that every statement offered as a research finding—and certainly every peer-reviewed article—has survived a process of challenge and vetting. That is no guarantee that it is true, but it *is* a reason to think that the statement is likely to be more reliable than alternative statements made by partisan think tanks, corporate marketers, or your opinionated uncle. It is only because of institutionalized disconfirmation that universities and groups of scholars can claim some authority to be arbiters of factual questions.[46]

Defining reality is not an endpoint but a constant process—propositions, tests, findings, challenges and critiques from the community, refined propositions and better testing in response to critiques, and on and on for eternity.

In the epistemic system, truth and reality are produced socially and collectively. The goal is to continuously stimulate as many new propositions as possible and then submit them to rigorous and systematic criticism in order to attempt to disconfirm them—knowing that truly valuable propositions will withstand even the most rigorous scrutiny.[47] Members aim to mistrust their senses, avoid certitude, and skeptically interrogate sacred values and beliefs (including those of the groups to which they belong). This is an open, public, and "social process of continuously comparing notes and spotting errors and proposing solutions."[48] Members should define what they know, and just as importantly, what they do not know.[49] Within this community, evaluation/disagreement/criticism/correction are expected and necessary.[50] Any proposition may be wrong and participants should expect intense scrutiny of their work, the point of which is to help identify both strengths as well as errors. While all people (including even the best researchers) have biases, the collective production of knowledge by a global community of scholars helps keep much of it in check. Strengths and errors identified in people's work provide lessons that are integrated into the existing literature, a body of knowledge that is now larger, more accurate, and more helpful to the world:

> [A] hypothesis passes through one screen after another: testing, editing, peer review, conference presentation, publication, and then—for the lucky few ideas deemed important—citation or replication. . . [A]fter a process which can take years or even decades, a kind of social valve admits the surviving propositions into the canon of knowledge by granting them prestige and recognition, indicated with designations like 'generally accepted' or 'well confirmed.'[51]

There are multiple layers of quality control and accountability,[52] from standardized credentialing processes, to internalized professional ethics which guide one's work, to peer review, to the expectation of transparency regarding one's methods (and increasingly their data, too), to dissemination of one's work to the larger community of experts for critiques and attempted replication, to sanctions by professional associations for misconduct, to name a few.[53]

In the epistemic system, authority rests not with individual people[54] but with propositions that the larger community has validated:

> It is not acceptable for a scholar to say, 'You have shown me convincing evidence that my claim is wrong, but I still *feel* that my claim is right, so I'm sticking with it.' When scholars cannot rebut or reconcile disconfirming evidence, they must drop their claims or else lose

the respect of their colleagues. As scholars challenge one another within a community that shares norms of evidence and argumentation and that holds one another accountable for good reasoning, claims get refined, theories gain nuance, and our understanding of truth advances.[55]

Even dominant propositions are always assumed to be imperfect, provisional, and tentative—the weight of the empirical evidence at any given moment can change in the future as new evidence emerges.

The network of knowledge-producing institutions within our modern epistemic system is something to behold, unimaginable to our ancestors. The advances taking place each year in areas such as science, technology, and medicine are enormous. And there are more high-quality news and information outlets than ever before. People from different historical eras would be awestruck to find out that we have so many high-quality sources of information available to us *at all times in our pockets.*

Of course, our epistemic system regularly gets things wrong. Mistakes are frequently made. Peer review will sometimes fail. Journals will sometimes publish work that is not at all rigorous. News outlets get stories wrong. Findings that cannot be reproduced are sometimes accepted as settled fact for decades. Many participants fail to meet high standards on a regular basis. Some frequently violate established norms. There are members who are very bad at their jobs and use flawed methods. Some let their biases pollute their work or their evaluation of others' work. Some participants commit outright fraud. Others kill important lines of inquiry for unethical reasons. Some will intentionally mask their partisanship or self-interest in order to engineer outcomes that they favor. Many make claims far greater than the empirical evidence warrants—and some make claims diametrically opposed to the best available evidence. Some attack researchers whose findings make them uncomfortable.

All of these things are true, yet on the whole, the modern epistemic system eventually self-corrects and gets it right at a far greater rate than any alternative way of knowing. Whatever mistakes are being made at the current moment, one can be assured that we are closer to "the truth" and "reality" now than we were 50 years ago (and they were closer than those 50 years before them and so on). Our understanding of reality at any given moment is always imperfect, always provisional, and always tentative. It can and will change in the future as more information becomes available. We keep working, always inching closer and closer to the truth, year after year after year.

The modern epistemic system, with its "open-ended, depersonalized checking by an error seeking social network," is "the only legitimate validator of knowledge":

Other communities, of course, can do all kinds of other things. But

THE POISONING OF THE AMERICAN MIND

they cannot make social decisions about objective reality. . . [This assertion] goes down very badly with lots of people and communities who feel ignored or oppressed by the Constitution of Knowledge: creationists, Christian Scientists, homeopaths, astrologists, flat-earthers, anti-vaxxers, birthers, 9/11 truthers, postmodern professors, political partisans, QAnon followers, and adherents of any number of other belief systems and religions. It also sits uncomfortably with the populist and dogmatic tempers of our time.[56]

The system's logic and structure ensure that, even though mistakes are made, the larger system will eventually identify, correct, and learn from these mistakes:

The advantage of the reality-based community is not that it catches every error immediately, but that it catches most errors eventually, and many errors very quickly. No other regime can make that claim, or come anywhere close.[57]

The modern epistemic system's track record is unmatched by any other way of knowing.[58]

CHAPTER 2
Epistemic Crisis[1]

By Lawrence M. Eppard

If what I say is true and the modern epistemic system is so great, then what's the problem? The problem is not with the system overall, but certain segments of that system which are currently malfunctioning. Despite the fact that the vast majority of the system is working just fine, the malfunctioning portions (such as some partisan media outlets on the right and some academic disciplines on the left) are exposing Americans to far too much misleading information.

Despite the unprecedented amount of high-quality information provided by our epistemic system in recent decades, major changes in both (a) how people access information (such as the rise of cable news, the internet, smart phones, and social media) and (b) the standards of evidence in some academic fields (such as the social sciences, where dubious claims have been gaining too much traction in recent years) have led to an explosion in bad information, too. We have plenty of good sources of information to choose from—the problem is separating them from the nonsense.

Concerning the astonishing amount of information being produced by our modern epistemic system, Jonathan Rauch writes:

> [B]y organizing millions of minds to tackle billions of problems, the epistemic constitution disseminates knowledge at a staggering rate. Every day, probably before breakfast, it adds more to the canon of knowledge than was accumulated in the 200,000 years of human history prior to Galileo's time.[2]

In fact, a 2003 study from researchers at the University of California, Berkeley found that more information was being produced in a single year in the early 2000s than *the cumulative total of all preceding human history*.³ If all of that information was reliable, or if people only stuck to the high-quality sources, there would be nothing to worry about. Unfortunately, far too many people are getting information from sources—such as partisan outlets (cable news, several internet websites) and some irresponsible academic fields (psychology, sociology, and others)—with questionable credibility and far too much bias. Despite enjoying easier access to more high-quality information than any other point in history, we also have easy (and often easier) access to more low-quality information than ever before: "A smartphone with social media apps is like a portable Thunderdome of argument. There are no teachers or editors, no gatekeepers or referees, no one to rule out lies, insults, illogical reasoning, or threats."⁴ Tom Nichols, commenting on the wild west of information that we find ourselves in, joked that: "Imagine what the 1920s would have sounded like if every crank in every small town had his own radio station."⁵

Adrift in this vast ocean of both good and bad information, many people have a difficult time identifying what is reliable and what is not, and millions have become hopelessly addicted to misinformation and disinformation that makes them feel good because they agree with it.

Imagine sitting at a table in a restaurant one evening. On this night, you have decided that you would really like to eat a healthy meal (maybe you, like me, are perpetually trying to get into better shape!). Along comes your server with the plate of healthy food you ordered and places it on your table. At this point, 100% of the food in front of you is healthy. But before you can take a bite, another server brings three more plates to your table—but these three contain *unhealthy* food. Now only 25% of the food on the table is good for you.

Have these additional plates made your goal of a healthy meal less attainable? Not necessarily. It is only more difficult if (a) you are unable to identify which plate contains the healthy food and/or (b) you are unable to resist the temptation to eat off of the other three plates. This is a good metaphor for the current information landscape—there is an abundance of healthy food (factual information with limited bias), but the market has been glutted with junk food, too (such as misinformation and disinformation).

Numerous powerful actors and institutions bombard Americans with a fire hose of misleading information every day—information that appears credible, is delivered by seemingly trustworthy/credentialed sources, and is framed in such a way (it confirms people's prior assumptions, stokes their anger/fear/resentment/ etc.) that gets the consumer hooked and wanting more. Human brains have always been wired to look for information that makes them feel good—this is not new. What changed was the rise of partisan talk radio and cable news in the 1980s and 1990s, along with technological changes like the internet, social media, and smart phones in the 2000s, which have made it possible to disseminate information that (supposedly) confirms any worldview—regardless of how fringe or detached from reality—in a cost-effective manner. It was much harder (and much less profitable) to reach tens of millions of people with misinformation and disinformation in the 1990s. No more.[6]

In addition, ideologically charged and empirically questionable research is being done in some academic fields around a variety of topics (perhaps most prominently about issues related to gender and race) at the same time that there is a growing tendency across academic fields to inject those findings into the public discourse. That is, there is a growing tendency in these fields not just to publish findings in academic journals with prohibitively expensive paywalls where only others with narrow expertise will see them, but to amplify these claims in the public square through television/radio/podcast appearances, op-eds, TED talks, etc.

In our current moment, cognitive biases that human beings have always had have now been both (a) weaponized by malicious actors (who spread disinformation, malinformation, and ideology disguised as facts—think Fox News)[7] and (b) unleashed by irresponsible actors (spreading information they do not know is low-quality) in dangerous ways (think fad psychology).[8] This is contributing to people being able to find sources which bend their "reality" to match their beliefs (instead of adjusting their beliefs to match the evidence), millions of Americans losing faith in notions of facts and expertise, and far too many being either ignorant of or rejecting accepted methods of establishing facts. Some have lost faith in the notion of reality altogether:[9] "[W]hat seems new in the post-truth era is a challenge not just to the idea of *knowing* reality but to the existence of reality itself."[10] As political philosopher Hannah Arendt famously wrote, "The ideal subject of totalitarian rule is not the convinced Nazi or the convinced Communist, but people for whom the distinction between fact and fiction. . . and the distinction between true and false. . . no longer exist."[11] There are valuable tools that can help in the battle against all of this, but many Americans are either unaware of them, unskilled in using them, or unwilling to use them.

My main thesis boils down to this: (a) our hard-wired cognitive biases make us dumber the more we surround ourselves with low-quality sources of information and (b) Americans are increasingly surrounding themselves with low-quality information sources, such as partisan media (cable news, some internet websites) and dubious information from some academic fields.

All human brains have hard-wired cognitive biases—biases which act like a monster who has an insatiable appetite for information that it agrees with (regardless of the information's veracity) and an intense hatred of information that makes it uncomfortable (even if that information is true). This monster can be constrained, but far too many of us don't know how to, don't care enough to, and/or don't want to, and instead we find ways to let the monster loose to do significant damage to our perception of reality.

Our Biased Brains

The human brain is not wired to do a very good job of identifying reliable news and information sources. This is true irrespective of political orientation, so it is not unique to Democrats or Republicans. Our hard-wired cognitive biases ensure that what we hope to be true about the world shapes our perceptions of what actually is true.[12] While this is a flaw in all human brains, we can in fact guard against this by surrounding ourselves with high-quality information. When we fail to do so and instead surround ourselves with questionable information, we become vulnerable to believing a lot of nonsense.

Humans are motivated to look for information that confirms their existing beliefs, avoid information that does not, and to interpret information to make it consistent with what they already believe. We look for information that makes us feel good about ourselves (makes us feel decent, intelligent, competent, informed, and so on) and sheds a positive light on the groups to which we belong:

> Too often, we assume that better information will improve the character of a democracy, despite the abundant evidence that the most educated and literate generations in American history are now less civic-minded than their under-educated progenitors. The problems of maturity and selfishness, however, are far more daunting for modern liberal democracies. In an age of cheap and abundant information, it is relatively easy to be a better-informed citizen. But the commitment to become such a citizen requires changes in even small habits that many people are unwilling to make, including reading a reputable newspaper and turning off the gladiatorial propaganda of social media, video postings, and cable shows. If making such changes means feeling less good about ourselves, or even thinking less often about ourselves, many of us will simply refuse to do it.[13]

When our beliefs and reality are misaligned, one would think we would change our beliefs to match reality—but instead we often try to bend reality to fit our preexisting views. We are more likely to believe information from people we trust and reject information from those we do not. We also have a hard time imagining that those we disagree with are operating in good faith.

Humans want their own beliefs, attitudes, and behaviors to be in harmony, and prefer for them to be in harmony with those of people around them. Indeed, we often just channel the people around us without thinking through issues ourselves. As Jonathan Rauch explains: "What matters most from an evolutionary perspective is not that a person forms beliefs which are true; it is that she forms beliefs which lead to social success." He goes on:

> We have hundreds of thousands of years of practice at believing what-

ever will keep us in good standing with our tribe, even if that requires denying, discounting, rationalizing, misperceiving, and ignoring the evidence in front of our nose.[14]

Humans try to avoid information that might destabilize their view of the world and/or threaten their core beliefs, identities, and deeply held opinions—after all, who wants to believe something that shatters their view of themselves, their deeply-held convictions, those they care about, and/or their way of life? As social psychologist David Dunning explains:

> Some of our most stubborn misbeliefs arise not from primitive child-like intuitions or careless category errors, but from the very values and philosophies that define *who we are* as individuals. Each of us possesses certain foundational beliefs—narratives about the self, ideas about the social order—that essentially cannot be violated: To contradict them would call into question our very self-worth. As such, these views demand fealty from other opinions. And any information that we glean from the world is amended, distorted, diminished, or forgotten in order to make sure that these sacrosanct beliefs remain whole and unharmed.[15]

He later went on:

> The most difficult misconceptions to dispel, of course, are those that reflect sacrosanct beliefs. And the truth is that often these notions can't be changed. Calling a sacrosanct belief into question calls the entire self into question, and people will actively defend views they hold dear.[16]

We want to be seen as smart and want to avoid threats to our status, reputation, self-image, or ego. When uncomfortable/disconfirming information makes it to us anyway, we tend to interpret it in a way that is as favorable to our sense of self as possible. As Jonathan Haidt notes, "When the facts conflict with. . . sacred values, almost everyone finds a way to stick with their values and reject the evidence."[17] And as Jonathan Rauch explains, "The more passionately we feel about something, the more likely it is that our reasoning is warped and unreliable," and "Often we think we are most rational and feel we can be most certain when we are in fact most mistaken and most deceived."[18] Additionally, he notes that: "When facts collide with beliefs which implicate our prestige or define our identity. . . the facts tend to bend."[19]

Human beings have several cognitive tendencies that can negatively influence how we seek and interpret information—here are some of the most frequently cited:

- **Availability heuristic:** A tendency to allow our judgement to be influenced by things that are readily available in our memory.
- **Dunning-Kruger effect:** A tendency for people with limited knowledge of a particular area to overestimate what they know in that area, because in order to possess accurate self-awareness of one's knowledge in a particular domain, one needs to have a baseline knowledge of that domain.[20]
- **Epistemic tribalism:** The tendency to evaluate information based not on conformity to common standards of evidence but to be consistent with our community's evaluation.
- **Equality bias:** The tendency for people, when making decisions together, to weight each participant's opinion equally, regardless of differences in each opinion's reliability, and even when this strategy leads to a suboptimal decision.
- **Familiarity/repetition bias:** A tendency to believe things which we hear often.
- **Fluency bias:** A tendency to believe statements which are easy to understand and assimilate.
- **Illusion of asymmetric insight:** The presumption that we understand others' thinking and motives better than they understand ours.
- **Illusion of explanatory depth:** The tendency to believe that one knows more than they actually do, especially about our modern, highly-complex world (ask yourself to explain in detail how a toilet or zipper works—this exercise makes me personally depressed at my lack of knowledge!).[21]
- **Motivated reasoning and confirmation bias:** A tendency to look for information that confirms one's existing beliefs, avoid information that does not, and to interpret information to make it consistent with what one already believes.
- **Perseverance bias:** A tendency to hold onto beliefs despite disconfirming evidence.
- **Source amnesia:** A tendency to misattribute where we learned information and how we know what we think we know.[22]

Jonathan Rauch notes that: "[B]ecause our biases evolved to guide us in some directions and away from others, they do not result in randomly distributed errors. Rather, the errors lead us down predictable pathways, again and again."[23]

Humans have always had these cognitive tendencies, so why are we so worried about them at this particular moment? Because aspects of our information ecosystem that used to constrain these hard-wired tendencies to some reasonable degree have been changed in ways that have unleashed them to be much more destructive.

America's Changing Information Ecosystem

Think back to the scene in the movie *Jurassic Park* where the tyrannosaurus rex escapes its enclosure, devours Donald Gennaro (the character of the lawyer representing the park's investors, played by Martin Ferrero), and nearly kills the other four patrons. Just minutes earlier, when the security systems were operating properly, everybody was safe despite the extraordinarily dangerous dinosaur lurking just a few feet away. Things went from perfectly safe to life-threatening when Dennis Nedry (Newman!) deactivated several park security systems so that he could steal dinosaur embryos. Had Nedry not done this, everybody could have enjoyed their time at the park (and the movie would have been much shorter and much less thrilling). The possibility of being eaten by dinosaurs would have still been a reality throughout their visit, but the risk would be very low as long as nothing about the security systems was changed.

Likewise, the cognitive tendencies discussed earlier are always present in our minds—whether or not they cause us harm is dependent upon the environments which surround us and whether these conditions unleash and amplify them or constrain them and lessen their impact.

When we only have a few sources of mostly high-quality information available to us, our cognitive biases are kept somewhat under control. This was the reality for me and my family when I was a child growing up in the Washington, D.C. area in the 1980s. A print edition of the *Washington Post* was delivered to our house early each morning and my parents watched a little bit of the evening network television news broadcast a few nights a week. My family did not listen to talk radio or watch the (very different) cable news that existed at the time, and it was not until I was much older that we had computers, smart phones, the internet, and social media. In the 1980s, my family and I were exposed to only a tiny fraction of the daily information that people today are exposed to, and a much higher percentage of it was reliable compared with today.

I had plenty of people I knew in the 1980s and early 1990s—whether they were family members or family friends—who believed things that were not true. But the massively different contours of the information ecosystem then compared with today's ensured that they would have a harder time having those ideas validated by others:

> I struggle to explain the scarcity of information [in the 1990s]. Nobody noticed what they couldn't yet imagine otherwise, as is the case with all historical change. . . Knowledge was different: Faced with an information problem, where could one shop for solutions? The library, or the bookstore, or the museum, or some other archive perhaps, but only if you already knew enough about the information you sought to know where to look.[24]

Finding ways to validate one's fringe beliefs was not impossible, but much harder. Which credentialed authorities would they turn to who would assure them that their beliefs were backed up by solid evidence? Where would they find a large community of people who agreed with them and could affirm their beliefs on a regular basis? Before the rise of cable news and the internet, this would have been much more difficult. So they kept much quieter about, and felt less confident in, their views than they would today. Today they can surround themselves with people who not only do not push back on what they espouse but actively validate and encourage their fringe beliefs. Today, they can find any number of (at least what they perceive to be) "credible" sources to validate their beliefs as facts. Today they can find many in-group communities on the internet, radio, and television to validate them and encourage them as well. Compared with the past, today they feel more confident in their version of reality.

Anybody who has seen a family member or friend radicalized by partisan media—as I have and I am sure many readers have as well—has seen how the changes in our information ecosystem have allowed our loves ones' cognitive tendencies, once constrained to a reasonable degree, to lead them down a dark path in recent years.

In our much larger and much more fragmented media landscape today, Americans face an unrelenting stream of information that spans the entire gamut from fact to disinformation—and millions have limited skills to help them (or have no desire to) differentiate the facts from the nonsense. This has unleashed our hardwired cognitive biases to do much more damage. As Ian Bogost writes: "Nowadays, too much information is on offer, most of it bad or wrong, and we spend our time either sifting for gold in the filth or mistaking the filth for gold."[25] Or as NewsGuard co-founder Steven Brill explains:

> Imagine you walked into a library, and there were a trillion pieces of paper flying around in the air, and you grabbed one, and you didn't know anything about it, or where it came from or who's financing it...That's the internet, that's your Facebook feed, that's your Google search.[26]

And as Martin Gurri notes, "When proof *for* and *against* approaches infinity, a cloud of suspicion about cherry-picking data will hang over every authoritative judgement."[27]

A variety of factors have deactivated the security systems that kept our cognitive biases somewhat at bay in earlier times. One factor of course is increasing polarization[28] and partisanship (including negative partisanship and affective polarization):

> The body politic is more fractious than at any time in recent mem-

ory. Over the past 25 years, both red and blue areas have become more deeply hued, with Democrats clustering in cities and suburbs and Republicans filling in rural areas and exurbs. In Congress, where the two caucuses once overlapped ideologically, the dividing aisle has turned into a chasm.[29]

As liberals and conservatives have moved further away from each other on the issues since the 1980s, they have less in common with each other and feel worse toward the other side: "If the people on the 'other side' are moving farther and farther away from you on a broad set of moral and political issues, it stands to reason that you would feel more and more negatively toward them."[3031]

Partisanship refers to people who see themselves as aligned *with* a political party, people who form their political opinions due to their agreement with and fondness for a particular group of people. Negative partisanship refers to people who see themselves as aligned *against* a political party, disfavoring particular people or points of view because they are associated with a group they dislike/hate.[32] As political scientists Alan Abramowitz and Steven Webster explain:

> The concept is pretty simple: Over the past few decades, American politics has become like a bitter sports rivalry, in which the parties hang together mainly out of sheer hatred of the other team, rather than a shared sense of purpose. Republicans might not love the president, but they absolutely loathe his Democratic adversaries. And it's also true of Democrats. . . Our research has shown that since the 1980s, supporters of both major parties, including independents who just lean toward one party or the other, have grown to dislike the opposing party and its elected leaders more than they like their own party and its elected leaders. . . Americans increasingly are voting against the opposing party more than they are voting for their own party. . . [P]artisans [have] come to see each other not just as political adversaries, but as enemies who want to harm the nation. . . [R]ather than seeking to inspire voters around a cohesive and forward-looking vision, politicians need only incite fear and anger toward the opposing party to win and maintain power. Until that fundamental incentive goes away, expect politics to get even uglier.[33]

Affective polarization refers to emotional hostility toward the other political party rather than non-hostile disagreement over issues.[34]

Other factors that have helped deactivate our cognitive security systems include the dawn of the internet,[35] a steep decrease in the cost of producing and disseminating information,[36] a decline in trust in (and often hostility toward) people and institutions which create and disseminate information,[37] the decline of traditional news outlets, the rise of partisan news outlets "detached from reality-based norms"[38] within a fragmented and siloed media ecosystem (including the rise of talk radio, cable news, and partisan websites),[39] growing outrage-/anger-/fear-driven partisan news reporting, the 24-hour news cycle,[40] the blending of entertainment and news (into "infotainment"), the advent of social media[41][42] (along with their algorithms[43] which often reward emotionally-charged content and are "sensitive to popularity but indifferent to truth"),[44] geographic sorting, and failures in academia (including increasing progressivism, questionable standards of evidence in some disciplines, and cancel culture) coupled with its increasing engagement with the public, among others.

While I am primarily concerned with the impact of changes to our media ecosystem and failures in academia, a number of other factors are important to consider as well,[45] including growing American affluence (and associated narcissism and entitlement),[46] civic disengagement, egalitarian/anti-authority cultural trends (nobody is smarter than me/should tell me what to do!),[47] illiteracy and anti-intellectualism, "emotional safetyism,"[48] political correctness, safe spaces and campus speech codes, DEI bureaucracies, the commodification of higher education, postmodern thought, credential inflation, increasing levels of educational attainment (and thus overestimation of one's knowledge), nostalgia, social resentment, demographic change, inequality, growing gender equality, changes to the economy, and the impact of an increasingly complex and globalized world.

The Comeback of Yellow Journalism

Partisan news is of course not new—in fact, misleading information has been disseminated since the invention of the printing press in the 15th century. Verified and objective news became the norm only during the 20th century. Jacob Soll notes that, "[A]s printing expanded, so flowed fake news, from spectacular stories of sea monsters and witches to claims that sinners were responsible for natural disasters."[49] Many people will likely remember learning in school about the incredibly low standards of journalism in 19th century America: "During the Gilded Age, yellow journalism flourished, using fake interviews, false experts and bogus stories to spark sympathy and rage as desired."[50] Such poor and unethical journalism caused a backlash and helped lead to the development of widespread use of objective and verifiable methods among news outlets in the U.S., and this became the dominant model in the 20th century. This was a tremendous accomplishment, and many trustworthy outlets still follow incredibly high standards—in fact, I believe we currently have access to more high-quality journalism than ever before. But changes in the media ecosystem have again flooded the market with partisan outlets spreading misleading information, and our society is paying the price. As Soll argues, "Digital news, you might say, has brought yellow journalism back to the fore."[51]

Since the late 1980s/early 1990s—with the rise of talk radio and cable news—and the 2000s—with the rise of the internet, smart phones, and social media—

there has been an explosion in low-quality news and information sources:

> Long ago is the time when everybody watched one of three national television networks. By the 1990s, there was a cable news channel for most points on the political spectrum, and by the early 2000s there was a website or discussion group for every conceivable interest group and grievance. By the 2010s, most Americans were using social media sites like Facebook and Twitter, which make it easy to encase oneself within an echo chamber. And then there's the 'filter bubble,' in which search engines and YouTube algorithms are designed to give you more of what you seem to be interested in, leading conservatives and progressives into disconnected moral matrices backed up by mutually contradictory informational worlds. Both the physical and the electronic isolation from people we disagree with allow the forces of confirmation bias, groupthink, and tribalism to push us still further apart.[52]

There are myriad questionable (and sometimes downright dangerous) news and information sources available to Americans, sources which will validate any and all beliefs, including (but not limited to):

- AlterNet
- The American Conservative
- American Greatness
- The American Spectator
- American Thinker
- The Blaze
- Breitbart
- Buzzfeed
- CNN
- Daily Mail
- Daily Wire
- Democracy Now!
- Drudge Report
- The Epoch Times
- The Federalist
- Fox News
- The Gateway Pundit
- Huffington Post
- InfoWars
- Jacobin
- Mother Jones
- MSNBC
- The Nation
- National Review
- New Republic
- New York Post
- Newsmax
- One America News Network (OAN)
- RedState
- Salon
- Slate
- ThinkProgress
- Townhall
- Truthout
- Vice
- Vox
- Washington Examiner
- Washington Times
- ZeroHedge

I will explain the rubric I used to produce this list later, but I can assure you that, to qualify for this list, an outlet must have clearly documented problems with accuracy and/or bias.

So while Americans have easier access to as many high-quality sources as probably ever before, many cannot (or don't care to or are unwilling to) distinguish the trustworthy ones (like the Associated Press and Reuters) from the ones in the list above and/or they've become addicted to the junk.

Many Americans consume news and information from untrustworthy outlets that pass themselves off as legitimate news sources. The Fox Corporation, for instance, insists that it "is uncompromisingly committed to being neutral arbiters of timely news, and we consider journalistic independence and editorial integrity to be sacrosanct," and that their "foremost principles are the accuracy of information, clarity of opinion and quality of our content."[53] A regular consumer of Fox News, however, will be exposed to outrageous lies and conspiracy theories:

> Fox News lies to its viewers. Its most prominent personalities, among the most influential in the industry, tell their viewers things they know not to be true. This is not accusation, allegation, or supposition. Today, we know it to be fact. . . With Fox News, examples of the network's commitment to knowingly misleading its viewers abound. . . In 2020, the network successfully beat a defamation lawsuit by arguing that Tucker Carlson is 'not 'stating actual facts' about the topics he discusses and is instead engaging in 'exaggeration' and 'non-literal commentary.'[54]

A true news organization, of course, would have no place for exaggerations, "non-literal commentary," lies, and conspiracy theories in its programming. Fox News is clearly not a legitimate news organization, despite its claims, having promoted wildly inaccurate information about climate change,[55] the "Great Replacement Theory,"[56] lies about "stolen" national elections,[57] and the ludicrous conspiracy theory that black helicopters are patrolling the U.S., "hunting" conservatives, "purging" them from society, and placing them in Guantanamo Bay.[58] These are just a few of the many examples of Fox promoting ideology presented as fact, misinformation, malinformation, and/or disinformation. As *The Bulwark's* Mona Charen writes, "Fox is not a news channel—it is the right's *Pravda*."[59] Yet millions of Americans consider Fox News a credible news organization and believe the untrustworthy information that it disseminates.

One of the most poisonous moments—of many—in the history of Fox News came in the aftermath of the 2020 election. The preponderance of evidence of course tells us that Joe Biden won the election, Donald Trump lost, and the number of election problems and irregularities was small, inconsequential to the result, and no worse than in previous elections.[60] But Trump claimed fraud anyway—a claim he had been laying the groundwork for among his supporters *before the election even took place*—and Fox News promoted this lie publicly on their airwaves despite knowing better privately:

> Top personalities, executives and producers at Fox News privately condemned 'reckless' claims from election fraud conspiracy theorists they dismissed as 'crazy' and 'insane.' But they were repeatedly invited on air on some of the most-watched cable news programs in the country, where they amplified bogus statements about the 2020 presidential election and a voting machine company.[61]

We know that people at Fox knew better behind the scenes based on a trove of emails, text messages, and depositions that emerged from Dominion Voting System's lawsuit against Fox News:

> The most compelling example of Fox News consciously lying to its viewers, however, arrived yesterday with the evidence in the defamation lawsuits filed by the voting-machine company Dominion, over claims aired on Fox News echoing Trump's lie that the 2020 election had been fixed by compromised voting machines. Dominion's latest filing argues that privately, Fox News hosts admitted that the allegations of election fraud being floated by Trump allies were baseless, but they kept airing them, in part because they feared that another right-wing network, Newsmax, was stealing their audience. The filing shows that when Fox News reporters shot down the allegations publicly, the network's big personalities were livid, complaining internally that telling their viewers the truth was hurting the network's brand. . . [I]nternally, the messages in Dominion's filing suggest that network officials knew they were exercising editorial judgment that would lead their audience to see the fictitious election-fraud allegations as not simply newsworthy, but legitimate, which they properly understood to be irresponsible.[62]

This trove included messages and testimony from Fox News hosts, producers, executives, and even Fox Corporation Chair Rupert Murdoch himself. Despite knowing the truth about the election, Fox News nonetheless helped Trump spread baseless lies in his attempt to overturn Biden's victory, which helped fuel the Capitol Insurrection of January 2021 and an even more divided and toxic American political culture that we are now burdened with.

Cable News and the Internet: A Fire Hose of Nonsense

Even the wackiest of ideas can find communities and "sources" that will "confirm" them on the internet, where an endless amount of both good and bad information exists side by side. As Lee McIntyre, author of *Post-Truth*,[63] explains:

> The cognitive bias has always been there. The internet was the ac-
> celerant which democratized all of the disinformation and misin-
> formation and diminished the experts. Democratization has led to
> the abandonment of standards for testing beliefs. It leads people to
> think they are just as good at reasoning about something as anybody
> else. But they're not. At the doctor's office, I don't ask for the data
> and reason through it myself and decide on the course of treatment.
> It takes expertise and experience to make that judgement. Just like I
> can't fly my own plane. There is a scene in *Indiana Jones and the Last
> Crusade* where he is in a room with all of these goblets and chalices
> and doesn't know which one is the Holy Grail. That's where we are
> right now. We have the truth right in front of us, but we don't know
> which one it is. There is a slogan that science deniers use, 'Do your
> own research.' If science is about facts, why can't I just go out and
> find my facts? But you need guidance to know what is factual, you
> need experts. Many Americans have an enormous misunderstand-
> ing about science generally. They misunderstand the term 'theory,'
> for instance, thinking that any theory is as good as any other, rather
> than realizing that some theories are more credible than others be-
> cause they are warranted by the evidence.[64]

Some of the best information in the world is on the internet—but so is some of
the most useless (such as the website Goop, which, among many other wild claims,
asserted you can cure depression by walking barefoot)[65] and downright dangerous
information (such as InfoWars, which, among many other deranged claims, alleged that the Sandy Hook school massacre was staged by "crisis actors")[66] as well.
As *The Death of Expertise* author Tom Nichols quipped, "The Internet lets a billion
flowers bloom, and most of them stink."[67] He went on:

> Some of the information on the Internet is wrong because of slop-
> piness, some of it is wrong because well-meaning people just don't
> know any better, and some of it is wrong because it was put there out
> of greed or even sheer malice. The medium itself, without comment
> or editorial intervention, displays it all with equal speed. The Inter-
> net is a vessel, not a referee.[68]

Without somebody and/or some level of personal knowledge to guide you, it is
easy to fall prey to misleading information in this overwhelming cacophony of
noise. Hyper-social beings with poor research skills—aka, most human beings—
are prime candidates to fall victim to the misguided opinions of people they like
who seem smart and are telling them exactly what they want to hear, and they are

especially susceptible when such information and the communities that share it are so plentiful on the world wide web.

There is a wonderful cartoon by Peter Steiner that has made the rounds on the internet for years. In the cartoon, a dog is sitting at a computer and turns to another dog and confides, "On the internet, nobody knows you're a dog." As the cartoon suggests, in real life it is much easier to pick up on whether somebody knows what they are talking about or not, to pick up on whether somebody is not to be trusted. But on the internet, misinformation/disinformation can be presented in beautiful font and perfect grammar with seemingly authoritative hyperlinked sources in an aesthetically pleasing web layout that looks no different than information presented by the Associated Press or Reuters. You need to either (a) know that the outlet is of low-quality and/or (b) already possess particular news literacy skills in order to tell the difference. If you don't, you might be following the advice of a dog (or worse). It is the wild west of information.

One of the more annoying sayings in the modern world is that you should "do your own research" on a controversial topic. The idea is that when we all have access to the internet, nobody can be lied to because all of the world's information is available to us online. There are numerous problems with this assertion. When the internet contains nearly 200 million active websites[69]—many of them aesthetically pleasing to the eye and seemingly authoritative despite containing faulty information—it takes some amount of knowledge to understand how to sift through the fire hose of information to determine what is factual and what is not.

Cable news is another place that will confirm extremely flawed ideas. To many viewers, cable news outlets appear to be legitimate news organizations that employ messengers who appear to be appropriately credentialed journalists. These channels then confirm the worldview of the viewer through the stories they choose to cover, the ones they avoid, and the ways in which they frame their stories. Viewers grow to trust these outlets since the information they present makes the viewer feel good and is presented to them by seemingly credentialed and knowledgeable sources who belong to the viewers' "tribe." But the journalistic standards of channels like Fox News, MSNBC, Newsmax, CNN, and One America News Network (OAN) are nowhere near the same as they are at places like the Associated Press and Reuters. Relying on cable news means taking in a lot of faulty information, and most of us do not have the time, knowledge, and/or desire to figure out what is true and what is not.

Commenting on the impact of cable news on our society, Ted Koppel wrote that:

> The commercial success of both Fox News and MSNBC is a source of nonpartisan sadness for me. While I can appreciate the financial logic of drowning television viewers in a flood of opinions designed to confirm their own biases, the trend is not good for the republic... Beginning, perhaps, from the reasonable perspective that absolute

objectivity is unattainable, Fox News and MSNBC no longer even attempt it. They show us the world not as it is, but as partisans (and loyal viewers) at either end of the political spectrum would like it to be. This is to journalism what Bernie Madoff was to investment: He told his customers what they wanted to hear, and by the time they learned the truth, their money was gone."[70]

Cable news takes advantage of the audience's motivated reasoning and confirmation bias. As Koppel told Fox News's Sean Hannity directly, "You have attracted people who are determined that ideology is more important than facts."[71]

Using social media, Americans spread the flawed information presented on cable news and partisan websites to their like-minded friends and family members, many of whom have already tailored their online social networks to contain a disproportionate number of people they agree with. When social media algorithms figure out the political orientation of these consumers, they then feed them more and more partisan information.

Yevgeny Simkin offers a valuable take on the rise of social media and its impact on American society:

> Let's take a short walk down memory lane. It's 1995. A man stands on a busy street corner yelling vaguely incoherent things at the passersby. He's holding a placard that says 'THE END IS NIGH. REPENT.' You come upon this guy while out getting the paper. How do you feel about him? You might feel some flavor of annoyance. Most people would also feel compassion for him as he is clearly suffering from something. No reasonable person would think of convincing this man that his point of view is incorrect. This isn't an opportunity for an engaging debate...Now fast forward to 2020. In terms of who this guy is and who you are absolutely nothing has changed. And yet here you are—arguing with him on Twitter or Facebook. And you, yourself, are being brought to the brink of insanity...Back in 2011 Chamath Palihapitiya left Facebook and said of his former company, 'It literally is a point now where I think we have created tools that are ripping apart the social fabric of how society works'... [Social media is] [a]n insidious malware slowly corrupting our society in ways that are extremely difficult to quantify, but the effects of which are evident all around us. Anti-vaxxers, anti-maskers, QAnon, cancel-culture, Alex Jones, flat-Earthers, racists, anti-racists, anti-anti-racists, and of course the Twitter stylings of our Dear Leader.[72]

Because of all of this—the internet and social media, the decline of traditional news outlets, the rise of partisan and siloed media, along with increased polarization—many Americans now have difficulty differentiating legitimate journalism from biased partisanship and are becoming addicted to low-quality information sources. They are exposed to a fire hose of information each day, some of it high quality but much of it misleading or just downright wrong. A large portion of the population either believes the faulty information or has lost faith in the notion of high-quality information altogether. Many Americans—exhausted, overwhelmed, and disoriented by the amount of misleading information and unsure how to judge fact from fiction—have resigned themselves to the belief that there are no objective facts and no sources of information can be trusted. This is not true, but people believe it nonetheless.

This is incredibly damaging to our society. Without some semblance of a shared reality, our society will be dysfunctional. We must find some meaningful and effective way to address this problem.

CHAPTER 3
Ideological Silos and Epistemic Secession[1]

By Lawrence M. Eppard

There is so much partisan information available on radio, television, and the internet, and it is made all the more damaging by the phenomenon of ideological silos—similar to what you might also have heard called "bubbles" or "echo chambers." Many Americans are increasingly locking themselves within ideological silos, meaning they are surrounding themselves with far too many like-minded people and partisan sources of information that leave them with an incomplete and flawed understanding of the world.[2] These silos are environments where people's beliefs and assumptions aren't sufficiently challenged because they are surrounded (in physical spaces, their social networks, and online) by people with similar beliefs and they get their information from partisan sources aligned with their worldview. This is of course a problem, because:

> The most reliable cure for confirmation bias is interaction with people who don't share your beliefs. They confront you with counterevidence and counterargument. John Stuart Mill said, 'He who knows only his own side of the case, knows little of that,' and he urged us to seek out conflicting views 'from persons who actually believe them.' People who think differently and are willing to speak up if they disagree with you make you smarter, almost as if they are extensions of your own brain.[3]

Let's explore ideological silos with two fictional characters. The first one we will call "Hannah." All of Hannah's friends are politically conservative, including those in her social media networks on Facebook and Twitter. The only news she watches is Fox News, and the only news stories her friends share with her are from conservative sources. Because of the people and information she has surrounded herself with, it would not be surprising for Hannah to have a very flawed understanding of the facts about climate change (perhaps she has been led to believe that it's wildly exaggerated or even a hoax). There just isn't enough factual information about this issue making its way to her, plenty of misleading or false information is always available, and everybody she knows (including those she loves and/or respects) seems to agree with her (and those who don't are people that Hannah distrusts and/or dislikes).

Likewise, let's explore the experiences of a fictional left-winger we will call "Bob." In Bob's left-wing silo, all of his friends and information sources are reliably progressive. When people ask Bob why he hates capitalism, he is able to immediately recite all of its shortcomings off the top of his head. But if he were asked to list its *strengths*, he would have a difficult time, not just because he has a negative view of it, but because he has never had to truly contend with the strongest arguments in favor of capitalism. Bob took several college courses critical of capitalism and was able to avoid any courses detailing its strengths. Nobody in his silo ever talks about (or is even aware of) capitalism's positive aspects, all of the sources he trusts have assured him that his negative view is accurate, and he's never seen any high-quality information detailing the strengths of this economic system.

This is what ideological silos can do to us—overwhelm us with information that is favorable to our side's beliefs, hide information that questions them, and provide us with constant ideological affirmation from people we love and respect.

Inside of ideological silos, partisan messages are repeated back to people constantly, while the silo prevents them from frequently confronting contradictory messages. Certain elements of these silos—such as algorithms used by YouTube and other social media platforms—make matters worse, learning people's biases, feeding them more and more misinformation and disinformation from a particular partisan perspective, and assuring they see less and less trustworthy information.[4]

People within these silos understand reality and truth to mean something different from people in bubbles that are ideologically different. They have different understandings of epistemic authorities, methods, and standards of evidence. When people from different silos talk to each other, it can seem like they inhabit different realities: "A group creates a consensual moral matrix as individuals interact with one another, and then they act in ways that may be unintelligible to outsiders."[5]

In some respects, our country is experiencing a full-blown "epistemic secession"[6] or even "epistemic cold war."[7] As Jonathan Haidt argues:

> The story of Babel is the best metaphor I have found for what happened to America in the 2010s, and for the fractured country we now inhabit. Something went terribly wrong, very suddenly. We are

disoriented, unable to speak the same language or recognize the same truth. We are cut off from one another and from the past. It's been clear for quite a while now that red America and blue America are becoming like two different countries claiming the same territory, with two different versions of the Constitution, economics, and American history. But Babel is not a story about tribalism; it's a story about the fragmentation of everything. It's about the shattering of all that had seemed solid, the scattering of people who had been a community. It's a metaphor for what is happening not only *between* red and blue, but within the left and within the right, as well as within universities, companies, professional associations, museums, and even families.[8]

This is incredibly socially corrosive, causing rifts between millions of Americans and even dividing families and damaging friendships.

We no longer have a single national conversation, but several conversations all happening at once in different silos, operating on different sets of "facts," and disconnected from each other in important ways. As *Twilight of Democracy* author Anne Applebaum explains:

> [T]he old newspapers and broadcasters created the possibility of a single national conversation. In many advanced democracies there is now no common debate, let alone a common narrative. People have always had different opinions. Now they have different facts. At the same time, in an information sphere without authorities—political, cultural, moral—and no trusted sources, there is no easy way to distinguish between conspiracy theories and true stories. False, partisan, and often deliberately misleading narratives now spread in digital wildfires, cascades of falsehood that move too fast for fact checkers to keep up. And even if they could, it no longer matters: a part of the public will never read or see fact-checking websites, and if they do they won't believe them.[9]

As Ben Sasse argues, "A republic will not work if we don't have shared facts." Former President Barack Obama similarly proclaimed that, "If we do not have the capacity to distinguish what's true from what's false. . . by definition our democracy doesn't work. We are entering into an epistemological crisis."[10] And as Jonathan Rauch argues, the rules of our reality-based epistemic system are "foundational to modern liberalism and instrumental to bringing the peace, prosperity, and freedom which liberal societies uniquely enjoy."[11]

Both the left-wing and right-wing ideological silos in the U.S. have their problems. I am not arguing that they are equally flawed, but I am also not arguing that one is worse than the other. It could certainly be the case that one is more

THE POISONING OF THE AMERICAN MIND

detached from reality, but I've yet to figure out how to reliably and objectively determine that. This may seem like a cop out, but I honestly do not know how to quantify which silo is causing more damage to our society. What I do know is that both rely on information of very questionable veracity, and both are contributing to our societal dysfunction. Regardless of which is "worse," they both have problems that must be fixed for the good of our country.

I will discuss some of the problems that exist within both silos, beginning with the right-wing.

Problems in Right-Wing Silos

While there are many problems in right-wing ideological silos, the most pressing seems to be too heavy a reliance among American conservatives on low-quality partisan sources of information like Fox News.

Fox News bills itself as a news organization, but it is hardly that, as its sole aim seems to have little to do with journalism. To repeat a Mona Charen quote, "Fox is not a news channel—it is the right's *Pravda*."[12] Instead of operating like a legitimate news organization, Fox focuses most of its efforts on promoting the Republican agenda and diminishing progressivism:

> The late conservative Roger Ailes (funded by conservative Rupert Murdoch) created Fox News, a channel that carried, and still carries, mostly talk radio-style right-wing commentary. Like talk radio, it is of the conservative movement, in a way that no mainstream media outlet would ever think of itself as of the left. . . Fox plopped down on cable and dared the mainstream media to say anything about it. It never saw itself as better mainstream media—it saw itself as a conservative competitor to a liberal incumbent. It started mainstreaming conservative talking points and conspiracies, quickly gained a huge (mostly white, mostly old) audience, and, through sheer chutzpah, was accepted as a legitimate news outlet. It's not that Fox News hasn't produced some good journalism and good journalists. It's that the ultimate axis around which the enterprise revolves is partisan. It is an instrument to advance the interests of the conservative movement.[13]

Fox cherry-picks stories that conservatives care about (especially ones that make them angry/scared/resentful), frames them in the most conservative-friendly manner possible, and either ignores stories that are uninteresting/unfavorable to conservatives or reports these stories but frames them in a partisan manner. A regular Fox News viewer will be overwhelmed with messages that make "others" look bad/dishonest/incompetent/dangerous/evil/un-American, along with stories that promote the Republican agenda. This is of course incredibly socially corrosive, as Mona Charen explains:

> All of us indulge the urge, at least sometimes, to hear news that con-
> firms our own views. What Fox's audience must grapple with is that
> choosing news is not like other consumer choices. It's not like choos-
> ing country music in preference to hip hop or preferring Android
> over iOS. Getting the truth from a news source is more analogous
> to getting the straight story from your doctor or financial adviser or
> home inspector. If your financial adviser told you what you wanted
> to hear rather than the truth, you'd have a legal case. He or she has a
> professional responsibility not to mislead you. If your doctor assured
> you that your skin lesion was benign because he thought this would
> be more welcome than the news that it was melanoma requiring
> immediate treatment, the doctor would be guilty of malpractice and
> you wouldn't thank him. When Fox News and its competitors lie
> to viewers, they are endangering not their physical health but their
> civic health and the good of the nation.[14]

The U.S. has been experiencing major changes in recent decades, including
globalization, demographic changes, shifting gender roles, and increasing progressivism in institutions and the culture at large—and many conservatives are react-
ing negatively to these developments:

> The United States is undergoing a transition perhaps no rich and
> stable democracy has ever experienced: Its historically dominant
> group is on its way to becoming a political minority—and its minori-
> ty groups are asserting their co-equal rights and interests. If there are
> precedents for such a transition, they lie here in the United States,
> where white Englishmen initially predominated, and the boundar-
> ies of the dominant group have been under negotiation ever since.
> Yet those precedents are hardly comforting. Many of these renego-
> tiations sparked political conflict or open violence, and few were as
> profound as the one now under way.[15]

As Tom Nichols writes:

> Cultural change is inevitable and sometimes invigorating, but it is
> also terrifying to those who feel themselves on the wrong side of it.
> One of the main drivers of authoritarian attacks on democracy is
> the sense among privileged groups that their grip on politics and
> the national culture is slipping away; the internet is their window on
> that process, distorted and amplified by clever entrepreneurs who
> know how to play on feelings of inferiority and fears of threats and

injuries, real or imagined.[16]

Nichols goes on to say that "When the citizens of a dominant culture come to believe that the end is near for their way of life, they search for scapegoats."[17]

The rise of partisan talk radio (with popular personalities like Rush Limbaugh), partisan cable news (such as Fox News, Newsmax, and OAN), and partisan websites (like the Drudge Report, Daily Wire, Gateway Pundit, Breitbart, and InfoWars) gave American conservatives a new, self-contained media ecosystem focused on their specific concerns, including the aforementioned societal changes—they subsequently fell in love with these new sources of information and became increasingly distrustful of traditional ones outside of their silo:

> Although each party's elites, activists and voters now depend on different sources of knowledge and selectively interpret the messages they receive, the source of this information polarization is the American conservative movement's decades-long battle against institutions that it has deemed irredeemably liberal.[18]

Unfortunately, many of these new outlets had much lower journalistic standards than traditional media of the past, and spread misleading information (ideology presented as fact, misinformation, disinformation, and malinformation) specifically designed to confirm the conservative agenda and stoke conservatives' uneasiness, fear, anger, and resentment around these issues. The right-wing media ecosystem became "an internally coherent, relatively insulated knowledge community, reinforcing the shared worldview of readers and shielding them from journalism that challenge[s] it."[19] This is driving conservatives further and further from reality: "[C]onservatives are pulled with increasing gravity into an information vortex that simply has no analogue elsewhere in American politics."[20] As David Roberts argues:

> The right hypes its base up with bullshit—it has for decades—until an already tribally inclined audience has now descended into near-total epistemic closure. It is contemptuous of outside fact-checking, no matter how assiduous, but endlessly gullible toward information shared on the inside. Consequently, it is an easy target.[21]

And as Harvard Law School's Yochai Benkler and his colleagues explain:

> What we find in our data is a network of mutually-reinforcing hyper-partisan sites that revive what Richard Hofstadter called 'the paranoid style in American politics,' combining decontextualized truths, repeated falsehoods, and leaps of logic to create a fundamentally misleading view of the world. . . By repetition, variation,

and circulation through many associated sites, the network of sites make their claims familiar to readers, and this fluency with the core narrative gives credence to the incredible.[22]

They go on: "It is a mistake to dismiss these stories as 'fake news'; their power stems from a potent mix of verifiable facts...familiar repeated falsehoods, paranoid logic, and consistent political orientation within a mutually-reinforcing network of like-minded sites."

Conservatives believe this information because it confirms their sacred beliefs,[23] makes them feel good, comes from people in their "tribe" who appear to be trustworthy (carrying credentials that *should* signify credibility), is oppositional to what liberals believe (Trigger the libs! Liberal tears!), portrays out-groups (such as Democrats) in a bad light, and is repeated many times by many different trusted sources within their ideological silo. When a trusted authority from your "team" crafts a convincing message specifically designed to confirm your preexisting beliefs while also activating your biggest fears and insecurities, your cognitive security systems are undermined and you become less skeptical of the message than you might normally be.

In right-wing ideological silos, you will hear many alarming things from news and information sources. It is not uncommon to hear unvarnished bigotry. You might hear that Western civilization is failing or that democracy is not all it is cracked up to be. You will hear that the other side is the enemy, a threat to you/your way of life/your family and children, as well as messages that dehumanize your opponents (such as the "groomer" rhetoric). You will also hear the outright rejection of objective truths, such as claims that climate change is not real (it is),[24] Donald Trump really won the 2020 presidential election (he didn't),[25] or immigrants are unusually violent (they aren't),[26] among other claims.

The extent to which many Republicans see their political opponents as an existential threat to civilization is alarming. The following are excerpts from Michael Anton's "The Flight 93 Election"[27] from the *Claremont Review of Books*, which received a lot of attention from the American right when it was published in September of 2016 (Rush Limbaugh even discussed it on his program):

> 2016 is the Flight 93 election: charge the cockpit or you die. You may die anyway. You—or the leader of your party—may make it into the cockpit and not know how to fly or land the plane. There are no guarantees. Except one: if you don't try, death is certain. To compound the metaphor: a Hillary Clinton presidency is Russian Roulette with a semi-auto. With Trump, at least you can spin the cylinder and take your chances.

The essay goes on to say that:

- If conservatives are right, America is "headed off a cliff."
- "[T]he opinion-making elements—the universities and the media above all—are wholly corrupt and wholly opposed to everything we want, and increasingly even to [conservatives'] existence."
- "[M]ost important, the ceaseless importation of Third World foreigners with no tradition of, taste for, or experience in liberty means that the electorate grows more left, more Democratic, less Republican, less republican, and less traditionally American with every cycle. As does, of course, the U.S. population. . . This is the core reason why the Left, the Democrats, and the bipartisan junta (categories distinct but very much overlapping) think they are on the cusp of a permanent victory that will forever obviate the need to pretend to respect democratic and constitutional niceties."
- "The Left and the Democrats seek ringers to form a permanent electoral majority."
- "This is insane. This is the mark of a party, a society, a country, a people, a civilization that wants to die."

Such ideas were espoused by other commentators as well. Eric Metaxas, a prominent evangelical author and talk radio host, argued in 2016 that the presidential election that year was an "existential struggle" for the U.S., and that a Clinton victory would indeed be the end of the republic itself.[28] Fox News personality Laura Ingraham has stated on her show that all of Western civilization is "tipping over the cliff."[29]

It is hard to know what politicians truly believe based upon what they say in public,[30] which makes leaked private correspondence, where they are presumably saying things much more closely aligned with what they truly believe, all the more interesting. Here is just a small sample from a batch of numerous text messages exchanged between then White House Chief of Staff Mark Meadows and Republican members of Congress in which they discuss attempts to overturn Joe Biden's legitimate victory in the 2020 presidential election:[31]

> Brian Babin (Republican House Member/TX): "Mark, When we lose Trump we lose our Republic. Fight like hell and find a way. We're with you down here in Texas and refuse to live under a corrupt Marxist dictatorship. Liberty!"

> —Sent November 6, 2020.

> Rick Allen (Republican House Member/GA): "Mark, please know that I have prayed for President Trump, his family, for you and the entire Administration. Our Nation is at war, it is a Spiritual War at the highest level. This is not a war that can be fought conventionally,

this is God's battle and He has used President Trump in a powerful way to expose the deceit, lies and hypocrisy of the enemy. The Trump family and all of us have paid a heavy price to be used by the Father but the War is just beginning. We have had a major set back and people are taking sides, and my plea to my fellow believers who want to cut and run is judge not less you be judged, we have all fallen short of the Glory of Almighty God. What I heard during my prayers is the Trump family and the Administration need to be surrounded by those great Pastors and Evangelicals who have and continue to love and support them. President Trump needs to be ministered to, he needs the love that only Jesus Christ offers! This is his opportunity to confess that he can no longer fight this battle alone, he must give it to Christ and God almighty will show him the way to victory. I will continue to pray for all of you, please let me know how I can help??"

—Sent January 8, 2021 (two days after the insurrection at the U.S. Capitol).

Ralph Norman (Republican House Member/SC): "Mark, in seeing what's happening so quickly, and reading about the Dominion law suits attempting to stop any meaningful investigation we are at a point of no return in saving our Republic !! Our LAST HOPE is invoking Marshall Law!! PLEASE URGE TO PRESIDENT TO DO SO!!"

—Sent January 17, 2021 (just three days before Joe Biden was to take office).[32]

Marjorie Taylor Greene (Republican House Member/GA): "In our private chat with only Members, several are saying the only way to save our Republic is for Trump to call for Marshall law. I don't know on those things. I just wanted you to tell him. They stole this election. We all know. They will destroy our country next."

—Sent January 17, 2021.

In another text, House Representative Mark Green (R-TN) argued that Republican state legislatures could simply "declare" Trump the winner of the presidential election—and his argument relied on a segment he had seen on Newsmax,[33] a far-right cable network and dangerous purveyor of misinformation/disinformation.[34]

Commenting on these texts, *The Bulwark's* Jonathan Last observed that, "What struck me is that they don't sound like elected officials. They sound like commenters on Breitbart."[35] These politicians are clearly victims of misinformation/disinformation. They are also clearly gripped by the widespread idea among conservatives that they are locked in an existential battle that, if they were to lose, would result in the end of their country forever. Commenting on the January 6, 2021 insurrection in December of 2022, Marjorie Taylor Green said, "I want to tell you something, if Steve Bannon and I had organized that, we would have won. Not to mention, we would've been armed."[36]

The fact that conservatives feel they are losing their grip on the country helps explain their weakening commitment to democracy and the growing appeal of authoritarianism for some. If you feel that you can no longer win a majority of the votes in a presidential election, you may turn to alternative means to stay in power and preserve your preferred way of life:

> [M]any conservatives, surveying demographic trends, have concluded that Teixeira wasn't wrong—merely premature. They can see the GOP's sinking fortunes among younger voters, and feel the culture turning against them, condemning them today for views that were commonplace only yesterday. They are losing faith that they can win elections in the future. With this come dark possibilities.[37]

Yoni Appelbaum goes on:

> [Trump's] defeat would likely only deepen the despair that fueled his rise, confirming his supporters' fear that the demographic tide has turned against them. That fear is the single greatest threat facing American democracy, the force that is already battering down precedents, leveling norms, and demolishing guardrails. When a group that has traditionally exercised power comes to believe that its eclipse is inevitable, and that the destruction of all it holds dear will follow, it will fight to preserve what it has—whatever the cost.[38]

I should note the influence of bad faith knowledge *producers* in right-wing silos, not just bad faith *disseminators* like Fox News. There is a long history of industry-backed researchers and partisan think tanks injecting misleading information into the public discourse in support of conservative priorities. Big Tobacco was perhaps most notorious, as David Michaels notes in *Doubt Is Their Product*:

> Without a doubt, Big Tobacco has manufactured more uncertainty over a longer period and more effectively than any other industry. The title of this book comes from a phrase unwisely committed to paper by a cigarette executive: 'Doubt is our product since it is the best means of competing with the 'body of fact' that exists in the minds of the general public. It is also the means of establishing a

controversy'…Whatever the story—global warming, sugar and obesity, secondhand smoke—scientists in what I call the 'product defense industry' prepare for the release of unfavorable studies even before the studies are published. Public relations experts feed these for-hire scientists contrarian sound bites that play well with reporters, who are mired in the trap of believing there must be two sides to every story. Maybe there are two sides—and maybe one has been bought and paid for."[39]

He goes on to note that: "[P]roduct defense consultants have shaped and skewed the scientific literature, manufactured and magnified scientific uncertainty, and influenced policy decisions to the advantage of polluters and the manufacturers of dangerous products."[40] Like Michaels, Erik Conway and Naomi Oreskes catalogue such industry tactics in their book, *Merchants of Doubt:*

For half a century the tobacco industry, the defenders of SDI, and the skeptics about acid rain, the ozone hole, and global warming strove to 'maintain the controversy' and 'keep the debate alive' by fostering claims that were contrary to the mainstream of scientific evidence and expert judgement. They promoted claims that had already been refuted in the scientific literature, and the media became complicit as they reported these claims as if they were a part of an ongoing scientific debate. Often the media did so without informing readers, viewers, and listeners that the 'experts' being quoted had links to the tobacco industry, were affiliated with ideologically motivated think tanks that received money from the tobacco industry (or in later years the fossil fuel industry), or were simply habitual contrarians.[41]

Industry-backed researchers and partisan think tanks have historically used a number of tactics to try to sway public opinion, including:

- Funding and then using front groups and third parties as public messengers (sometimes called "information laundering") so that the interests of those spreading partisan and/or misleading information aren't obvious (such as ExxonMobil funding the climate change denying Heartland Institute),
- Funding front groups and third parties to manufacture scientific debate by carrying out methodologically flawed studies designed to confirm a partisan conclusion,
- Flooding the public discourse with flawed but seemingly legitimate contrarian opinions to mischaracterize the weight of the scientific evidence,
- Demanding balance, even when an issue does not have two equally valid

arguments (as my colleague Lee McIntyre likes to say, the midpoint between the truth and a lie is still a lie),

- Exaggerating the level of uncertainty and controversy within the scientific community around particular issues,
- Impugning the motives of scientists and/or creating the impression that all science is biased and agenda-driven, thus eroding trust in *all* sources of information,
- Framing the implications of scientific findings in ways that violate core American values, align with other issues, and/or create false dichotomies (such as the idea that addressing climate change would require unacceptable regulation of our capitalist economy),
- Using colorful imagery to suggest that the solution to the problem is worse than the problem itself,
- Diminishing the severity of the problem,
- Attacking the messengers instead of the messages,
- Shifting blame (such as arguing that it's flammable furniture that is the problem in house fires, not cigarettes),
- Repeating flawed claims over and over and over again,
- Intimidating scientists,
- Investing in lobbyists and donating to politicians,
- Keeping the debate alive by any means necessary for as long as possible,
- Delaying action by any means for as long as possible.[42]

Problems in Left-Wing Silos

Like conservatives, liberals also frequent questionable sources of information, such as CNN and MSNBC. Compared with conservatives, however, liberals are more likely to include other higher-quality sources in their media diets as well (such as trustworthy newspapers or the network news).[43] So why do so many American liberals believe so many questionable things? There are many plausible contributing factors, but there is one in particular that I think deserves a lot of attention: the ideological capture of some segments of the American research community.

As I have argued, the size and quality of our epistemic system would be hard to imagine even just a few decades ago, with major advances in science, medicine, and technology happening with an astonishing frequency. The problem is not with the system as a whole—it remains impressive and unparalleled and should be allowed to continue to grow and better our world. The problem is that in *certain areas* of this epistemic system—perhaps most notably in the academic social sciences— some researchers and institutions have allowed their methods and analyses to be undermined by ideology. Addressing the failings of these bad actors so that they conform to the high standards of the rest of our epistemic system should be a top priority moving forward—because, as Jonathan Rauch argues, "[Academia] may well be the most important of the institutions that comprise the constitution of knowledge."[44]

Many liberals like to criticize conservatives for denying established evidence, and there is no doubt that many conservatives deny facts. A recent Gallup poll, for instance, found that while 92% of liberals and 76% of moderates believed that global warming was primarily caused by human activities—which is what the current weight of the scientific evidence suggests[45]—only 35% of conservatives agreed.[46] But there is plenty of evidence that liberals believe questionable things about a variety of issues as well—they are just different issues than the ones they criticize conservatives for.[47] Both groups, when discussing issues that are sacred to their side, will often bend reality to their beliefs.

I have personally witnessed numerous conservatives push back against criticism that they reject reality—like their refusal to acknowledge the legitimacy of the 2020 presidential election—by highlighting that liberals do the same thing on different issues. One of the most common retorts I hear relates to sex and gender. I've heard some version of this statement countless times: "Why should I believe what liberals say about [whatever issue is being debated] when they cannot even tell me what a woman is?" They argue that liberals' rejection of biological contributions to differences between men and women, and their advocacy for overly social constructionist explanations, is far from settled fact. Yet liberals often weaponize selective evidence in debates in order to claim it is settled objective truth (and label those who disagree as sexists or misogynists).

As an example, GLAAD recently tweeted the following: "A reminder that healthcare for transgender people is settled science."[48] This is demonstrably false, as there is significant controversy and scientific debate about gender identity as well as gender-affirming care (such as the use of puberty blockers and hormones). But liberals can find plenty of scholars who will affirm this statement and can thus weaponize ideology masquerading as settled science against their opponents.

None of this should be much of a surprise, as Jonathan Haidt explains: "On the left, including the academic left, the most sacred issues involve race and gender. So that's where you find the most direct and I'd say flagrant denial of evidence."[49]

On the left, academics, partisan media personalities, and activists are guilty of frequently spreading "virtuous lies"[50]—that is, many on the left make claims (that they insist are scientifically authoritative) that further a social justice agenda without realizing/acknowledging the preliminary, weak, or nonexistent empirical support behind their assertions. Many liberals who hear/read these claims will believe them because they see them repeated often by various credentialed sources who they trust, they assume the claims are backed by credible evidence, and they fit their worldview/make them feel good.

Additionally, for a liberal to oppose a virtuous lie would be to align oneself with "bad" people on the other side (supposed bigots, know-nothings, etc.). Occidental College's Jacob Mackey argues that to correct a virtuous lie is to oppose the noble goals of one's tribe and/or to signal that one does not take the problem seriously.

As Dorian Abbot and his colleagues argue, "[I]n the 'right' circles, one can make almost any ridiculous claim, as long as one frames it as advancing 'Social Justice.'"[51]

Many virtuous lies come from academia. Some of the research behind these flawed assertions is just the result of sloppiness (in research design and/or the interpretation of results), some the result of confirmation bias, and some the result of researchers intentionally designing and/or interpreting studies so that they reach a specific desired conclusion (and some a combination of these):

> In complex areas like the study of racial inequality, a fundamentalism has taken hold that discourages sound methodology and the use of reliable evidence about the roots of social problems. We are not talking about mere differences in interpretation of results, which are common. We are talking about mistakes so clear that they should cause research to be seriously questioned or even disregarded. A great deal of research. . . rigs its statistical methods in order to arrive at ideologically preferred conclusions.[52]

Michael Jindra and Arthur Sakamoto go on:

> [I]deologically driven abuse of statistics happens all across the social sciences. Why? In left-leaning academic discourse, there are strong biases toward 'structural' causes, in part because scholars face strong pressures to avoid 'blaming' people and cultures for social problems. But social theory must recognize both structure and agency, alongside intermediary forces of social influence such as culture. . . Again, we are not talking about normal differences in the interpretation of results. We are talking about clear errors, or at least very poor scholarship that should not have passed peer review. It is easy to question some of these results because they often don't make intuitive sense... Research simply shouldn't be directed by a priori ideological commitments. It should follow the evidence. Often, that evidence won't lead to clear-cut or definitive results. Some of these articles should be candidates for retraction, but retraction is rare...Some scholars even received major promotions, perhaps partly because their findings fit favored narratives. Instead, papers that violate ideological beliefs, more than those with errors of fact, receive pressure for cancellation, often from Twitter activists."

The authors note that in the social sciences, the entire system of research, funding, publication, and promotion strongly values findings that support current social justice goals. Because so many of the career rewards (and sanctions) are aligned with these goals, "people will go to extraordinary lengths to achieve them."

If virtuous lies were simply confined to academia, it would be worrisome enough. But as Dorian Abbot and his colleagues argue, these flawed claims have escaped the lab: "For decades, Critical Theories had been confined to humanities and Studies departments of universities. But the ideas have spread to other disciplines and the outside world, where they have been picked up by activists and the press."[53]

The left tells many virtuous lies, particularly about issues related to race and gender, including claims regarding the gender pay gap, gender identity, micro-aggressions, implicit bias, police shootings, and genetic fallacies, to name a few. While the larger epistemic system is working well, in some fields—like psychology and sociology—current social justice goals are blinding far too many researchers to (and scaring others from speaking up about) the flaws in many studies.

I suspect that part of the problem is that many social scientists are simply ill-equipped to identify flaws in major academic studies. In my own field of sociology, for instance, you can earn a Ph.D. and spend an entire career teaching and publishing in a tenured university position without ever developing even a rudimentary grasp of quantitative research methods. Many sociologists do so. At many universities across the U.S., sociology professors are presenting information to their students that they incorrectly assume is strongly supported by empirical evidence because, while the professors themselves may not understand the research behind the claims, *the authorities in their field have assured them it is sound.* This information passed peer review, was published by leading journals/book presses, was accepted by the larger field, made its way into textbooks, etc. Most sociology professors have not seen the empirical research behind much of the information they present in class, likely would not fully understand it if they did, and are unlikely to question it anyway because it aligns with current left-wing social justice assumptions.

I'm not picking on sociology—I assume a number of academic disciplines face this same problem—it's just that I can speak confidently about my own discipline because I have seen all of this firsthand.

Another possible (and likely even more important) culprit in all of this is a glaring lack of intellectual diversity within many academic fields and institutions. Liberal professors and researchers far outnumber conservative ones at American universities (where much of our knowledge is produced), an imbalance that has grown in recent decades.

The ratio of Democrats to Republicans in disciplines like math and chemistry has been reported to be around 5:1, while estimates are much higher in the social sciences and humanities.[54] In the field of psychology the ratio was estimated to be as low as 2:1 earlier in the 20th century but around 17:1 in recent years (and even worse at more prestigious universities and in New England).[55] In my own discipline of sociology, one estimate puts the ratio at 40:1.[56] The imbalance is likely worse at elite institutions, as Jonathan Rauch explains:

> A recent study of top-ranked liberal-arts colleges by the National Association of Scholars found that 39% had zero Republican professors, and that almost 80% of the academic departments had 'either

zero Republicans, or so few as to make no difference.'[57]

Increasing progressivism is no doubt limiting the quality of both the scholarship produced by academics as well as the education their students receive: some research questions get investigated and others are avoided, some methods utilized and others ignored, information gets interpreted in biased ways, and some legitimate viewpoints are marginalized while others are amplified:

> [W]hen the majority of scientists in a discipline share the same sacred values, then the checks and balances of peer review and peer skepticism that science relies upon can fail. Peer review, critical engagement, skepticism, and the other virtues of science...become tyrants that promote and protect the sacred values of the scientific community.[58]

This leads to a left-biased understanding of many issues, especially in places like the social sciences: "[S]tudents in politically homogenous departments will mostly be exposed to books and research studies drawn from the left half of the range, so they are likely to come down to the 'left' of the truth, on average."[59] Greg Lukianoff and Jonathan Haidt go on to note that: "[V]iewpoint diversity is necessary for the development of critical thinking, while viewpoint homogeneity (whether on the left or the right) leaves a community vulnerable to groupthink and orthodoxy."[60] All of this, of course, helps to further erode conservatives' faith in higher education and science in general:

> Conservative voters are not going to consent forever to sending tax dollars to support institutions at odds with their values. They are losing confidence in higher education's benefits for the country. And, in the past few years, Republican states have increasingly been legislating against left-wing indoctrination in colleges.[61]

If there is enough intellectual diversity in academia, flawed partisan ideas will have a difficult time gaining traction without being revised in a more nuanced direction. But while the academy has long had problems with the conservative/liberal ratio, it is much more imbalanced today than in the past, increasing the number of ideological blind spots among its members. As Jonathan Haidt argues, "[W]e can't count on 'institutionalized disconfirmation' anymore because there are hardly any more conservatives or libertarians in the humanities and social sciences."[62] This extreme imbalance in academia today has seriously eroded empirical standards of evidence for truth claims in some fields. There just aren't enough skeptical voices pushing back, and the very real possibility of severe career and personal consequences one could face for saying the wrong thing makes those few who might speak up think twice.[63]

That leads me to other related problems in the left-wing silo: growing dog-matism/purity tests, mischaracterizing good faith disagreements as bigotry,[64] and cancel culture: "[Wokeism] fosters a kind of leftist illiberalism that is almost reli-gious in nature, in that it brooks no dissent—the sort of ideology that center-left liberals have historically opposed."[65] Thomas Chatterton Williams goes on: "Can-cel culture is quite real in the U.S., and its effects have been toxic to debate and, in many cases, to institutional decision making."

Nicholas Christakis defines cancel culture as (1) forming a mob, to (2) seek to get someone fired or disproportionately punished, for (3) statements within the Overton window (or within the spectrum of ideas considered reasonable/accept-able/mainstream by the general public at a given time).[66] David French argues that:

> The appeal of Christakis's formulation was that it concisely cap-tured the precise public fear—that a person can be cast out of polite society for saying something completely conventional, normal and in good faith. But there's a problem—the more that America po-larizes, the more it contains not one but two Overton windows, the 'red' window and the 'blue' window. Speech that is squarely main-stream in Red America is completely out of bounds in Blue Ameri-ca, and vice versa.[67]

When those within the left-wing tribe attempt to question specific orthodoxies of their side, they run the risk of being publicly smeared in a manner that unjusti-fiably ruins their reputation (being called a racist, sexist, transphobe, etc.): "Many professors say they now teach and speak more cautiously, because one slip or one simple misunderstanding could lead to vilification and even threat from any num-ber of sources."[68] There is reason for somebody to experience reputational harm if they are intentionally making obvious, overtly racist or sexist statements. In-creasingly, however, people are getting into trouble for asking reasonable, good faith questions about issues that, despite the claims of some on the left, are far from being empirically settled. As David French notes:

> Americans have read story after story (from across the political spec-trum) of activists, corporations and colleges targeting individuals for speech that is squarely within the mainstream of either progressive or conservative thought. In other words, dissent—even thoughtful dissent—has become dangerous, in both right- and left-leaning America. Private organizations are acting punitively when the gov-ernment cannot. This is the essence of cancel culture, the wide-spread use of private power to punish allegedly offensive speech.[69]

Throughout my career at various academic institutions, I have routinely felt pressure—from both students and colleagues—to self-censor in the classroom and in my research. This was especially true *before* I had tenure (there is zero chance I would have published this before tenure given the risk that doing so could have posed to my career and my family's financial security). Even though most of my students and colleagues would probably never attempt to hurt my career, even a small minority have the power to cause professional, financial, and reputational ruin for me with a single tweet.

As an example of the pressure I have personally faced, I recently shared a draft of an article with a colleague for feedback while I was fine-tuning it before submitting it to an academic journal. I had included a paragraph in the draft arguing that professors should be clear when they are discussing certain issues in the classroom—issues where there is no objective and empirically demonstrable "right" or "wrong" answer—that the debates around those issues involve subjective value judgements, not objective truths. In this example, I specifically cited the abortion debate in America. I wrote that, while there are many facts one could use to support a variety of positions, abortion policy ultimately reflects the subjective manner in which we prioritize those facts based upon our values and preferences. I do not know of an objective way to settle the question of whether the life of the unborn child or the rights of the mother should take precedence—it comes down to values. While giving me feedback on my draft, my colleague zeroed in on the abortion paragraph and said the following to me in a tense exchange:

> Pro-lifers hold their views for only *one* reason: they want to control women. Period. If I had read your article in a journal, I would have stopped reading when I saw the line about the abortion debate being about subjective values and would never have read any of your work in the future—and encouraged others not to, either.

Upon hearing this and other related criticisms from my colleague—and knowing that many sociologists think this way and could severely damage my career if they desired—I regret to say that I caved. I removed that line from the article before submitting it to the journal (where it was eventually published).

"Pro-lifers hold their views for only *one* reason: they want to control women. Period." This was not just some one-off personal belief shared with me by a colleague in private—I have heard professors present this empirically questionable claim to college students as objective fact on numerous occasions. This is an example of the highly questionable claims frequently presented as settled fact not only in college classrooms but in major academic journals, books from prestigious presses, at major academic conferences, and elsewhere. Radical and empirically shaky claims about not only abortion but capitalism, gender identity, racial/gender/economic inequalities, and many other topics are misleadingly presented as empirically settled and those who dare step outside of the acceptable range of liberal thought on such topics face very serious personal and professional risks.

I do not always cave when pressured to conform—and I am feeling much more comfortable challenging the orthodoxies of academia now that I have tenure—but the pressure is always present. For instance, I once submitted an article—about community-level factors which impact children's success—to a peer-reviewed academic journal. My findings were rather uncontroversial and aligned with what a number of other scholars have found: that community-level factors—including a community's social capital, rate of single parenthood, school quality, and degree of racial segregation, among others—are associated with children's likelihood of success later on in life as adults (independent of individual- and family-level factors). Echoing an anonymous reviewer's comments, the editor of the journal was concerned about the inclusion of one variable in particular: community single parenthood rates. The editor was worried that its inclusion would suggest that single parents contribute to the poor outcomes of their children. They did not ask me to remove that finding from the study, but they did ask me to include commentary that I felt I could not support with my data.

In the case of the aforementioned article that discussed abortion, I was able to replace the abortion example with a different one without changing any of the substance of my argument. To cave here, however, would have been unethical—single parenthood was one of the strongest variables in my study, and to downplay or ignore that altogether would mean altering my findings to say something that they didn't really say in order to appease the personal beliefs of an anonymous reviewer.

For obvious reasons, I could not agree to this. I decided to stand firm, explain my reasoning for doing so, and simply submit the article to another journal if the editor was displeased. Luckily, the editor published my article without any changes to or distortions of my findings, but it was a delicate and unnecessary negotiation due to the inappropriate influence of a reviewer's personal beliefs.

Regarding the manner in which the social sciences have been captured by ideologues, Lee McIntyre argues: "It is unfortunately true that a good deal of social science today is unreliable, due to its infection by political ideology. Even in universities, in some fields there is no clear line between 'research' and political advocacy."[70] From personal experience I can report that I believe McIntyre is correct. I have numerous examples from my own career in addition to what I have discussed here—many of them much more serious—that I'd rather not mention publicly.

Because of growing progressivism in the academy and the rise of cancel culture, professors are increasingly self-censoring: avoiding posing questions in the classroom and in their research that might get them called out publicly by liberal students, colleagues, administrators, and DEI[71] staff. This is especially true when it comes to classroom discussions and research questions related to race, gender, and sexual orientation. As Rebecca Tuvel—a Rhodes College professor and victim of a social media pile-on related to an academic article she published defending transracialism—noted:

I know professors who will not touch certain topics with a ten-foot pole in the classroom for fear of getting a report filed against them. Self-censorship is everywhere. It's a serious problem that makes me concerned for the future of academia.[72]

Northwestern University professor Laura Kipnis, who faced protests from students and a Title IX investigation over an article she wrote about consensual-relations codes governing professor-student dating,[73] argued that on today's college campuses:

Most academics I know—this includes feminists, progressives, minorities, and those who identify as gay or queer—now live in fear of some classroom incident spiraling into professional disaster. After [my] essay appeared, I was deluged with emails from professors applauding what I'd written because they were too frightened to say such things publicly themselves. . . I learned that professors around the country now routinely avoid discussing subjects in classes that might raise hackles. A well-known sociologist wrote that he no longer lectures on abortion. . . A tenured professor on my campus wrote about lying awake at night worrying that some stray remark of hers might lead to student complaints, social-media campaigns, eventual job loss, and her being unable to support her child. I'd thought she was exaggerating, but that was before I learned about the Title IX complaints against me.

She went on:

What's being lost, along with job security, is the liberty to publish ideas that might go against the grain or to take on risky subjects in the first place. With students increasingly regarded as customers and consumer satisfaction paramount, it's imperative to avoid creating potential classroom friction with unpopular ideas. . . [P]retty much everyone now self-censors.

I'll end this section with a long but I believe important quote from the "Harper's Letter":

The free exchange of information and ideas, the lifeblood of a liberal society, is daily becoming more constricted. While we have come to expect this on the radical right, censoriousness is also spreading more widely in our culture: an intolerance of opposing views, a vogue for public shaming and ostracism, and the tendency to dissolve complex policy issues in a blinding moral certainty. We uphold the value of robust and even caustic counter-speech from all quarters. But it is now all too common to hear calls for swift and severe retribution in response to perceived transgressions of speech and thought. More troubling still, institutional leaders, in a spirit of panicked damage control, are delivering hasty and disproportionate punishments instead of considered reforms. Editors are fired for running controversial pieces; books are withdrawn for alleged inauthenticity; journalists are barred from writing on certain topics; professors are investigated for quoting works of literature in class; a researcher is fired for circulating a peer-reviewed academic study; and the heads of organizations are ousted for what are sometimes just clumsy mistakes. Whatever the arguments around each particular incident, the result has been to steadily narrow the boundaries of what can be said without the threat of reprisal. We are already paying the price in greater risk aversion among writers, artists, and journalists who fear for their livelihoods if they depart from the consensus, or even lack sufficient zeal in agreement. This stifling atmosphere will ultimately harm the most vital causes of our time...As writers we need a culture that leaves us room for experimentation, risk taking, and even mistakes. We need to preserve the possibility of good-faith disagreement without dire professional consequences. If we won't defend the very thing on which our work depends, we shouldn't expect the public or the state to defend it for us."[74]

I. DEFENDING TRUTH

CHAPTER 4
The Constitution of Knowledge[1]

By Jonathan Rauch

Long before Donald Trump began his political career, he explained his attitude toward truth with characteristic brazenness. In a 2004 television interview with Chris Matthews on MSNBC, he marveled at the Republicans' successful attacks on the wartime heroism of Senator John Kerry, the Democrats' presidential candidate. "[I]t's almost coming out that [George W.] Bush is a war hero and Kerry isn't," Trump said, admiringly. "I think that could be the greatest spin I've ever seen." Matthews then asked about Vice President Dick Cheney's insinuations that Kerry's election would lead to a devastating attack on the United States. "Well," replied Trump, "it's a terrible statement unless he gets away with it." With that extraordinary declaration, Trump showed himself to be an attentive student of disinformation and its operative principle: Reality is what you can get away with.

Trump's command of the basic concept of disinformation offers some insight into how he approaches the truth as president. The fact is that President Trump lies not only prolifically and shamelessly, but in a different way than previous presidents and national politicians. They may spin the truth, bend it, or break it, but they pay homage to it and regard it as a boundary. Trump's approach is entirely different. It was no coincidence that one of his first actions after taking the oath of office was to force his press secretary to tell a preposterous lie about the size of the inaugural crowd. The intention was not to deceive anyone on the particular question of crowd size. The president sought to put the press and public on notice that he intended to bully his staff, bully the media, and bully the truth.

In case anyone missed the point, Sean Spicer, Trump's press secretary, made it clear a few weeks later when he announced favorable employment statistics. In the Obama years, Trump had been fond of describing monthly jobs reports as "phony" and "totally fiction." But now? "I talked to the president prior to this and he said to quote him very clearly," Spicer said. "They may have been phony in the past, but it's very real now." The president was not saying that the Bureau of Labor Statistics had improved its methodology. He was asserting that truth and falsehood were subject to his will.

Since then, such lies have only multiplied. Fact checkers say that, if anything, the rate has increased. For the president and his enablers, the lying reflects a strategy, not merely a character flaw or pathology.

America has faced many challenges to its political culture, but this is the first time we have seen a national-level *epistemic* attack: a systematic attack, emanating from the very highest reaches of power, on our collective ability to distinguish truth from falsehood. "These are truly uncharted waters for the country," wrote Michael Hayden, former CIA director, in the *Washington Post* in April. "We have in the past argued over the values to be applied to objective reality, or occasionally over what constituted objective reality, but never the existence or relevance of objective reality itself." To make the point another way: Trump and his troll armies seek to undermine the constitution of knowledge.

The Problem of Reality

The attack, Hayden noted, is on "the existence or relevance of objective reality itself." But what is objective reality?

In everyday vernacular, *reality* often refers to the world out there: things as they really are, independent of human perception and error. Reality also often describes those things that we feel certain about, things that we believe no amount of wishful thinking could change. But, of course, humans have no direct access to an objective world independent of our minds and senses, and subjective certainty is in no way a guarantee of truth. Philosophers have wrestled with these problems for centuries, and today they have a pretty good working definition of objective reality. It is a set of *propositions*: propositions that have been validated in some way, and have thereby been shown to be at least conditionally true—true, that is, unless debunked. Some of these propositions reflect the world as we perceive it (e.g., "The sky is blue"). Others, like claims made by quantum physicists and abstract mathematicians, appear completely removed from the world of everyday experience.

It is worth noting, however, that the locution "validated in some way" hides a cheat. In *what* way? Some Americans believe Elvis Presley is alive. Should we send him a Social Security check? Many people believe that vaccines cause autism, or that Barack Obama was born in Africa, or that the murder rate has risen. Who should decide who is right? And who should decide who gets to decide?

This is the problem of social epistemology, which concerns itself with how societies come to some kind of public understanding about truth. It is a fundamental problem for every culture and country, and the attempts to resolve it go back at least to Plato, who concluded that a philosopher king (presumably someone like Plato himself) should rule over reality. Traditional tribal communities frequently use oracles to settle questions about reality. Religious communities use holy texts as interpreted by priests. Totalitarian states put the government in charge of objectivity.

There are many other ways to settle questions about reality. Most of them are terrible because they rely on authoritarianism, violence, or, usually, both. As the great American philosopher Charles Sanders Peirce said in 1877, "When complete agreement could not otherwise be reached, a general massacre of all who have not thought in a certain way has proved a very effective means of settling opinion in a country."

As Peirce implied, one way to avoid a massacre would be to attain unanimity, at least on certain core issues. No wonder we hanker for consensus. Something you often hear today is that, as Senator Ben Sasse put it in an interview on CNN, "[W]e have a risk of getting to a place where we don't have shared public facts. A republic will not work if we don't have shared facts."

But that is not quite the right answer, either. Disagreement about core issues and even core facts is inherent in human nature and essential in a free society. If unanimity on core propositions is not possible or even desirable, what is necessary to have a functional social reality? The answer is that we need an elite consensus, and hopefully also something approaching a public consensus, on the *method* of validating propositions. We needn't and can't all agree that the same things are true, but a critical mass needs to agree on what it is we *do* that distinguishes truth from falsehood, and more important, on who does it.

Who can be trusted to resolve questions about objective truth? The best answer turns out to be no one in particular. The greatest of human social networks was born centuries ago, in the wake of the chaos and creedal wars that raged across Europe after the invention of the printing press (the original disruptive information technology). In reaction, experimenters and philosophers began entertaining a radical idea. They removed reality-making from the authoritarian control of priests and princes and placed it in the hands of a decentralized, globe-spanning community of critical testers who hunt for each other's errors. In other words, they outsourced objectivity to a social network. Gradually, in the scientific revolution and the Enlightenment, the network's norms and institutions assembled themselves into a system of rules for identifying truth: a constitution of knowledge.

Our Epistemic Constitution

Though nowhere encoded in law, the constitution of knowledge has its own equivalents of checks and balances (peer review and replication), separation of powers (specialization), governing institutions (scientific societies and professional bodies), voting (citations and confirmations), and civic virtues (submit your beliefs for checking if you want to be taken seriously). The members of the community that supports and upholds the constitution of knowledge do not have to agree on facts;

the whole point, indeed, is to manage their disagreements. But they do need to agree on some rules.

One rule is that any hypothesis can be floated. That's free speech. But another rule is that a hypothesis can join reality only insofar as it persuades people after withstanding vigorous questioning and criticism. That's social testing. Only those propositions that are broadly agreed to have withstood testing over time qualify as knowledge, and even they stand only unless and until debunked.

The community that follows these rules is defined by its values and practices, not by its borders, and it is by no means limited to scholars and scientists. It also includes journalism, the courts, law enforcement, and the intelligence community— all evidence-based professions that require competing hypotheses to be tested and justified. Its members hold themselves and each other accountable for their errors. When CNN, in 2017, fired three senior journalists for getting a story wrong, President Trump gloated that the "Fake News" media's dishonesty had been exposed (His tweet: "So they caught Fake News CNN cold, but what about NBC, CBS & ABC?"). In fact, the opposite was true: By demanding evidentiary accountability, CNN showed that, unlike Trump, it adheres to standards of verification.

On any given day, of course, we won't all agree on what has or has not checked out. The speed of light is widely agreed upon, but many propositions are disputed, and in some cases, such as man-made climate change, there is even a dispute about whether the proposition is in dispute. The community that lives by the standards of verification constantly argues about itself, yet by doing so provides its members with time and space to work through their disagreements without authoritarian oversight.

The results have been spectacular, in three ways above all. First, by organizing millions of minds to tackle billions of problems, the epistemic constitution disseminates knowledge at a staggering rate. Every day, probably before breakfast, it adds more to the canon of knowledge than was accumulated in the 200,000 years of human history prior to Galileo's time. Second, by insisting on validating truths through a decentralized, non-coercive process that forces us to convince each other with evidence and argument, it ends the practice of killing ideas by killing their proponents. What is often called the marketplace of ideas would be more accurately described as a marketplace of *persuasion*, because the only way to establish knowledge is to convince others you are right. Third, by placing reality under the control of no one in particular, it dethrones intellectual authoritarianism and commits liberal society foundationally to intellectual pluralism and freedom of thought.

Together, these innovations have done nothing less than transform our way of living, learning, and relating to one another. But they have always had natural enemies. One, an ancient parasite, has recently mutated into something like an epistemic super-virus.

Troll Epistemology

There is nothing new about disinformation. Unlike ordinary lies and propaganda, which try to make you believe *something*, disinformation tries to make you disbelieve *everything*. It scatters so much bad information, and casts so many aspersions on so many sources of information, that people throw up their hands and say, "They're all a pack of liars." As Steve Bannon, a former Trump aide and former leader of *Breitbart News*, succinctly put it in an interview with *Bloomberg*, "[T]he way to deal with [the media] is to flood the zone with shit."

Although disinformation is old, it has recently cross-pollinated with the internet to produce something new: the decentralized, swarm-based version of disinformation that has come to be known as trolling. Trolls attack real news; they attack the sources of real news; they disseminate fake news; and they create artificial copies of themselves to disseminate even more fake news. By unleashing great quantities of lies and half-truths, and then piling on and swarming, they achieve hive-mind coordination. Because trolling need not bother with persuasion or anything more than very superficial plausibility, it can concern itself with being addictively outrageous. Epistemically, it is anarchistic, giving no valence to truth at all; like a virus, all it cares about is replicating and spreading.

Still, trolling is epistemically low-tech. It is antisocial, even sociopathic, and therefore difficult to direct toward any constructive goal. Unmoored from all epistemic standards, it is incapable of establishing that anything is true or that anyone is right. All it can do is spread confusion and demolish trust.

Why would someone want to do that? Some trolls find it amusing to give offense (what they call "triggering"); some style themselves protesters against political correctness; and some love the thrill of vandalism and defiance. But there are other, less-nihilistic reasons.

To understand troll epistemology, think of the constitution of knowledge as a funnel. At the wide end, millions of people float millions of hypotheses every day. Only an infinitesimal fraction of new ideas will be proven true. To find them, we run the hypotheses through a massive, socially distributed error-finding process. Only a tiny few make it to the narrow end of the funnel. There, often years later, a kind of social valve—call it prestige and recognition—admits the surviving propositions into the canon of knowledge. People who successfully bring a proposition into the canon are greeted with publication, professorships, promotions, and prizes. Those who follow the rules without scoring a breakthrough receive honorable mention. Those who flout the rules are simply ignored.

The constitution of knowledge makes a very strong claim: a claim to supremacy in organizing social decision-making about what is and is not reality (much as the U.S. Constitution claims supremacy in organizing political decision-making). Of course, it's a free country, and anyone can *say* he has knowledge. But the constitution of knowledge is defined by a social pact: In return for the freedom and peace and knowledge the system confers, we ignore alternative claims on reality where social decision-making is concerned. We let alt-truth talk, but we don't let it write textbooks, receive tenure, bypass peer review, set the research agenda, dominate the front pages, give expert testimony, or dictate the flow of public dollars. That is why we don't mail Elvis a Social Security check, no matter how many people think he is alive.

Notice the delicate balance here. To protect the wide end of the funnel, we disallow censorship. We say: *Alt-truth is never criminalized.* At the same time, to protect the narrow end of the funnel, we regulate influence. We say: *Alt-truth is always ignored.* You can believe and say whatever you want. But if your beliefs don't check out, or if you don't submit them for checking, you can't expect anyone else to publish, care about, or even notice what you think. Striking this balance is difficult, and maintaining it involves a lot of implicit social cooperation. The constitution of knowledge requires high degrees of both toleration and discipline, neither of which is easy to come by.

With that in mind, the implications of troll epistemology come into sharper focus. By insisting that all the fact checkers and hypothesis testers out there are phonies, trolls discredit the very possibility of a socially validated reality, and open the door to tribal knowledge, personal knowledge, partisan knowledge, and other manifestations of epistemic anarchy. By spreading lies and disinformation on an industrial scale, they sow confusion about what might or might not be true, and about who can be relied on to discern the difference, and about whether there *is* any difference. By being willing to say anything, they exploit shock and outrage to seize attention and hijack the public conversation.

That last tactic is especially insidious. The constitution of knowledge is organized around an epistemic honor code: Objective truth exists; efforts to find it should be impersonal; credentials matter; what hasn't been tested isn't knowledge; and so on. Trolls violate all those norms: They mock truth, sling mud, trash credentials, ridicule testing, and all the rest. Instinctively, the champions of the constitution of knowledge defend their values—but when they do, they "feed the trolls," providing attention and airtime that the trolls use to redouble their attacks. In this way, Trump and his troll army delighted in repurposing the charge that they were purveying "fake news."

In 2013, someone using the handle @backupwraith tweeted, "i firmly believe that @realDonaldTrump is the most superior troll on the whole of twitter." Whereupon @realDonaldTrump took the trouble to tweet back: "A great compliment!" We can't say he didn't warn us.

A Perfect Storm

If trolling is sociopathic and disinformation is parasitic, how did this ancient but usually containable bug become a super-virus?

George Orwell thought that making us doubt the truth that's in front of our noses required bureaucracies and police agencies marshalling the might of a state.

In his age of big business and big unions and big government and the other "bigs," disinformation and propaganda seemed unlikely to succeed without large-scale institutional support—and even for states as overbearing as the Soviet Union, the lift was heavy. Liberalism's diffuse, decentralized model thrives on dissent, whereas a single Andrei Sakharov threatened the brittle Soviet system.

To be sure, fake news existed and entrepreneurs found ways to profit from it. Who can forget the *Weekly World News*? From 1979 to 2007 it treated us to headlines like "Clinton Hires 3-Breasted Intern," "Hillary Clinton Adopts Alien Baby," and "Bat Child Found in Cave." In 1992, politicos knew George H. W. Bush's re-election campaign was in trouble when *WWN*'s beloved space alien endorsed Bill Clinton for president. But that august publication had to employ writers and editors to make up stuff, artists to doctor photos, and sales staff to round up ads for penile enhancement; then it had to pay for printing and buy rack space in supermarkets. The bat child was expensive to create and distribute, and the market for him was small and costly to reach. By contrast, the Associated Press could bundle reporting from reputable papers everywhere and distribute it to outlets around the world. Economies of scale favored real news.

In the heyday of the bigs, reality defenders became complacent about disinformation. There didn't seem to be a private-sector business model for it, and the state actors were weakening. What we could not foresee was a perfect storm of technological, economic, and political changes, all working to the disadvantage of the constitution of knowledge.

First, social media created a distribution platform for disinformation. Putting stuff out there costs effectively nothing. Mobilizing troll armies of humans and bots is easy and cheap. As the digital-media critic Frederic Filloux writes:

> For a few hundred bucks, anyone can buy thousands of social media accounts that are old enough to be credible, or millions of email addresses. Also, by using Mechanical Turk or similar cheap crowd-sourcing services widely available on the open web, anyone can hire legions of 'writers' who will help to propagate any message or ideology on a massive scale.

Second, software learned to hack our brains. Sophisticated algorithms and granular data allowed messages and images to be minutely tuned and targeted. These are powerful new tools that humans are not designed to encounter or resist (Coming soon, according to Filloux: "weaponized artificial intelligence propaganda," fake or hyperpartisan content that is customized for particular individuals and distributed by swarms of bots. Do you feel ready?).

Third, the clickbait economy created a business model. Disinformation went from vandalistic to profitable. Google Ads and Facebook (among others) monetized page views, thereby monetizing anything that generates clicks, regardless of truth value. At the same time, traditional media's business model crumpled. Because accurate reportage is orders of magnitude more expensive to produce than disinformation, the economic advantage of real news vaporized.

Together, those changes democratized and economized disinformation in ways Orwell could not have imagined. One more step was then required to complete the process: Politicians and nation-states weaponized trolling. Russia, as we now all know, was ahead of the curve in understanding how to mechanize and merchandize disinformation. Orwell wasn't wrong: A nation-state is still an impressive force multiplier. As state-based actors and independent trolls and bots cued each other with fake news, they created an echo chamber that proved deafening and disorienting.

All of which was compounded by one other actor. A student of disinformation and a self-described troll, Trump established his political celebrity with a lie about President Obama's birth and never stopped lying. The outrage and bewilderment evoked by his tsunami of balderdash dominated the 2016 campaign and afforded him unprecedented free media. Like an epistemic virus, Trump commandeered the media and reprogrammed them to pump out his memes.

Trump's most important contribution to the trolling of the American mind is not what he says, but that it is impossible to ignore what he says. In the past, the constitution of knowledge dealt with and contained alt-truth by ignoring and sidelining it. For generations, such marginalization allowed Christian Scientists and astrologists and conspiracy theorists and many other purveyors of alternative realities to believe what they believe without disrupting science and society. But there is just no way to marginalize an American president. He can set the agenda and dominate the news. He can turn the White House into a baloney factory. He can impanel a public commission to investigate a claim he completely made up. All of which, and more, he has done.

All Downside

Will Trump and the trolls triumph? I doubt it. Weaponized trolling has enjoyed the advantage of surprise, but as that diminishes, the troll army will encounter a disadvantage. Trolls have swarms, but the constitution of knowledge has institutions.

Creating knowledge is inherently a professionalized and structured affair. Whether you are engaged in bench chemistry, daily journalism, or intelligence analysis, testing hypotheses requires time, money, skill, expertise, and intricate social interaction. Of course, ordinary people can and should participate, and the constitution of knowledge welcomes their efforts. Anyone who follows the rules can make a contribution, as amateur astronomers and geologists have been doing for centuries, and no one is jailed for being wrong. But at the core of the constitution of knowledge, by its very nature, are professional networks.

The distinguishing characteristic of journalism is professional editing, and its institutional home is the newsroom, which curates and checks stories, trains reporters, organizes complex investigations, inculcates professional ethics, and more. The distinguishing characteristic of academic research is professional review: a sophisticated, multilayered project distributed among university faculties, journals, credentialing organizations, scholarly conferences, and so on. Modern jurisprudence, policy development, and intelligence collection would be unthinkable without institutions like the courts, law schools, and think tanks, as well as agencies like the Congressional Budget Office, Bureau of Labor Statistics, Central Intelligence Agency, and many others—all staffed and run by elaborately trained people who exchange detailed knowledge across specialized channels, using protocols developed over decades and centuries. To be an accomplished scholar or journalist requires years of training and acculturation, which only institutions can provide.

Troll networks are acephalous, which makes them self-organizing and persistent. They do have some institutional nodes, such as Russia's Internet Research Agency and President Trump's Twitter account. And they are nothing if not ingenious. So they are in a position to spring a lot of unpleasant surprises. But they cannot approach the institutional depth of the communities built up around the constitution of knowledge, nor do they try. Instead, they relentlessly attack the institutions at the heart of those communities, hoping to make the public see professional academics and journalists as scammers peddling biased personal opinions. On that score, they have had some success.

Charges that academia, journalism, and other evidence-based enterprises are bogus, biased, illegitimate, racist, oppressive, secular-humanist, and so on are nothing new, and they contain important grains of truth. Although the marvel of our knowledge-making institutions is how well they have functioned (especially compared to the alternatives), it's reasonable to worry about, for example, liberal bias in traditional media and a replication crisis in establishment science. The answer, however, is to remediate the defects, not to trash the institutions. How much damage the troll attack inflicts depends on a lot of things, but it depends most on how successfully the institutions rally to improve their performance and defend their values.

Most of those institutions appear to be rising to the challenge. Mainstream media organizations, for example, have responded well to Trump's unprecedented populist attacks. They have shown no signs of being intimidated or deterred; if anything, just the opposite. The public seems to be responding with new, if sometimes grudging, respect. Between 2016 and 2017, according to polling by the Freedom Forum Institute, the percentage of the public saying that media outlets try to report news without bias jumped by an impressive 20 percentage points, from 23% to 43%. *Politico* reports that even young subscribers are flocking to old media. Trump's attacks on the press seem to have strengthened its resolve and its popularity.

The courts and law enforcement have also responded resolutely, even bravely. The judicial system has gone about its business with unperturbed professionalism, much to the frustration of the White House. Still more frustrating to the president has been the determination of professionals within the Justice Department and the FBI to maintain their integrity in the face of his unrelenting campaign to demonize and politicize them and bend them to his will. The same appears to be true of the intelligence community. Republicans charge the so-called "deep state" with one impropriety after another, yet each investigation only bolsters confidence that the law-enforcement and intelligence communities are on the level, and the Republicans are not. It's no coincidence that some of the most outspoken defenders of the constitution of knowledge—such as Hayden, the former CIA director, and James Comey, the former FBI director—have come from the intelligence and law-enforcement worlds. Although the government's statistical and research agencies—places like the Centers for Disease Control and Prevention, the Bureau of Labor Statistics, and the Congressional Budget Office—have not come under direct attack (with the possible and partial exception of the Census Bureau), my guess is that, when the attack comes, they too will stand their ground.

New media and social platforms have not performed as well, but they are scrambling to do better. Trolls and bots stole a march on them. Their own mistakes and blind spots left them vulnerable, and they lack the deep institutional cultures and defenses that old media have evolved. Fortunately, Facebook and Google—the industry titans—have declared their commitment to the constitution of knowledge and are working fast to demote fake news, kick out bots, and deter abusive behavior. Whether they can get a handle on the problem remains to be seen, but they are trying, and that is important and good.

But then, in the not-so-hot category, there is academia, which may well be the most important of the institutions that comprise the constitution of knowledge. A recent study of top-ranked liberal-arts colleges by the National Association of Scholars found that 39% had zero Republican professors, and that almost 80% of the academic departments had "either zero Republicans, or so few as to make no difference." You need to go about with a lantern in broad daylight, Diogenes-style, to find a conservative in a humanities department. Many academics and students who do lean right are closeted. The university does not reliably feel like a safe space for them.

On campus, conservative speakers are often shunned, shouted down, and denounced in hysterical terms. An unguarded statement, even if not obviously controversial—say, a suggestion that grown-up students at Yale should not need university guidance about their Halloween costumes—can ignite a firestorm. Many otherwise outspoken students, including many who do not think of themselves as particularly conservative, say they will not discuss race or gender on campus, for fear of being called out. As one recent Ivy League graduate told me, "It's all downside."

The large majority of professional scholars strive to conduct gold-standard research, and many if not most students quietly resent the call-out culture. But theirs are not the dominant voices on campus or in the media. News stories about campus intolerance and unreason ricochet throughout the media to portray the university as a place that puts political standards ahead of professional ones. No wonder much of the public has formed the impression that academia is not trustworthy.

It should be routine for universities to welcome conservative scholars and champion conservative scholarship; to engage civilly and even appreciatively with controversial speakers; to shrug off provocations and reject censorship in all its forms; to eschew the politicization of research; to define safety as something other than intellectual conformity; to teach students to transcend their tribal identities rather than to burrow into them; to regard diversity of perspective as a reason to have conversations, not to shut them down. Universities are the mainstays of the constitution of knowledge. They train students and scholars in the methods and mores of structured inquiry; they build and safeguard knowledge; they ask the questions that others overlook or avoid.

And so if universities are rackets, merely imposing some opinions on everyone else or pursuing someone's political agenda, then the constitution of knowledge is a racket, too. If universities foster cultures of conformity rather than of criticism, if they traffic in politicized orthodoxies and secular religions, then the winner is not social justice but trolling. Which is all downside.

CHAPTER 5
Why Should We Trust Science?[1]

By John Wright

Many of us accept that science is a reliable guide to what we ought to believe—but not all of us do. Mistrust of science has led to skepticism around several important issues, from climate change denial to vaccine hesitancy during the COVID pandemic. And while most of us may be inclined to dismiss such skepticism as unwarranted, it does raise the question: why ought we to trust science? As a philosopher with a focus on the philosophy of science, I'm particularly intrigued by this question. As it turns out, diving into the works of great thinkers can help provide an answer.

Common Arguments

One thought that might initially spring to mind is we ought to trust scientists because what they say is true. But there are problems with this. One is the question of whether what a scientist says is, in fact, the truth. Skeptics will point out that scientists are just humans and remain prone to making mistakes.

Also, if we look at the history of science, we find that what scientists believed in the past has often later turned out to be false. And this suggests what scientists believe now might one day turn out to be false. After all, there were times in history when people thought mercury could treat syphilis,[2] and that the bumps on a person's skull could reveal their character traits.[3]

Another tempting suggestion for why we ought to trust science is because it is based on "facts and logic." This may be true, but unfortunately it is of limited help in persuading someone who is inclined to reject what scientists say. Both sides in a dispute will claim they have the facts on their side; it is not unknown for climate change deniers to say global warming is just a "theory."

Popper and the Scientific Method

One influential answer to the question of why we should trust scientists is because they use the scientific method. This, of course, raises the question: what is the scientific method? Possibly the best-known account is offered by science philosopher Karl Popper, who has influenced an Einstein Medal-winning mathematical physicist and Nobel Prize winners in biology and physiology and medicine.

For Popper, science proceeds by means of what he calls "conjectures and refutations." Scientists are confronted with some question and offer a possible answer. This answer is a conjecture in the sense that, at least initially, it is not known if it is right or wrong. Popper says scientists then do their best to refute this conjecture or prove it wrong. Typically, it is refuted, rejected, and replaced by a better one. This too will then be tested, and eventually replaced by an even better one. In this way science progresses.

Sometimes this process can be incredibly slow. Albert Einstein predicted the existence of gravitational waves more than 100 years ago, as part of his general theory of relativity. But it was only in 2015 that scientists managed to observe them.[4]

For Popper, at the core of the scientific method is the attempt to refute or disprove theories, which is called the "falsification principle." If scientists have not been able to refute a theory over a long period of time, despite their best efforts, then in Popper's terminology the theory has been "corroborated."

This suggests a possible answer to the question of why we ought to trust what scientists tell us. It is because, despite their best efforts, they have not been able to disprove the idea they are telling us is true.

Majority Rules

Recently, an answer to the question was further articulated in a book by science historian Naomi Oreskes.[5] Oreskes acknowledges the importance Popper placed on the role of attempting to refute a theory, but also emphasizes the social and consensual element of scientific practice. For Oreskes, we have reason to trust science because, or to the extent that, there is a consensus among the (relevant) scientific community that a particular claim is true—wherein that same scientific community has done their best to disprove it and failed.

Here is a brief sketch of what a scientific idea typically goes through before a consensus emerges that it is correct. A scientist might give a paper on some idea to colleagues, who then discuss it. One aim of this discussion will be to find something wrong with it. If the paper passes the test, the scientist might write a peer-reviewed paper on the same idea. If the referees think it has sufficient merit, it will be published. Others may then subject the idea to experimental tests. If it passes a sufficient number of these, a consensus may emerge that it is correct.

A good example of a theory undergoing this transition is the theory of global warming and the human impact on it. It had been suggested as early as 1896 that increasing levels of carbon dioxide in Earth's atmosphere might lead to global warming.[6] In the early 20th century, another theory emerged that not only was this happening, but carbon dioxide released from human activities (namely fossil fuel burning) could accelerate global warming. It gained some support at the time, but most scientists remained unconvinced.

However, throughout the second half of the 20th century and what has so far passed of the 21st, the theory of human-caused climate change has so successfully passed ongoing testing that one recent meta-study found more than 99% of the relevant scientific community accept its reality.[7] It started off perhaps as a mere hypothesis, successfully passed testing for more than a hundred years, and has now gained near-universal acceptance.

The Bottom Line

This does not necessarily mean we ought to uncritically accept everything scientists say. There is of course a difference between a single isolated scientist or small group saying something and there being a consensus within the scientific community that something is true.

And, of course, for a variety of reasons—some practical, some financial, some otherwise—scientists may not have done their best to refute some idea. And even if scientists have repeatedly tried, but failed, to refute a given theory, the history of science suggests at some point in the future it may still turn out to be false when new evidence comes to light.

So when should we trust science? The view that seems to emerge from Popper, Oreskes, and other writers in the field is we have good, but fallible, reason to trust what scientists say when, despite their own best efforts to disprove an idea, there remains a consensus that it is true.

CHAPTER 6
Understanding Science[1]

By Tim Dean

If I told you that science was a truth-seeking endeavor that uses a single robust method to prove scientific facts about the world, steadily and inexorably driving towards objective truth, would you believe me? Many would. But you shouldn't.

The public perception of science is often at odds with how science actually works. Science is often seen to be a separate domain of knowledge, framed to be superior to other forms of knowledge by virtue of its objectivity, which is sometimes referred to as it having a "view from nowhere."[2]

But science is actually far messier than this—and far more interesting. It is not without its limitations and flaws, but it's still the most effective tool we have to understand the workings of the world around us.

In order to consume science effectively as a reader, it's important to understand what science is, how the scientific method (or methods) work, and also some of the common pitfalls in practicing science and interpreting its results.

What is Science?

Science is special, not because it claims to provide us with access to the truth, but because it admits it can't provide truth. Other means of producing knowledge, such as pure reason, intuition, or revelation, might be appealing because they give the impression of certainty, but when this knowledge is applied to make predictions about the world around us, reality often finds them wanting.

Rather, science consists of a bunch of methods that enable us to accumulate evidence to test our ideas about how the world is, and why it works the way it does. Science works precisely because it enables us to make predictions that are borne out by experience.

What makes science so powerful is that it's intensely self-critical. In order for a hypothesis to pass muster and enter a textbook, it must survive a battery of tests designed specifically to show that it could be wrong. If it passes, it has cleared a high bar.

The Scientific Method(s)

There is a method for conducting science—in fact, there are many. And not all revolve around performing experiments.

One method involves simple observation, description, and classification, such as in taxonomy (Some physicists look down on this—and every other—kind of science, but they're only greasing a slippery slope).

However, when most of us think of The Scientific Method, we're thinking of a particular kind of experimental method for testing hypotheses. This begins with observing phenomena in the world around us, and then moves on to positing hypotheses for why those phenomena happen the way they do. A hypothesis is just an explanation, usually in the form of a causal mechanism: X causes Y. An example would be: gravitation causes the ball to fall back to the ground.

A scientific theory is just a collection of well-tested hypotheses that hang together to explain a great deal of stuff.

Crucially, a scientific hypothesis needs to be *testable* and *falsifiable*. An untestable hypothesis would be something like "the ball falls to the ground because mischievous invisible unicorns want it to." If these unicorns are not detectable by any scientific instrument, then the hypothesis that they're responsible for gravity is not scientific.

An unfalsifiable hypothesis is one where no amount of testing can prove it wrong. An example might be the psychic who claims the experiment to test their powers of ESP failed because the scientific instruments were interfering with their abilities. (Caveat: there are some hypotheses that are untestable because we choose not to test them. That doesn't make them unscientific in principle, it's just that they've been denied by an ethics committee or other regulation).

Experimentation

There are often many hypotheses that could explain any particular phenomenon. Does the rock fall to the ground because an invisible force pulls on the rock? Or is it because the mass of the Earth warps spacetime, and the rock follows the lowest-energy path, thus colliding with the ground? Or is it that all substances have a natural tendency to fall towards the center of the Universe, which happens to be at the center of the Earth?

The trick is figuring out which hypothesis is the right one. That's where experimentation comes in. A scientist will take their hypothesis and use that to make a prediction, and they will construct an experiment to see if that prediction holds.

But any observation that confirms one hypothesis will likely confirm several others as well. If I lift and drop a rock, it supports all three of the hypotheses on gravity above.

Furthermore, you can keep accumulating evidence to confirm a hypothesis, and it will never prove it to be absolutely true. This is because you can't rule out the possibility of another similar hypothesis being correct, or of making some new observation that shows your hypothesis to be false. But if one day you drop a rock and it shoots off into space, that ought to cast doubt on all of the above hypotheses.

So while you can never prove a hypothesis true simply by making more confirmatory observations, you only one need one solid contrary observation to prove a hypothesis false. This notion is at the core of the hypothetico-deductive model of science.[3]

This is why a great deal of science is focused on testing hypotheses, pushing them to their limits, and attempting to break them through experimentation. If the hypothesis survives repeated testing, our confidence in it grows. So even crazy-sounding theories like general relativity and quantum mechanics can become well accepted because both enable very precise predictions, and these have been exhaustively tested and come through unscathed.

Significance Testing

The null-hypothesis is just a baseline hypothesis that typically says there's nothing interesting going on, and the causal relationship underpinning the scientist's hypothesis doesn't hold. It's like a default position of skepticism about the scientist's hypothesis. Or like assuming a defendant is innocent until proven guilty.

Now, as the scientist performs their experiment, they compare their results with what they'd expect to see if the null-hypothesis were true. What they're looking for, though, is evidence that the null-hypothesis is actually false.

An example might help. Let's say you want to test whether a coin is biased towards heads. Your hypothesis, referred to as the alternate hypothesis (or H_1), that you want to test is that it is biased. The null-hypothesis (H_0) is that it's unbiased.

We already know from repeated tests that if you flip a fair coin 100 times, you'd expect it to come up heads around 50 times (but it won't always come up heads precisely 50 times). So if the scientist flips the coin 100 times and it comes up heads 55 times, it's pretty likely to be a fair coin. But if it comes up heads 70 times, it starts to look fishy.

But how can they tell 70 heads is not just the result of chance? It's certainly *possible* for a fair coin to come up heads 70 times. It's just very unlikely. And the scientist can use statistics to determine how unlikely it is.

If they flip a fair coin 100 times, there's a 13.6% chance that it'll come up heads 55 or more times. That's unlikely, but not enough to be confident the coin is biased. But there's only a 0.1% chance that it'll come up heads 70 or more times.

Now the coin is looking decidedly dodgy. The probability of seeing this particular result is referred to as the "p-value," expressed in decimal rather than percentage terms, so 13.6% is 0.136 and 0.01% chance is 0.0001.

Typically, scientists consider a p-value of 0.05 or lower to be a good indication you can reject the null-hypothesis (e.g., that the coin is unbiased) and be more confident that your alternative hypothesis (that the coin is biased) is true. This value of 0.05 is called the "significance level." A result with a p-value of 0.05 or lower is considered "significant."

P-Hacking

A good experiment will clearly define the null and the alternate hypothesis before handing out the drugs and placebos. But many experiments collect more than just one dimension of data. A trial for a headache drug might also keep an eye on side-effects, weight gain, mood, or any other variable the scientists can observe and measure. And if one of these secondary factors shows a "significant" effect—like the group who took the headache drug also lost a lot of weight—it might be tempting to shift focus onto that effect. After all, you never know when you'll come across the next Viagra.

However, if you simply track 20 variables in a study, you'd expect one of them to pass the significance threshold. Simply picking that variable and writing up the study as if that was the focus all along is dodgy science.

It's why we sometimes hear stuff that's too good to be true, like that chocolate can help you lose weight (although that study turned out to be a cheeky attempt to show how easy it is for a scientist to get away with blatant p-hacking).[4]

Publishing

Once scientists have conducted their experiment and found some interesting results, they move on to publishing them. Science is somewhat unique in that the norm is towards full transparency, where scientists effectively give away their discoveries to the rest of the scientific community and society at large. This is not only out of a magnanimous spirit, but because it also turns out to be a highly effective way of scrutinizing scientific discoveries and helping others to build upon them.

The way this works is typically by publishing in a peer-review journal. It starts with the scientist preparing their findings according to the accepted conventions, such as providing an abstract, which is an overview of their discovery, and outlining the method they used in detail, describing their raw results and only then providing their interpretation of those results. They also cite other relevant research.

They then send this "paper" to a scientific journal. Some journals are more desirable than others, i.e., they have a "high impact." The top tier, such as *Nature, Science, The Lancet,* and *PNAS,* are popular, so they receive many high-quality papers and accept only the best (or, if you're a bit cynical, the most flashy). Other journals are highly specialist and may be desirable because they're held in high esteem by a very specific audience. If the journal rejects the paper, the scientists move on to the next most desirable journal and keep at it until it's accepted or remains unpublished.

Journals employ a peer review process, where the paper is typically anonymized and sent out to a number of experts in the field. These experts then review the paper, looking for potential problems with the methods, inconsistencies in reporting or interpretation, and whether they've explained things clearly enough such that another lab could reproduce the results if they wanted to. The paper might bounce back and forth between the peer reviewers and authors until it's at a point where it's ready to publish. This process can take as little as a few weeks, but in some cases it can take months or even years.

Journals don't always get things right. Sometimes a paper will slip through with shoddy methods or even downright fraud. A useful site for keeping tabs on dodgy journals and researchers is Retraction Watch.[5]

Balance and Debate

Balance is oft touted as a guiding principle of journalistic practice. However, it's often misapplied in the domain of science. Balance works best when there are issues at stake involving values, interpretation, trade-offs, or conflicts of interest. In these cases, there is either no fact of the matter that can arbitrate between the various views or there is insufficient information to make a ruling one way or another.

In these cases, a reporter does their job by allowing the various invested parties to voice their views and, given appropriate care and background information, the reader can decide for themselves whether any have merit. This might be appropriate in a scientific context if there is a debate about the interpretation of evidence, or which hypothesis is the best explanation for it in the absence of conclusive evidence. But it's not appropriate when directly addressing some empirical question, such as which is the tallest mountain in the world. In that case, you don't call for a debate or take a straw poll, you go out and measure it.

It's also not appropriate when comparing the views of a scientist and a non-scientist on some scientific issue. An immunologist ought not be balanced with a parent when it comes specifically to discussing the safety or efficacy of vaccines.

Many reporters like to paint a vignette using an individual example. This can be a useful tool to imbue the story with emotional salience. But it also risks the introduction of an emotive anecdote into a subject that ought to be considered on the weight of the evidence.

However, balance is called for when going beyond the scientific evidence and speaking to its societal or policy implications. Science can (and should) inform policy debates, to the extent they rely on empirical facts, but policy is also informed by values and involves costs and trade-offs. Scientists can certainly weigh in on such issues—they are citizens, too. But one thing to be wary of is scientists who step outside of their areas of expertise to advocate for some personally held belief. They are entitled to do so—but they are no longer an expert in that context.

Red Flags

While it's unlikely that you'll be qualified to judge the scientific merits of the study in detail, you can look for red flags. One is the language used in the study.

Most scientists have any vestige of personality hammered out of their writing by a merciless academic pretension that a dry passive voice is somehow more authoritative than writing like a normal human being. It's not, but nevertheless if the paper's tone is uncomfortably lively, vague, or verging on the polemical, then treat it with suspicion.

You can also look for a few key elements of the study to assess its quality. One is the character of the cohort. If it's a study conducted on U.S. college students (who are known to be "WEIRD"),[6] don't assume the results will generalize to the broader population, especially outside of the United States.

Another is sample size. If the study is testing a drug, or describing some psychological quirk, and the sample size is under 50, the findings will not be very strong. That's just a function of statistics.

If you flip a coin only 10 times and it comes up heads 7 times (the p-value, or chance of it coming up 7, 8, 9 or 10, is 0.17, so not quite "significant"), it's a lot harder to be confident that the coin is biased compared with flipping it 100 times and it coming up heads 70 times (p-value 0.000039, or very, very "significant").

Also check what the study says about causation. Many studies report associations or correlations, such as that college students who drink and smoke marijuana tend to have lower grades than their peers.[7] But correlation doesn't imply causation. It might be that there is a common cause for both phenomena. Perhaps those students who are more likely to choose to drink and smoke are predisposed towards distraction, and it's the distraction that causes the lower grades rather than the content of the distraction per se. So never imply causation when a study only reports correlation. You can speculate as to causation—many studies do— but do so in context and with appropriate quotes from experts.

Many studies are also conducted on animals, especially medical studies. While it's tempting to extrapolate these results to humans, don't. It's not the case that we've cured cancer because a drug made it disappear in a mouse. It's not even the case that we've cured cancer in mice (which would still be big news in some circles).

What we've found is that application of some drug corresponded with a shrinkage of tumors in mice, and that's suggestive of an interesting interaction or mechanism that might tell us something about how the drug or cancers work, and that might one day inform some new treatment for cancers in people.

The Foundations of Science

Explaining what science is, and entertaining all the debates about how it does or should work, would take up an entire book. Rather than tackling such issues head-on, this section will give a broad overview of what science is.

While it doesn't get mentioned often outside of scientific circles, the fact is there is no one simple definition of science, and no single definitive method for conducting it. However, virtually all conceptions of science lean on a couple of underlying philosophical ideas.

The first is a commitment to learning about the world through observation, or empiricism. This is in contrast to alternative approaches to knowledge, such as rationalism—the notion that we can derive knowledge about the world just by thinking about it hard enough—or revelation—that we can learn from intuition, insight, drug-induced hallucinations, or religious inspiration.

Another philosophical basis of science is a commitment to methodological naturalism, which is simply the idea that the best way to understand the natural world is to appeal to natural mechanisms, laws, causes, or systems, rather than to supernatural forces, spirits, immaterial substances, invisible unicorns, or other deities.

This is why scientists reject the claim that ideas like creationism or intelligent design fall within the purview of science. Because these ideas posit or imply supernatural forces, no matter how scientific they try to sound, they break methodological naturalism, so they aren't science.

As a side point, science doesn't assume or imply the stronger claim of philosophical or ontological naturalism. This is the idea that only natural things exist—which usually means things that exist in spacetime—and that there are no supernatural entities at all. This is a strictly philosophical rather than scientific claim, and one that is generally agreed to be beyond the ken of science to prove one way or the other. So, if cornered, most scientists would agree it's *possible* that intangible unicorns might exist, but if they don't exist in spacetime or causally interact with things that do, then they're irrelevant to the practice of science and can be safely ignored. See Pierre Laplace's apocryphal—but no less cheeky—response to Napoleon, who remarked that Laplace had produced a "huge book on the system of the world without once mentioning the author of the universe," to which Laplace reputedly replied: "Sire, I had no need of that hypothesis."

This is where we come to the role of truth in science: there isn't any. At least in the absolute sense. Instead, science produces facts about the world that are only held to be true with a certainty proportional to the amount of evidence in support of them. And that evidence can never give 100% certainty.

No matter how certain we are of a particular theory, and no matter how much evidence we've accrued to support it, we must leave open the possibility that tomorrow we will make an observation that contradicts it. And if the observation proves to be reliable (a high bar, perhaps, but never infinitely high), then it trumps the theory, no matter how dearly it's held.

Scientific Progress

The steady accumulation of evidence is one reason why many people believe that science is constantly and steadily progressing. However, in messy reality, science rarely progresses smoothly or steadily. Rather, it often moves in fits and spurts. Sometimes a new discovery will not only change our best theories, it will change the way we ask questions about the world and formulate hypotheses to explain them. Sometimes it means we can't even integrate the old theories into the new ones. That's what is often called a "paradigm shift."

For instance, sometimes a new observation will come along that will cause us to throw out a lot of what we once thought we knew, like when the synthesis of urea, of all things, forced a rewrite of the contemporary understanding of what it means to be a living thing. That's progress of a sort, but it often involves throwing out a lot of old accepted facts, so it can also look regressive. In reality, it's doing both. That's just how science works.

Science also has its limits. For one, it can't say much about inherently unobservable things, like some of the inner workings of our minds or invisible unicorns. That doesn't mean it can only talk about things we can directly observe at the macroscopic scale. Science can talk with authority about the microscopic, like the Higgs boson, and the distant, like the collision of two black holes, because it can scaffold those observations on other observations at our scale.

But science also has limits when it comes to discussing other kinds of things for which there is no fact of the matter, like questions of subjective preference. There are similar limits when it comes to moral values. Science can describe the world in detail, but it cannot by itself determine what is good or bad. To do that, it needs an injection of values, and they come from elsewhere. Some say they come from us, or from something we worship (which many people would argue means they still come from us), or from some other mysterious non-natural source. Arguments over which source is the right one are philosophical, not scientific (although they can be informed by science).

That said, to the extent that anyone makes an empirical claim—whether that be about the movement of heavenly bodies, the age of Earth, or how species change over time—science has proven to be our best tool to scrutinize that claim.

CHAPTER 7
How Science Works[1]

By the Australian Academy of Science

- Scientific knowledge is an aggregate of research-based evidence; it is not based on any single source of information.

- Although different scientific disciplines may have different ways of gathering knowledge, in general, the scientific method comprises observation, experimentation, and then analysis of experimental data. This may be followed by reformulating the original hypothesis or idea and sometimes synthesis to formulate natural laws.

- When research papers are published, they are first scrutinized by peers in the discipline. After they are published, they are scrutinized by the broader scientific community and other researchers will try to reproduce, analyze, and challenge what is presented. This is an ongoing process and ensures rigor and integrity of the scientific process. It is an essential part of the peer-review process.

- As new knowledge emerges, newer publications supersede older ones and they become the new reference point.

- Advances in scientific knowledge or understanding are usually communicated through research publications in specialized outlets. These are often too detailed, out of the reach of the broader community, or highly specialized, so social media platforms and other forms of public communication are used to share scientific knowledge with non-specialists.

* * * * *

Science is a system of knowledge: knowledge about the physical and natural world, knowledge gained through observation and experimentation, knowledge organized systematically. It is knowledge gained using the scientific method, commonly involving a hypothesis that can be proved or disproved, or a question that can be answered. Science-based knowledge is usually subjected to discussion, debate, and further examination and review over time, especially as new information becomes available.

This process of testing, contesting, and reviewing is what gives scientists confidence in the state of knowledge at a particular time; it is what they use to explain the physical world. The knowledge that we retain and build on ("systematized knowledge") can explain phenomena robustly.

The scientific method is often thought of as a straightforward process: form a hypothesis, test or try to disprove the hypothesis through experimentation, and then revise the hypothesis. But this view can discount the role of purely observational research and pattern recognition—so-called "discovery science"—and understate the role of analysis and synthesis of concepts.

Scientists do not often use the word "proven" to describe a current level of understanding. This is reserved for the well-tested laws of nature. Science works on the basis that in many areas there will always be more to know. Even an overwhelming body of evidence may be expanded, or modified, as further work is completed and evidence compiled. That body of evidence usually becomes more complete with more work but is rarely overturned. This is science at work.

The Processes of Science

Different scientific disciplines approach the task of gathering knowledge in different ways. For example, an astronomer does not have the same opportunity to experiment that a chemist or physicist might have. A neuroscientist has a different approach to medical knowledge from an epidemiologist. There are, however, three main and mutually compatible approaches to gathering scientific knowledge. These are often combined and most scientists will use all three approaches in their research. The knowledge gained is then tested against established understandings, reviewed, and contested, all in order to ensure that the new knowledge is robust.

Observation
Scientific observation involves the close examination of phenomena. Historically, natural philosophers watched, learned, and recorded their observations using only their senses, sometimes assisted by simple instruments. Over time, devices that assist observation have become increasingly sophisticated, ranging, for example, from simple magnifying lenses to scanning electron microscopes that can detect and examine objects at finer resolutions than the human eye, through to radio

telescopes that can observe space objects well beyond the limit of visible light and well beyond the visible light spectrum.

Observations are no longer limited to human senses. Technology allows us to gather and record data on any number of physical properties. Such technology ranges from the simple and everyday—such as a thermometer or a rain gauge—to the highly advanced—such as the IceCube Neutrino Observatory in Antarctica,[2] which detects subatomic particles (neutrinos) that barely interact with other matter. Scientific observation might include identifying gene sequences and comparing them across species, or measuring radio bursts from distant stars, lasers or crystallography to identify the structures of molecules, or large-scale observatories to identify subatomic particles.

Observations need to be meticulously recorded and reported so that they can be compared across time periods, with or against the observations of others, or against benchmarks and standards. Knowledge is drawn from these comparisons.

Scientific disciplines that rely heavily on observations include astronomy, genetics, taxonomy, anatomy and medical science, and subatomic physics.

Experimentation

Experimentation is the deliberate, procedural testing of the physical world. It can be thought of as extending observations by changing aspects of a system to see what effects those changes have. Experiments are carefully designed to ensure that the conclusions drawn are derived directly from the changes made and the observed results. An experimental system is usually designed to retain as much control of the system as possible, so that deliberate changes are under the control of the experimenter and the resulting observations can be assumed to result from those changes.

Again, the methods and results of experiments must be meticulously recorded and reported. Experiments need to be reproducible by others so that their veracity can be tested and results examined.

In experimental disciplines, knowledge is gained by testing hypotheses and exploring different aspects of a system. As the understanding of the various interactions grows, predictions can be made with greater confidence. Systems can then be harnessed in reproducible, reliable ways. In this way, an experimental system becomes an applied technology, as in a medical or engineering device.

Examples of experimental disciplines include chemistry, biochemistry and molecular biology, agricultural science, physics, and medical science.

Analysis

The data gathered and recorded from observational and experimental sciences provide insights beyond their immediate context. Scientists can gather and synthesize data from different sources and conduct analyses on the aggregated dataset. Using the greater statistical power of more massive datasets, we can be more confident of the patterns and relationships that we find within them.

The starting dataset does not necessarily need to be a scientific one. For example, medical records used in hospital administration might reveal patterns of disease prevalence, which could lead to knowledge about how those diseases are caused and transmitted.

Analytical disciplines include statistics, epidemiology, atmospheric science, data science, genomics, and proteomics.

Conceptualizing and Testing

All knowledge gained through scientific processes must be contextualized within the current understanding. Science means testing: testing assumptions, testing knowledge, testing boundaries, testing evidence. Regardless of the approach taken or the methods used, a scientist must maintain an essential skepticism, constantly examining their work to ensure it is robust.

Publishing and Communication

Scientists usually publish their work as research papers in specialized journals. These provide a record of a discrete piece of work: a set of observations, a series of experiments, or a full analysis.

Academic journals have always had an essential role in the quality control of research. Journals do not publish material without analysis and comment by people skilled in the field of the research to be published, a process known as peer review. Reviewers usually remain publicly anonymous to allow comments to be made without fear of repercussion. Based on advice from the reviewers, a paper can be published or not published, or the author can make changes based on the reviewers' concerns and resubmit to the journal.

Many scientists also archive their work in data and research repositories to make it available to other researchers. This is mandatory for much of publicly funded research. Such repositories—including preprint servers for papers that have been submitted but not peer reviewed—are beyond the scope of this article, but provide other opportunities to disseminate work beyond formal journal publication.

Once a paper is published, it is subject to scrutiny by anyone working in the field. Research results can be integrated into other scientists' research and may be reproduced, analyzed, and challenged. It is common to publish research that contradicts (or appears to contradict) another paper. By recording and analyzing these differences and discrepancies, scientists can identify flaws and errors that need to be corrected. A paper found to have major flaws will be withdrawn, either by the authors or by the journal, with the reasons being outlined. Withdrawal of a paper is seen as a correction of the scientific record—a necessary and appropriate action in certain circumstances, but it is a rare occurrence. Expert peer review usually exposes flaws and misinterpretations prior to publication.

As knowledge grows, newer papers with additional evidence generally take the place of older papers. Older papers remain in the scientific record so that the lines of reasoning that led to the current knowledge can still be traced and understood.

Any given paper is open to challenge. Peer review provides only a certain minimum quality standard and does not raise the research above criticism. Once published, the paper and the data on which it rests can be scrutinized by the wider international scientific community. There is, however, something of a hierarchy of trust: a peer-reviewed paper is considered more reliable than a description of research which has not been reviewed, and a heavily scrutinized and cited paper may be regarded as more reliable (unless the citations point to flawed work) than a less-cited paper.

Other methods can be used to communicate scientific results. Communication papers are short peer-reviewed summaries of research that generally provide results in advance of a full paper. Review articles collect the results of several papers on a particular subject, providing a detailed summary of the available knowledge while citing the original papers. Monographs (books) do the same on a larger scale, addressing a broader branch of knowledge. And models are shared, synthesized collections of data that describe a particular system in detail.

In some fields, it is normal to release papers on preprint servers ahead of peer review and formal publishing. Papers on preprint servers conform to the standards of their discipline and meet academic publishing and format standards, but are not peer reviewed. Publication on these servers allows early community scrutiny and rapid dissemination of results ahead of publication, and provides a record of active research. Papers on preprint servers are often cited, but are treated with the caution owed to research that has not been peer reviewed.

News articles, essays, videos, magazines, websites, social media, and other forms of public communication help communicate scientific knowledge to non-specialists. The Australian Academy of Science produces videos and articles for this purpose. Importantly, these are not research publications and are not afforded the same status as peer reviewed research. However, they can provide valuable opportunities for scientists to share their knowledge widely and to encourage an interest in science.

* * * * *

Scientific knowledge is an aggregate: it is not based on any single publication or work, but rather on continual conversation that publishing represents. A scientist can only communicate what they know and understand; the scientific system ensures that knowledge will continue to expand and mature, and that new knowledge will be created.

CHAPTER 8
A Skeptical Manifesto[1]

By Michael Shermer

On the opening page of the splendid little book, *To Know a Fly*, biologist Vincent Dethier makes this humorous observation of how children grow up to become scientists:

> Although small children have taboos against stepping on ants because such actions are said to bring on rain, there has never seemed to be a taboo against pulling off the legs or wings of flies. Most children eventually outgrow this behavior. Those who do not either come to a bad end or become biologists.[2]

The same could be said of skepticism. In their early years children are knowledge junkies, questioning everything in their view, though exhibiting little skepticism. Most never learn to distinguish between inquisitiveness and credulity. Those who do either come to a bad end or become professional skeptics.

But what does it mean to be skeptical? Skepticism has a long historical tradition dating back to ancient Greece when Socrates observed: "All I know is that I know nothing." But this is not a practical position to take. Modern skepticism is embodied in the scientific method, that involves gathering data to formulate and test naturalistic explanations for natural phenomena. A claim becomes factual when it is confirmed to such an extent it would be reasonable to offer temporary agreement. But all facts in science are provisional and subject to challenge, and therefore skepticism is a method leading to provisional conclusions. Some claims, such as water dowsing, ESP, and creationism, have been tested (and failed the tests) often enough that we can provisionally conclude that they are false. Other claims, such as hypnosis and chaos theory, have been tested but results are inconclusive so we must continue formulating and testing hypotheses and theories until we can reach a provisional conclusion. The key to skepticism is to continuously and vigorously apply the methods of science to navigate the treacherous straits between "know nothing" skepticism and "anything goes" credulity. This manifesto—a statement of purpose of sorts—explores these themes further.

The History, Meaning & Limits of Skepticism

The modern skeptical movement is a fairly recent phenomenon dating back to Martin Gardner's 1952 classic, *In the Name of Science.* Gardner's copious essays and books over the past four decades debunking all manner of bizarre claims, coupled to James "the Amazing" Randi's countless psychic challenges and media appearances throughout the 1970s and 1980s (including 36 appearances on *The Tonight Show*), pushed the skeptical movement to the forefront of public consciousness. The philosopher Paul Kurtz helped create dozens of skeptics groups throughout the United States and abroad, and his Committee for the Scientific Investigation of Claims of the Paranormal (CSICOP) inspired me to found the Skeptics Society and *Skeptic Magazine,* now with both national and international membership and circulation. There is today a burgeoning group of people calling themselves skeptics—scientists, engineers, physicians, lawyers, professors and teachers, and the intellectually curious from all walks of life—who conduct investigations, hold monthly meetings and annual conferences, and provide the media and general public with natural explanations for apparently supernatural phenomena.

But skepticism as a way of thinking has a long historical tradition that can be traced back at least 2,500 years. The foremost historian of skepticism, Richard Popkin, tells us: "Academic scepticism, so-called because it was formulated in the Platonic Academy in the third century, B.C., developed from the Socratic observation, 'All I know is that I know nothing.'"[3] Two of the popular received meanings of the word by many people today are that a skeptic believes nothing, or is closed minded to certain beliefs. There is good reason for the perception of the first meaning. The Oxford English Dictionary (OED) gives this common usage for the word skeptic: "One who, like Pyrrho and his followers in Greek antiquity, doubts the possibility of real knowledge of any kind; one who holds that there are no adequate grounds for certainty as to the truth of any proposition whatever."[4]

Since this position is sterile and unproductive and held by virtually no one (except a few confused solipsists who doubt even their own existence), it is no wonder that so many find skepticism disturbing. A more productive meaning of the word skeptic is the second usage given by the OED: "One who doubts the validity of what claims to be knowledge in some particular department of inquiry; one who maintains a doubting attitude with reference to some particular question or statement."

The history of the words "skeptic" and "skepticism" is interesting and often amusing. In 1672, for example, the *Philosophical Transactions VII* records this passage: "Here he taketh occasion to examine Pyrrhonisme or Scepticisme, professed by a Sect of men that speak otherwise than they think." The charge is true. The most ardent skeptics enjoy their skepticism as long as it does not encroach upon their own cherished beliefs. Then incredulity flies out the window. I once received a call from a gentleman who professed to be a skeptic, wanted to support the organization, and agreed with our skepticism about everything except the power of vitamins to restore health and attenuate disease. He hoped I would not be organizing any skeptical lectures or articles on this field, which, he explained, has now been proven scientifically to be effective. "Your field wouldn't be vitamin therapy would it?," I inquired. "You bet it is!" he responded.

It is easy, even fun to challenge others' beliefs, when we are smug in the certainty of our own. But when ours are challenged, it takes great patience and ego strength to listen with an unjaundiced ear. But there is a deeper flaw in pure skepticism. Taken to an extreme, the position by itself cannot stand. The OED gives us this 1674 literary example: "There is an air of positiveness in all scepticism, an unreserved confidence in the strength of those arguments that are alleged to overthrow all the knowledge of mankind."[5]

Skepticism is itself a positive assertion about knowledge, and thus turned on itself cannot be held. If you are skeptical about everything, you would have to be skeptical of your own skepticism. Like the decaying sub-atomic particle, pure skepticism uncoils and spins off the viewing screen of our intellectual cloud chamber.

Nor does skepticism produce progress. It is not enough simply to reject the irrational. Skepticism must be followed with something rational, or something that does produce progress. As the Austrian economist Ludwig von Mises warned against those anti-communists who presented no rational alternative to the system of which they were so skeptical:

> An anti-something movement displays a purely negative attitude. It has no chance whatever to succeed. It's passionate diatribes virtually advertise the program they attack. People must fight for something that they want to achieve, not simply reject an evil, however bad it may be.[6]

Carl Sagan sounded a similar warning to skeptics: "You can get into a habit of thought in which you enjoy making fun of all those other people who don't see things as clearly as you do. We have to guard carefully against it."[7]

The Rational Skeptic

The second popular notion that skeptics are closed-minded to certain beliefs comes from a misunderstanding of skepticism and science. Skeptics and scientists are not necessarily "closed-minded" (though they may be since they are human).

They may once have been open-minded to a belief, but when the evidence came up short, they rejected it. There are already enough legitimate mysteries in the universe for which evidence provides scientists fodder for their research. To take the time to consider "unseen" or "unknown" mysteries is not always practical. When the non-skeptic says, "You're just closed-minded to the unknown forces of the universe," the skeptic responds: "We're still trying to understand the known forces of the universe."

It is for these reasons that it might be useful to modify the word skeptic with "rational." Again, it is constructive to examine the usage and history of this commonly used word. Rational is given by the OED as: "Having the faculty of reasoning; endowed with reason." And reason as, "A statement of some fact employed as an argument to justify or condemn some act, prove or disprove some assertion, idea, or belief."[8] It may seem rather pedantic to dig through the dictionary and pull out arcane word usages and histories. But it is important to know how a word was intended to be used and what it has come to mean. They are often not the same, and more often than not, they have multiple usages such that when two people communicate they are frequently talking at cross purposes. One person's skepticism may be another's credulity. And who does not think they are rational when it comes to their own beliefs and ideologies?

It is also important to remember that dictionaries do not give definitions; they give usages. For a listener to understand a speaker, and for a reader to follow a writer, important words must be defined with semantic precision for communication to be successful. What I mean by skeptic is the second usage above: "One who doubts the validity of what claims to be knowledge in some particular department of inquiry." And by rational: "A statement of some fact employed as an argument to justify or condemn some act, prove or disprove some assertion, idea, or belief." But these usages leave out one important component: the goal of reason and rationality. The ultimate end to thinking is to understand cause-and-effect relationships in the world around us. The goal is to know the universe, the world, and ourselves. Since rationality is the most reliable means of thinking, a rational skeptic may be defined as: "One who questions the validity of particular claims of knowledge by employing or calling for statements of fact to prove or disprove claims, as a tool for understanding causality." In other words, skeptics are from Missouri—the "show me" state. When we hear a fantastic claim we say, "That's nice, prove it."

Let me offer an example of how a rational skeptic might analyze a claim. For many years I had heard stories about the so-called "Hundredth-Monkey phenomenon" and was fascinated with the possibility that there might be some sort of collective consciousness into which we can tap to decrease crime, eliminate wars, and generally unite as a single species. In the last presidential election, in fact, one candidate—Dr. John Hagelin from the Natural Law Party—claimed that if elected he had a plan solve the problems of our inner cities: meditation. Hagelin and others (especially proponents of Transcendental Meditation) believe that thought can somehow be transferred between people, especially in a meditative state; if enough do it at the same time, some sort of critical mass will be reached and thereby induce significant planetary change. The Hundredth-Monkey phenomenon is commonly cited as empirical proof of this astonishing claim. In the 1950s, so the story goes, Japanese scientists gave monkeys on Koshima Island potatoes. One day one of the monkeys learned to wash the potatoes and then taught the skill to others. When about 100 monkeys had learned the skill—the so-called critical mass—suddenly all the monkeys automatically knew it, even those on other islands hundreds of miles away. The belief is widespread in New Age circles: Lyall Watson's *Lifetide* (1979) and Ken Keyes's *The Hundredth Monkey* (1982), for example, have been through multiple printings and sold millions of copies; and Elda Hartley made a film called *The Hundredth Monkey*.

As an exercise in skepticism, we should start by asking if these events really happened as reported. They did not. In 1952, primatologists began providing Japanese macaques with sweet potatoes to keep them from raiding local farms. One of them did learn to wash dirt off the potatoes in a stream or the ocean, and other monkeys learned to model the behavior (modeling is a normal part of primate behavior—"monkey see, monkey do" predates the New Age). Now let's examine Watson's claim more carefully. He admits that, "One has to gather the rest of the story from personal anecdotes and bits of folklore among primate researchers, because most of them are still not quite sure what happened. So I am forced to improvise the details." Watson then speculates that, "An unspecified number of monkeys on Koshima were washing sweet potatoes in the sea," hardly the level of precision required to justify so far-reaching a conclusion. He then makes this astonishing statement:

> Let us say, for argument's sake, that the number was 99 and that at 11:00 a.m. on a Tuesday, one further convert was added to the fold in the usual way. But the addition of the hundredth monkey apparently carried the number across some sort of threshold, pushing it through a kind of critical mass.

At this point, says Watson, the habit "seems to have jumped natural barriers and to have appeared spontaneously on other islands."

One need go no further. Scientists do not "improvise" details or make wild guesses from "anecdotes" and "bits of folklore." But there is more. In fact, some real scientists did record exactly what happened. The troop began with 20 monkeys in 1952 and reached 59 by 1962, and every monkey on the island was carefully observed. By March of 1958 exactly 17 of 30 monkeys, and by 1962 exactly 36 of 49 monkeys, had modeled the washing behavior. The "sudden" acquisition of the behavior actually took four years, and the "100 monkeys" were actually only 17 in 1958 and 36 in 1962. And while there are some reports of similar behavior on other islands, the observations were made between 1953 and 1967. It was not sudden, nor was it connected in any way to Koshima. The monkeys on other islands could have discovered this simple skill themselves; or researchers or inhabitants of the islands might have taught them; or monkeys from Koshima might have been taken there. In any case, there is nowhere near the evidence necessary to support this extraordinary claim. There is not even any real phenomenon to explain.

Science & Skepticism

Skepticism, then, is a vital part of science. Reviewing the usages and history of the word science would be inappropriately long here. For purposes of clarity science will be taken to mean "a set of mental and behavioral methods designed to describe and interpret observed or inferred phenomenon, past or present, aimed at building a testable body of knowledge open to rejection or confirmation."

In other words, science is a specific way of thinking and acting—a tool for understanding information that is perceived directly or indirectly ("observed or inferred"). "Past or present" refers to both the historical and the experimental sciences. Mental methods include hunches, guesses, ideas, hypotheses, theories, and paradigms; behavioral methods include background research, data collection, data organization, colleague collaboration and communication, experiments, correlation of findings, statistical analyses, manuscript preparation, conference presentations, and publications. What then is the scientific method? One of the more insightful and amusing observations was made by the Nobel laureate and philosopher of science, Sir Peter Medawar:

> Ask a scientist what he conceives the scientific method to be and he will adopt an expression that is at once solemn and shifty-eyed: solemn, because he feels he ought to declare an opinion; shifty-eyed, because he is wondering how to conceal the fact that he has no opinion to declare.[9]

A sizable body of literature exists on the scientific method and there is little consensus among the authors. This does not mean that scientists do not know what they are doing. Doing and explaining may be two different things. For the purpose of outlining a methodology for the rational skeptic to apply to questionable claims, the following four step process may represent, on the simplest of levels, something that might be called the "scientific method":

- **Observation:** Gathering data through the senses or sensory enhancing technologies.
- **Induction:** Drawing general conclusions from the data. Forming hypothesis.
- **Deduction:** Making specific predictions from the general conclusions.
- **Verification:** Checking the predictions against further observations.

Science, of course, is not this rigid; and no scientist consciously goes through such "steps." The process is a constantly interactive one between making observations, drawing conclusions, making predictions, and checking them against further evidence. This process constitutes the core of what philosophers of science call the hypothetico-deductive method, which involves:

1. Putting forward a hypothesis.
2. Conjoining it with a statement of "initial conditions."
3. Deducing from the two a prediction.
4. Finding whether or not the prediction is fulfilled.[10]

It is not possible to say which came first, the observation or the hypothesis, since we do both from childhood, through school, to college, into graduate training, and on the job as scientists. But observations are what flesh out the hypothetico-deductive process and serve as the final arbiter for the validity of the predictions, as Sir Arthur Stanley Eddington noted: "For the truth of the conclusions of science, observation is the supreme court of appeal."[11] Through the scientific method we may form the following generalizations:

- **Hypothesis:** A testable statement to account for a set of observations.
- **Theory:** A well-supported testable statement to account for a set of observations.
- **Fact:** Data or conclusions confirmed to such an extent it would be reasonable to offer temporary agreement.

A hypothesis and theory may be contrasted with a construct: a non-testable statement to account for a set of observations. The observation of living organisms on Earth may be accounted for by God or by evolution. The first statement is a construct, the second a theory. Most biologists would even call evolution a fact by the above definition.

Through the scientific method we aim for objectivity: the basing of conclusions on external validation. And we avoid mysticism: the basing of conclusions on personal insights that lack external validation. There is nothing wrong with personal insight. Many great scientists have attributed important ideas to insight, intuition, and other equally difficult-to-define concepts. Alfred Wallace said that the idea of natural selection "suddenly flashed upon" him during an attack of malaria. Timothy Ferris called Einstein, "the great intuitive artist of science." But insightful and intuitive ideas do not gain acceptance until they are externally validated, as Richard Hardison explained:

Mystical 'truths,' by their nature, must be solely personal, and they can have no possible external validation. Each has equal claim to truth. Tea leaf reading and astrology and Buddhism; each is equally sound or unsound if we judge by the absence of related evidence. This is not intended to disparage any one of the faiths; merely to note the impossibility of verifying their correctness. The mystic is in a paradoxical position. When he seeks external support for his views he must turn to external arguments, and he denies mysticism in the process. External validation is, by definition, impossible for the mystic.[12]

Science leads us toward rationalism: the basing of conclusions on the scientific method. For example, how do we know the Earth is round?:

1.   The shadow on the moon is round.
2.   The mast of a ship is the last thing seen as it sails off the horizon.
3.   The horizon is curved.
4.   Photographs from space.

And science helps us avoid dogmatism: the basing of conclusions on authority rather than science. For example, how do we know the Earth is round?:

1.   Our parents told us.
2.   Our teachers told us.
3.   Our minister told us.
4.   Our textbook told us.

Dogmatic conclusions are not necessarily invalid, but they do pose another question: how did the authorities come by their conclusions? Did they use science or some other means?

The Essential Tension Between Skepticism & Credulity

It is important that we recognize the fallibility of science and the scientific method. But within this fallibility lies its greatest strength: self-correction. Whether mistakes are made honestly or dishonestly, whether a fraud is unknowingly or knowingly perpetrated, in time it will be flushed out of the system through the lack of external verification. The cold fusion fiasco is a classic example of the system's swift consequences for error and hasty publication.

Because of the importance of this self-correcting feature, there is in the profession what Richard Feynman calls "a principle of scientific thought that corresponds to a kind of utter honesty—a kind of leaning over backwards." Feynman says: "If you're doing an experiment, you should report everything that you think might make it invalid—not only what you think is right about it: other causes that could possibly explain your results."[13]

Despite these built in mechanisms, science is still subject to a number of problems and fallacies that even the most careful scientist and rational skeptic are aware can be troublesome. We can, however, find inspiration in those who have overcome them to make monumental contributions to our understanding of the world. Charles Darwin is a sterling example of a scientist who struck the right balance in what Thomas Kuhn calls the "essential tension" in science between total acceptance of and devotion to the status quo, and an open willingness to explore and accept new ideas.[14] This delicate balance forms the basis of the whole concept of paradigm shifts in the history of science. When enough of the scientific community (particularly those in positions of power) are willing to abandon the old orthodoxy in favor of the (formerly) radical new theory, then, and only then can the paradigm shift occur.

This generalization about change in science is usually made about the paradigm as a system, but we must recognize that the paradigm is only a mental model in the minds of individuals. Historian of science, Frank Sulloway, identifies three characteristics of Darwin's intellect and personality that mark him as one of the handful of giants in the history of science who found the essential tension between skepticism and credulity: "First, although Darwin indeed had unusual reverence for the opinions of others, he was obviously quite capable of challenging authority and thinking for himself." Second, "Darwin was also unusual as a scientist in his extreme respect for, and attention to, negative evidence."[15] Darwin included, for example, a chapter on "Difficulties on Theory" in the *Origin of Species;* as a result his objectors were rarely able to present him with a challenge that he had not already confronted or addressed. Third, Darwin's "ability to tap the collective resources of the scientific community and to enlist other scientists as fellow collaborators in his own research projects."[16] Darwin's collected correspondence numbers greater than 16,000 extant letters, most of which involve lengthy discussions and question-and-answer sequences about scientific problems. He was constantly questioning, always learning, confident enough to formulate original ideas, yet modest enough to recognize his own fallibility.

A fourth characteristic that might be added is that Darwin maintained a good dollop of modesty and cautiousness that Sulloway sees as "a valuable attribute" that helps "prevent an overestimation of one's own theories." There is much to be learned in this regard from Darwin's autobiography. Darwin confesses that he has "no great quickness of apprehension or wit which is so remarkable in some clever men," a lack of which makes him "a poor critic: a paper or book, when first read, generally excites my admiration, and it is only after considerable reflection that I perceive the weak points." Unfortunately, many of Darwin's critics have selectively quoted such passages against him, not seeing the advantage Darwin saw in the patient avoidance of regrettable mistakes made in haste:

> I think that I have become a little more skillful in guessing right ex-
> planations and in devising experimental tests; but this may probably
> be the result of mere practice, and of a larger store of knowledge.
> I have as much difficulty as ever in expressing myself clearly and
> concisely; and this difficulty has caused me a very great loss of time;
> but it has had the compensating advantage of forcing me to think
> long and intently about every sentence, and thus I have been often
> led to see errors in reasoning and in my own observations or those
> of others.

His is a lesson in science well worth learning. What Sulloway sees as particularly special about Darwin was his ability to resolve the essential tension within
himself. "Usually, it is the scientific community as a whole that displays this essential tension between tradition and change," Sulloway observes, "since most people
have a preference for one or the other way of thinking. What is relatively rare in
the history of science is to find these contradictory qualities combined in such a
successful manner in one individual."[17]

Carl Sagan summed up this essential tension:

> It seems to me what is called for is an exquisite balance between two
> conflicting needs: the most skeptical scrutiny of all hypotheses that
> are served up to us and at the same time a great openness to new
> ideas. If you are only skeptical, then no new ideas make it through to
> you. You never learn anything new. You become a crotchety old per-
> son convinced that nonsense is ruling the world (There is, of course,
> much data to support you). On the other hand, if you are open to
> the point of gullibility and have not an ounce of skeptical sense in
> you, then you cannot distinguish the useful ideas from the worthless
> ones. If all ideas have equal validity then you are lost, because then,
> it seems to me, no ideas have any validity at all.[18]

There is some hope that rational skepticism, and the vigorous application of the
scientific method, can help us find this balance between pure skepticism and un-
mitigated credulity.

The Tool of the Mind

Science is the best method humankind has devised for understanding causality.
Therefore, the scientific method is our most effective tool for understanding the
causes of the effects we are confronted with in our personal lives as well as in nature. There are few human traits that most observers would call truly universal.

Most would consent, however, that survival of the species as a whole, and the achievement of greater happiness of individuals in particular, are universals that most humans seek. We have seen the interrelationship between science, rationality, and rational skepticism. Thus, we may go so far as to say that the survival of the human species and the attainment of greater happiness for individuals depend on the ability to think scientifically, rationally, and skeptically.

It is assumed that human beings are born with the ability to perceive cause-and-effect relationships. When we are born, we have no cultural experience whatsoever. But we do not come into the world completely ignorant. We know lots of things—how to see, hear, digest food, track a moving object in the visual field, blink at approaching objects, become anxious when placed over a ledge, develop a taste aversion for noxious foods, and so on. We also inherit the traits our ancestors evolved in a world filled with predators and natural disasters, poisons and dangers, and risks from all sides. We are descended from the most successful ancestors at understanding causality.

Our brains are natural machines for piecing together events that may be related and for solving problems that require our attention. One can envision an ancient hominid from Africa chipping and grinding and shaping a rock into a sharp tool for carving up a large mammalian carcass. Or perhaps we can imagine the first individual who discovered that knocking flint would create a spark with which to light a fire. The wheel, the lever, the bow and arrow, the plow—inventions intended to allow us to shape our environment rather than be shaped by it—started civilization down a path that led to our modern scientific and technological world.

Vincent Dethier, whose words opened this manifesto, in his discussion of the rewards of science, recounts a pantheon of the obvious ones—monetary, security, honor—as well as the transcendent: "a passport to the world, a feeling of belonging to one race, a feeling that transcends political boundaries and ideologies, religions, and languages." But he brushes these aside for one "more lofty and more subtle." This is the natural curiosity of humans in their drive to understand the world:

> One of the characteristics that sets man apart from all the other animals (and animal he indubitably is) is a need for knowledge for its own sake. Many animals are curious, but in them curiosity is a facet of adaptation. Man has a hunger to know. And to many a man, being endowed with the capacity to know, he has a duty to know. All knowledge, however small, however irrelevant to progress and well-being, is a part of the whole. It is of this the scientist partakes. To know the fly is to share a bit in the sublimity of Knowledge. That is the challenge and the joy of science.[19]

Children are naturally curious and inquisitive, and love to explore their environment. It is normal to want to know how things work and why the world is the way it is. At its most basic level, this is what science is all about. As Richard Feynman observed:

> I've been caught, so to speak—like someone who was given something wonderful when he was a child, and he's always looking for it again. I'm always looking, like a child, for the wonders I know I'm going to find—maybe not every time, but every once in a while.[20]

The most important question in education, then, is this: what tools are children given to understand the world? On the most basic of levels we must think or die. Those who are alive are thinking and using reason to a greater or lesser extent. Those who use more reason and employ rational skepticism will attain greater satisfaction because they understand the cause of their satisfaction. It cannot be otherwise. As Ayn Rand concluded in her magnum opus *Atlas Shrugged:*

> Man cannot survive except by gaining knowledge, and reason is his only means to gain it. . . Man's mind is his basic tool of survival. Life is given to him, survival is not. His body is given to him, its sustenance is not. His mind is given to him, its content is not. To remain alive, he must act, and before he can act he must know the nature and purpose of his action. He cannot obtain his food without a knowledge of food and of the way to obtain it. He cannot dig a ditch—or build a cyclotron—without a knowledge of his aim and of the means to achieve it. To remain alive, he must think.[21]

Over three centuries ago the French philosopher and skeptic René Descartes, after one of the most thorough skeptical purges in intellectual history, concluded that he knew one thing for certain: "*Cogito ergo sum*"—"I think therefore I am." By a similar analysis, to be human is to think. Therefore, to paraphrase Descartes:

> Sum Ergo Cogito —
> I Am Therefore I Think

CHAPTER 9
Common Tactics of Science Denialism[1]

by Lee McIntyre

While watching the House impeachment hearings, I realized my two decades of research into why people ignore, reject, or deny science had a political parallel. From anti-evolutionists to anti-vaccine advocates (known as "anti-vaxxers"), climate change deniers to Flat Earthers, science deniers all follow a common pattern of faulty reasoning that allows them to reject what they don't want to believe—and accept what they favor—based on a misunderstanding of how science deals with evidence. As I've been watching the hearings, I've noticed that a number of characteristics of this type of reasoning are now being embraced by President Donald Trump and his congressional supporters.

Characteristic Acts

Mark and Chris Hoofnagle (a lawyer and a physiologist) wrote an early blog post about science denialism.[2] That was followed by further work by econometrician Pascal Diethelm and public health scholar Martin McKee[3] and cognitive scientists John Cook[4] and Stephan Lewandowsky.[5] All identified the following five characteristic acts of science deniers:

- Believing in conspiracy theories;
- Relying on cherry-picked evidence;
- Relying on fake experts (and dismissal of actual experts);
- Committing logical errors;
- Setting impossible standards for what science should be able to deliver.

These elements are present when those who deny the Earth is round or who believe vaccines cause autism insist that there is a governmental cover-up of the real evidence on their topics. They can be seen when Ted Cruz tries to discredit climate change with talk about the anomalous world weather pattern in 1998 due to El Niño.[6] And they're evident when intelligent design theorists complain that evolution by natural selection still has not been proven.

Alternative Reality

Trump and his defenders in Congress echo this pattern. Even though Trump has firsthand knowledge of some of the facts under dispute—whereas his supporters may not—all seem to have bought in fully to the idea that the actual political situation is not the one pictured in the mainstream consensus of facts and evidence, but instead is based on an alternative reality.

Here are the five ways Trump and his allies use the same strategies as science deniers:

1. *Conspiracy theories*: During his questioning of Ambassador Bill Taylor and other witnesses at the impeachment hearings, Republican counsel Steve Castor repeatedly pursued a debunked conspiracy theory involving an alleged plot in which the Ukrainian government—and not the Russians—interfered with the 2016 presidential election because they were out to get the president.

2. *Cherry-picking*: Gordon Sondland, U.S. ambassador to the European Union, testified before the House Intelligence Committee that President Trump told him, "I want nothing from Ukraine. I want no quid pro quo." Trump and his supporters focused on this statement as evidence of his innocence, despite the fact that in other testimony by Sondland that day he said, "Mr. Giuliani's requests were a quid pro quo for arranging a White House visit for President Zelensky. . . Mr. Giuliani was expressing the desires of the president of the United States, and we knew that these investigations were important to the president."

3. *Discrediting experts:* President Trump has repeatedly—and falsely—claimed that State Department and CIA employees such as Bill Taylor, George Kent, Fiona Hill, Alexander Vindman, and others who have testified in the impeachment hearings are "Never Trumpers," a term for Republicans who do not support Trump—and who therefore have no credibility. His supporters have latched onto this tactic. GOP Sen. Josh Hawley of Missouri said on September 20 after the whistleblower complaint was made public: "It looks to me like another deep-state attack."

4. *Illogical reasoning*: Trump supporters have claimed that Ukrainian President Volodymyr Zelensky never complained that he felt pressured by

Trump to do the investigations into the Bidens that Trump sought. Trump himself has described the July 25 conversation he had with Zelensky in which he asked for the investigations as "perfect." But news reports have shown that Zelensky did in fact feel pressured, and analysts have pointed out that Zelensky would risk losing crucial U.S. support were he to anger Trump by saying that he felt pressured.

5. *Double standard for opponents*: Trump claimed that written testimony from the whistleblower was unacceptable, despite the fact that he himself had only given written testimony in the Mueller investigation. Some of his supporters seem to agree and have tried to compel the whistleblower's in-person testimony.

Partisan Logic

What might be behind the similarities between Trump defenders and science deniers? Perhaps, like science denial, all fact denial is basically the same. All ideology supports the reflex to believe what you want to believe. Scholars have studied the role of identity in shaping belief and concluded that sometimes even empirical beliefs can be tribal, reflecting what the other people on your team want you to believe. Adherence to a belief is not always based on evidence.

The danger, of course, is that even as new facts come in, people won't change their minds. This is the direct opposite of good empirical reasoning. It is the hallmark of science that beliefs should be based on evidence, and that people should be willing to change their beliefs based on new evidence. This means that people should be able to specify in advance what evidence, if it existed, would be sufficient to get them to change their minds.

But are Trump and his congressional supporters doing that? Like science deniers, no amount of evidence seems sufficient to change their partisan beliefs that the phone call with Zelensky was proper and that Trump "did nothing wrong." Even when the facts are overwhelming, congressional Republicans seem, like science deniers, willing to contort their beliefs and torture their logic, to stick to the party line because that is who they are. As Sen. Lindsey Graham recently put it, "I don't care what anybody else says about the phone call. . . The phone call, I've made up my own mind, is fine." In science, such behavior means that one is eventually read out of the profession—you're not fired, your tenure isn't revoked, but you're no longer taken seriously anymore. In politics, it is not yet clear what the consequences might be.

CHAPTER 10
There is Plenty of Trustworthy Journalism[1]

By Lawrence M. Eppard

Americans have easier access to reliable information and high-quality journalism, and more of it, than ever before. It is true that there has been an explosion in the number of questionable outlets in recent decades, from cable news channels (such as Fox News, MSNBC, Newsmax, CNN, and the One America News Network) to partisan websites (Huffington Post, Breitbart, InfoWars, Truthout, etc.) to numerous radio talk shows.

But there are as many high-quality outlets as ever before—we've identified over 50 trustworthy news and information outlets using a rigorous rubric at our website, ConnorsForum.org. What separates these high-quality outlets from the rest? What follows are general reflections on how real journalists at trustworthy news outlets get to the facts based on several conversations I have had on this topic with Jason Adrians, the Vice President of Local News at Lee Enterprises.[2]

* * * * *

There is a lot that goes into getting a news story to print, and how it gets there depends upon the particular story. Some stories are basic and rather straightforward. A good example might be a local university putting out a press release announcing an upcoming event or important date (say an application deadline or big sporting event). There is no reason to doubt the accuracy of this information, so this story can go to print very quickly. Obviously, if the event is cancelled or changed in some way, the newspaper can run a follow-up piece alerting readers to what has been changed and why.

Many stories are more complicated, however, and involve more investigation to figure out the truth about something newsworthy that has happened. These stories typically come from sources in the community that journalists have developed relationships with over years and sometimes decades. These sources have a strong record of credibility based upon a firmly established history of truthfulness.

That does not mean journalists just take a source's word for it and simply repeat what they are told. Receiving this information is just the beginning of the investigation. Journalists and editors take time to vet the story, explore all of the angles, and make sure the sourcing is rock solid. No matter how much a journalist may trust a source, he or she always wants to verify the information. After all, different people involved in a story have different backgrounds, perspectives, motivations, and interests, and some are themselves stakeholders in a particular story. The journalist's job is not to be the spokesperson for a particular politician or business or organization—their job is to deliver to readers a factual account of what is happening in their community. Journalists therefore consider the weight of all of the evidence and available information in order to figure out the facts.

Trustworthy news outlets[3] have quality journalists who eat, sleep, and breath news, and they are relentless in corroborating their stories with as many credible sources as possible. They collect as much additional information as they possibly can to corroborate a news story. This not only includes multiple additional sources but can also mean sorting through numerous documents and databases as well.

Once a journalist has written a draft of a story, multiple editors will then subject the story to a rigorous editing process. My colleague and former *Chicago Tribune* editor Michael Anthony Deas says that as an editor he would "cross-examine the story like a prosecuting attorney, vet all sources, and try to discredit the content," and only if it withstood his scrutiny did it make it to print. This is a useful description of what news editors do. This means double- and triple-checking the credibility of the sources as well as the accuracy, thoroughness, attribution, and fairness of the information they provide. If a story needs more information, editors and journalists work collaboratively to identify and contact as many additional credible sources as necessary in order to nail down the story.

Newspapers also write much more in-depth investigative pieces on sensitive and/or controversial issues that they may work on over the course of several weeks or months. These stories rely on dozens of sources and sometimes go through a dozen rounds of editing, revisions, and rewrites. These stories also usually lead to anywhere between five and 50 follow-up stories given the importance and complexity of the issue at hand.

These types of stories involve not only journalists and editors, but sometimes representatives from the legal and human resources teams as well. When in doubt, journalists and editors contact these folks and have them review and help with the story. Sometimes lawyers are involved in not only making sure the paper gets the story right, but in helping journalists get access to critical information in the first place. A good example would be when a governmental or other source is resisting the paper's efforts to get access to information that the public is legally entitled to.

Regardless of whether the story is basic and innocuous or complex and sensitive/controversial, if the news outlet makes a mistake or there are additional developments in a story, the good ones will strive to quickly, clearly, and publicly indicate what the mistake or development is and alert readers to the new information that they have uncovered and how this further illuminates the issue at hand. It is inevitable that mistakes will sometimes be made—what is important is that news outlets are transparent and honest when this happens, and that they quickly rectify the mistake with information that gets readers closer to the truth.

In summary, trustworthy news outlets have numerous guardrails and safeguards in place to ensure that most of the time they are getting the facts right. These guardrails and safeguards include committed journalists all over the country relentlessly corroborating their stories with multiple sources, documents, and databases. They include editors double- and triple-checking stories for their sourcing, accuracy, thoroughness, and fairness. And these guardrails and safeguards include legal and human resources representatives who are on call around the clock to make sure the outlets are getting stories right.

At numerous news outlets across the country there are journalists who, whether they feel like it or not, suit up and show up every single day. They are committed to making sure their communities are well-informed and getting the information that they need. They want to provide readers with information that is useful in their everyday lives. They want them to know that those in power will be held accountable to the public. They refuse to lose the public's trust by taking shortcuts and so they make sure to go through the proper steps to provide their communities with accurate information. And when they are wrong, they stand up and admit their mistake and explain the additional information that they have uncovered.

At this moment in our country's history, it is incredibly important for Americans to consume credible information and to support the many trustworthy outlets that provide it.

CHAPTER 11
Identifying Reliable News Sources[1]

By Alison Dagnes and Daniel Herndon

With all the reporting, news content, and commentary out there, many of us struggle to separate the fake from the fair. If you're like me, it is a part-time job to parse the balanced, the breaking, and the bad.

Well, I've got good news. And bad news, but let's start with the positives. The good news is that we now have an abundance of media options from which to choose our news, entertainment, and social connections. We are rich with content, and some of it is fabulous. The bad news is that there are too many media options, which can be paralyzing when we try to find something to watch, stream, listen to, or read. More bad news: some of the content out there is total dreck. Even worse, some is riddled with lies, misinformation, and downright dangerous garbage.

It is time consuming to find quality entertainment and tricky to find actual "good news." By this, I do not mean finding stories that make us happy but news and political information that is legit.

This begs the question: what, exactly, is "legit?" And when is it so legit we simply cannot be convinced to quit? To me, quality news has to be well-sourced, fact-checked, and balanced journalism. I am frequently asked the question: Where can we find this "good" news because, with so many options, it feels overwhelming? Fret not! I am here to help. The doctor is in.

I have carefully constructed a 3-step program and guide for those looking for the kind of quality news that informs instead of entertains and provides context instead of controversy. The Dag Dawg Method (patent pending) demands introspection and action, but at the end of it, you will have the tools to go find legit news and political information.

Grab a pencil, and away we go!

Step 1: Admitting We Have a Problem

Too many choices allow Americans to select and consume news that is chosen, formed, and delivered in a manner to inspire righteous indignation. Confirmation bias is a theory describing the partiality for information that validates existing beliefs, and modern technology affords us media that tell us what we want to hear instead of what we actually need to know. Between cable news channels, podcasts, newsletters, and Substacks, we can find the outlets that serve up the exact political content that makes us feel clever and morally superior to others. Righteous indignation, by the way, is the most wonderful feeling in the world.

But wonderful feelings are normally activated by things that should be consumed in moderation, and the pleasant buzz of moral ire, like the heady kick that comes from beer, cocktails, and nachos, is best achieved in small amounts. Thus, it is healthiest to seek out news and information that is not *purposely* antagonistic against partisan opponents.

- **Action #1:** Step away from the computer and put down the cell phone and remote control.
- **Action #2:** Ask yourself, "Do I *really* need to follow this closely? Is George Santos stealing my credit card information? Was Rep. Matt Gaetz correct that Democrats will "disarm you, empty the prisons, lock you in your home and invite MS-13 to live next door?"[2] If not, you can walk away because following politics is a choice, not your job.
- **Action #3:** To quote the philosophers Public Enemy: "Don't believe the hype." These hyperbolic outlets are trying to scare us all into Crazy Gluing our phones to our hands.

Results: Admitting you are hooked on anger is the first step toward understanding the role this polarizing content plays in our current political dysfunction. Falling prey to what the Poli Sci Nerd Herd refers to as "partisan selective exposure"[3] makes us more extreme and less likely to compromise with those with whom we disagree. It also spreads misinformation, and watching information that does *not* confirm existing beliefs can increase greater fact-based knowledge.[4]

Step 2: Separate Ballers from Bawlers

There is some *incredible* journalism being done today, AND we have an opinion problem. The **Ballers** are the journalists who do incredible research and win awards for their tenacity and clarity. The **Bawlers** are the partisans who yell a lot on cable & podcasts and use ALL CAPS in type.

The old joke goes that "opinions are like assholes: everyone's got one." These days every asshole has an opinion they share on social media, which turns the old joke into an impossible math problem involving exponentiality. As I do for most things, I blame Mark Zuckerberg. People have taken their opinions way too seriously ever since the moment they became convinced that the guy who helped them at Staples was their "friend" and that everyone wanted to hear their thoughts about absolutely everything.

An even larger problem is that we now have a tangle of news and opinion, and it's tough to tell the difference. We get news and commentary confused because the lines blur constantly:

- **Journalists Give Their Opinions Widely**, which goes against one of the important tenets of journalism. We hear from reporters on Twitter, on podcasts, on shows like *This Week, Fox News Sunday, Face the Nation,* and *Meet the Press,* and everywhere we know exactly who they like and whom they do not. This leads to the very real critique of media bias and then the less credible accusation of fake news.
- **Some "News" Organizations Feature More Opinion than Journalism.** Just because it's called "InfoWars" doesn't mean there's real information there. Most of the cable news prime time lineups consist entirely of punditry, even when "News" is in their channel name. This is confusing for the audiences, and probably purposely so. Colorful storytelling is more interesting than just the facts, even when the stories are complete fiction.

Here are the differences:

Opinion:

Comes in many forms but is not the news.

- **Punditry** = A viewpoint from someone paid to give their opinion, be it credible or unsubstantiated, found on cable news, blogs, Substacks, or talk radio. Famous pundits include Tucker Carlson, Rachel Maddow, Sean Hannity, Don Lemon, Laura Ingraham, and Rush Limbaugh.
- **Analysis** = An opinionated, ostensibly "expert" assessment of a news event found mostly in online versions of newspapers. Used to be called "Op-Eds," now leads to arguments about "journalistic punditry," which isn't really a thing.
- **Social Media Posts by Your Family Members** = These should not be taken with even a grain of salt because salt is either bad for you or it will cure herpes, according to my Uncle Harmon. This is the kind of second-third-hundredth-hand opinion that is not verified or even real, and the reason we now have a QAnon problem in America. Thanks, Uncle Harmon!

Journalism:

Sourced, verified, factual information provided without opinion or bias.

- **Print, Online, Broadcast** = Brought to us by journalists who gather the news and do so with a series of rules that guide their behavior, including story verification and fact-checking.
- **Anonymous Sources** = In general, these should not be concerning since they are only anonymous to the reader. Arguably, the reporters and their editors know who the sources are and have verified their claims with corroboration from other sources.

How Can You Tell It Is Journalism?

Journalism is a very different beast than commentary, and the bottom line comes down to money. It takes money to produce well-sourced, interesting, ground-breaking news, and it costs nothing to have an opinion about it.

The easiest way to determine if something is journalism is to follow the money. A real journalistic outlet scores its revenue from the legitimacy of its product. In other words, ask: How does the outlet bring in readers or viewers? The real newspapers that make their reputation by breaking stories will lose readership by making things up or by pressing their thumb on the scale. Conversely, the political content outlets that drum up interest by pissing off their audience make their money through outrage. If this is the case, it's not journalism. If it involves long-form reporting, it probably is.

When a publication is openly commentary or opinion, that doesn't mean it can't provide journalistic value. The question is whether they are a source that can be trusted to practice journalistic integrity, regardless of whether they break the news or summarize it with their take. An outlet like this will go out of its way to be fair or accurate. When a news outlet runs an error, they bend over backward to acknowledge it. When a GOOD news outlet runs an error, they run a ten-page story and a podcast explaining where they went wrong to correct the record.

Conversely, if a political outlet says the Clintons murdered someone and, after a lawsuit, does not apologize (ahem), it's not news. When an outlet makes a mistake and they run a correction, it is journalism—or at least credible commentary.

Step 3: Trust the Professionals for Valid News

Now that you're looking inside yourselves and recognizing the kinds of info available, it's time to hand it over to the pros because you've worked hard enough. There are two excellent avenues for outsourcing the media selection decision-making process to the people who are trained, experienced, and (perhaps most importantly) paid to be experts.

First Avenue: Hit the Bias Charts

Biased media is more than just the unseasoned opinion of one person, and two highly respected, well-credentialled organizations rate news and political information outlets for fairness and validity.

- **Ad Fontes Media** (located at <u>adfontesmedia.com</u>) rates news organizations for original fact reporting and ideological bias. You can sort through TV, podcasts, and online sources to find the most unbiased and trustworthy news and political content.
- **AllSides** (located at <u>allsides.com/media-bias</u>). If Ad Fontes is too much, check out the easier to read chart from AllSides that lays out the ideological perspective of the big online outlets (not radio, TV, or audio).

Some people will doubt the validity of the bias charts themselves, but each site has a good explanation of their methodology for you to plagiarize when you're explaining trustworthiness to a relative who is convinced that Democrats, Hollywood celebrities, and most Jews are actually lizard people bent on destruction.[5]

Second Avenue: Trust the News Services

If you don't have the time or inclination to be introspective, analytical, and chart literate, here's a fast and easy way to get straight facts without fear of any kind of ideological or structural bias: Get your news from a news service.

News services are the agencies that gather news stories and distribute them for print or broadcast to outlets that subscribe to the service. Getting a good story from a news service used to require a subscription, but these days you can hit the news service website and help yourself. Here are two:

- The Associated Press (AP) (located at <u>apnews.com</u>).
- Reuters (located at <u>reuters.com</u>).

One thing to be wary of: *many* websites purport to be unbiased "news services" and are really boloney in disguise. Stick with the knowns, and you're good to go.

The next time you find yourself scrolling or flipping channels just to get that sweet, juicy feeling of haughty self-satisfaction, check yourself before you wreck yourself and get the truth. It may not be as sweet a feeling, but at least you'll know that you're playing with a full deck.

CHAPTER 12
How NewsGuard Works[1]

By NewsGuard

NewsGuard employs a team of journalists and experienced editors to produce reliability ratings and scores for news and information websites based on nine journalistic criteria. The criteria assess basic practices of credibility and transparency. Based on a site's performance on these nine apolitical criteria, which are each weighted differently with the points for all adding up to 100, it is assigned a 0-100 score, also expressed as 0% to 100%, and a rating level indicating the degree to which it adheres to the weighted criteria. The accompanying Nutrition Label, accessible by clicking through from the listed score, then explains how NewsGuard arrived at its assessment.

* * * * *

Score and Rating Levels

For NewsGuard's browser extension users, each site's score is displayed next to links on search engines and social media platforms in the form of an icon.

The language that introduces and summarizes each website's score varies, depending on the score, as follows:

- **100** (or 100%): **High Credibility**: This website adheres to all nine standards of credibility and transparency.

- **75-99** (or 75%-99%): **Generally Credible**: This website mostly adheres to basic standards of credibility and transparency.

- **60-74** (or 60%-74%): **Credible with Exceptions**: This website generally maintains basic standards of credibility and transparency—with significant exceptions.

- **40-59** (or 40%-59%): **Proceed with Caution**: This website is unreliable because it fails to adhere to several basic journalistic standards.

- **0-39** (or 0% to 39%): **Proceed with Maximum Caution**: This website is unreliable because it severely violates basic journalistic standards.

In addition, some websites by their nature do not receive a score based on their adherence to the nine criteria because the criteria are not directly relevant to them. However, they do receive a Nutrition Label that describes the website more generally. There are two such categories of websites:

- Satire: A humor or satire site receives a satire rating, indicating that while it may use news as a basis for satire, it is not a traditional news website. We do not rate these sites according to the nine journalistic criteria, but we do provide a description of each site including, if possible, who is behind it.

- Platform: A site receives a platform rating if it primarily hosts content directly published by users with limited vetting. Information from platform sites may or may not be reliable. We do not rate these sites according to the nine journalistic criteria, but we do provide a description of each site and its practices.

* * * * *

Rating Criteria

NewsGuard's scores and ratings for news and information sites are based on nine apolitical criteria that assess the website's credibility and transparency. As noted, each criterion is worth a certain number of points out of 100, weighted based on importance, as indicated below. All criteria are pass-fail, meaning that a site either receives all of the points associated with the criterion or receives no points for that criterion. In some instances, this may make the scores less precise, but the alternative of giving sites some but not all of the relevant points is not feasible for a process that involves rating thousands of news sites.

In some specific cases described below, a site can receive an "N/A" for a criterion that NewsGuard determines does not apply to the website, in which case the publisher receives the points associated with that criterion. Again, satire sites and platforms are given separate designations and are not scored using the nine criteria.

Each score is described in detail in the Nutrition Label, which explains why NewsGuard made its determination on each of the criteria, provides evidence and examples to back up its assessments, includes any relevant comments from the publisher, and indicates the history of the sites' ratings. We always seek feedback from publishers that appear to fail any of our criteria before we publish a rating or an updated rating, ensuring a publisher ability to reply.

The criteria below are listed in order of their importance in determining a site's 0-100 score.

Credibility
Does not repeatedly publish false content: The site does not repeatedly and currently produce content that has been found to be clearly and significantly false, and which has not been quickly and prominently corrected. There is a "high bar" for failing this criterion. In practice, it means that on any given day the website is likely to display significantly false content. (**22 points**)

Here are some reasons that a site might pass this criterion:

- The site has not been found currently and repeatedly to publish clearly and egregiously false information, even if it may have published such content in the past or even recently, whereupon it is likely to fail the criteria for not gathering and presenting news responsibly.
- Factual errors or misstatements on the site are generally minor.
- Major mistakes are generally quickly and transparently corrected or retracted.
- If the website repeatedly published significantly false content in the past, it has not regularly published such content in recent months.
- If the website repeatedly and accurately quotes other publications or sources making significantly false claims, it generally does not present those false claims as fact. However, doing so, especially without questioning the quoted false claim or presenting an alternative view, might mean that it will fail the criterion for gathering and presenting news responsibly.
- If the website sometimes publishes significant false claims, those claims represent a small proportion of its overall content, which otherwise generally adheres to journalistic standards.

Here are some reasons that a site might fail this criterion:

- The site has displayed a pattern of publishing egregiously false claims on a regular and ongoing basis—meaning that a user is likely to encounter such a false claim on any given visit to the site. Egregiously false means that there is clear, credible evidence contradicting the claim such that a reasonable person taking care to get the facts right would be unlikely to make the false claim.

- The site repeatedly states as fact claims that are contradicted by an abundance of scientific evidence.
- The site repeatedly promotes conspiracy theories that cannot be disproven but have no basis in fact and are contradicted by an abundance of credible evidence.
- In some cases, a government-owned outlet that repeatedly and accurately, but uncritically, quotes the false claims of its government owner will fail this criterion. This is especially likely to be the case where the news outlet does not have an effective charter enabling it to publish independently of the views of the government.

Note: In assessing this criterion, NewsGuard reviews both claims made in news articles and factual statements made in opinion pieces, even if those pieces are clearly labeled as opinion.

Gathers and presents information responsibly: Content providers are generally fair and accurate in reporting and presenting information. They reference multiple sources, preferably those that present direct, firsthand information on a subject or event or from credible secondhand news sources, and they do not egregiously distort or misrepresent information to make an argument or report on a subject. (**18 points**)

Here are some reasons that a site might pass this criterion:

- The site generally reports on events factually and presents information in context.
- The site generally attributes information to credible sources and credits content that it republishes to the original source.
- The site generally publishes claims that can be verified, either by attributing information to reliable sources or providing evidence or firsthand reporting.
- When articles quote someone making a clearly false claim, the site typically notes the falsehood to readers.
- When articles quote someone making an unsubstantiated claim for which there is significant countervailing evidence, the site typically includes countervailing evidence or notes that the claim is unsubstantiated.
- If the site has made some false or unsubstantiated claims, it has not repeatedly done so.

Here are some reasons that a site might fail this criterion:

- The site egregiously distorts or misrepresents facts—for example, taking quotes out of context or citing a scientific study to make a false point not supported by the research.
- The site fails NewsGuard's criterion for not repeatedly publishing false content.
- The site regularly quotes sources or other publications making clearly false claims without noting that those claims are false.
- The site regularly quotes sources or other publications making unsubstantiated claims about which there is credible countervailing evidence without noting that the information is unsubstantiated or providing some countervailing evidence.
- The site has published numerous older, clearly false claims on significant topics that remain online uncorrected, even if it has not published such claims recently.
- The site publishes one-sided coverage of issues, such as politics, without clearly disclosing that it is owned or financed by a government or organization that supports the site's views—for example, a website owned by a political campaign that publishes negative stories about other candidates without disclosing that conflict of interest.
- The website publishes poorly sourced information that is difficult to verify and omits context such as times, places, and names.
- The site routinely republishes content from other publishers without attribution or credit to the original source.
- The website predominantly cites anonymous sources whose connection to the information is not clearly described.

Regularly corrects or clarifies errors: The site has effective practices for identifying errors and for publishing clarifications and corrections, transparently acknowledges errors, and does not regularly leave significant false content uncorrected. (**12.5 points**)

Here are some reasons that a site might pass this criterion:

- There is evidence that the site has a regular practice of correcting errors in its stories, publishing at least one correction a year and publishing previous corrections in past years.
- Corrections are visible and the error being corrected generally is clearly described to the reader.
- The site has not yet been publishing content for a full year and, while it has not published corrections, NewsGuard's review did not find clearly false claims that would require a correction—making it too early for NewsGuard to find a failure on this criterion.

Note: A Nutrition Label may note that a site has published a corrections policy, but the existence of such a policy is not necessary to pass this criterion.

Here are some reasons that a site may fail this criterion:

- The site does not regularly correct errors, meaning NewsGuard could not find evidence of at least one correction issued per year in recent years.
- The site repeatedly deletes or edits inaccurate content to remove errors instead of transparently issuing corrections.
- The site previously published transparent corrections but has not done so in the last 12 months.
- The site only corrects errors as a result of NewsGuard's review process.
- Even if the site regularly issues corrections for minor errors, it repeatedly leaves significantly false claims uncorrected.

Handles the difference between news and opinion responsibly: Content providers who convey the impression that they report news or a mix of news and opinion distinguish opinion from news reporting, and when reporting news, do not egregiously cherry pick facts or stories to advance opinions. Content providers who advance a particular point of view disclose that point of view. (**12.5 points**)

Here are some reasons that a site might pass this criterion:

- The site publishes opinion content in a designated section clearly labeled as opinion using terminology that would be understood by the average reader, such as "opinion," "editorial," "commentary," "analysis" or another label that an average reader would understand.
- The content signals that it is the opinion of the author by providing the author's name with a colon in the headline.
- If the site has an overall agenda or point of view in its news coverage that it advances by its choice of the news it covers and the opinion it publishes, it clearly discloses and describes its perspective to readers somewhere prominent on the site—such as on an about page or the site's homepage.
- Content presented as news generally does not contain opinionated language.
- The site clearly describes itself as an opinion site, does not purport to publish straightforward news content, and does not present any of its content as news.

Here are some of the reasons that a site might fail this criterion:

- Content presented as news frequently contains opinionated language.
- The site advances a particular point of view through clearly one-sided story selection or opinionated content without disclosing that point of view to readers.
- The site mixes news stories and opinion stories throughout the site without clearly distinguishing between the two types of stories.
- The site inaccurately labels its news or opinion content.

Sites might receive an "N/A" on this criterion if:

- The site is clearly the website of an advocacy organization and is transparent about its mission.

Avoids deceptive headlines: The site generally does not publish headlines that include false information, significantly sensationalize, or otherwise do not reflect what is actually in the content under the headline. (**10 points**)

Here are some reasons that a site might pass this criterion:

- The site publishes accurate, factual headlines that properly communicate the content they represent.
- If the site publishes buzzy, slightly sensational headlines, they generally do not misrepresent facts or misdescribe the content to which they refer.
- If the website has published some deceptive headlines, it has not done so frequently enough that a user would be likely to encounter the headlines on a regular basis.

Here are some reasons that a site might fail this criterion:

- The site frequently runs headlines that do not accurately reflect the content.
- The site regularly publishes headlines that contain significant falsehoods.

Sites might receive an "N/A" on this criterion if:

- The site does not publish headlines.

Transparency
Website discloses ownership and financing: The site discloses in a user-friendly manner its ownership and/or financing, as well as any notable political affiliations or financial interests relevant to the site's coverage held by those with a significant financial interest in the site. Put simply, the reader should know who is

funding the content and what relevant interests the owner or funder might have in the content. **(7.5 points)**

Here are some reasons that a site might pass this criterion:

- The website clearly identifies its owner in a prominent, easily accessible section of the site.
- If any of the site's owners or major funders has a notable political affiliation, financial interest, or other role or affiliation that might present a conflict of interest with the site's coverage, that information is disclosed clearly to readers.
- The site discloses its ownership and financing in specific stories that refer to the owner or to subjects of coverage connected to the owner or funder.
- If the site is owned by a nonprofit organization, the site identifies major donors in a place where a user can find that information easily.

Here are some reasons that a site might fail this criterion:

- The site does not clearly identify its owner, including any parent company.
- The site's only mention of its owner is in a place that an average user would not be likely to look, notice, or understand, such as a copyright notice or on a "Terms of Service" page.
- The site is owned by a nonprofit but does not identify its major donors, if any.
- The site does not disclose potential conflicts of interest involving its owners and financers in individual stories related to the owner or funders.

Clearly labels advertising: The site makes clear which content is paid for and which is not. **(7.5 points)**

Here are some reasons that a site might pass this criterion:

- Advertising is distinguished from editorial content either with clear visual cues or explicit labels such as "advertisement," "paid content," "sponsored," or another label an average reader would understand indicates that the content is paid.
- If the site publishes a sponsored or promotional article alongside straightforward news content, it distinguishes the article by disclosing to readers that the content is paid in a prominent place, such as at the beginning of the sponsored article or at the headline. A disclosure at the bottom of a long article or in a small, hard-to-notice typeface does not meet this standard.

- If the site publishes content via a commercial content-sharing arrangement or partnership, the site discloses that arrangement or partnership.
- If the site publishes an article with affiliate links, it clearly discloses somewhere on the article page, in a location and manner that an average reader could find, that the site may earn revenue from purchases made through the links.

Here are some of the reasons that a site might fail this criterion:

- The site presents sponsored and promotional articles alongside straightforward news content on the site without clearly distinguishing which is which.
- The site includes links to buy products within its articles for which it receives affiliate or referral payments without clearly and prominently disclosing that commercial arrangement to readers.
- The site publishes paid content, affiliate links, and other commercial content that is labeled in a manner that the average reader would not understand to mean that the content is commercial — such as "From Our Partners" or "Around the Web."
- The site is paid to run promotional articles on behalf of a company or organization but does not disclose the commercial relationship to a reader.

Sites receive an "N/A" on this criterion if:

- The site does not publish advertisements or sponsored content.

Reveals who's in charge, including possible conflicts of interest: Those in charge of the content are identified on the site, and there is a way for readers to contact the site about editorial issues. In other words, the reader is told who is in charge of deciding what content is published. (**5 points**)

Here are some of the reasons that a site might pass this criterion:

- The website identifies someone in charge of editorial decisions in an easily accessible section of the site and provides some way for readers to contact the site about editorial issues.
- If the site's editorial leaders have a significant potential conflict of interest, such as involvement in a political campaign or with a company on which the site reports, any such conflicts are disclosed to readers.

Here are some reasons that a site might fail this criterion:

- The website does not identify someone who oversees editorial content, or only does so on a page that is not easily accessible to an average visitor to the site.
- Even if the site lists the name of a person in charge of editorial content, it does not provide any way for users to contact the site about editorial issues.
- One or more of the site's editorial leaders has a significant potential conflict of interest, such as involvement in a political organization or with a company about which the site reports, that is not disclosed to readers.

The site provides the names of content creators, along with either contact or biographical information: Information about those producing the content is made accessible on the site, and it is generally clear who produces which content. (**5 points**)

Here are some reasons that a site might pass this criterion:

- Content is typically attributed to an author or content creator whose full name is provided, and the site provides either contact information or relevant biographical information for most content creators (Examples of contact information include the content creator's phone number, email address, Twitter handle, or other method through which the content creator can be contacted).
- If content is not typically attributed to a specific author or content creator, the website provides a staff directory listing the names, relevant biographical information, and contact information for its content creators, along with an indication of the general topics or areas of coverage to which each content creator contributes.

Here are some reasons that a site might fail this criterion:

- Content never or rarely is attributed to a specific author or content creator.
- Content often is bylined with only the author or content creator's first name, initials, or a pseudonym.
- Content is attributed to specific authors or content creators, but the site does not provide contact information or relevant biographical information about its content producers.

Note: Some publications tell NewsGuard that they decline to name their content creators for fear that they will be subject to reprisal or that doing so is an invasion of their privacy. In some instances, this is a legitimate concern and constitutes a strong argument against this criterion. However, NewsGuard believes that as a general matter journalists should stand behind, and be accountable for, their work. Thus, it remains a weakness of the NewsGuard system that otherwise highly professional news websites operating in areas where journalists may be in jeopardy will get a 95 Green score instead of a 100. This reflects the fact that operating in certain regions or countries means this disclosure is impractical, depriving readers of this information.

✶ ✶ ✶ ✶ ✶

Scoring Process

Our scoring process is designed to ensure our nine journalistic criteria are applied equally and accurately to all sites, regardless of the site's topic, tone, or political leaning if any, and regardless of whether the site is a long-established large news operation or a small digital startup.

1. **A NewsGuard analyst assesses the contents of the site against our nine criteria.** Our analysts are trained journalists who conduct reporting to determine relevant details of the website's ownership, financing, credibility, and transparency practices.

2. **The analyst drafts the "Nutrition Label" for the site based on their reporting.** Nutrition labels consist of a grid showing the site's performance on each of the nine criteria and a written explanation of the content on the site, who's behind it, and why it received its score.

3. **We call the website for comment.** If a NewsGuard analyst believes a site may fail one or more of the nine criteria, it is NewsGuard's practice to contact the website's proprietor to attempt to seek comment before publishing the rating. If the website provides a comment, that comment is included in the written assessment of the site to provide users with the website's perspective.

4. **The score is reviewed and fact-checked by experienced editors.** At least one senior editor and NewsGuard's co-CEOs review every Nutrition Label prior to publication to ensure that the rating is as fair and accurate as possible.

5. **The site's score is determined solely based on its performance on each of the nine criteria.** The criteria are apolitical (For example, there is no "liberal" or "conservative" way to have a systemic, transpar-

ent process for posting corrections, which is one of the nine criteria).

6. **We update scores and the associated Nutrition Labels periodically.** NewsGuard periodically updates its score and rating of each site. If a site changes its practices, its performance on one or more of News-Guard's nine criteria may change. More than 2,000 websites have improved their transparency or credibility practices as a result of engaging with NewsGuard's analysts through the scoring process. Such updates are noted in an editor's note on the Nutrition Label.

7. **We practice accountability and show our work.** Each Nutrition Label contains the names of the writer and editors who worked on the rating. The backgrounds of the analysts and editors named, as well as those of the supervising editors, can be found by clicking on their names or going to the Our Team page of our website. If a website disagrees with NewsGuard's score for its site, it can comment as part of the assessment process, and relevant comments will be included in the site's Nutrition Label. The publisher also may write a more detailed response or complaint using NewsGuard's contact page. Any such complaints will be published on NewsGuard's website and linked from the site's Nutrition Label.

CHAPTER 13
How the Media Bias Chart is Created[1]

By Vanessa Otero

Ad Fontes Media's founder, Vanessa Otero, created the first Media Bias Chart in October of 2016 (check out the current chart at https://adfontesmedia.com/). She initially created it as a hobby, for the purpose of creating a visual tool to discuss the news with friends and family, so she created the taxonomy and analyzed the initial set of news sources herself. However, because it grew to be extremely popular, she sought out to improve the methodology, make the process more data-driven, and mitigate bias (hers and that of any new analysts). To do so, she recruited teams of politically diverse analysts and trained them in the methodology. Over time, this process evolved into Ad Fontes Media's current method of multi-analyst content analysis ratings.

Ad Fontes finished our first extensive multi-analyst content ratings research project in June 2019. From June 2019 to August 2020, a group of nine analysts from that initial project continued to rate several dozen articles per month to add new sources and update previously existing ones. From August to October of 2020, we conducted a second large multi-analyst content ratings project to rate over 2,000 articles and 100 new news sources with some existing analysts and over 30 new analysts. From October 2020 to present, we have used our team of nearly 40 paid, trained analysts to continuously rate new sources and update ratings on existing sources. Our current data set includes nearly 20,000 multi-analyst ratings of articles, and episodes from over 1,600 Web, podcast, and TV shows, and growing.

All the scores we collect in our analysis rely on an assumption that the taxonomy of the Media Bias Chart is a valid way of rating news sources on the dimensions of reliability and political bias. This taxonomy was created by Vanessa

Otero, the founder of Ad Fontes Media, who has a B.A. in English from UCLA and a J.D. from the University of Denver Sturm College of Law. Most of her educational and career background focused on analytical reading and writing. Aspects of the systems and methods described herein are patent pending.

Since the release of the original Media Bias Chart in 2016, millions of observers have found the system of classification to be useful, regardless of whether they personally agree with where news sources are placed on the Chart. Social scientists, data scientists, statisticians, and news organizations may find areas of our work to be improved, and we welcome criticisms and suggestions, recognizing there is always sharpening that may be done, and that the news landscape itself is always shifting. Some observers take issue with aspects of the taxonomy itself; for example, some object that a left-right spectrum doesn't capture the full extent of political positions. Such points may be (and likely will be) debated forever, but based on the proven utility of this taxonomy for so many, and with increasing demand for the underlying data, we continue to use it while improving and refining it along the way.

Core Taxonomy

Otero also created the original content analysis methodology. However, the methodology has evolved over time and with input from many thoughtful commentators and experts, including Ad Fontes Media Advisor and long-time journalist and journalism professor Wally Dean. Professor Dean co-authored *We Interrupt This Newscast*, a book detailing one of the largest content analysis studies ever done—a study of local news broadcasts from 1998 to 2001.[2]

We currently provide in-depth discussions of our taxonomy and methodology in various public-facing webinars. For example, we teach ongoing news analysis training that is available for members of our site and free teacher training which we conduct from time to time.

Framework

Our taxonomy continues to be a two-dimensional framework for rating the reliability and bias of content, shows, and sources.

The horizontal axis (political bias, left to right) is divided into seven categories, three of which represent the spectrum on the left, three of which represent the spectrum on the right, and one in the middle. Each category spans 12 units of rating, so the total numerical scale goes from -42 on the left to +42 on the right. These values are somewhat arbitrary, though there are some good reasons for them, including that they (1) allow for at least seven categories of bias, (2) allow for more nuanced distinction between degrees of bias within a category (allowing analysts to categorize something as *just a bit* more biased than something else), and (3) they correspond well to visual displays on a computer screen or a poster.

Bias scores are on a scale of -42 to + 42, with higher negative scores leaning more to the left, higher positive scores leaning more to the right, and scores closer to zero being either centrist, minimally biased, and/or balanced (It should be noted that centrism, neutrality, and balance are not the same thing from our point of view. For example, an article may score near 0 because it contains an even-handed debate between multiple similarly informed and authoritative sources).

The vertical axis (overall reliability, top to bottom), is divided into eight categories, each spanning eight rating units, for a total numerical scale of 0 to 64. Again, these are somewhat arbitrary, but the eight categories provide sufficient levels of classification of the types of news sources we are rating and sufficient distinction within the categories. Reliability scores are on a scale of 0-64, with source reliability being higher as scores go up.

Overall source ratings are composite weighted ratings of the individual article and show scores. There are many specific factors our analysts take into account when considering the reliability and bias of an article, episode, or other content. The main ones for *Reliability* are defined metrics we call "Expression," "Veracity," and "Headline/Graphic," and the main ones for *Bias* are ones we call "Political Position," "Language," and "Comparison."

Observers may argue that numerical scales for bias and reliability should be more or less granular, but our ratings are based on the scale described above. Therefore, an underlying premise of the scoring is that this scale is useful for conveying its meaning to its observers.

Definitions

The horizontal (or "bias") categories are defined by the policy positions of current U.S. elected officials (For more on why, see the methodology video in the following footnote.[3] This video also discusses how the U.S. left-right spectrum shifts over time—which relates to a concept known as the Overton Window—and how that affects our rating of contemporary media content). There are three important definitions we use for defining areas of the horizontal axis, which are as follows:

1. The line between "Most Extreme Left/Right and Hyper-Partisan Left/Right" is defined by the policy positions of the most extreme *elected* officials significantly relevant to the scope of the issue being considered. Any position in a news source that is more extreme than what that official advocates falls in the "Most Extreme" category.

2. Most of the categories of "Hyper-partisan Left/Right and Skews Left/Right" are defined by the current positions of Democratic and Republican party politicians, with the midpoint position in each party (the policy positions held by the leaders of each party, respectively) represented by the line between "skews left/right" and "hyper-partisan left/right."

3. The "middle" position on the horizontal axis represents narratives with no discernable political position taken, a relatively complete and balanced survey of key competing positions on a given issue, as well as narratives representing a "centrist" political perspective, which is itself a political bias. An article, episode, or source placing near the midpoint on the horizontal axis may land there for any of these reasons; thus the position does not necessarily represent "neutrality." Nor is the midpoint on the horizontal axis intended to imply that the position is best or most valid.

The vertical (or "reliability") axis represents a continuum between fact and falsehood, as follows:

1. Analysts score content they deem to be primarily fact reporting between 48 and 64, with the highest scores reserved for encouraging the hard (and socially essential) work of original fact reporting that is subsequently corroborated by additional sources. However, fact-based content that is widely corroborated has the highest likelihood of veracity, so fact reporting generally falls between 48 and 56 on the vertical axis.

2. Content that includes analysis scores between 32 and 48, with the higher scores in this range reserved for analysis that is supported by well-argued fact reporting. In terms of "reliability," the taxonomy places opinion (24-32) below analysis. However, as with analysis, opinion that is well-argued and defended based with facts also scores higher within the category.

3. Content scoring below 24 generally has a reliability problem. When it scores between 16 and 24, very likely an important part of the story was omitted. It is likely (and literally) a "partial" story representing—at least in that sense—an "unfair" attempt at persuasion. Content scoring below 16 has been determined by our analysts to be misleading or downright false, at least based on the best evidence presented to date.

It should be noted that our taxonomy and methodology constitute a rubric used to *describe* content on both the horizontal ("bias") and vertical ("reliability") axes. Bias scores are *descriptive* in relation to the current politics of the country as a whole. They are not intended to rate the moral quality of a position; nor are they measured against a timeless or universal norm. Reliability scores are similarly *descriptive*, though veracity is one of the metrics considered on the vertical axis. While veracity is part of what we consider when rating the reliability of content, there is a categorical difference between the "rightness" or "wrongness" of content expressing an opinion and the "truth" or "falsehood" of content stated as fact. Moreover, there are limits to human knowledge, and our methodology considers "likelihood of veracity" to be more accurate than a "true/false" toggle when considering the accuracy of content presented as fact.

The overall source rating is a result of a weighted average, algorithmic translation of article raw scores. Low-quality and highly-biased content weight the overall source down and outward. The exact weighting algorithm is not included here because it is proprietary, but generally, lower reliability and more biased content is weighted more heavily. Aspects of what is disclosed here are patent pending.

Analysis

Prior to October 2020, all analysts were volunteers receiving perks and/or small stipends. Since October 2020, Ad Fontes Media has contracted and hired a team of analysts to rate news content on an ongoing basis. At the time of this 2021 revision, we have 33 active professional analysts.

Currently, our analyst application process requires the following:

- Submission of a professional resume, CV, or similar written summary of qualifications.
- Completion of an online application enabling further assessment of qualifications.
- Completion of a political viewpoint assessment used to build an analyst team that can provide equal input from those leaning politically to the left, those leaning to the right, and those with centrist leanings. A self-reported classification of their political leanings. Each analyst submitted a spreadsheet about their political views overall and per listed political topic. The "political position assessment" can be viewed on our site on the analyst application page.

Submission of basic demographic information is optional but helpful in maintaining an analyst team that is relatively representative of the country as a whole.

Education and Qualifications
Our current qualification expectations for new applicants are as follows:

Minimum Qualifications

- Has completed minimum high school + 2 years (60 hours) of undergraduate work
- Lives in the United States, and is politically/civically engaged
- Has a personal computer and reliable internet, and is able to troubleshoot basic technical issues
- Is familiar with a range of news sources

- Is familiar with party platforms and government systems in the U.S.
- Is willing to divulge political leanings internally as required by our approach to analysis
- Demonstrates excellent reading comprehension skills
- Demonstrates excellent analytical skills
- Demonstrates ability to engage in sometimes difficult conversations, including on sensitive issues
- Demonstrates ability to see issues from multiple perspectives while also respectfully expressing a dissenting perspective when applicable

Strong Qualifications

- Demonstrates a passionate interest in news media and contemporary U.S. politics
- Demonstrates a desire to make a positive difference.
- Has achieved an advanced degree, or a highly relevant undergraduate degree, in Media, Journalism, Political Science, Linguistics, History, Sociology, Philosophy, or other field requiring strong skills in analyzing information content.
- Helps contribute to the diversity of our team
- Helps contribute to the range of special subject expertise within our team
- Helps contribute to the range of skills within our team
- Demonstrates familiarity with identifying bias and reliability in news sources
- Demonstrates interest in Ad Fontes Media and our mission

The extent to which applicants demonstrate the qualifications above is assessed by a politically balanced team of application reviewers using a shared rubric to identify the most qualified applicants.

All of our current analysts hold at least a bachelor's degree, and most have completed at least one graduate degree program. Approximately one third have completed a doctoral degree program or are current doctoral students.

While education is an important qualification, a number of other factors are considered as well, particularly familiarity with U.S. politics and the ability to engage in rigorous critical reflection on written and spoken content. Analysts come from a wide range of professional backgrounds—including federal service, law, and management—the backgrounds represented most within the team are media and communications, education, and research.

Political Leanings

Because analysts use a shared methodology (described below), the descriptive placement of each piece of content on the Media Bias Chart is generally quite close regardless of the analyst's political bias. However, since we moved to a multi-analyst approach in 2019, each piece of content we rate has been rated by an equal number of analysts who identify as left-leaning, center-leaning, and right-leaning politically.

To arrive at the classification of the analysts, we lean heavily on their own sense of political identity, along with a self-assessment currently using the following categories:

1. Abortion-related policy
2. Affirmative Action & reparations
3. Campaign finance
4. Climate-related policy
5. Criminal justice reform
6. Defense/military budget
7. Subsidized food & housing
8. Gun-related policy
9. Higher education policy
10. Immigration
11. International affairs
12. K-12 education policy
13. LGBTQ related policies
14. Marijuana policy
15. Private/public healthcare funding
16. Regulation of corporations
17. Social security
18. Tax related policies

For each of the issues above, we request that each analyst identify their perspective as:

- "Decidedly to the left"
- "Moderately to the left"
- "Centrist or undecided"
- "Moderately to the right"
- "Decidedly to the right"

For each issue in which the analyst identifies their perspective as "decidedly to the left," they score "-2," for each "moderately to the left," they score "-1," for each "centrist or undecided," they score "0," and so on.

Analysts scoring more than 10 points from 0 are initially categorized as left-leaning or right-leaning. Analysts scoring fewer than 4 points from 0 are initially categorized as centrist. Analysts falling between 4 and 10 points from 0 are considered on a case-by-case basis, with the analyst's political identity being considered most heavily.

While individuals' political outlooks are generally quite complex, and are often varied across issues, the analysts are generally able to identify their own perspective on these issues quickly using the framework above. To do so assumes a level of familiarity with U.S. politics, which is assessed during the application process. When combined with the practice of having each piece of content analyzed by an equal number of left-, center-, and right-leaning analysts, we have found that this system of classifying analysts yields a diversity of perspectives represented when analyzing content, though the horizontal axis analysis is politically descriptive and not intended to judge the moral value of political positions.

Training

Before joining the analyst team, each analyst trainee reads an article overviewing each step within Ad Fontes Media's eight-step core analysis methodology. The eight steps are made up of Veracity, Expression, Headline/Graphics, and Overall Reliability for the "Reliability" (vertical) metric, along with Political Position, Language, Comparison, and Overall Bias for the "Bias" (horizontal) metric. For each of these eight metrics, analysts also attend a 60-minute presentation on the same topic.

As they complete the assignments above, trainees also practice rating content using the methodology as a rubric. They also observe live analysis shifts where experienced analysts consider content together. Trainee ratings are observed; however, during this time, trainee scores are not included in the data used in our overall source and content ratings.

Upon successful completion of 20-25 hours of training described above, and once significant outlier scores are rare, trainees enter a probationary period where they score articles along with two experienced analysts. At this point, trainee scores are included in source and content ratings, and any outlier scores are managed as described below.

All analysts attend periodic additional training, which may include occasional fine-tuning to the methodology and awareness of the shifting meaning of categories such as "left" and "right" when applied to specific issues over time.

Process of Analysis

Content selection

To date, we have fully rated nearly 1000 sources and shows, including Web/print, podcast, and television. Members of our team use reach data, source lists, and user requests in order to select sources to be rated. While all sources gain additional article and episode scores over time, some sources have many more data points than the minimum, no source or show is considered to be "fully rated" until our team has rated a minimum of 15 articles for web/print content or 3 complete episodes of podcast or television content. This being the case, our team has scored over 20,000 articles and episodes to date in order to arrive at approximately 1,000 sources fully rated, and analysis is ongoing with several shifts of live analysis running daily.

Upon selecting a source to be rated, sample articles or episodes are selected for analysis, and these samples are used to arrive at an overall source score.

Articles are currently selected manually based on their "prominence," as determined by page placement, size of print headline, or when available, based on reach. In the future, we would like to consider reach more systematically when selecting sample content to be rated. Prominence functions partly as a proxy for reach when necessary currently, though prominence is also an important part of our methodology because many publishers feature highly opinionated or biased articles to drive engagement, even if most content they publish is more fact-based and neutral. Public perceptions of bias of large publishers are often driven by the extensive reach of lower-reliability, highly biased content.

For TV networks, content is similarly selected based on reach and its prominence in terms of when it is scheduled to air. For podcasts and TV shows, sample episodes are selected based on representativeness of the show overall.

For some sources, current ratings are based on a small sample size from each source. We believe these sample articles and shows are representative of their respective sources, but these rankings will certainly get more accurate as we rate more articles over time.

We rate all types of articles, including those labeled analysis or opinion by the news source. Not all news sources label their opinion content as such, so regardless of how it is labeled by the news source, we make our own methodology determinations on whether to classify articles as analysis or opinion on the appropriate places on the chart.

The content rating period for each rated news source is performed over multiple weeks in order to capture sample articles over several news cycles. Sources that have appeared on our Media Bias Chart for longer have articles over much longer periods of time.

Often, our sample sets of articles and shows are pulled from sites on the same day, meaning that they were from the same news cycle. Doing so allows analysts to incorporate evaluations of bias by omission and bias by topic selection.

We update all sources periodically by adding new articles. Because we have so many news sources, and because the most popular sources are important to the public, we generally update the most popular sources the most frequently and less popular sources less frequently. For example, we update a tier of the top 15 sources with about 15 new articles each month, and the next tier of 15 sources with about 7 articles per month. The top 200 get updated with about 5 articles per quarter and the next 200 about 5 articles per 6 months. We strive to balance rating new sources and updating existing ones.

Analysis

Each individual article and episode is rated by at least three human analysts with balanced right, left, and center self-reported political viewpoints. That is, at least one person who has rated the article self-identifies as being right-leaning, one as center-, and one as left-leaning.

The main principle of Ad Fontes (which means "to the source" in Latin) is that we analyze content. We look as closely as possible at individual articles, shows, and stories, and analyze what we are looking at: pictures, headlines, and most importantly, sentences and words.

In 2020, we began to rate most content live because the live process requires each analyst to justify their score when needed, aids in exposing analysts to multiple perspectives, and allows analysts to point out features that may have been missed by a single person in the group.

Articles and episodes are rated in three-person live panels conducted in shifts over Zoom, with each pod containing a left-leaning analyst, a center-leaning analyst, and a right-leaning analyst. Analysts first read each article and rate it on their own, and then they immediately compare scores. If there are notable discrepancies in the scores, they discuss and adjust scores if convinced. The three analysts' ratings are then averaged to produce the overall article rating. Sometimes articles are rated by larger panels of analysts for various reasons—for example, if significant outlier scores remain, the article may be sent to an additional pod to receive additional input.

Occasionally, content is rated asynchronously by experienced analysts, as was our initial multi-analyst rating project of 2019. However, when analysis is done asynchronously, the commitment to a politically-balanced multi-analyst approach to each piece of content remains. Additionally, though rare, an outlier score continues to move the content into a review stage for additional input.

The type of rating we ask each analyst to provide is an overall coordinate score on the chart (e.g., "40, -12"). The rating methodology is rigorous and rule based. There are many specific factors we take into account for both reliability and bias because there are many measurable indicators of each. The main ones for Reliability are defined metrics we call "Expression," "Veracity," and "Headline/Graphic," and the main ones for Bias are ones we call "Political Position," "Language," and "Comparison." There are several other factors we consider for certain articles. Therefore, the ratings are not simply subjective opinion polling, but rather methodical content analysis.

The "Veracity" factor is of particular importance in the reliability score. Our analysts use a veracity-checking methodology which incorporates best practices of fact-checking, such as lateral reading and consulting primary sources, but which is designed to be broad enough to cover claims that are not fact-checkable and quick enough to make an evaluation on every article (For more information on our veracity evaluation methodology, see the video in the following footnote).[4] Overall source ratings are composite weighted ratings of the individual article and show scores.

We continue to refine our methodology as we discover ways to have analysts classify rating factors more consistently. Our analysts use our software platform called CART. This ratings software is currently available for use by educators in classrooms, and by individual adult learners in our news literacy courses. Educators and individuals can learn how to rate news articles like Ad Fontes Media. Our courses include detailed video and written explanations of the factors we use to rate articles.

Data Analysis Results

The easiest way to see the resulting ratings for each article and show is, of course, on the Interactive Media Bias Chart at our website. By clicking on a button for a particular source, you can see a scatter plot of each article or episode rated for that source. The overall score of an article or show is the average of at least three individual scores.

To see an individual article or TV show and its score, you can search the table function just below the chart. Searching for a source name will pull up all the individual articles for that source along with their scores, so if you like, you can click on the URL to read the story and compare it to the score.

Close observers of the Interactive Media Bias Chart will notice that, particularly for low-scoring sources, the overall source scores appear to be lower than what would be expected from a straight average. As previously mentioned, this is because in our overall source-ranking methodology, we weight extremely-low-reliability and extremely-high-bias article scores very heavily.

The reason is this: the lowest rows of the chart indicate the presence of content that is very unreliable, including selective or incomplete stories, unfair persuasion, propaganda, misleading information, inaccurate, and even fabricated information (these are listed in order of egregiousness). Therefore, it is unacceptable for reputable news sources to include this type of content, even if it is infrequent or not the majority of the content. A source that has even 5% inaccurate or fabricated information is highly unreliable. A source that "only" publishes misleading or inaccurate content 33% of the time is terrible. In our system, they do not get credit for the 67% of stories that are merely opinion, but factually accurate.

A straight average, in such cases, would result in a higher overall source score—one that is inconsistent with the judgment of most savvy news consumers. Therefore, article scores of less than 24 for reliability are weighted very heavily.

We also rate bias scores more heavily the further the scores are away from zero. This results in sources with left or right leaning opinion content mixed with neutral/balanced content skewing more overall toward the bias of their opinion content. For example, *The New York Times and Wall Street Journal* skew left and right, respectively, due in large part to their opinion section content.

All other article scores for sources were straight-averaged. For example, if a news source had a mix of "fact reporting," "complex analysis," "analysis," and "opinion" articles, those would be straight averaged. As shown, our taxonomy rewards high percentages of fact reporting and complex analysis in sources and slightly down-ranks them for high percentages of opinion content (via straight averages). It does not punish a source for opinion content, because opinion content does have a useful place in our information ecosystem. However, our system does punish unfair opinion and worse content—that which we view as most polarizing "junk news."

CHAPTER 14
The Harper's Letter

Published by *Harper's Magazine*[1]

Our cultural institutions are facing a moment of trial. Powerful protests for racial and social justice are leading to overdue demands for police reform, along with wider calls for greater equality and inclusion across our society, not least in higher education, journalism, philanthropy, and the arts. But this needed reckoning has also intensified a new set of moral attitudes and political commitments that tend to weaken our norms of open debate and toleration of differences in favor of ideological conformity. As we applaud the first development, we also raise our voices against the second. The forces of illiberalism are gaining strength throughout the world and have a powerful ally in Donald Trump, who represents a real threat to democracy. But resistance must not be allowed to harden into its own brand of dogma or coercion—which right-wing demagogues are already exploiting. The democratic inclusion we want can be achieved only if we speak out against the intolerant climate that has set in on all sides.

The free exchange of information and ideas, the lifeblood of a liberal society, is daily becoming more constricted. While we have come to expect this on the radical right, censoriousness is also spreading more widely in our culture: an intolerance of opposing views, a vogue for public shaming and ostracism, and the tendency to dissolve complex policy issues in a blinding moral certainty. We uphold the value of robust and even caustic counter-speech from all quarters. But it is now all too common to hear calls for swift and severe retribution in response to perceived transgressions of speech and thought. More troubling still, institutional leaders, in a spirit of panicked damage control, are delivering hasty and disproportionate punishments instead of considered reforms. Editors are fired for running controversial pieces; books are withdrawn for alleged inauthenticity; journalists are barred from writing on certain topics; professors are investigated for quoting works of literature in class; a researcher is fired for circulating a peer-reviewed academic study; and the heads of organizations are ousted for what are sometimes just clumsy mistakes. Whatever the arguments around each particular incident, the result has been to steadily narrow the boundaries of what can be said without the threat of reprisal. We are already paying the price in greater risk aversion among writers, artists, and journalists who fear for their livelihoods if they depart from the consensus, or even lack sufficient zeal in agreement.

This stifling atmosphere will ultimately harm the most vital causes of our time. The restriction of debate, whether by a repressive government or an intolerant society, invariably hurts those who lack power and makes everyone less capable of democratic participation. The way to defeat bad ideas is by exposure, argument, and persuasion, not by trying to silence or wish them away. We refuse any false choice between justice and freedom, which cannot exist without each other. As writers we need a culture that leaves us room for experimentation, risk taking, and even mistakes. We need to preserve the possibility of good-faith disagreement without dire professional consequences. If we won't defend the very thing on which our work depends, we shouldn't expect the public or the state to defend it for us.

II. PROBLEMS IN RIGHT-WING SILOS

CHAPTER 15
Deceit and the Danger to Democracy[1]

By William Saletan

Americans like to think our country is immune to authoritarianism. We have a culture of freedom, a tradition of elected government, and a Bill of Rights. We're not like those European countries that fell into fascism. We'd never willingly abandon democracy, liberty, or the rule of law.

But that's not how authoritarianism would come to America. In fact, it's not how authoritarianism *has* come to America. The movement to dismantle our democracy is thriving and growing, even after the failure of the January 6th coup attempt, because it isn't spreading through overt rejection of our system of government. It's spreading through lies.

It turns out that you don't have to renounce any of our nation's founding principles to betray them. All you have to do is believe lies: that real ballots are fake, that prosecutors are criminals, and that insurrectionists are political prisoners. Once you believe these things, you're ready to disenfranchise your fellow citizens in the name of democracy. You're ready to cover up crimes in the name of fighting corruption. You're ready to liberate coup plotters in the name of justice.

And that's where we are. Donald Trump and his party have sold these lies to more than 100 million Americans. He has built an army of authoritarian followers who think they're saving the republic.

* * * * *

As president, Trump abused every power he could, from pardons to control of the military. And as he lays the groundwork to run for re-election, he continues to advocate and threaten such abuses. But for the most part, he's careful to frame them as the opposite of what they are. "I am not the one trying to undermine

American Democracy," he declared last month in a statement marking the anniversary of January 6th. "I am the one trying to SAVE American Democracy."[2]

At a rally in Arizona this past January 15,[3] Trump repeated his standard lie that "the real insurrection took place on Election Day," through voter fraud. From that standpoint, he noted, the January 6th uprising was an attempt to restore democracy, and the people arrested in the uprising were "political prisoners." The House January 6th Committee is, in Trump's words, a partisan cabal that trampled innocent people "like this is. . . a communist country." So are the federal and state prosecutors looking into Trump's possible financial and political crimes. In the name of law and order, he urged his supporters to rise up against these agents of the state: "We must protect our nation from these monsters that are using law enforcement for political retribution."

Trump continued his Orwellian themes at a January 29 rally in Texas.[4] He argued that President Joe Biden had been installed by fake ballots, not real voters, and that legislation to make voting easier would just lead to more fake ballots. Democrats "don't have a voting rights bill," Trump scoffed. "They have a voting fraud bill."

This strategy—inserting lies into conventional moral appeals, so that his listeners think they're doing the right thing when they're actually doing the opposite—is central to Trump's propaganda. Without the lies, the evil would be exposed. That's what happened a week ago, when Trump forgot to lie. In a statement, he complained that when Congress counted electoral votes on January 6th, Vice President Mike Pence could have, and should have, "change[d] the results" and "overturned the Election." The words "change" and "overturn" revealed Trump's despotic intent. So, in a follow-up statement two days later, he replaced them. His true purpose, he insisted, was to "ensure the true outcome" and "ensure the honest results."[5]

* * * * *

Trump isn't alone in peddling these lies. The Republican party stands behind him. On Friday, the Republican National Committee, following his lead, censured Reps. Liz Cheney and Adam Kinzinger for telling the truth about January 6th. The party's censure resolution adopted Trump's upside-down account of the insurrection and the investigation. It accused Cheney and Kinzinger, who sit on the House January 6th Committee, of "participating in a Democrat-led persecution of ordinary citizens engaged in legitimate political discourse."[6]

The party has also adopted Trump's broader strategy of using lies to induce and disguise authoritarian behavior. Instead of arguing that laws should be tightened to make it harder to vote, Republicans pretend that ballots blocked by such laws wouldn't come from real or legal voters. For example, Sen. Ted Cruz has falsely asserted that voting rights legislation would enfranchise "illegal aliens," not "American citizens"—and, therefore, the legislation "doesn't protect voting rights, it steals voting rights."[7] Instead of arguing that people who committed crimes on January 6th should be let off the hook, Republicans pretend that the real criminals are the investigators themselves. Lawmakers and staffers on the committee are "running over the law, pursuing innocent people," former House Speaker Newt Gingrich told Fox News on January 23. "They're the ones who. . . face a real risk of jail for the kind of laws they're breaking."[8]

The committee has requested interviews, unsuccessfully, with two top Republicans who spoke directly to Trump on January 6th and who witnessed his refusal to call off the mob. One is Rep. Kevin McCarthy, who's in line to become the next speaker, which would give him the power to end the congressional investigation. Three weeks ago, when McCarthy refused the committee's request for an interview, he didn't bother to justify protecting Trump. Instead, he pretended that Cheney and Kinzinger weren't real Republicans. This allowed him to dismiss the committee as "purely an arm of the DCCC"[9]—the Democratic Congressional Campaign Committee—and therefore "illegitimate."

Mark Meadows, Trump's former chief of staff, has also refused to answer questions from the committee, claiming executive privilege. The claim is hollow for many reasons, starting with the fact that Trump isn't president anymore. But in a speech defending Meadows, Rep. Jim Jordan—who's in line to become chairman of the House Judiciary Committee if the GOP takes over—didn't even acknowledge that Meadows was trying to conceal facts from the public. Instead, taking a cue from Trump, Jordan suggested that the former president *was* the public. "Executive privilege serves the public interest," said Jordan. "It's for us. It's for we the people."[10]

*　*　*　*　*

In a country immune to authoritarianism, this campaign of lies would fail. But the campaign isn't failing. It's working. Rank-and-file Republicans, joined by many independent voters, believe the lies. They're ready to put Republicans back in charge of Congress. They're ready to support McCarthy when he shuts down the January 6th investigation. And many are ready to re-elect Trump.

These people don't think they're betraying democracy. They think they're saving it. In polls, Republicans are significantly more likely than Democrats to say that "American democracy is under a major threat,"[11] that "there is a serious threat to the future of our democracy,"[12] and that "the nation's democracy is in danger of collapse."[13] What makes these Republicans functionally authoritarian is that they're completely wrong about who poses the threat. In October, when a Quinnipiac survey asked whether "Donald Trump has been undermining democracy or protecting democracy," 94% of Democrats said he was undermining it. But 85% of Republicans said he was protecting it.[14]

Today, three-quarters of Republicans continue to insist that Biden "did not legitimately win the election."[15] When they're asked why, they cite Trump's lies, which they think are true. In a December survey by the University of Massachusetts Amherst, 61% of Republicans said Biden was illegitimate because "fraudulent ballots supporting [him] were counted by election officials."[16] Forty-six percent said "ballots supporting Donald Trump were destroyed by election officials." Forty-one percent said "voting machines were re-programmed by election officials to count extra ballots for Biden."

Once you believe these lies, it's easy to believe Trump's lies about January 6th, since the point of the January 6th uprising was to block certification of the election. In a Politico/Morning Consult poll taken last month, more than 60% of Republicans said that in terms of violating the Constitution, the election was at least as bad as "the January 6th attack on the U.S. Capitol."[17] Two-thirds of these people—43% of all Republicans—said the election was worse. In other surveys, most Republicans have maintained that people who committed violence on January 6th—those who "forced their way into the U.S. Capitol" or were "involved in the attack on the U.S. Capitol"—were "defending freedom"[18] or "protecting democracy."[19]

Some of these fictions haven't just permeated the Republican base. They've infected the broader electorate. In the last four Economist/YouGov polls, most White Americans without a college degree have said Biden didn't legitimately win the presidency.[20] In a Quinnipiac survey taken last month, a plurality of independents agreed with the statement that "too much is being made of the storming of the U.S. Capitol on January 6, 2021, and it is time to move on."[21] In a Harvard CAPS/Harris poll taken two weeks ago, most independents said the Department of Justice was prosecuting January 6th defendants primarily "for political reasons"[22]—not "because they should be prosecuted"—and 54% of registered voters said the House January 6th Committee's investigation was "more of a partisan exercise" than "an independent inquiry."

Among voters as a whole, Trump's party—despite its embrace, defense, and extension of his authoritarianism—is seen as no worse than Democrats in adhering to democracy. In a Marist poll taken in October,[23] when voters were asked which party was a "bigger threat to democracy in the United States," 41% named the Republican Party, but 42% named the Democratic Party. And in a Fox News survey taken three weeks ago,[24] when voters were asked which party would do a better job of "protecting American democracy," 50% chose Democrats, but 48% chose Republicans. In both surveys, by margins of four to five percentage points, independents viewed the GOP as the more democracy-friendly party.

These numbers, combined with the corresponding patterns in Trump's, McCarthy's, and the RNC's propaganda, teach an important lesson. We're in a battle to save democracy, but the battleground isn't values. It's facts. We're up against a party that spreads, condones, excuses, tolerates, and exploits lies—lies about our political process, and lies about an attempt to overthrow our government—in order to make Americans think that the party of authoritarianism is the party of democracy. And we're in serious danger of losing.

CHAPTER 16
A Fire Hose of Dishonesty[1]

By Alison Dagnes and Daniel Herndon

We live in an age of alternative facts and dishonest brokers who "just ask questions" that are (at best) duplicitous. There is monster distrust all around. Into this setting comes *Dominion v. Fox News*, the lawsuit filed by the voting machine company against the most profitable cable news company on the planet alleging the TV channel spread bald face, destructive lies. The bad news for Fox is that the legal maneuverings have produced more receipts than a CVS self-checkout.

The lawsuit filings and discovery have shed some light on the Fox News juggernaut, the 900-pound gorilla in conservative media. It also has exposed many of the ancillary satellite media outposts that claim to be an antidote to liberal media, rather than journalistic endeavors. Seeing their job not as "real news" providers but as a cudgel against the mainstream press, *Fox* and friends played fast and loose with the facts to keep an audience who had been lured into believing a scheme that was repeatedly proven in court to be false.

Shocked. I'm shocked.

Look, this has been in development for decades. Fox News made its bones by scattering grievance politics and government distrust among the weeds of negative partisanship and conspiracy theories it had rooted. The approach has been so good for business that Fox News continues to toe the line of partisan lunacy even when faced with rock-solid evidence that disproves it. One email sent by the Fox executive in charge of prime-time programming warned that the network should fan the flames of conspiracies: "Do not ever give viewers a reason to turn us off. Every guest and topic must perform."[2] Doing otherwise would lose their audience. As Adam Serwer wrote in *The Atlantic* "The network inflames right-wing conspiracism, but it also bows to it out of partisan commitment and commercial incentive."[3] There are reasons for this.

The claim of liberal media bias began softly in the mid-Twentieth Century and has grown in volume and pitch ever since, which is how a dedicated audience segment primed for conservative content was built and preserved. The technological advancements merely caught up with the purpose of providing an "antidote" to the so-called liberal press. This mostly took the form of conservative commentary, beginning with the wild west of talk radio in the 1980s. The post "Fairness Doctrine" media landscape let big mouthed talking heads use partisanship as entertainment, and the public began to see politics as entertaining. Audiences flocked to Rush Limbaugh, and then to cable news since Rush was the not-so-secret inspiration for Rupert Murdoch's creation of Fox, which launched in 1996. The whole point of conservative media was to challenge the libs while bucking the professional, impartial norms of journalism. They hoovered up profits and spawned imitators.

After cable news took over the airwaves and Al Gore invented the internet, right-wing media content exploded in scope and scale. With so many options, many Americans just wanted the news that went down as easy as a Slurpee on a hot day, which meant that politically interested people flocked to the partisan networks and websites that supported their views. This is how the right-wing media circle we have today developed, and it is profitable. With Fox News in the center, this right-wing media circle features websites, radio shows, podcasts, and streaming services that all make the same fundamental argument: the left is an insane clown posse of socialists and identity politics obsessed radicals. This line of reasoning works: Fox News has been the #1 cable news channel for 20 uninterrupted years,[4] and of the top websites in the U.S., FoxNews.com comes in at #27, beating *The New York Times*.[5]

All of this is to say that Fox News is extremely popular. The narratives set by Fox then bounce around the outlets within the right-wing media circle, and fairly quickly these stories are set in stone. Which gets us back to the *Dominion* lawsuit.

On Election Night in 2020, Fox News was the first to call Biden as the winner. It was an early call, and it turned out to be a correct call, but it was a call that made former President Trump furious. Numerous accounts report that Trump and his staff called Fox News and begged them to retract the call, but to no avail. This is where Trump's "Frankly, we did win this election" line came to pass. It was in response to the Fox News Decision Desk call.

Legal depositions revealed the following:

- Fox News viewers began to abandon the network for more conspiracy-laden fare found on Newsmax and OANN.

- The well-paid Fox staff howled in protest and insisted that they further the election conspiracy they apparently knew was a lie.

Since Donald Trump had planted the seeds of mistrust well before Election Day 2020, there were unsubstantiated stories about election fraud circulating on the right. Many of these rumors had been reinforced on Fox News, but the conspiracy theory about Dominion was a real corker. Pundits fortified the falsity that the Dominion Voting Machine company was in cahoots with the Democrats to change votes from Trump to Biden. Allegations against Dominion included connections to the (late) Hugo Chavez, treacherous behavior traced to foreign interference, and all-around nefarious action on the part of a once-unknown voting machine company.

After so many Fox News segments, Dominion was no longer unknown and they had enough: the company sent formal notices (more than 3,600 requests to Fox News) asking Fox to stop name checking their company in their wild (and unsubstantiated) story telling. Spoiler alert: Fox did not stop spreading the fabrications even though their most popular (and highest paid) pundits knew they were, in legal terms, totally banana-pants. To win back their audience that couldn't handle the truth, Fox News continued to amplify the stolen election invention in earnest, with appearances on the network by Trump surrogates, in order to regain their audience.

- Testimony from Rupert Murdoch and emails from Fox employees all show that nobody at the network believed these fabrications but they aired them anyway.

- They did this to save their stock price and because money mattered most. As Murdoch himself stated, it was not a matter of ideology. It was: "not red or blue. It is green."[6]

The bottom line of this legal dump is that the financial imperatives of Fox News rest on spreading misinformation, even though the power structure knew it was incorrect. In other words, Fox knew what their audience wanted, and they took a hard U turn after they behaved like a real news organization and their audience bolted. They fired the real news people who had properly called the election, threw shade at the journalists from their network, and they shuffled their schedule to lose the news and add more opinion. It worked. Fox won their audience back.

Immediately following the election, according to the Brookings Institute: "Unsubstantiated and false claims tied to the 2020 U.S. presidential election spiked dramatically after the election and did not abate in the following months, despite multiple failed legal challenges."[7] This was the result of harmonization between right-wing outlets. Fox News might be the undisputed center of the right-wing media universe, but there needs to be message corroboration in order for an argument to congeal, and this is where the podcasts, websites, and streaming services stayed on message to perpetuate the "Big Lie" about election fraud.

That's how ideas have become fact: that January 6 was really an heroic effort by patriots to tour the U.S. Capitol, that there's a conspiracy afoot to replace White American voters with people of color, and that former President Donald Trump is the victim of political persecution. These narratives spread around the right-wing media circle, from guest to host to commentary, and they are consistently echoed since so many of the right-wing personalities do double and triple duty on the air, on podcasts or talk radio programs, and on the web. The misinformation and storylines spread with alarming alacrity because there is so much airtime to fill. And much like cement, these opinions solidify over time having been buttressed by numerous personalities on many different outlets.

Studies and polling data show little overlap between the right-wing media and the mainstream press,[8] mostly because of the deep distrust mentioned at the top. This means that consumers of right-wing media are locked in a bubble of confirmation bias that is corroborated everywhere they go for political content, as long as they stay within their bubble. It's not fair to blame these Americans for believing the fake news and misinformation they get, because it's everywhere they go. I play my own version of "Name That Tune" where I can identify someone's media diet from one phrase. The moment I hear "Biden Crime Family," I know what I'm dealing with.

The real villains are not our friends and neighbors who buy into the fire hoses of dishonesty. As one cable executive said to a reporter off the record,[9] the Dominion lawsuit will not do much to dissuade the Fox News audience: "Fox may be forced to read an apology on air or something, but the audience still loves the product. It's basically the W.W.E. for this kind of world." You can't blame the public for wanting entertainment, even from their politicians. The real offenders are the media figures who peddle the dreck.

In the days after the 2020 election, former President Trump tweeted to his millions of followers: "@FoxNews daytime ratings have completely collapsed. Very sad to watch this happen, but they forgot what made them successful, what got them there. They forgot the Golden Goose." Quickly thereafter, Fox remembered their Goose and their ratings rose once again, proving that they will be okay as long as Fox News supports Trump. But this is the problem: If Fox champions Trump, their audience will stay loyal and hear even more biased content that further distorts the truth.

It is already evident that Trump's third presidential campaign is built upon resentment and retribution, both of which fit into Fox News' lib trolling mission. Vengeance programming will spread from Fox News throughout conservative media outlets because it sells, and in selling the anger the revenge narrative will be strengthened and solidified. We will learn a great deal from the Dominion lawsuit, and it will all point to the irrefutable fact that Fox News manipulates the truth to satisfy their audience. In the end, these revelations might not matter too much because ratings will probably remain solid. In the right-wing media circle, it's not who you support, but who you oppose, that counts.

CHAPTER 17
Fox's Pander-for-Profit Business Model[1]

By Amanda Carpenter

Fox News loves to project bravado, but the Dominion Voting Systems defamation lawsuit shows how deeply threatened the network is by flimsy, fringe competitors and how executives and hosts talked themselves into dishonestly pandering to viewers to keep ratings and profits up.

Court filings released by Dominion[2] reveal frantic discussions inside the network about losing viewers by correctly calling Arizona for Joe Biden in the 2020 election. Leaders at Fox then hushed truth-tellers and latched on to election conspiracy theories to lure viewers back.

Dominion must meet a high standard to win its $1.6 billion case. But the filings are already proving something significant, beyond the shadow of a doubt: that Fox casually *and knowingly* feeds its viewers lies. Dominion has documented how their leading voices don't believe what they say on the air. How they are afraid to tell you what they *really* think. Therein lies the peril of Fox's pander-for-profit model. The filings tell the story.

Fox fatefully declared Biden the victor in Arizona on election night in 2020 (November 3), ahead of the other networks. As the House January 6th Committee found, the Trump campaign inveighed heavily against Fox for it. But the Dominion filings show for the first time how much angst network leaders felt about reporting that news.

Fox News Senior Executive Vice President for Corporate Communications Irena Briganti acknowledged how their audience reacted to the Arizona call in an email on Saturday, November 7, that read, "[O]ur viewers left this week after AZ."

On November 7, Fox—like the other networks—called the overall election for

Biden. But there continued to be a great deal of handwringing inside the company about the Arizona call. Around that time, Tucker Carlson texted his producer, "Do the executives understand how much credibility and trust we've lost with our audience? We're playing with fire, for real. . . an alternative like newsmax could be devastating to us." And on November 9, he texted Fox News CEO Suzanne Scott: "I've never seen a reaction like this, to any media company. Kills me to watch it."

Scott quickly flew into action. She kicked up Carlson's concerns to Fox Corporation Chief Lachlan Murdoch and explained: "Viewers going through the 5 stages of grief. It's a question of trust—the AZ [call] was damaging but we will highlight our stars and plant flags letting the viewers know we hear them and respect them." Scott told Briganti that Bill Sammon, then a senior vice president at Fox and the managing editor of the Washington bureau, did not understand "the impact to the brand and the arrogance in calling AZ," which she found "astonishing" given that as a "top executive," it was Sammon's job "to protect the brand."

It is worth dwelling on that point for a moment: In his role at Fox News, perhaps Bill Sammon did have a corporate responsibility "to protect the brand," but in his role as the managing editor of the Washington bureau, he had a higher responsibility—a responsibility to deliver the news in a timely and accurate way, with integrity. Those roles will always have some tension between them. In this case, it's clear that Suzanne Scott cared little for the integrity of the news side. The same goes for Fox chair Rupert Murdoch: "Maybe best to let Bill go right away," he said—which would "be a big message with Trump people." By November 20, Sammon was told his days at Fox were numbered. Two months later, he was axed, along with fellow Decision Desk editor Chris Stirewalt.

So how would Fox, as Suzanne Scott put it, "[let] the viewers know we hear them and respect them"? How would it, as she promised Rupert Murdoch, "make sure they know we aren[']t abandoning them and still champions for them"? That plan to do so involved booking guests who could air their election conspiracies. Fox executives defended the practice by saying they were "newsworthy."

It took a little time for the executives to implement the plan and for others to get up to speed. In the interim, some hosts, like daytime host Neil Cavuto, attempted to cover the election news responsibly, which set off more internal firestorms at Fox.

What happened on the airwaves on November 9 shows how the conflict played out in real time. Trump and his allies continued to spread his lies in a way that was so blatant that Cavuto cut the cameras from Trump aide Kayleigh McEnany's press conference that day. Cavuto told viewers, "Whoa, whoa, whoa. . . She's charging the other side as welcoming fraud and welcoming illegal voting, unless she has more details to back that up, I can't in good countenance continue showing you this," and "that's an explosive charge to make."

That didn't go over well behind the scenes. Dominion's filings show that Raj Shah—a former Trump White House staffer who by this point was an executive at the Fox Corporation that owns Fox News—labeled Cavuto's action a "Brand

Threat." Porter Berry, Sean Hannity's former producer who by this point was running Fox News Digital, looked at Newsmax's ratings and found they were getting a good response from "hitting Cavuto" and "just whacking us."

CEO Scott once again went into protective mode. She instructed an analyst to "keep an eye" on Newsmax and monitor its ratings. She then flagged the Newsmax ratings for Fox News president Jay Wallace. He took it very seriously: "The Newsmax surge is a bit troubling—truly is an alternative universe when you watch, but it can't be ignored. . . Trying to get everyone to comprehend we are on war footing."

The execs weren't the only ones fuming about the truth-tellers at Fox and scrambling to fend off competitors. So were Fox's big three primetime hosts. The latest Dominion filing includes new revelations about the group discussions among Tucker Carlson, Sean Hannity, and Laura Ingraham.

In a November 12 group chat, Hannity told Carlson and Ingraham, "In one week and one debate they destroyed a brand that took 25 years to build and the damage is incalculable." Carlson called it "vandalism." Hannity was anxious for the network to work to prevent loonier competitors from taking advantage: "[S]erious $$ with serious distribution could be a real problem. Imho they need to address but wtf do I know." Carlson replied: "That could happen."

That night, Fox reporter Jacqui Heinrich fact-checked a tweet from Trump about Dominion, quoting a government statement that said, "There is no evidence that any voting system deleted or lost votes, changed votes, or was in any way compromised."[3] Carlson wanted consequences for Heinrich's tweet. He texted Hannity: "Please get her fired. Seriously. . . What the fuck? I'm actually shocked. . . It needs to stop immediately, like tonight. It's measurably hurting the company. The stock price is down. Not a joke." Hannity confirmed that he had elevated the issue to Scott and described Heinrich's tweet as another strike against the network. He summed up their recent woes: "I'm 3 strikes. [Chris] Wallace shit debate[.] Election night a disaster[.] Now this BS? Nope. Not gonna fly. Did I mention Cavuto?"

The executives kept tracking the negative reaction Fox truth-tellers were getting from viewers. On November 13, Shah reported to the executives that there was "strong conservative and viewer backlash to Fox that we are working to track and mitigate." He said that "[b]oth Donald Trump and Newsmax have taken active roles in promoting attacks on Fox News" and that "[p]ositive impressions of Fox News among our viewers dropped precipitously after Election Day to the lowest levels we've ever seen." Shah later followed up with more specific metrics, saying, "We are now underwater with our viewers in 3-day tracking, and continue to show declines in 1- and 2-week averages."

A few days later, on November 18, Ron Mitchell, senior vice president of Fox primetime programming, had an idea. They should take their lead from spurious sources to entice viewers. He emailed Scott and Wallace about how Newsmax "sourced websites like Gateway Pundit while talking about voter fraud." "This type of conspiratorial reporting might be exactly what the disgruntled FNC viewer is looking for," Mitchell said. He said the network should "not ever give viewers a reason to turn us off. Every topic and guest must perform. [Fox cannot afford any] 'unforced errors' in content—example: Abruptly turning away from a Trump campaign press conference."

The next day, November 19, Trump's legal team, led by Rudy Giuliani, held a press conference to promote myriad lies. Unlike the McEnany press conference, Fox News did exactly as Mitchell suggested to Fox executives. The network stayed on Giuliani and did not cut away. A Fox reporter again fact-checked the lies being spread.[4] And just like Heinrich before her, Kristin Fisher was rebuked by her bosses for it. The Dominion filings also reveal that Fisher got a call from her supervisor and was told (as she recalls it) that the "higher-ups" at Fox News were "unhappy with" her fact-checking of the Trump campaign lies and that she "needed to do a better job of—this is a quote—'respecting our audience.'"

Fox anchor Dana Perino also set off the "higher-ups" when she, quite presciently, suggested that baseless allegations Giuliani made during his press conference could provide Dominion a reason to sue. The Dominion filings state that Perino's remarks, coupled with Fisher's fact-checking, caused Scott to start "screaming about Dana's show and their reaction to the Rudy presser." Scott fired off an email about their coverage that said: "[Y]ou can't give the crazies an inch right now. . . they are looking for and blowing up all appearances of disrespect to the audience."

In other emails, Mitchell expressed more sympathy for Fisher and Perino but a similar desire to pander to the election delusions. He wrote: "I'm not mad at either of them. I'm mad at those clowns at the conference who put us in a terrible place. . . those clowns put us [in] an awkward place where we're going to need to thread the needle."

The idea of "respecting the audience" or "threading the needle" comes up quite a bit in the Dominion filings. Network Chairman Rupert Murdoch similarly testified that he saw it as "trying to straddle the line between spewing conspiracy theories on one hand, yet calling out the fact they are actually false on the other." Except that the substantive "calling out" was kept private.

While Fox gave license to its most-watched hosts—primarily Carlson, Ingraham, Hannity, Lou Dobbs, Jeanine Pirro, and Maria Bartiromo—to elevate conspiracy theorists and lend credibility to guests such as Sidney Powell, they revealed their true thoughts only to each other. Around November 18, while Trump and his allies were in the throes of promoting his lies, Carlson told his producer Alex Pfeiffer: "Sidney Powell is lying. Fucking bitch." Carlson told Ingraham, "Sidney Powell is lying by the way. I caught her. It's insane." The filings show that Ingraham responded: "Sidney is a complete nut. No one will work with her. Ditto with Rudy." Carlson replied: "It's unbelievably offensive to me. Our viewers are good people and they believe it." But Fox still put Powell, Trump, Giuliani, and guests who said similar things on the air and declined to rebut their claims. Dominion says it flooded Fox with over 3,600 separate communications asking them to cease smearing their company. The requests went unheeded.

On December 2—six weeks before they were fired—Bill Sammon discussed Fox's "supposed election fraud" with his colleague Chris Stirewalt and concluded, "It's remarkable how weak ratings make[] good journalists do bad things." They got steamrolled as Trump continued to spread his election lies through December 2020 and early January 2021; Fox continued to go along with it all, giving its viewers the false hope that the election could somehow be overturned.

Perhaps sensing something bad was on the horizon, Rupert Murdoch told Scott on January 5 that "it's been suggested our prime time three should independently or together say something like 'the election is over and Joe Biden won,' [which] would go a long way to stop the Trump myth that the election [was] stolen." Scott forwarded the email to Fox News Executive President for Primetime Programming Meade Cooper, stating, "I told Rupert that privately they are all there—we need to be careful about using the shows and pissing off the viewers but they know how to navigate." When it came to their viewers' sensitivities, Fox did, indeed, play it carefully. No statement went out. So the big names at Fox did not issue that authoritative refutation of what Murdoch himself called the "Trump myth." And the next day, motivated by the very lies Fox promoted, Trump's mob stormed the Capitol.

After the insurrection, it appears that Rupert Murdoch felt uncomfortable about the gap between what Fox hosts believed and what they told viewers. He told Scott that it was "All very well for Sean [Hannity] to tell you he was in despair about Trump but what did he tell his viewers?" But even then, Fox didn't change its ways. Rather than tell the truth, the network pivoted to promoting even more lies about how Antifa had actually invaded the Capitol on January 6th, injured police officers were "crisis actors," and well-meaning Trump supporters were set up by the "deep state."

After Sammon and Stirewalt were shown the door for correctly calling Arizona, and others were chastised for demonstrating similar basic journalistic ethics, Kayleigh McEnany, whose November 9 White House presser alleging fraud had so alarmed Cavuto that he cut away from it, was welcomed as a new on-air paid talent. Since April 2021, she has co-hosted a talk show for the network.

Kristin Fisher left her job as Fox White House correspondent in May 2021 and is now a space and defense reporter at CNN.

Also in 2021, Fox would deploy resources to allow Carlson to produce an unhinged documentary titled *Patriot Purge,* which depicted jailed January 6th rioters as being unfairly targeted, prosecuted, and imprisoned for their political beliefs.[5]

And now, Republican House Speaker Kevin McCarthy is giving Carlson exclusive access to footage from the riot to create even more content.

It all seems like good business for Fox, which is why Murdoch has embraced it.

After the riot, Fox courted election conspiracist Mike Lindell. Scott sent him a personal note and a "gift," which the MyPillow founder claims to have never received. Scott also told shows to put him on air because he would "get ratings." Dominion's lawyers asked Rupert Murdoch why they gave Lindell this special treatment, and Murdoch said that Fox makes a lot of money from the commercials Lindell buys to promote his products. He testified, "The man is on every night. Pays us a lot of money." "It is not red or blue," Murdoch said. "It is green."

Jury selection for Dominion's case is scheduled to begin in April. Given the high standard to prove defamation, even with Dominion's strong case, no one can predict whether the company will win. But there is no question of Fox's fundamental deceit, which is now coming fully into view because Dominion has the legal standing, deep pockets, and temerity to fight its case.

Fox routinely commits similar smears against other targets who lack the resources to pursue similar recourse. And while the company is protecting its own interests, not fighting purely for the sake of American democracy, it's also true that by defending itself, Dominion is challenging Fox's pander-for-profit business model. That model has many imitators—so many that Fox is constantly worried it will lose its grip on its audience.

There's a big market for media that lies to its audience under the guise of reporting the news. This case will decide, in part, whether those media put themselves at risk by embracing contempt and deception as a ratings strategy. Regardless of the outcome, the filings show how cynical the model is.

CHAPTER 18
Please Lie to Me, Tucker Carlson[1]

By Mona Charen

Oh, how conservatives loved to hate the media. I witnessed it firsthand for decades. In any speech before a conservative audience, the jokes about media bias got the loudest laughs and heartiest applause. Among conservative writers and thinkers, examples of bias were a staple of our output. It was evergreen. In 1992, conservatives sported bumper stickers reading "Annoy the Media: Reelect George Bush."

I certainly did my share of press criticism. The leftward tilt of the big prestige press was irritating for those of us on the other side, and compounding the offense were ritualistic denials that emanated from the likes of CBS and the *New York Times*. We'd cite chapter and verse of slanted reporting; we'd reference surveys showing that only 7% of reporters and editors called themselves Republicans;[2] and still we'd be waved away with the patronizing explanation that reporters' personal views didn't taint their work.

Does it strike you as outrageous to suggest, as Fox News host Tucker Carlson has, that President Joe Biden's slow response to the toxic spill in East Palestine, Ohio is evidence that he doesn't care about White people? Carlson put it this way:

> East Palestine is overwhelmingly white, and it's politically conservative. That shouldn't be relevant, but it very much is. . . [It's] a poor benighted town whose people are forgotten, and in the view of the people who lead this country, forgettable.[3]

Not to be outdone in the racial sweepstakes, Charlie Kirk denounced Biden's "war against white people."[4]

If you're disgusted by that, you may understand how some conservatives felt in 2005 when Hurricane Katrina became the occasion for charging George W. Bush with racism. Jesse Jackson told CNN, "I saw five thousand African Americans on the I-10 causeway. It looked like Africans in the hull of a slave ship."[5] He also claimed that when churches were contacted about offering aid, they first demanded to know whether the victims were Black or White. During NBC's telethon for hurricane relief, Kanye West famously declared that "George W. Bush doesn't care about Black people." Those sentiments got a good airing on major TV outlets (That West wound up on the Mar-a-Lago patio 17 years later in company with a Nazi suggests that perhaps he shouldn't have been treated as an oracle back then).

George W. Bush was smeared as a racist despite his "No Child Left Behind" education bill; his appointment of the first African American secretary of state; the first Black, female secretary of state; and the PEPFAR program that has saved 25 million lives in Africa—so far.

My own writing featured many objections to liberal media bias. I objected to widespread reporting during the Clinton years about a spate of church burnings that were nearly universally attributed to White racists. In fact, many churches, not just African American churches, had experienced fires and most were not the result of arson. When the Bureau of Alcohol, Tobacco, Firearms, and Explosives tracked down the arsonists, they could find only 2 out of 39 church fires that were the work of racists (and both of those fires were set by the same two individuals).[6]

Conservatives were dismayed that Mitt Romney's anodyne comment about having "binders full of women" (as potential hires when he was governor of Massachusetts) was transformed by many in the press into some kind of misogynist slur. And even *Saturday Night Live* mocked press sycophancy toward Barack Obama.[7]

* * * * *

Like most conservatives, I initially welcomed Fox News to the airwaves. A media world that included Jennifer Griffin at the Pentagon, Neil Cavuto on Wall Street, and Charles Krauthammer every evening on *Special Report* was an overdue counterbalance. An enormous audience had been underserved, and Fox was able to exploit an opening.

But then things went sideways. While we can't say the Fox News effect was entirely responsible—talk radio too played a role, as did social media—it started to become evident during the Obama years that the right's impatience with press bias had curdled into something more ominous. Instead of seeking to fact check and balance coverage, Republican and conservative audiences demanded combat. Newt Gingrich turbocharged his anemic presidential campaign in 2011 by using the primary debates not as an opportunity to draw contrasts with his opponents but as a forum for attacking the press.[8] When *Politico's* John Harris asked Gingrich about a philosophical dispute regarding health insurance, Gingrich wheeled on him:

> I hope all of my friends up here are going to repudiate every effort
> of the news media to get Republicans to fight each other to protect
> Barack Obama, who deserves to be defeated, and all of us are com-
> mitted as a team—whoever the nominee is—we are for defeating
> Barack Obama.[9]

The crowd vibrated with pleasure, and the belligerent seed that would later bloom into Donald Trump's war on truth itself was planted.

The revelations in the Dominion Voting Systems legal filings[10] demonstrate the full corruption of Fox News. The channel that debuted with the tagline "fair and balanced" has become completely untethered to any standard of integrity. Its own bias bears no comparison to that of the "mainstream media." CNN, ABC, and *USA Today* have their flaws, but at least remain within the bounds of reality. Fox is not a news channel—it is the right's *Pravda*. Among the frank acknowledgments of what the channel had become were rebukes to reporters who attempted to tell the simple truth. When reporter Kristin Fisher noted on the air that Rudy Giuliani and Sidney Powell's howler of a press conference on November 19 contained allegations that did not align with what Trump's lawyers were pleading in court and were not supported by evidence, she was rebuked by higher-ups at the network and told to do a better job of "respecting the audience."

Respecting the audience in Fox speak meant telling the audience exactly what it wanted to hear and nothing that would ruffle its delicate feathers. In private, Sean Hannity would confide that "Rudy is acting like an insane person," but in public—to Fox's vast audience—Rudy's ravings were laundered and legitimized. In private, Tucker Carlson fumed that a reporter telling the truth—that the election had not been stolen—was "measurably hurting the company. The stock price is down."

The executives and others who clung to their integrity, most notably Chris Stirewalt and Bill Sammon, were cashiered. Those who could "protect the brand" by lying were rewarded. Dominion's thorough airing of internal communications reveals executives who were total cynics, ready to serve the rubes whatever was required to maintain their market share. Fox News President Jay Wallace, after catching a bit of *Lou Dobbs Tonight*, noted tartly that "The North Koreans do a more nuanced show."

We know what to think of Fox News hosts and executives. But what about the audience? All of us indulge the urge, at least sometimes, to hear news that confirms our own views. What Fox's audience must grapple with is that choosing news is not like other consumer choices. It's not like choosing country music in preference to hip hop or preferring Android over iOS. Getting the truth from a news source is more analogous to getting the straight story from your doctor or financial adviser or home inspector. If your financial adviser told you what you wanted to hear rather than the truth, you'd have a legal case. He or she has a professional responsibility not to mislead you. If your doctor assured you that your skin lesion was benign because he thought this would be more welcome than the news that it was melanoma requiring immediate treatment, the doctor would be guilty of malpractice and you wouldn't thank him. When Fox News and its competitors lie to viewers, they are endangering not their physical health but their civic health and the good of the nation.

For decades, conservatives longed to get the whole story into the national news, but by demanding agreeable fiction instead of accepting complex fact, they have embarrassed themselves and undermined the case—still relevant—for fair and balanced coverage.

CHAPTER 19
How We Know Recent Elections Were Not Stolen[1]

By Isaac Saul

Over the last six years, allegations of stolen elections and massive election fraud have proliferated in the United States. While former President Donald Trump and his allies have been most responsible for this proliferation, it is certainly not a phenomenon limited to conservatives. Hillary Clinton still doesn't accept the results of the 2016 election,[2] and Democrats have spread election-related conspiracy theories in 2016 and 2020 as well.[3]

The significance of claims that the results of one election—let alone several—were fraudulent cannot be overstated. In the United States, order depends on faith in its electoral system. Globally, and in the wake of 2020, we see what happens when citizens believe an election has been stolen: chaos, riots, and the potential collapse of political systems. That means the question of whether an election was stolen or rigged should demand the highest level of scrutiny and the highest degree of skepticism. It also means the answer is not only vitally important but also has many consequences.

When analyzing allegations of stolen elections or fraud, the biggest difficulty is that you are often trying to demonstrate to someone that a *feeling* they have is wrong, not that the evidence they have is lacking. As a reporter who has written a lot about claims of voter fraud (the corruption of a single vote, usually purported by one person acting alone) and election fraud (the systemic corruption of an election, usually through some pre-planned scheme), it often feels like trying to prove that aliens *don't* exist. It's not really about evidence, it's about overcoming a belief someone has even when there is little or no evidence to support that belief. Put differently, proving that aliens do exist—like proving that the 2020 or 2016 election was stolen—is difficult because there is so little evidence for it. The burden of proof must be upon the asserter.

Still, that's not to say voter and election fraud claims can't be analyzed. On the contrary, many specific allegations which offer purported evidence have been presented over the last six years. However rare, election fraud and voter fraud do occur, and have been alleged, investigated, and prosecuted even within the last few years.[4] However, many of the allegations that have become the most popular have been sufficiently investigated and, upon the basis of the evidence, disproven.[5] Meanwhile, the fraud we know about—the fraud for which there is solid evidence—doesn't come remotely close to being sufficient to have changed the results of any recent presidential election.[6]

Russia, Russia, Russia

The 2016 election was unlike any others in recent memory. Most notably, it was marred by allegations of "Russian interference," including the leaking of internal communications from Hillary Clinton's campaign team—an unprecedented breach of accepted presidential electoral ethics.[7]

It should be said explicitly that the hack of the Democratic National Committee was very real, as were the documents published by WikiLeaks. While elements of it were a tad bit rudimentary—for example, Hillary Clinton campaign chairperson John Podesta's assistant falling for a spear-phishing email (that is, a fraudulent email sent ostensibly from a known or trusted sender in order to induce targeted individuals to reveal confidential information) to reset his password—the fervor over all of it led to some rather bizarre and unfounded allegations.[8] Perhaps one of the most prominent was the idea that Russia actually *hacked into* U.S. voting systems in order to help Trump.

This claim was, in part, popularized by former Clinton advisor and now Joe Biden senior advisor Neera Tanden. In the weeks after Trump's victory, Tanden repeatedly called on electors to ignore their states' votes and refuse to elect Trump as president. She insisted Clinton only lost the election because Russia "did enough damage to affect 70,000 votes in three states." And, perhaps most critically, she repeatedly suggested that Russian hackers changed actual vote tallies in the election.[9]

In fact, there is no evidence that any Russian hackers ever changed a single vote in the 2016 election. In Robert Mueller's sweeping indictment of Russian intelligence agents, he never even *alleged* U.S. voting machines were ever compromised—let alone produced evidence of such. Rather, Russia's role in the 2016 election amounted almost entirely to the dissemination of some real and damaging information, as well as the spreading of disinformation and the organization of fake political meetups.[10] Unfortunately, misleading headlines about these hacks led many voters to believe otherwise. In May of 2019, National Public Radio (NPR) published a piece headlined "Florida Governor Says Russian Hackers Breached 2 Counties in 2016." However, in the body of the piece, the reporter emphasized that "no data were tampered with and vote tallies were not affected."

While specific Florida counties weren't named, officials also said the data accessed by the hackers were already publicly available.[11]

Nonetheless, that false claim enjoyed a life of its own. Shortly after the 2016 election, 67% of Democrats reported believing that it's "definitely true" or "probably true" that Russia tampered with votes in order to help elect Trump.[12]

Democrat Allegations of Fraud in 2020

In 2020, while Donald Trump began spreading his election fraud conspiracy claims, Democrats briefly latched onto conspiracy theories of their own. First, rumors persisted online that 300,000 ballots for Democrats had "gone missing."[13] This claim originated when some online sleuths were trying to understand why hundreds of thousands of ballots had not been scanned for delivery. It turned out that USPS workers were manually postmarking the ballots and delivering them quickly, without scanning them into the system.[14] Before reporters made that information clear, however, the theory that hundreds of thousands of ballots had gone missing due to a corrupt USPS being run by a hand-picked Trump appointee was going viral.

In another instance from the 2020 election, a progressive Twitter user attempted to frame the results in Kentucky as rigged, arguing that Senate Majority Leader Mitch McConnell had facilitated a stolen election.[15] "The GOP seem to have used 'a bag of tricks' to mess with the results," Allison Greene tweeted. "It's a combination of things that includes somehow getting more Republican votes then there are Republican voters, significant absentee votes not being counted, suppressing the Vote in key Democrat counties."

Greene came to these conclusions by making claims such as, "Ballard County Kentucky the State Board of Elections shows 2285 registered REPUBLICAN voters as of Oct 2020 yet 3155 people voted for Mitch McConnell?" The progressive website Daily Kos republished her claims and her thread was shared more than 13,000 times as of this writing, likely seen by millions of users.[16]

However, her Twitter thread was filled with misconceptions. Greene was making basic mistakes, such as misreading voter registration files or misunderstanding Kentucky politics (and assuming no Democrat would vote for McConnell). As elections reporter Grace Panetta put it:

> This thread is proof that harmful election conspiracy theories are by no means limited to the right. Especially in a place like Kentucky, people don't vote perfectly in line with their party registration, ticket-splitting is common, and there are voters who aren't registered with either party.

None of Greene's claims ever held up to scrutiny. They were immediately refuted by Kentucky voters who replied to her tweet, and thoroughly debunked in the comments sections of articles like the one posted by Daily Kos.[17] Yet the narrative persisted and Greene never replied to her critics. She continues to make those claims today in publications such as D.C. Report.[18]

Of course, in 2020, that was just the beginning.

Trump's Big Lie

One of the first viral claims was that thousands of votes had been "dropped" in the "middle of the night" by Democrats in states like Michigan and Wisconsin to overcome Donald Trump's early lead.[19] These votes supposedly evaded detection from Republican poll watchers at every poll in every swing state and were then counted and illegally added to the Democrats' tally.

For those of us who reported on the election, however, we know the late surge from Biden was quite predictable. In fact, I reported this weeks before the election, because in most swing states mail-in ballots were going to be tabulated last. Two days before the election, BBC News explained:

> Early tallies may be deceptive. This is due in part to more differences between states in reporting. Some states, like Florida and Arizona, begin pre-processing ballots weeks before November 3rd. Others, like Wisconsin and Pennsylvania, won't touch these votes until election day, meaning they'll likely be slower to count. . . In some states, ballots cast in person on election day will be counted first. These counts are expected to favour Mr. Trump, as his supporters are expected to be more likely to vote on the day.[20]

Since mail-in ballots were predominantly coming from Democratic voters, who were more fearful of COVID-19 and more encouraged by their preferred candidates to vote by mail, it was obvious that the votes counted last were going to disproportionately favor Biden. This was especially relevant given that Trump repeatedly told supporters that mail-in voting was unreliable.

So, the fact that some people went to bed when Trump was ahead and woke up (after the mail-in ballots were counted) to find Biden leading should not have been surprising. It played out exactly as reporters and election experts expected it would. It should be noted, also, that the *only reason* this happened was that Republicans in states such as Wisconsin and Pennsylvania refused to tally, process, and count mail-in votes before Election Day.

You may have noticed that in Florida and Ohio, where elections are also run by Republicans, we did not have allegations of votes being "dumped" to favor Biden. That is probably, in part, due to the fact that Trump won those states. But it's mostly because those Republicans passed bills to allow mail-in votes to be processed and counted before election day.[21]

Dead Voters

Another common voter and election fraud allegation from 2020 was the claim of "dead people voting." More precisely, this is the allegation that dead people's ballots were being stolen and cast without detection. This allegation is harder to parse in a broad way because the ways by which states ensure votes are legally cast vary. Nonetheless, we can look at some specific allegations made by Donald Trump. Consider, for instance, his claim that "at least" 5,000 dead people voted in Georgia's presidential election in 2020.[22]

These claims started almost immediately after the election when President Trump's team claimed four "dead people" had their ballots cast: Linda Kesler, Deborah Jean Christiansen, James Blalock, and Edward Skwiot.[23] It began with a series of viral internet posts and that was amplified by Fox News host Tucker Carlson, who did an entire segment on the purported dead voters. "Mr. James Blalock of Covington, Georgia, a World War II veteran, voted in the election," read one of the posts. "The only problem? He passed away 14 years ago, in January 2006. Sadly, Mr. Blalock is a victim of voter fraud." However, it became apparent to investigators that three of the four, including Blalock, did not actually have their ballots cast:

> Linda Kesler died in 2003 and didn't vote—but *Lynda* Kesler, a nearly identical name but a person with a different address, birthday and zip code—did vote. Similarly, Deborah Jean Christiansen voted in 2018, died in 2019, and had her registration canceled before the election (voter rolls are regularly matched with death records and then updated). However, a woman with the same name born in the same year, but with a different birthday and social security number, did vote in 2020. Finally, James Blalock, who died in 2006, was purged from the voter rolls that year. But in 2020, his widow voted under the name 'Mrs. James E. Blalock Jr.,' which she did even when her husband was alive.

As it turns out, Edward Skwiot *did* have his ballot cast, despite dying in 2015.[24] Skwiot's vote was illegally cast in a county where 6,000 of the 7,327 votes were cast for Trump. In total, Georgia officials have found four voters who had died but whose ballots were cast in 2020—despite the fact Trump alleged "at least" 5,000 dead people's votes were cast.[25] These few "phantom" voters were discovered after election officials investigated allegations from the public.[26]

In each of those four cases, the ballots were not enmeshed in some vast Democratic conspiracy to overturn the election, but were cast by family members of the deceased, according to sworn testimony from Republican Secretary of State Brad Raffensperger. In most cases, election officials find that dead people's ballots being cast are from family members who purport to know how the person in whose name they voted would have wanted to vote, and so justified their illegal action that way.[27]

How do we know more dead people aren't voting? Every state has different rules, but since so many of the dead people voting allegations were in Georgia, we can discuss specifics there.

First, the only way a dead person's ballot could be cast is by absentee voting. The first step toward getting an absentee ballot is requesting an application. It's worth noting here that because of COVID-19, mail-in and absentee voting proliferated across the country. Many Americans were sent absentee ballot *applications* in 2020 for the first time, and confused them for *actual ballots*, thus helping to spread the rumor that dead people were being sent ballots. It's legal for voting groups to send out applications to people without requests, and many groups do so in order to ramp up voter participation. Even so, only one single ballot can actually be requested and can be cast by a legal, living voter.

In Georgia, in order to receive that ballot, a person must send in an application with voter information that identifies them by name, date of birth, and either Social Security Number or Driver's License Number. When that application is sent in, the person must sign it, affirming they are who they say they are (under penalty of prosecution), and their signature is matched against a signature that Georgia has on file. If the person is approved for a ballot, they will receive it by mail. They then have to vote and have to sign it again (with this signature also matched against the one on file). Moreover, once your ballot is cast, it is still subject to an audit.

At each one of these steps, Georgia election officials use voter rolls to ensure that each vote is legitimate. Voter roll maintenance happens in every state, but as it is directly related to deaths, states use various methods to ensure voters on their rolls are still alive: They check state death records, obituaries, vital records, and/or Social Security data. Six states receive updates from the state health department every month on who has died. Most states have "inactive voter" lists—that is, voters who aren't voting—and purge those voters from the rolls.[28]

Recounts and Election Audits

There are additional reasons for confidence in the voting system: First, the reason you heard about claims of dead people voting in Georgia is that Georgia voter rolls are public—meaning anyone can investigate whether a person voted who is also dead. While this allows a lot of inexperienced online sleuths to make erroneous claims about voter fraud, it also allows campaigns, journalists, and investigators to scrutinize those allegations. Further, it makes it extremely unlikely that any huge irregularities would get past election officials, investigators, campaigns, journalists, and the public.[29]

In 2020, Georgia also performed a "risk-limiting audit" (RLA). This is a process where investigators pull a sample of ballots from the state for close inspection, and then extrapolate to the entire election based on that investigation. Ballots are chosen for audit by rolling twenty 10-sided dice, which produce random numbers that are input into risk-limiting software. The results inform counties as to which ballots to pull and where, until enough ballots are pulled to form a statistically representative sample.[30]

Georgia also performed a full hand recount of millions of voters to ensure there wasn't any machine error. The state also performed signature matching audits, which would turn up all kinds of fraud—from organized election interference to dead people voting. All of the results of these audits indicate that votes had been tabulated fairly.

For instance, Trump and his team levied many allegations about Cobb County, Georgia. So investigators pulled 15,118 absentee ballot envelopes from 30 randomly-selected boxes. There were a total of 150,431 absentee ballots returned in Cobb County, so the sample was large enough to produce representative results, with a 99% confidence level and a one percent margin of error. Investigators formed 18 two-member teams to look at voter signatures, and compare them to voter registration forms, absentee ballot applications, passports, and other government documents.[31]

Collectively, the investigators found 396 questionable signatures on ballot envelopes. All but 10 were accepted as valid, and then voters were contacted and given the opportunity to verify those ballots. There were zero cases of fraud in the entire batch. Meanwhile, county-by-county results of the RLA are also live and accessible to the public on Georgia Secretary of State's website.[32]

Given that nearly every swing state conducted hand recounts and audits in close races, any machine error would have immediately been caught by auditors—as it was in two counties in Michigan and Georgia (In both cases, it was human error—not corrupted software—that caused the miscount).[33]

Curing Ballots

As it happens, the transparency of the 2020 election itself is part of what created such controversy. In many polling stations, there were livestreams of the ballots being sorted and counted. There were security cameras at drop boxes and nonstop news coverage of any allegation of fraud across the country. In several instances, this transparency actually resulted in people misunderstanding typical election procedures as something more nefarious.

In one example, President Trump shared a video where election workers were curing ballots, and raised the prospect that they were actually illegally filling out ballots. Ballot curing happens when a machine fails to read a ballot someone submitted—usually because a person filled in a bubble outside the lines, tried to correct a mistake, or accidentally marked the paper somewhere and so confused the scanner.

In this process, two election workers sit across from each other, one with the invalid ballots and the other with a new ballot. If they can, they "cure" the ballot by recreating the voter's intended vote and putting it back through the machine. This process is overseen by poll watchers (an even number of Republicans and Democrats) and is only performed on ballots where the intent of a voter is clear. The remade ballot is then attached to the original ballot that had readability problems so that the vote can be audited after the election.[34]

Since we had live access to many polling stations, some Americans unfamiliar with the process saw ballot curing taking place—again, out in the open, under the watch of poll watchers and on livestreams of polling places—and erroneously believed they were witnessing vote fraud.

Similarly, ballots are often sorted at polling stations. Given that some more populous counties handle tens or hundreds of thousands of ballots, the process can be laborious. In one video from the 2020 election, a poll worker threw out instructions that were inside a ballot while being filmed. Voters who witnessed this process online believed that *votes* were being thrown out in front of their eyes. What they really were witnessing was just a normal part of the sorting process before votes are opened and counted. Sadly, the election worker in question had to go into hiding and his boss had to go on the nightly news to clear his name.[35]

Perhaps one of the most popular allegations from the 2020 election was the claim that Dominion Voting Systems had corrupted machines that would somehow switch votes from Trump to Biden. President Trump himself helped popularize this claim after the election when he tweeted:

> REPORT: DOMINION DELETED 2.7 MILLION TRUMP VOTES NATIONWIDE. DATA ANALYSIS FINDS 221,000 PENNSYLVANIA VOTES SWITCHED FROM PRESIDENT TRUMP TO BIDEN. 941,000 TRUMP VOTES DELETED. STATES USING DOMINION VOTING SYSTEMS SWITCHED 435,000 VOTES FROM TRUMP TO BIDEN.[36]

This allegation was first made by One America News Network, who published a report saying:

> an unaudited analysis of data obtained from Edison Research, states using Dominion Voting Systems may have switched as many as 435,000 votes from President Trump to Joe Biden. And the author also finds another 2.7 million Trump votes appear to have been deleted by Dominion, including almost 1 million Trump votes in Pennsylvania alone.

However, when reporters reached out to Edison Research about this claim, they responded unequivocally: "Edison Research created no such report and we are not aware of any voter fraud," President Larry Rosin said. It was a "game of telephone" going all the way back to the source, who then denied even making the initial allegation. The claim was, literally, concocted out of thin air.[37]

As we learned from investigations into January 6, even Trump-affiliated lawyers such as Sidney Powell never actually obtained evidence of Dominion Voting machines corrupting the vote, despite the fact they claimed that evidence was forthcoming. Trump eventually dropped Powell, and text messages subpoenaed by the January 6 committee show Trump's chief of staff and allies discussing privately the fact Powell never showed them any evidence of Dominion voting machines helping facilitate fraud, despite claiming otherwise publicly. Dominion is now successfully advancing a defamation lawsuit against Powell and conservative news networks who elevated her claims, and allegations of Dominion switching votes have all but disappeared. President Trump does not even make these allegations anymore.[38]

2000 Mules

The most recent popularized story of voter fraud comes from Dinesh D'Souza in his film *2000 Mules*, in which he claims that hundreds of thousands of illegal votes were cast by at least 2,000 people—and as many as 50,000—who were operating across major swing states in order to stuff drop boxes with illegal ballots to help Biden win.

D'Souza's evidence for these claims consists of GPS cell phone-tracking data purchased by his team, which allegedly shows 2,000 mules repeatedly passing by drop boxes and the offices of political organizations leading up to the 2020 election. In his analysis, for the period from October 1, 2020 to election day, D'Souza isolated every person who passed or stopped at 10 or more drop boxes in a day, and every person who passed or stopped at five or more nonprofit organizations tied to political entities. Using these criteria, he claims to have found over 2,000 people across several Democratic strongholds in swing states, mainly Philadelphia and Atlanta. These "2,000 mules" are then credited with delivering hundreds of thousands of ballots that threw the election to Biden.

Along with the cell phone data, D'Souza shows various clips from security footage of people dropping off ballots late at night, taking photos of the ballot box after they've submitted them, or wearing gloves when they drop the ballots off—all of which is supposed to create suspicion that the voters were doing something illegal.

I've published an entire 8,000-word piece examining the claims in D'Souza's film, which do not hold up under scrutiny. Among the many issues with his film, the main problems are as follows.[39]

First, D'Souza never once in the film concedes that the Georgia Bureau of Investigation (GBI) actually looked into a few of the so-called mules and found that all of the ones they investigated were turning in legal ballots for family members. In Georgia, it is legal to drop off ballots for family members, people who are disabled, or people in your care. Several of the people featured in D'Souza's film were investigated by the GBI and found to be casting legal ballots, yet D'Souza never informs his viewers of this fact. The GBI has requested more information from the producers of the *2,000 Mules* film about the purported scheme, but they have so far declined to cooperate.[40]

Second, D'Souza (and his team) alleged repeatedly that these "mules" were making *several stops at several drop boxes in the same day.* That is the entire premise of their geo-tracking cell phone data. Nowhere in the movie, however, do they show the same "mule" twice. When pressed on this point, D'Souza—to his credit—produced still images of one person visiting a ballot box on two separate days. That would be easily explainable if the person was, as it appears, some kind of health care worker turning in ballots for people in his care or turning in ballots for family members on two separate days. Still, the person is not at the same ballot box on the same day, which—again—is the entire premise of D'Souza's film.

This leads to the other, more obvious reasons to question its claim. Why would a vast conspiracy of political operatives use drop boxes to commit their scheme? Absentee ballots in Georgia can be submitted by mail, and by using drop boxes the schemers would allow themselves to be seen on security camera footage when they could have just mailed in the ballots or dropped them off at a post office.

Further, where are the witnesses? D'Souza claims as many as 50,000 mules participated in this scheme and were likely paid off by Democrats. Yet not a single whistleblower or witness has come forward. In election fraud cases that have been prosecuted in recent years, members of politicians' own staff often testify against them, even in cases where they are incriminating themselves. D'Souza purports to have the cell phone data on over 2,000 criminals, but his team hasn't been able to identify even a single one of them to authorities. Nor has a single one come forward or confessed on tape, in a text message, or in an email to a friend. None have been outed by family members or colleagues who they confided in.

Simply put: Where are the mules? Where is the smoking gun?

Victor Reynolds, the director of the Georgia Bureau of Investigation, looked into some of these claims. In a letter to the chairman of the Georgia Republican Party on September 30, 2021, he wrote: "Saliently, it has been stated that there is 'a source' that can validate ballot harvesting. Despite repeated requests that source has not been provided to either the GBI or to the FBI."

Finally, the actual geo-tracking data at the center of their allegations is a questionable foundation on which to build. While D'Souza mostly used general terms such as "GPS data" to describe what he purchased, the data expert in the film, Gregg Phillips, told investigators that the data they bought was Cell Site Location Information—that is, CSLI data. Historical CSLI data cannot track someone's movements within three-to-five foot accuracy, as D'Souza has claimed. In reality, there is no way to pinpoint a cellphone's precise geographic location from CSLI data and no known validation methods or error rates for the methodologies used to collect that data.[41]

Given that there are political nonprofits and drop boxes placed all across cities like Atlanta and Philadelphia, the place where the creators of *2,000 Mules* focused their attention, data showing people coming near those locations is actually an invalid metric for proving some kind of illicit election fraud scheme.

Even More Allegations of Fraud

These allegations are just the tip of the iceberg of what has been alleged in the 2020 and 2016 elections. Others include claims such as three to five million un-documented immigrants voting, or fake ballots being printed and used, or sta-tistical anomalies that make it impossible for Biden to have won, or ballots cast outnumbering registered voters. In every one of these allegations, similar logical fallacies, misunderstandings, or falsehoods are at the core of the story—not actual evidence of voter or election fraud. Passage of time and accumulation of evidence have only reinforced that null hypothesis.

In July of 2022, perhaps the most damning, expansive, and conclusive report analyzing these claims was published. It was the work of a group of conserva-tives—eight prominent former attorneys general, judges, Republican senators, and Republican-appointed officials. They examined all 64 cases of election fraud Trump and his legal team tried to file in court, and then issued a 72-page report on the details and outcomes of those cases.[42]

In total, the group found 20 of those cases were dismissed before a hearing on the merits, 14 were voluntarily dismissed by Trump and his allies before a hearing on the merits, 30 were dismissed that included a hearing on the merits, leaving only one case involving far too few votes to impact the election in which Trump's team did prevail in Pennsylvania. It was a case about a voter ID deadline, not election fraud.[43]

In all, 22 federal judges appointed by Republican Presidents, including 10 ap-pointed by Trump himself and at least 24 elected or appointed Republican state judges, dismissed the President's claims. At least 11 lawyers have been referred for disciplinary proceedings due to bad faith and baseless efforts to undermine the outcome of the 2020 Presidential election. Several prominent conservative news outlets and magazines have had to issue retractions.[44]

One Trump-appointed judge said of the allegations: "Charges require specific allegations and proof. We have neither here."[45]

Another Trump-appointed judge warned that if cases like these succeeded, "Any disappointed loser in a Presidential election able to hire a team of clever lawyers could flag claimed deviations from election results and cast doubt on elec-tion results."[46]

As President Trump's own former attorney general William Barr put it to in-vestigators, after examining evidence with the full power of the Justice Depart-ment, he believes the claims of election fraud were "bullshit," "complete non-sense," and "a great, great disservice to the country." He went on that Trump is "detached from reality" if he believes them.[47]

While voter fraud and election fraud cases have been prosecuted in recent years, nearly two years after the 2020 election there is still no credible evidence that the race was stolen—just as six years after the 2016 election we still know Donald Trump won that race fairly. No court has validated a stolen election in 2020, no claim has withstood scrutiny from election experts, and yet each time an allegation is disproven another one emerges, which is how we went from Dominion Voting Systems to *2000 Mules.*

Was It All Above Board?

Over time, the claim that the 2020 election was "stolen" has taken on different meaning to different people. Some supporters of former President Trump have attached themselves to many of the allegations above, which—as demonstrated above—don't contain any merit.

Others, though, have used the word "stolen" to imply something different: That the election was *unfair*—that the deck was stacked against Trump. Rather than argue that "mules" stole the election or voting machines flipped ballots or election workers rigged races, this claim carries a bit more nuance.

In this telling, the unfairness of the 2020 race is about a combination of legal but unusual factors: the suppression of the Hunter Biden scandal story, the banishing of high-profile Trump supporters from major social media platforms, the rapid and unprecedented expansion of mail-in voting access (which benefits Democratic candidates), and the hundreds of millions of dollars provided by wealthy liberals such as Mark Zuckerberg to fund the facilitation of elections in predominantly Democratic districts.

If there is an argument that the 2020 election was unfair, these angles certainly carry more weight than the ones that preceded them. Yet, are they anything more than somewhat aged and more sophisticated sour grapes?

Among many other excuses, Hillary Clinton blamed her 2016 loss on then-FBI Director James Comey's decision to announce a reopening of the investigation into her email scandal just weeks before voters cast their ballots. Some pollsters have demonstrated a statistically significant drop in Clinton's support immediately following that announcement. It was highly unusual, and Comey is a registered Republican. On top of that, WikiLeaks did actually disseminate DNC emails, which really were hacked in an effort to damage her. If you believe the 2020 election was stolen from Trump, it might be worth considering that such an allegation sounds a lot like Clinton's claims the 2016 election was stolen from her—not because the vote was compromised, but because her campaign was hurt by a series of extraordinary events.

What's critical in all this is to separate the wheat from the chaff. The burden of proof rests on those who claim the 2020 election was marred by widespread election fraud, committed in some sort of vast, Democrat-run conspiracy. So far, the claimants haven't come close to supporting such an allegation, and the evidence they've tried to bring forward dissolved under even slightest mild scrutiny.

For Americans of all stripes, that should first and foremost be encouraging. In nearly every election of recent memory, the losing side has alleged a range of shenanigans. No elections are perfect, and fraud is not as uncommon as some want you to believe. Nonetheless, America's political process thrives because citizens and politicians are able to view the evidence, trust the checks and balances, and move forward as a single nation. If the last election had been truly rigged, if such evidence did exist, it would be a calamity.

That is what makes this exercise frightening. It's encouraging that we can have confidence in the result of the 2020 election. Yet it's frightening that such flimsy allegations captured such a massive and gullible audience. And it's worrisome that, with such little evidence to support those claims, articles like this remain necessary.

CHAPTER 20
Truth and Consequences[1]

By Jonathan V. Last

There's an interesting coda to the *Fox v. Dominion* story.

You may recall that in August of 2021 the MyPillow guy, Mike Lindell, offered a $5 million bounty to anyone who could "Prove Mike Wrong" about his claims of Chinese interference in the 2020 election.

Well, someone did. Then Mike Lindell tried to stiff him. And yesterday an arbitrator ruled that Lindell had to pay the guy. Here's what happened, per the *Washington Post:*[2]

- Lindell claimed to have data proving that the Chinese hacked the election.
- Robert Zeidman, a computer forensics expert (and Trump voter!) "examined Lindell's data and concluded that it not only did not prove voter fraud, it had no connection to the 2020 election."
- He submitted a claim.
- Lindell rejected it.
- Zeidman took the dispute to arbitration.

From the *Post:* "In their 23-page decision, the arbitrators said Zeidman proved that Lindell's material 'unequivocally did not reflect November 2020 election data.' They directed Lindell's firm to pay Zeidman within 30 days."

Say what you will about Mike Lindell, but unlike Rupert Murdoch and many of the executives and talent at Fox, he seems to *genuinely believe* everything he says in public.

The Fox people have to pay their parking ticket—$787.5 million, some large portion of which will come out of their $4 billion war chest. These ducats will quickly be replenished by the roughly $4 billion in revenue[3] that Fox News brings in yearly just from cable carriage fees.[4] None of the money will come from the personal accounts of the people who defamed Dominion.

I don't know what Lindell's finances are, but I suspect that $5 million is a *much* more significant sum to him, personally, than the $787.5 million corporate tariff is to the personal finances of the various people in and around Fox Corp. In the Game of Trump, only the true believers ever really get hurt.

Truth is, I have more respect for Mike Lindell and Marjorie Taylor Greene (MTG) and the other true believers than I do for the Laura Ingrahams and Elise Stefaniks of the world. At least the true believers *believe* the stuff they say. I would be shocked if there exists a bunch of texts between Mike Lindell and MTG in which they rant about how passionately they hate Donald Trump and can't wait for him to go away.

Yet one persistent aspect of the Trump years is that the cynical class of professionals who make their money and careers off of Trump never seem to suffer any real consequences. But the true believers? They often get the short end. On January 6, thousands of regular folks who truly believed that the election was stolen were told by the president and various elites to march on the Capitol and "take their country back" with "strength." So they did. And now hundreds of them are in jail and have had their lives upended.

But the cynics who told them to do it so that they could make money from ratings and clicks and carriage fees? Not a single one of them has faced any real consequences. I suspect it'll be the same with Mike Lindell and Dominion. Three months from now the Fox machine will still be printing money, without admitting fault or changing behavior. No one is going to lose their show for having exposed the company to legal jeopardy. Yet I suspect that Mike Lindell will reach a different outcome. He's already out $5 million. When Dominion is finished with him, he'll be a husk.[5] Another true believer wrecked because he wasn't smart enough to understand what was happening and wasn't elite enough to have a moat protecting him from consequences.

The worst part in all of this is that it proves the cynics were right. When Trump came to power, nearly all of the elites in Conservatism Inc. and the Republican party decided to go along with him. They reasoned that they could prosper under Trump and that they were unlikely to suffer any adverse effects should the experiment go pear-shaped. They were correct. The consequences were only experienced further down the food chain:[6] By the rubes who actually believed that COVID was just the common cold and vaccines were dangerous. Or that the election was stolen and could be overturned. Or that you could defame businesses with impunity.

CHAPTER 21
The "Great Replacement" and the "Big Lie"[1]

By Theodore R. Johnson

Conspiracy theories rarely grow alone. They are like vines: when placed next to one another, they entwine and mature together—the worldviews and communities where they thrive are trellises they climb to the heights of absurdity. Which is why Donald Trump's "Big Lie"—the belief that the 2020 election was illegitimate and that he was its real winner—cannot be understood on its own. It is tangled up with the conspiratorial Great Replacement theory and with the anti-democratic notion that state legislatures have the sole authority to elect presidents.

These three ideas are distinct enough that they can be discussed separately—but people who embrace one of them are more likely to embrace the others. That is, a person who believes that the 2020 election was stolen from Donald Trump is more likely than not to reject, at least tacitly, the idea of a multiracial United States and to repudiate the intrinsically American principle that government derives its just powers from the consent of the governed.

This realization is especially troubling given recent reporting from the *New York Times* showing that 44% of Republican lawmakers in nine swing states—that's 357 sitting legislators—"took concrete steps to discredit or overturn the results of the 2020 presidential election."[2] And in Pennsylvania, where Big Lie enthusiast and January 6th insurrectionist Doug Mastriano won the Republican gubernatorial primary, the overwhelming majority of the party's state legislators sought to reverse the election outcome or delay the vote count.

The easy explanation is that Republican incumbents and candidates, in the name of political expedience, have gone all in on the Big Lie merely as a show of loyalty to the former president in hopes of winning over his supporters and securing election victories.

But that superficial explanation for the GOP's direction is belied by the fact that many of these Republicans endorse not just the narrow Big Lie about the election but also two other un-American theories—the Great Replacement and the independent state legislature.

Recall that the Trump-induced myth of election fraud was grounded in the bogus idea that areas with high concentrations of Black and Hispanic voters were the source of the illegitimacy.[3] Trump lost Michigan, Wisconsin, and Georgia thanks in no small part to lopsided margins in the Detroit, Milwaukee, and Atlanta metro areas in a high-turnout election. The subtext of the Big Lie could not be clearer: Trump and his acolytes were accusing Black and Hispanic voters of being foot soldiers in the Democratic plot to steal the election. And, should one need more information to connect the dots, we can turn again to Pennsylvania: During the first presidential debate, Trump previewed his election denialism by suggesting that "tens of thousands of ballots" could be manipulated there because "bad things happen in Philadelphia,"[4] a plurality-Black city. And sure enough, just over a month later, Philadelphia was the first city Trump targeted in the Big Lie.[5]

The fingerprints of the Great Replacement theory, which suggests that there's an intentional political strategy being implemented to have racial and ethnic minorities take the place of White people and culture in America, are all over this framing. Replacement theorists accuse the Democratic party of using Black and Hispanic voters to displace the electoral voice of *real* Americans. As replacement evangelist Tucker Carlson proclaimed last year, "This is a voting rights question. I have less political power because [Democrats] are importing a brand-new electorate. Why should I sit back and take that?"[6] Indeed, Republican Congresswoman Elise Stefanik declared Democrats, who have received the lion's share of the Black vote for decades, are attempting a "permanent election insurrection" by exploring pathways to citizenship for immigrants—an odd proposition given that a year ago many pundits and GOP officials couldn't stop pointing out the party's gains among Hispanic and Black voters.[7]

Through this lens, the very participation of people of color is viewed as a threat to American democracy and a distortion of the social order that replacement theorists believe the Constitution established. The Big Lie is a product of the belief that the Americans these theorists deem undesirable have too much influence on election outcomes.

If the Big Liars and replacement theorists feel political losses are imminent and enduring, they suddenly become more accepting of anti-democratic actions to rig the game by weighting the areas where they hold power. Enter the independent state legislature theory—a fanatical interpretation of the Constitution's Elections and Electors Clauses suggesting that, among other things, state legislatures are authorized to act independently of the popular vote when selecting presidential electors. In practice, this means that a state assembly can ignore the votes of their constituents and unilaterally determine which presidential candidate should receive its Electoral College votes.

This theory is linked to some Republicans' longstanding mantra "America is a republic, not a democracy"—the idea being that the representative nature of a republic is the true means by which the governed provide consent, not through casting their votes directly for candidates for a particular office like the presidency. Rather, the republic serves to moderate the voice of the people, who, as Alexander Hamilton put it, "seldom judge or determine right."[8] This was part of the reason for which the Framers devised the Electoral College: to dilute the democratically expressed will of the populace. Better to empower the enlightened men of principle—"the rich and well born," in Hamilton's words—than to permit an obtuse public to decide who should lead. In this construction, the best and truest Americans are the proper caretakers of the country and its people (It is worth noting just as a historical footnote that the idea of the Electoral College originated with a Pennsylvanian—James Wilson, also one of the creators of the Three-Fifths Compromise).

The independent state legislature theory gaining steam in Republican circles not only self-designates whose voices matter most, but also undercuts the ability of the governed to provide consent and dismisses the participation of those Americans who experience the world differently on account of race or ethnicity.

Considering the three together—the Big Lie, replacement theory, and the independent state legislature doctrine—demonstrates how they work to assert one undeniably un-American view: It is not only permissible to prevent a democracy governed by an increasingly racially and ethnically diverse cohort, it is imperative because of the existential threat multiracial politics poses to "real Americans." The Big Lie not only insists the election was stolen but names the groups it believes are culpable and endorses anti-democratic means to exclude them from the electoral process.

It is said that Pennsylvania Avenue—the boulevard that connects the White House and the U.S. Capitol where Congress and the early Supreme Court convened—was given its name as a concession for moving the nation's capital from Philadelphia to Washington, D.C.[9] It is perhaps the most symbolically democratic street in America.

Centuries later, Pennsylvania remains a centerpiece. Republican gubernatorial candidate and Big Lie proponent Mastriano has said that he will appoint a secretary of state who will carry out his desire to rescind every Pennsylvanians voter registration and "start all over again."[10] Meanwhile, in Pennsylvania's extremely tight Republican senatorial race, now heading into a recount, a dispute has arisen around whether the commonwealth should count undated mail-in ballots, which have been considered both a vehicle for voter fraud by the right and voter suppression by the left. Pennsylvanian Republicans submitted an alternate slate of electors for the 2020 presidential election[11]—and the state is the site of the replacement theory-motivated May 2018 shooting at a synagogue.

When Ben Franklin, Pennsylvania's favorite son, emerged from the Constitutional Convention, he is famously quoted as saying the delegates had created "a republic, if you can keep it." Whether we can "keep it" remains a live question. We are on the cusp of answering his charge, and our answer hinges on the nation's willingness to be governed by a multiracial cohort or its insistence that the current slate of leaders can let the promise of America wither on the vine.

CHAPTER 22
The "Ground Zero Mosque" Presaged Today's GOP[1]

By Jim Swift

With the twentieth anniversary of the September 11 terrorist attacks upon us, it's worth looking back at one of the many ways this defining moment in American history shaped our politics—by creating an opening for the racism and xenophobia that later came to characterize the Trump years.

You don't have to venture far from where the Twin Towers once stood—where President Biden will be visiting on the anniversary this weekend—to find the site of one of the major controversies of the post-9/11 era: the planned location of what would have been the "Ground Zero mosque," so dubbed by some evil genius of political branding.

By way of background: Buildings at 45-51 Park Place were damaged by debris on 9/11. In 2009, the *New York Times* reported on plans to replace some of the buildings at "Park51" with a mosque and Islamic cultural center.[2]

The proposal quickly became the focus of intense criticism. Some of the criticism was raw and reflexive—*radical Muslim terrorists had killed thousands of people, and now Muslims want to put up a mosque nearby?*—but the controversy was soon cynically exploited by Republicans looking to position themselves against the Democrats and President Barack Obama. Some critics suggested the planned building was a "victory mosque"—as if Muslim Americans were erecting a Dome of the Rock in lower Manhattan.

At the time, Newt Gingrich said: "Nazis don't have the right to put up a sign next to the Holocaust Museum in Washington. . . We would never accept the Japanese putting up a site next to Pearl Harbor. There's no reason for us to accept a mosque next to the World Trade Center."[3] He would later warn that "we're in grave danger of losing our liberty and losing our religious liberty" over the lawsuits against Obamacare—apparently he cared only for the government's protection of his own religion and not the protection of others'.

Regardless of how sound Gingrich's and his fellow Republicans' arguments about religious rights were, they do not jibe with the undertones of xenophobia that characterized Republican rhetoric at the time.

Back in 2011, the Center for American Progress put together a nifty look at six House members who traded a lot on anti-Islamic sentiment.[4] It's worth checking out—but my recollection is that the craziest Republicans who pumped the "Ground Zero mosque" controversy into the right-wing bloodstream were Reps. Pete King of New York and Renee Ellmers of North Carolina.

Rep. King eventually backtracked on his inflammatory rhetoric.[5] Rep. Ellmers ran an ad that was probably the defining feature of her campaign in her first race (you can watch it for yourself by following the link in this footnote[6]). It worked for Ellmers: She was elected in 2010 and served three terms in the House.

Of course, there's a Trumpian twist:

> On Sept. 9, 2010, Trump wrote a letter to Hisham Elzanaty and offered to purchase his $4.8 million stake in the [Park51] project for $6 million—around 25% more—per *The Wall Street Journal*. Trump also specified that any agreement would require that a mosque be built at least five blocks from the former World Trade Center. 'I am making this offer as a resident of New York and citizen of the United States, not because I think the location is a spectacular one (because it is not) but because it will end a very serious, inflammatory, and highly divisive situation that is destined, in my opinion, to only get worse,' Trump reportedly wrote in a letter to Elzanaty at the time, according to the *Journal*.[7]

Trump's first response to the 9/11 attacks was to congratulate himself (on the radio) for now having the tallest building in downtown Manhattan, the two taller structures having been destroyed[8] (Naturally, the boast was false). His bid to buy the Park51 project seemed about as serious as his pledges to ease tension, or his bizarre insistence that he saw people in New Jersey on 9/11 celebrating on rooftops: just more Trumpian bluster.[9]

It is one thing to oppose radical Islamist terrorism. But when Republican politicians, for short-term political gain, redefined the enemy not as violent jihadists but Muslims in general, they also began to redefine their party as one welcoming xenophobic rhetoric and candidates. Remember, this was also the era when Republicans went out of their way to emphasize the middle name of "Barack *Hussein* Obama," and when Donald Trump, with an eye on the White House, was helping to spread lies about Obama's birth certificate and hinted that Obama was secretly Muslim.[10] The GOP became the sort of party that would stand by Donald Trump when he told Democratic members of Congress to "go back" to where they came from.[11] The sort of party that would stand by his "Muslim ban."

It didn't have to be that way. Not all Republicans were as irresponsible: After 9/11, President George W. Bush made every effort to communicate that America's war was not against Muslims—and many of the Muslims who have come here from Iraq, Afghanistan, and elsewhere over the past two decades got that message.[12]

But too many Republicans ensured that their party's base heard a very different message. And they still are: Some are rightly criticizing Biden's botched response to the Afghanistan withdrawal that Trump sought, but others are demeaning the very people who will be great Americans.[13]

And what of the planned "Ground Zero mosque"? The uproar a decade ago was apparently enough to kill the project—condominiums have been constructed on the site, but no mosque has been built, and even the more modest plans for an Islamic cultural center seem to have been canceled.

CHAPTER 23
Anti-Immigrant Lies[1]

By Lawrence M. Eppard

On his television show recently on Fox News, host Tucker Carlson was discussing the Russian invasion of Ukraine, or as he called it, Vladimir Putin's "border dispute" with Ukraine (it is in fact an invasion and violation of international law,[2] not a "border dispute," and it is likely that war crimes are occurring[3]). That comment certainly caught my ear, but it was not the only one. During his show Carlson also lamented that: "Biden has pledged to defend Ukraine's borders even as he opens our borders to the world. That's how it works: invading America is called 'equity,' invading Ukraine is a war crime."[4] He went on to say that American leaders "are allowing your country to become polluted and overrun."[5]

None of this is at all new for Carlson. He frequently claims that immigrants are overrunning the U.S., that Democrats want to replace White voters with non-White ones (the "Great Replacement Theory"),[6] and that unauthorized immigrants commit a lot of crime.[7]

This last claim in particular piques my interest as a scholar of economic and racial inequalities. No matter how many times scholars debunk this claim, it stubbornly lives on in the public and political discourse and plays a major role in how many Americans think about immigration.

Carlson is not alone in spreading this disinformation of course. Former President Donald Trump was one of the most high-profile disseminators of this myth, making it a central theme of his campaign and presidency. You'll remember that he kicked off his presidential campaign in June 2015 with this claim: "When Mexico sends its people, they're not sending their best. . . They're sending people that have lots of problems, and they're bringing those problems with us. They're bringing drugs. They're bringing crime. They're rapists."[8] He followed that up in a television interview the next month by saying:

> I'm talking not about Mexico, I'm talking about illegal immigration. And it has to be stopped. . . It's killing our country. . . People are pouring over the borders. Pouring. . . By the way, they come from the Middle East. We don't even know where they come from. . . If you look at the statistics on rape, on crime, on everything, coming in illegally into this country, they're mind-boggling. . . All I'm doing is telling the truth.[9]

He would return to this theme again and again throughout his presidency: "Thanks to Democrat immigration policies, innocent Americans in all 50 states are being brutalized and murdered by illegal alien criminals."[10]

These claims about immigrants and crime are demonstrably false and they distort what should be a factual, honest, and good faith policy debate.

What the Data Tell Us

Unauthorized immigrants (often referred to as "illegal" immigrants by many on the right and "undocumented" immigrants by many on the left), like native-born Americans, do indeed commit crimes. But looking at all of the best data available to us, the weight of the evidence suggests that they do not commit crimes at a higher rate than native-born Americans.

While a number of high-quality studies exist, some of the best and most frequently cited studies come from Michael Light at the University of Wisconsin and Alex Nowrasteh at the Cato Institute. These studies not only reject the notion that immigrants are more criminally oriented than native-born Americans, but reveal the opposite to be true: across the major crime categories, native-born Americans as a group have higher crime rates than unauthorized immigrants.

Michael Light and his colleagues' research,[11] for example, revealed that compared with unauthorized immigrants, native-born Americans were about 2.2 times more likely to be arrested for violent crimes, about 4.3 times more likely to be arrested for property crimes, about 2.5 times more likely to be arrested for drug violations, and about 1.8 times more likely to be arrested for traffic violations (see Table 23.1 on next page).

Table 23.1 Felony Arrest Rates By Citizenship Status
Felony arrest rate (per 100,000 Persons)

Crime Category	Native-born Americans	Legal-immigrants	Unauthorized-immigrants
Violent crime	213.0	185.3	96.2
Property crime	165.2	98.2	38.5
Drug Violations	337.2	235.6	136.0
Traffic Violations	68.3	86.7	38.1

Michael T. Light, Jingying He, and Jason P. Robey, "Comparing Crime Rates Between Undocumented Immigrants, Legal Immigrants, and Native-born U.S. Citizens in Texas," PNAS 117, no. 51 (2020): 32340-32347.

On detailed measures of violent and property crimes, native-born Americans were more likely than unauthorized immigrants to be arrested for homicide (2.5 times), assault (2.1 times), robbery (5.6 times), and sexual assault (1.6 times).[12] There was not a single crime category where unauthorized immigrants had a higher crime rate than native-born Americans. As Light and his coauthors explained in their article:

> [U]ndocumented immigrants have substantially lower rates of crime compared to both native U.S. citizens and legal immigrants. . . Debates about undocumented immigration will no doubt continue, but they should do so informed by the available evidence. The results presented here significantly undermine the claims that undocumented immigrants pose a unique criminal risk. In fact, our results suggest that undocumented immigrants pose substantially less criminal risk than native U.S. citizens. . . [U]ndocumented immigrants are driven by economic and educational opportunities for themselves and their families, and the decision to migrate necessarily requires a considerable amount of motivation and planning. As such, undocumented immigrants may be selected on qualities such as motivation to work and ambition to achieve, attributes that are unlikely to predispose them toward criminality. . . [U]ndocumented immigrants have strong incentives to avoid criminal involvement for fear of detection and deportation.[13]

In a different study with another colleague, Light examined the issue differently. Rather than look at the criminal arrest rates of different groups, he instead looked at whether the size of unauthorized immigrant populations living in particular areas was associated with crime rates there. His findings revealed *a strong negative correlation* (-0.65) between the size of unauthorized immigrant populations and violent crime across the U.S. The higher the proportion of unauthorized immigrants in a community, the lower the violent crime rate. In other words: unauthorized immigration does not increase violence.[14]

We hear about horrible individual cases, such as the killing of Kate Steinle in San Francisco by an unauthorized immigrant in 2015,[15] but those are tragic exceptions. Steinle herself would not have been killed had that unauthorized immigrant never come to the U.S.—but at the macro level, the presence of unauthorized immigrants does not increase crime because they are not particularly crime-prone as a group. Politicians and partisan commentators like to use these awful cases to magnify their claims that immigrants are dangerous criminals, but they are just exploiting tragedy for political gain.

Trump and Carlson and their allies also like to insinuate that terrorists are pouring over the southern U.S. border in order to murder Americans. The weight of the evidence again suggests this is not true. Some of the most well-known research in this area comes from Cato Institute scholar Alex Nowrasteh. He conducted an analysis of foreign-born terrorism in the U.S. from 1975-2017. Unauthorized immigrants represented about 5% of all terrorists in his analysis. Of the over 3,000 murders and over 17,000 injuries that occurred at the hands of foreign-born terrorists over that time period, zero could be attributed to an unauthorized immigrant.[16]

People like Trump and Carlson should (and probably do) know better—we've had access to data like these for years. The question is why they continue to make these claims in the face of a significant amount of disconfirming evidence.

There is no "right" or "wrong" answer to the question of how to structure our immigration system. Nothing that I have discussed in this chapter tells us anything about what should be done about unauthorized immigration or how we should feel about it. In a constitutional republic like the U.S., public policies depend upon the preferences of voters and their elected representatives. You can recognize the facts that I have laid out here and still wish to restrict unauthorized immigration for other reasons if you choose, for crime may not be the only reason that you are concerned about it. These data simply tell us that increased violence is not a concern that is warranted by the best available evidence that we have at the moment.

While red and blue Americans may differ on what should be done regarding immigration, we should not differ in our desire for these decisions to be based on facts. We need to embrace facts and shun misinformation and disinformation in order to craft public policies that will solve real problems. If we all rely on well-sourced data, groups with different opinions can come together, find common ground, and create successful policy.

CHAPTER 24
QAnon and the Satanic Panics of Yesteryear

By Daniel Nicholas Gullotta

Drive along the highways of Missouri and you're bound to see a few Trump 2020 signs and flags. Many of them are coupled with other staples of Missouri paraphernalia, such as Confederate flags and yellow "Don't Tread on Me" Gadsden flags. Exposed to the elements, these signs and flags are often in a state of decay, their colors fading and fabric unraveling, yet still proudly on display for as many travelers as possible to see.

You might also see, as I did on a recent weekend, something a little more confusing. On the way to Stockton Lake, my wife, who was driving, asked if I had read what the Trump banner we just passed read. Distracted by my phone, I hadn't noticed it. She told me it looked like gibberish, just a bunch of hand-painted letters and numbers. On our way home, I was on the lookout for it, suspecting it had something to do with the conspiracy theory QAnon. Sure enough, the hand-painted phrase was "WWG1WGA"—the initialism for the QAnon slogan "Where We Go One, We Go All."

Much as the Unite the Right rally in Charlottesville in August 2017 resulted in a surge of books explaining the alt-right, it was inevitable that publishers would start putting out stacks of books about QAnon. Its story is so strange and sprawling that authors have a lot to work with: the shadowy way in which QAnon began and spread; the wild claims concerning Satan-worshiping pedophiles and the coming "storm" that will see these villains arrested, imprisoned, and executed; the eye-catching personalities (and costumes) of figures like Jake Angeli, the "Q Shaman"; the relationship between QAnon and the January 6 attack on the U.S. Capitol; QAnon's rapidly growing popularity within the Republican party; and the election to Congress of QAnon supporters Marjorie Taylor Greene and Lauren Boebert.

Mike Rothschild's *The Storm Is Upon Us*[1] is among the first serious books about QAnon to be published since the storming of the Capitol, with more and more following, not to mention HBO's recent documentary *Q: Into the Storm* and the popular podcast QAnon Anonymous. For those who have not closely followed news coverage concerning QAnon or who are puzzled by its bizarre claims, Rothschild's book serves as a helpful primer, covering QAnon's mysterious origins, rapid evolution, and basic tenets.

As he describes it, QAnon:

> is a complex web of mythology, conspiracy theories, personal interpretations, and assumptions featuring a vast range of characters, events, symbols, shibboleths, and jargon. It can be understood as a conspiracy theory, for sure, but it also touches on aspects of cultic movements, new religions, Internet scams, and political doctrine.

Many details concerning the beliefs of QAnon are bizarre and difficult to piece together. Ambitious works of journalism, decent explainer articles, and even a vast and messy Wikipedia page can't quite do justice to its tangled, knotted, shifting conspiracy theories. But in its most simplistic form, QAnon holds that a secret group of Satan-worshipping, cannibalistic pedophiles has been running a global child sex-trafficking ring. This supposed cabal is linked to the power brokers of the Democratic Party; Hillary and Bill Clinton are typically said to play some kind of prominent role. There is more—much, much more—but that charge is at the core of QAnon.

At the heart of this phenomenon is the mysterious "Q," whom Rothschild describes as an "unknown figure claiming to be a military intelligence officer who posts purposefully vague and cryptic messages on imageboards about an upcoming great purge of the deep state." We now know, thanks to the investigation led by HBO filmmaker Cullen Hoback, that the individual behind Q's "drops" is in all likelihood the thirtysomething provocateur Ron Watkins.[2]

In Q's first posts, dated October 28, 2017, he claimed that Hillary Clinton would be arrested two days later. This fiction, like many of those that followed, was embellished with made-up government-military-techno details of the sort you might see in a Michael Crichton or Tom Clancy novel. Though no Clinton arrest took place, Q continued to post. As Rothschild rightly obverses, "Even a sampling of Q's predictions and conspiracy theories shows that, contrary to Q's believers, this is an Internet persona who not only has no feel for events to come, but quite the opposite." The unremittingly bold predictions—claiming that Trump's enemies would commit mass suicide on February 10, 2018, or that Pope Francis would resign—were at first posted on the 4chan imageboard, where anonymous users engaged with them. Soon, though, discussions about Q's promises and predictions found their way onto Twitter, Reddit, and YouTube. QAnon rapidly grew from some obscure posts into a fledgling online conspiracy movement and then into what some might call a new religious movement or a cult.

While it is difficult to know QAnon's exact numbers, Rothschild notes that there are probably "hundreds of thousands who buy into at least some part of the complex mythology." Indeed, according to a large PRRI survey conducted in March and published last month, perhaps 15% or 20% of Americans believe some of the central QAnon claims.[3]

But why—what's the appeal?

While QAnon undoubtedly attracts trolls, grifters, and the mentally ill, Rothschild notes that "there is a strain of critical thinking and writing that sees Q believers. . . as searchers yearning for answers and authenticity." QAnon offers the hope of order in an apparently orderless world; it offers a confusing though coherent explanation for the world's wrongs; perhaps most importantly, it promises retribution when justice seems lacking. A sense of belonging is another draw, as adherents develop their own cultural touchstones, insider lingo, in-jokes, and communal practices. All of this reinforces their shared sense of purpose and their group identity.

As circles of trust develop, deep and intimate friendships form inside the conspiratorial community, even romance. Rothschild shares tales of hospitality among QAnon followers trying to find places to rest while heading to a Trump rally and expressions of solidarity during tough emotional times. While it was played for laughs, some of this kindness was on display in *Borat Subsequent Moviefilm*, when Sacha Baron Cohen's Borat was welcomed to stay with a group of QAnon believers, informing them he had no place to quarantine during the start of the COVID-19 pandemic. Yet for every one of these stories of friendship and camaraderie, Rothschild shares tales of families between torn apart, loved ones becoming increasingly isolated from their old friends. Rothschild manages to convey some of the allure of QAnon, but does not stint in expressing the cost—the wasted hours, dollars, and lives.

Of course, the belief that the country is in a state of moral decline, full of corrupt elites and ungodly politicians, is nothing new in American politics. But it is worth remembering that even the more wild and unhinged accusations of Satan-worshipping have a long history in this country—and by studying the precedents, we might be able to better understand the dynamics and future of QAnon.

When, at an NBC town hall event last October,[4] former President Trump was asked if he would disavow QAnon, he professed ignorance and a touch of apparent admiration:

> I know nothing about it. I do know they are very much against pedophilia. They fight it very hard. . . I just don't know about QAnon. . .
> What I do hear about it, is they are very strongly against pedophilia.
> And I agree with that. I mean, I do agree with that.[5]

Even though Trump occasionally retweeted QAnon messages,[6] and even though he was a central figure in the QAnon mythos (and was even believed by some true believers to be "Q" himself), it seems plausible that he really was unaware of much about it beyond its opposition to pedophilia. Someone with superficial knowledge of QAnon, mostly encountering its anti-child-abuse social media hashtag (#SaveOurChildren), might come away thinking that its activism against pedophilia was reasonable and commendable. It is not surprising, then, that some curious Christians, concerned about child welfare, might initially find themselves drawn to it for that reason.

QAnon is on the political fringes but its beliefs about mysterious Satan worshipers fall into a well-established pattern of Christian theology concerning conspiracies dating back to the medieval church and the witch hunts of the early modern era. The fear that children are being morally corrupted, sexually abused, and physically harmed is one of the most recognizable Satanic conspiracy tropes. In the witch trials of early modern Europe, accusations of killing infants and harming young children were common. For centuries, Jews throughout the Holy Roman Empire and Reformation Europe were accused of ritually murdering Christian children for magical purposes and cannibalism.[7] Under stress and torture, both men and women—but mostly women—confessed to such Satanic crimes as using babies' blood for spells, murdering children at witches' sabbaths, and having sex with the devil (Ironically, similar tropes had been deployed against the early church by its Greco-Roman critics: Ancient Christians were accused of cannibalism and sexual perversion).[8]

America's most infamous witch hunt had its origin in the fear of Satanic harm befalling children. Beginning in 1692, Salem minister Samuel Parris and his wife Elizabeth were alarmed at their daughter Betty and niece Abigail's declining health. The Reverend John Hale suspected a Satanic attack: "These Children were bitten and pinched by invisible agents."[9] Believing them bewitched, fears of a Satanic conspiracy against the colony took hold—ultimately costing twenty lives.

Often, Satanic panics occur in the context of apocalyptic environments. Storms, famine, and war were common precursors for witch hunts in the medieval world. The Salem witch trials were preceded by the devastation of King Philip's War and the political unrest of the Glorious Revolution.[10] Before the Satanic panic of the 1980s in the United States, there had been more than a decade of political upheaval, economic recession, and energy disruption, not to mention the sexual revolution and a quickly changing youth culture.

More proximate factors connected to the 1980s panic included the rise of heavy metal bands, some of which adopted morbid imagery; the success of Dungeons & Dragons; and the growing pop-culture fascination with the demonic and the occult, as in the films *Rosemary's Baby, The Devil Rides Out, The Wicker Man,* and *The Exorcist.* Further contributing to the cultural milieu were the gruesome and bizarre violent crimes that had captured national attention in the preceding years—the Manson murders, the Zodiac Killer, the Night Stalker. There was worry about copycat killings. The AIDS scare, the growing awareness of such spiritual alternatives as New Age and Wicca, and concerns about child safety ("stranger danger") added to the sense of dread.

It was in this context that memoirs began to be published concerning supposed Satanic cults and survivors of demonic possession, the most famous being *Michelle Remembers* (1980).[11] Crimes with supposed connections to Satanic activity began to emerge, with the only evidence derived from the (subsequently discredited) practice of "recovered memory." There arose a shocking, and frankly implausible, volume of accusations of child abuse by devil-worshipping cults at day cares, like those in Kern County, California.[12] Soon an industry of so-called Satanic cult experts emerged, ready to offer their "expertise" to law enforcement and in courtrooms, as well as offering seminars and classes for the masses. For example, Dale W. Griffis offered his testimony as an expert on Satanic cults in the notorious trial of the West Memphis Three, despite having received his degree from an unaccredited university (a point the defense made).[13]

An exhaustive Department of Justice report[14] concluded in 1992 that "there is little or no evidence" for allegations of "large-scale baby breeding, human sacrifice, and organized satanic conspiracies." Given the lack of evidence and the backlash from friends and families of some of the people being accused, the Satanic panic eventually began to subside. But it left behind enormous damage—including families splintered by false accusations and innocent lives wasted in prison after false accusations of Satanic ritual pedophilia.

The past several years have again been a time of unsettledness—of war, recession, the tumultuous Trump presidency, constant talk of planetary ecological ruination, and now a global pandemic—so no one should be surprised that fears of Satanic activity have once again sprouted up. To put it another way, it might not take much nowadays to convince a person that we are living in the end times.

One of the reasons why doomsday thinking is important to the promulgation of Satanic panics is how it complements a feeling of intensified persecution. On issues ranging from abortion to marriage to drugs to how history is taught, many conservative Christians feel like cultural walls are closing in on them—a feeling of persecution encouraged by talk radio, cable news, and online personalities. Liberals may disregard these concerns as overblown and progressives may consider them illegitimate, but many conservative political and religious figures find themselves hopeless or even panicked.

As I mentioned, while QAnon undoubtedly attracts trolls, grifters, and the mentally ill, it also offers the hope of order in an apparently orderless world; it offers a confusing though coherent explanation for the world's wrongs; and it promises retribution when justice seems lacking. A sense of belonging is another draw. All of this reinforces members' shared sense of purpose and their group identity.

Rothschild warns against casting judgment. Relying on the work of Rob Brotherton,[15] Rothschild explains how conspiracy theorizing is not a psychological aberration but rather the biases of the human brain at work. When bad things happen to us, we prefer to blame our travails not on mere chance nor our own shortcomings but rather on other people; it's not unnatural to suspect that people are plotting against us, that there is some scheme that deserves blame. Writes Rothschild:

> A person doesn't get cancer because of some randomly misfiring cells—they got it because of chemtrails or 5G Internet or microchips poisoning them. Our beloved candidate didn't lose an election because they ran a poor campaign—they lost because of the conspiracy of a corrupt cabal to keep them from power.

According to Brotherton, this cognitive tendency toward conspiracy-mindedness has its roots in our species' evolutionary past, as a healthy amount of paranoia would have helped keep us alive when we heard rustling in the foliage or bumps in the night. As disturbing as it might seem, a certain amount of conspiracy theorizing is just normal human instinct.

Conspiracy theorists who think the moon landings were faked, ancient aliens were real, or the JFK assassination was covered up tend to be benign, Rothschild explains, because they are focused on the past, fixing what they believe to be errors in the historical record. Because of this, they have little interest in changing the future or even serious proselytizing. For many of them, knowing "the truth" gives them enough smug satisfaction.

But if the rest of the world is sliding into damnation, QAnon's supposed fight against Satan's followers can be seen as pure, faithful, and defiant. QAnoners see themselves as heroes, the faithful remnant as spoken of in Revelation.

As historian John Fea has argued,[16] the fear that America's Christian identity is eroding can partly explain the appeal of Trump as a "fighter" trying to win back the country for conservative Christians. This perception of a Christian nation in religious freefall fits almost seamlessly with QAnon's conviction that the United States is under spiritual assault. What makes QAnon so different (and so dangerous) is its belief in an ongoing war of good and evil in which the stakes are as high as they are real—an ever-unfolding drama concerning the "deep state," Q's apocalyptic hopes for the future, and the role adherents can play in bringing about the coming "storm." Even when compared to more violent groups like Aum Shinrikyo and al Qaeda, QAnon is distinctive in how quickly the movement has turned violent.

Due to QAnon's broadness and changing dynamics—it is "fairly easy to understand" yet "slippery to pin down"—Rothschild remains unsure what to label it. He is open to thinking of QAnon as a new religious movement. And he notes that sociologists and scholars of religion are wary of the term "cult" due to its historical baggage: There have been many instances of people pejoratively labeling as a cult any religious tradition they don't like, as when evangelical and atheist critics called Mormonism a cult. In this nonjudgmental view now standard in the academy, one man's cult is another man's religion. Even so, the word "cult" has remained an easy shorthand for much of the coverage of QAnon and undoubtedly such a provocative term (used in the book's subtitle) will help drive more clicks and sell more books.

Though Rothschild touches upon QAnon's religious elements, he doesn't do a deep dive into its theological convictions. Because of QAnon's growing appeal among White evangelicals,[17] I think it is best understood as a kind of para-Christianity—that is, something that "goes with" or "side by side" an evangelical Christian worldview. For many believers, QAnon is not a significant *alternative* to their orthodoxy or orthopraxy, but a complicating add-on. If one already believes that the world is besieged by demonic forces, then fine-tuning that conviction into ideas concerning a secret cabal of cannibalistic Satan-worshiping pedophiles is not a great leap of faith, as we have already seen during previous Satanic panics. QAnon might even be thought of as a kind of Trumpian gnosticism,[18] with seemingly "ordinary" Christians indulging in unconventional extracurricular activities beyond the supervision of their clergy. One can keep going to weekly Bible study and maintaining regular Sunday attendance while logging on each night to await the latest drops from Q and praying for the coming storm.

In short, it is my sense that QAnon isn't a cult or a new kind of religion, but rather part of a well-established Christian tradition of seeking secret knowledge and yearning for apocalyptic combat.

So, if QAnon is less an anomaly than it is the next chapter in America's horrified fascination with the devil, fitting within the Christian framework of apocalypticism, persecution, and demonology, what might we expect to come of it in the months and years ahead?

First, future incidents of violence should not surprise us. The "Pizzagate" conspiracy theory that was a precursor to QAnon nearly led to bloodshed, and among the January 6 rioters at the Capitol were QAnon true believers. When the stakes are believed to be so high—with children's welfare and lives, not to mention the spiritual and temporal fate of the world, supposedly on the line—a resort to violence may seem not desperate but reasonable.

Second, the most novel aspect of this Satanic panic—the wide reach and rapid evolution of the conspiracy theories, made possible by social media's ability to rapidly spread misinformation—will continue to be a factor. There are all sorts of ways that these conspiracy theories can start to reach new mainstream audiences, as certain Facebook, Instagram, and Twitter accounts create bridges between the most rabid participants and the uninitiated. One area to stay focused on is parental influencers,[19] especially given the power of simplistic ideas that can be distilled in catchy hashtags like #SaveOurChildren.

Third, we have reason to hope that QAnon will eventually spend itself out. If the Satanic panics of the past can teach us anything, it is that many of these individuals—including many whose beliefs are bizarre or seem like they must be ironic—are sincere in their convictions and mean well. They want wrongs to be righted and they want justice to be done. But eventually, they will move on. We don't know when that will be; it's entirely possible that the climax of QAnon already came on January 6, or perhaps the movement will linger on for years in ever-shifting forms. But Satanic panics tend eventually to peter out, and to be looked back upon with some mix of shame and horror.

The trouble is they tend to be forgotten, until Satan supposedly strikes again.

CHAPTER 25
How Industry Undermines Public Health[1]

By Rob Moodie

There are numerous examples of governments trying to introduce policies that improve health and/or to protect the environment, only to find their efforts undermined by unhealthy corporations and their industry associations. If you are working to improve public health and the environment, you need to know what your opponents are up to.

Below is a quick guide to their tactics, which I have assembled as a summary from three sources: Naomi Oreskes and Eric M. Conway, *Merchants of Doubt*,[2] William Wiist's "The Corporate Playbook, Health, and Democracy,"[3] and Nicholas Freudenberg's *Lethal But Legal*.[4]

1. **Attack Legitimate Science**
    *   Accuse science of deception, calling it "junk science" or "bad science," claiming science is manipulated to fulfill a political agenda.
    *   Attack the scientific institutions and government agencies perceived to be acting against corporate interests.
    *   Insist that the science is uncertain by claiming scientists don't know what's causing it, and that more research is needed.
    *   Withholding any data unfavorable to the corporate product.
    *   Using information in a misleading way; cherry-picking by using facts that are true but irrelevant.
    *   Insist that there are many causes to a health or environmental problem, and that addressing just one of them will have minimal impact.
    *   Exaggerate the uncertainty inherent in any scientific endeavor to under-

mine the status of established scientific knowledge.
- Use corporate-funded studies.
- Fund researchers sympathetic to corporate causes or products.

2. **Attack and Intimidate Scientists**
- Create doubt by attacking the authenticity and integrity of the author.
- Attack the credibility of the messenger and allege ulterior motives.
- Have "attack dogs" intimidate opponents.
- Smear the enemy—for example, by calling environmentalists "watermelons" (green on the outside and red on the inside), use hatred and fear of communism to transfer animosity to the environmental movement.
- Threaten to sue—or actually sue—scientists and advocates but avoid or delay hearings of the facts.
- Make accusations using the rhetoric of political suppression.
- Infiltrate scientific groups and monitor prominent scientists.
- Create enough doubt to forestall litigation and regulation.
- Constantly repeat the doubt, using surrogates or "message force multipliers."
- Use pejorative terms repeatedly such as "excessive" regulation, "over" regulation, "unnecessary" regulation, "nanny state," and "health Nazis" to promote fear and disdain.
- Always demand more proof.
- Alternatively, aim for self-regulation instead of regulation; introduce corporate voluntary codes to forestall government regulation.

3. **Create Arm's Length Front Organizations**
- Create front groups.
- Run projects through front groups ("information laundering")—especially law firms, because they can avoid scrutiny due to attorney-client privilege.
- Create research institutes that can create their own scientific studies.
- Sponsor conferences and workshops.
- Create "independent" newsletters, magazines, and journals (not subject to peer review).
- Publish findings selectively.
- Manipulate research funding, design, and authorship.
- Distribute materials—targeted pamphlets and booklets, social media.
- Use public opinion polling.

4. **Manufacture False Debate and Insist on Balance**
- Create the impression of a controversy.
- Maintain the controversy, keep the debate alive.

- Create false dichotomies.
- Insist that responsible journalists cover both sides of the argument equally.
- Demand balance, relying on the Fairness Doctrine.
- Divert attention from harmful products.
- Focus on corporate social responsibility.
- Set up corporate social responsibility foundations; find small-scale, apparently well-meaning community activities.
- Focus on other issues as the problem, like physical activity instead of diet, for example.

5. **Frame Issues in Highly Creative Ways**
- Insist that the problem is very complex, thus implying it can't have a simple solution, if any.
- Insist it is premature to suggest remedies.
- Constantly repeat that technological advances will obviate the need for regulations and that the problem can be solved only through the marketplace.
- Insist on personal or parental responsibility and insist that government should have no role in influencing individual health behavior.
- Use colorful imagery (such as "a billion-dollar solution to a million-dollar problem"); use words like "speculative," "oversimplified," "premature," and "unbalanced."
- Use the creation of fear as a tool for change of policy.
- Diminish the severity of the problem while giving some ground.
- Admit that it is a serious problem, but not a life-threatening one.
- Admit that there may be a problem, but it is less severe than everyone says.
- Argue that the problem is less severe than other problems—those should be the priority.
- Argue that the cost to fix the problem is too high.
- Argue that the benefits of the problem haven't been considered.
- Argue that other options haven't been considered.
- Understand and use the power of language—the other side's language is filled with uncertainties, so make sure yours is certain.

6. **Fund Industry Disinformation Campaigns**
- Run industry disinformation campaigns using new and creative forms.
- Pay and co-opt celebrities and sympathetic expert witnesses.
- Sponsor conferences to challenge scientific consensus.
- Align with other issues—employment discrimination, antitax groups.

7. **Influence the Political Agenda**

- Donate to political parties across the political spectrum.
- Get representatives from unhealthy industries around the policy table, for guideline development or standard setting.
- Invest heavily in paid lobbyists.
- Get "friends" in important and influential government roles—for example, by targeted hiring of politicians, their advisers, or senior administration officials once they leave office.
- Aim to reduce government budgets for regulatory, scientific, or policy activities against corporate interests.

CHAPTER 26
I Was an Exxon-funded Climate Scientist[1]

By Katharine Hayhoe

ExxonMobil's deliberate attempts to sow doubt on the reality and urgency of climate change[2] and their donations to front groups to disseminate false information about climate change[3] have been public knowledge for a long time now.

Investigative reports in 2015 revealed that Exxon had its own scientists doing its own climate modeling as far back as the 1970s: science and modeling that was not only accurate, but that was being used to plan for the company's future.[4]

Now a peer-reviewed study has confirmed that what Exxon was saying internally about climate change was quantitatively very different from their public statements.[5] Specifically, researchers Geoffrey Supran and Naomi Oreskes found that at least 80% of the internal documents and peer-reviewed publications they studied from between 1977 and 2014 were consistent with the state of the science—acknowledging that climate change is real and caused by humans, and identifying "reasonable uncertainties" that any climate scientist would agree with at the time. Yet over 80% of Exxon's editorial-style paid advertisements over the same period specifically focused on uncertainty and doubt, the study found.

The stark contrast between internally discussing cutting-edge climate research while externally conducting a climate disinformation campaign is enough to blow many minds. What was going on at Exxon?

I have a unique perspective—because I was there.

From 1995 to 1997, Exxon provided partial financial support for my master's thesis, which focused on methane chemistry and emissions. I spent several weeks in 1996 as an intern at their Annandale research lab in New Jersey and years working on the collaborative research that resulted in three of the published studies referenced in Supran and Oreskes' new analysis.

Climate Research at Exxon

A scientist is a scientist no matter where we work, and my Exxon colleagues were no exception. Thoughtful, cautious, and in full agreement with the scientific consensus on climate—these are characteristics any scientist would be proud to own.

Did Exxon have an agenda for our research? Of course—it's not a charity. Their research and development was targeted, and in my case, it was targeted at something that would raise no red flags in climate policy circles: quantifying the benefits of methane reduction.

Methane is a waste product released by coal mining and natural gas leaks; wastewater treatment plants; farting and belching cows, sheep, goats, and anything else that chews its cud; decaying organic trash in garbage dumps; giant termite mounds in Africa; and even, in vanishingly small amounts, our own lactose-intolerant family members.

On a mass basis, methane absorbs about 35 times more of the Earth's heat than carbon dioxide. Methane has a much shorter lifetime than carbon dioxide gas, and we produce a lot less of it, so there's no escaping the fact that carbon has to go. But if our concern is how fast the Earth is warming, we can get a big bang for our buck by cutting methane emissions as soon as possible, while continuing to wean ourselves off carbon-based fuels long-term.

For the gas and oil industry, reducing methane emissions means saving energy. So it's no surprise that, during my research, I didn't experience any heavy-handed guidance or interference with my results. No one asked to review my code or suggested ways to "adjust" my findings. The only requirement was that a journal article with an Exxon co-author pass an internal review before it could be submitted for peer review, a policy similar to that of many federal agencies.

Did I know what else they were up to at the time? I couldn't even imagine it.

Fresh out of Canada, I was unaware that there were people who didn't accept climate science—so unaware, in fact, that it was nearly half a year before I realized I'd married one—let alone that Exxon was funding a disinformation campaign at the very same time it was supporting my research on the most expedient ways to reduce the impact of humans on climate.

Yet Exxon's choices have contributed directly to the situation we are in today, a situation that in many ways seems unreal: one where many elected representatives oppose climate action, while China leads the U.S. in wind energy, solar power, economic investment in clean energy, and even the existence of a national cap and trade policy similar to the ill-fated Waxman-Markey bill of 2009.

Personal Decisions

This latest study underscores why many are calling on Exxon to be held responsible for knowingly misleading the public on such a critical issue. For scientists and academics, though, it may fuel another, different, yet similarly moral debate.

Are we willing to accept financial support that is offered as a sop to the public conscience?

The concept of tendering literal payment for sin is nothing new. From the indulgences of the Middle Ages to the criticisms some have leveled at carbon offsets today, we humans have always sought to stave off the consequences of our actions and ease our conscience with good deeds, particularly of the financial kind. Today, many industry groups follow this familiar path: supporting science denial with the left hand, while giving to cutting-edge research and science with the right.

The Global Climate and Energy Project at Stanford University[6] conducts fundamental research on efficient and clean energy technologies—with Exxon as a founding sponsor. Philanthropist and political donor David Koch gave an unprecedented $35 million to the Smithsonian National Museum of Natural History in 2015, after which three dozen scientists called on the museum to cut ties with him for funding lobbying groups that "misrepresent" climate science.[7] Shell underwrote the London Science Museum's "Atmosphere" program and then used its leverage to muddy the waters on what scientists know about climate.[8]

It may be easy to point a finger at others, but when it happens to us, the choice might not seem so clear. Which is most important—the benefit of the research and education, or the rejection of tainted funds?

The appropriate response to morally tainted offerings is an ancient question. In the book of Corinthians, the apostle Paul responds to a query on what to do with food that has been sacrificed to idols—eat or reject?

His response illustrates the complexity of this issue. Food is food, he says—and by the same token, we might say money is money today. Both food and money, though, can imply alliance or acceptance. And if it affects others, a more discerning response may be needed.

What are we as academics to do? In this open and transparent new publishing world of ours, declaration of financial supporters is both important and necessary. Some would argue that a funder, however loose and distant the ties, casts a shadow over the resulting research. Others would respond that the funds can be used for good. Which carries the greatest weight?

After two decades in the trenches of climate science, I'm no longer the ingenue I was. I'm all too aware, now, of those who dismiss climate science as a "liberal hoax." Every day, they attack me on Facebook, vilify me on Twitter, and even send the occasional hand-typed letter—which begs appreciation of the artistry, if not the contents. So now, if Exxon came calling, what would I do?

There's no one right answer to this question. Speaking for myself, I might ask them to give those funds to politicians who endorse sensible climate policy—and cut their funding to those who don't. Or I admire one colleague's practical response: to use a Koch-funded honorarium to purchase a lifetime membership in the Sierra Club.

Despite the fact that there's no easy answer, it's a question that's being posed to more and more of us every day, and we cannot straddle the fence any longer. As academics and scientists, we have some tough choices to make; and only by recognizing the broader implications of these choices are we able to make these decisions with our eyes wide open, rather than half shut.

CHAPTER 27
The Alt-Right and Moral Righteousness[1]

By Kevin McCaffree

> The surest way to work up a crusade in favor of some good cause is to promise people they will have a chance of maltreating someone. To be able to destroy with good conscience, to be able to behave badly and call your bad behavior 'righteous indignation'—this is the height of psychological luxury, the most delicious of moral treats.
> —Aldous Huxley[2]

The Alt-Left and the Alt-Right are secular religious ideologies. For both, if only the right group is subjugated and the government purged of their influence, history will take a new turn toward righteousness. The similarities between the two ideologies are troubling. The Alt-Left and Alt-Right are two panicked grasps for power, sharing a seething distrust of people, government, and society. I will endeavor to explain these dynamics as I see them.

The Ideology of the Alt-Right

The roots of Alt-Right ideology begin with those various 19th century writers attempting to apply the logic of Darwin's work to the project of genetically re-engineering human society. Today, this legacy is manifested in an insistence on the importance of genetic/biological differences between men and women and between members of different racial groups. Alt-Righters also assert that there has been biological Darwinian selection for types of societies, with the pinnacle of culture resting in the European Enlightenment. The Alt-Right thus sees biologically based hierarchies (of race, of gender, of societies) where the Alt-Left sees socially constructed oppression. The bedrock axiom of the Alt-Right is that equality and democracy are false idols.

For example, in the Alt-Right mindset, racial differences in wealth exist entirely due to differences in biology. Here, they point to research on race and IQ[3] as proof that this is about honest biological truth and not pseudo-intellectual White supremacy. Alt-Right ideology will tend to concede that the research shows Ashkenazi Jews and East Asians to have higher IQs than European Caucasians. They note however that Black and Hispanic people score even lower. The important implication of all of this for the Alt-Right is that such genetic differences in cognitive ability make it difficult for people of different racial groups to share expectations, goals, and values. Different genes mean we are unlikely to benefit from living near each other.

As for their critique of democracy, Alt-Righters parrot Churchill who famously said, "The best argument against democracy is a five-minute conversation with the average voter." They cite interesting work by Bryan Caplan[4] to argue, again with a nice-sized kernel of truth, that the average American (of any race or sex) just isn't incentivized to spend the long hours it takes to become educated enough to cast an informed vote. Given that one vote cannot sway an election, and given that there are no immediate penalties for ignorance, the democratic process itself incentivizes individuals to become preposterously uneducated, overzealous political warriors. Over time, people reasoning in this way have eroded the infrastructure of American democracy and mutiny hovers on the horizon.

The Alt-Left and Alt-Right have a nearly identical view of the sinister nature of popular culture. Where Adorno saw a "culture industry" pacifying the masses, the Alt-Right sees a "Cathedral" of Alt-Left professors, entertainers, and politicians working in tandem to promote the false ideals of equality and democracy. The Alt-Right also shares with the Alt-Left a grim view of life in America. For the Alt-Left, America is institutionally racist, sexist, homophobic, violent, and exploitive. For the Alt-Right America is experiencing rising suicide rates among Whites, men, and boys struggling in education, plummeting rates of civic participation (and uninformed voters), declining birth rates, rising rates of single motherhood, and pernicious immigration. Again, it is not the falsity here that we ought to take most issue with, it is the extremeness of the characterization and the cynicism about our collective ability to care.

I also suspect the Alt-Right (again in parity with the Alt-Left) has an ardent anti-religious streak. Alt-Right Millennials and GenZ inherited a Republican party which, mired in Evangelical Christianity, seemed to have lost the culture wars of the past half century over prayer in school, access to birth control and abortion, women in the workplace, and others. In response to this catastrophic failure of Republicans to influence mainstream culture, the Alt-Right often avoids or even critiques traditional religion. Yet, the Alt-Right shares Evangelical Christianity's yearning for strong male leadership and the values of hierarchy and loyalty ("America First," "Family First"). Compared to the Alt-Left's contradictory view of religion (Western religions are a tool of oppression, non-Western religions contain beautiful sacred communities), the Alt-Right is more proximately embarrassed by mainstream Republican party politics and their overlong commitment to fundamentalist religion.

The Alt-Right sees salvation in business. If one needed any further demonstration of this conviction, look no further than the election of Donald Trump, who is in many ways the opposite of his Republican voters—from money, only ever lived on the coasts, and only casually religious, at best. Yet, he spoke to them on another level—a level that the Alt-Right thrives on, which recognizes financial power as the ultimate determinant of authority. Business acumen takes brains, and countries are expensive things to run, true. But their distorted conclusion is that, therefore, our flawed democracy should be jettisoned in favor of plutocratic rule by businessmen and financiers. On this matter, the Alt-Left and Alt-Right are oil and water—the Alt-Left's core Marxism is diametrically opposed to the Alt-Right's regard for elite business interests.

* * * * *

In a later chapter in this book, I explain what I perceive to be the causes of both the Alt-Left and the Alt-Right. The answer, in brief, is that secularization, increasing income and wealth inequality, along with declining trust and civic engagement, are giving rise to charismatic authorities with dark utopian dreams on both the Left and the Right.

III. PROBLEMS IN LEFT-WING SILOS

CHAPTER 28
Virtuous Lies[1]

By Jacob L. Mackey

"Live not by lies."
—Aleksandr Solzhenitsyn

A "virtuous lie" is a false, misleading, or highly contestable claim that is promulgated without qualification as flatly true in order to serve a purportedly emancipatory end, despite the fact that evidence of its falsehood, deceptiveness, or contestability is readily available.

We live by these lies. They underlie a great many communications at elite institutions like my college. For example, a recent announcement for a talk read: "In this lecture, [the guest] asks, what can we do about unkindness? How can [we] grapple with this messy, borderless concept, which has influenced so much of our post-1492 era?" The announcement does not so much assert as simply *presuppose*, and ask readers to accept, that "unkindness" is a distinctive characteristic of the post-Columbian world. Readers are invited to draw the inference that "unkindness" had less "influence" in the world before Europeans arrived in the Americas. Like much of the messaging on elite campuses, this one implies that the West in general and perhaps the U.S. in particular are uniquely culpable in history's evils.

Another example. I attended a talk by a prominent author, a journalist, at a super-elite private high school. He took pains to paint North American slavery in the most gruesome of colors, as well one might for the edification of young people, who are inevitably ignorant of its true toll. However, in so doing, he told two virtuous lies: first, that slave-farmed cotton drove the expansion of the antebellum U.S. economy and, second, that increases in cotton productivity resulted from increases in the torture of enslaved people.

These two claims, both of which come straight out of the New History of

Capitalism and, via Matthew Desmond's contribution, are central to the 1619 Project, have been debunked.[2] And yet these lies are virtuous. North American slavery *is* a moral abyss. One can never overstate its horror or overdo one's condemnation of it. . . even if one lies. The lies of the New History of Capitalism are virtuous, serving noble goals like reparations, as the speaker took care to make explicit in his talk.

A third example. On May 21, 2020, as if to foreshadow the murder of George Floyd that was to come four days later, Kimberlé Crenshaw, a professor of law at both UCLA and Columbia and coiner of the concept of intersectionality, wrote in *The New Republic* that anti-Black police and vigilante violence represented "modern embodiments of racial terror dating back to. . . the reign of White impunity rooted in slavery and Jim Crow" and opined that such violence was part of a pattern that amounts to "a kind of genocide."[3] In a similar vein, star attorney Ben Crump titled his 2019 book *Open Season: Legalized Genocide of Colored People.* Chapter two is titled "Police Don't Shoot White Men in the Back." Note that this was the tone of the discourse *before* George Floyd.

What we see in this catastrophizing rhetoric about genocide is the product of the virtuous lie that Black people, and Black men in particular, are being murdered by racist police with wild abandon. As Derecka Purnell put it in *The Guardian*: "We know how we die—the police."[4] This perception is the result of a virtuous lie. The lie promotes a distorted view of reality. It is a well-meaning distortion but a distortion nonetheless, designed to bring attention to the cause, worthy in itself, of police brutality against Black people.

The reality, of course, easily accessible by all, is that while there are indeed disturbing anti-Black disparities in the police use of nonlethal force,[5] there do *not* appear to be racial differences in the way police deploy lethal force. In other words, police are, overall, no more disposed to kill a Black person than a White person. This basic finding has been discovered and rediscovered again,[6] and again,[7] and again,[8] and again,[9] and again,[10] and again,[11] and again.[12] And yet so taboo is this finding and so sacred is the lie that people have been fired for noting the former in order to correct the latter. Such was the fate of Zac Kriegman, a director of data science at the news and information company Thomson Reuters. When he pointed out that BLM was promoting a virtuous lie,[13] he was fired.[14]

Indeed, Kriegman was not the only casualty of the virtuous lie that lethal police violence specifically targets Black people. In 2019, a paper was published in *Proceedings of the National Academy of Sciences* (*PNAS*) that found "no evidence of anti-Black or anti-Hispanic disparities across shootings."[15] However, due to an unusual set of circumstances, including a Congressional hearing about policing, the article quickly became a flashpoint. First, it was officially "corrected," though its findings were not altered. A few weeks later, George Floyd was murdered. Soon after, as the article began to be cited and contested in the ensuing debate about policing, *PNAS* asked two independent researchers to look into the article's data and methods. They found that the article "does not contain fabricated data or serious statistical errors warranting a retraction." Nevertheless, the article's authors themselves retracted it, citing "continued use of our work in the public debate" about policing as their reason. *PNAS* chimed in, too, saying that "partisan political use" of the article warranted retraction.[16] The virtuous lie and the political program it serves must be protected at all cost.

Virtuous lies are not confined to high schools, colleges, major media companies, and scholarly journals. Our government and medical establishment increasingly run on virtuous lies as well.

For example, in 2019, California passed a bill, AB 241, that requires "implicit bias" training as part of routine continuing education for physicians, nurses, and physician assistants.[17] The bill asserts the following:

> Implicit bias, meaning the attitudes or internalized stereotypes that affect our perceptions, actions, and decisions in an unconscious manner, exists, and often contributes to unequal treatment of people based on race, ethnicity, gender identity, sexual orientation, age, disability, and other characteristics.

And in case you missed the causal chain running from implicit bias through behavior to health outcomes:

> Implicit bias contributes to health disparities by affecting the behavior of physicians and surgeons, nurses, physician assistants, and other healing arts licensees.

AB 241 is wholly based on a string of interconnected virtuous lies about implicit bias. The first virtuous lie is that researchers have settled on a coherent and consistent understanding of what the term "implicit bias" means.[18] The second lie is that whatever implicit bias may be, we know that it influences behavior.[19] The third falsehood is that we know that disparities in health outcomes are caused by the behavior of implicitly biased medical personnel.

The truth about implicit bias is easy to state: "[I]t is not clear precisely *what* is being measured on implicit attitude tests; implicit attitudes do not effectively predict actual discriminatory behavior."[20]

Moreover, with respect to disparate racial outcomes, it is important to note that measures that attempt to use implicit bias "to predict behavior find little or no anti-Black discrimination specifically."[21] This is good news! It means that racial health disparities are likely not wholly or even significantly attributable to the implicit bias of medical personnel.

What discrimination there is in medicine—and there surely is discrimination—is based on entirely *explicit* attitudes supported by pseudoscientific theories. For example, it used to be a common practice for the laboratories that physicians use to adjust the renal values of Black patients to take into account Black people's supposedly greater muscle mass relative to White people.[22] Such adjustments might, however, have caused doctors to overlook kidney failure in Black patients. Again, some White physicians are said to believe that Black patients are less susceptible to pain than White patients because they have longer nerve endings and thicker skin.[23] These are not "implicit biases." These are wholly conscious false beliefs that can be dispelled by acquaintance with the truth.

Nevertheless, California's medical personnel now must pay the opportunity cost of submitting to training for *implicit* biases that we know to be useless. In a sense, the mandating of implicit bias training is a fourth virtuous lie, for the fact is, "most interventions to attempt to change implicit attitudes are ineffective."[24] What we have, then, is an entire government-mandated regime of healthcare education built atop the foundational virtuous lie of implicit bias.[25] Articles appear regularly to bolster the lie in journals that could once be trusted. If everything you knew about implicit bias in medicine came from the latest article about it in *Science*,[26] for example, you'd know very little indeed.[27]

We live by lies like implicit bias because doing so makes us good people. To question them is to align oneself with all that is oppressive. Our moral credentials are burnished if we condemn European contact with the Americas as the moment at which "unkindness" became a force in human affairs. We signal our ethical seriousness with respect to American slavery and continuing Black socioeconomic inequality if we applaud rather than quibble when debunked theories are presented as plain facts to high school students. We stand ostentatiously on "the right side of history" if we endorse BLM's narrative that Black people are "intentionally targeted for demise" by police.[28] Similarly, medical personnel in California now attest their racial innocence by submitting, ironically enough, to the proposition that their implicit bias is causing them to mistreat racial minorities and to a highly profitable training industry that purports to remedy it.

As in the case of the narrative about police killings, to question any of the claims built upon the virtuous lie of implicit bias is to court personal and professional disaster. Edward Livingston, then a deputy editor at the *Journal of the American Medical Association* (*JAMA*), discovered this in early 2021 when he went on a *JAMA* podcast and made the mistake of suggesting that accusing doctors of racism was perhaps not the best way to resolve inequities in health outcomes and that the solution might instead lie in addressing socioeconomic disparities.[29] [30] This marked him for destruction. A petition against *JAMA* garnered 9,000 signatures, the podcast episode was scrubbed from the web, an investigation was announced, he was asked to resign his editorship, which he did,[31] and he was made the subject of a "restorative justice session" at UCLA medical school,[32] where he teaches. However, the spread of the miasma was not stopped by these expiations. *JAMA's* editor-in-chief Howard Bauchner, who had had nothing to do with the ill-fated podcast episode, fell over himself apologizing for the incident but was investigated by an AMA committee and soon had to resign his editorship.[33]

The fates of Kriegman, Livingston, and Bauchner, as well as my own reticence to push back on the high school speaker, reveal a central feature of the logic of the virtuous lie: To correct these lies is tantamount to opposing noble goals. Nobody wants to be the one who points out that a virtuous lie is not true. In the case of the high school speaker, any pushback would have come across as a defense of American slavery. In the case of "our post-1492 era," to ask for evidence would be to minimize the enormity of the post-Columbian devastation of Native Americans and of the Trans-Atlantic slave trade, just for starters. In the case of a state-sanctioned genocide of Black people, to gesture toward research to the contrary would be to affirm the status quo and to oppose much-needed reforms.

The Epistemology of the Virtuous Lie

Let us distinguish the virtuous lie from two adjacent phenomena—Plato's noble lie and Rob Henderson's luxury belief—and then consider the choice of the term "lie."

The Noble Lie

Plato introduces the noble lie in Book 3 of his *Republic*. Socrates, Plato's spokesman in the dialogue, urges that in order to found his proposed ideal city, they would need to craft "one noble lie which may deceive" the city's three social classes, that is, the ruler class, the soldier class, and the producer class:

> "Citizens,' we shall say to them in our tale, 'you are brothers, yet god has framed you differently. Some of you have the power of command, and in the composition of these he has mingled gold, wherefore also they have the greatest honour; others he has made of silver, to be auxiliaries; others again who are to be husbandmen and craftsmen he has composed of brass and iron.' (Jowett trans.)

The point of Plato's noble lie is to reconcile people to inequality and their place in the social hierarchy. The mechanism of reconciliation is a naturalization of the hierarchy not by analogy or comparison to metals but through the assertion that people of differing stations are quite literally made of different metals. The rulers are golden, the soldiers silver, and the workers brass and iron. (This is Plato's "Myth of the Metals.")

Luxury Beliefs

Rob Henderson defines luxury beliefs as follows: "Luxury beliefs are ideas and opinions that confer status on the upper class, while often inflicting costs on the lower classes."[34]

People crave status symbols and signs of distinction. Some such signs are expensive clothing or tastes that can only be cultivated by those with surplus time and material resources. However, another status symbol is *belief*. Henderson uses the example of "defund the police," which is endorsed disproportionately by those of high socioeconomic status, who, as a result of living in places relatively invulnerable to crime, would suffer the least from defunding. This belief is a luxury for them. It has no material impact on them, but it signals their high status to their peers, who are equally safe from crime. However, this belief is often unaffordable for poorer people, who tend to live in places that leave them vulnerable to crime. "Defund" is a luxury beyond their means. If the elites, who dominate the media discourse and exert control in government, get their way and succeed in defunding the police, the costs of the policy will be borne disproportionately by the poor.

Virtuous Lies Versus Noble Lies and Luxury Beliefs

Virtuous lies differ from both Plato's noble lies and Rob Henderson's luxury beliefs. Plato's noble lie promotes acceptance of an inequitable social order, depicting it as natural, inevitable, and just. In contrast, the virtuous lie invariably produces dissatisfaction with the social order, which it depicts as illegitimate or unjust. The noble lie reconciles us to social inequality whereas the virtuous lie is intended to serve a project of dismantling inequality. Finally, the noble lie is ultimately *metaphysical*. That is, it purports to offer an account of the underlying nature of reality that can be adduced to explain social arrangements. The virtuous lie, in contrast, is concerned with matters historiographical, sociological, economic, and psychological, as the four examples offered above show.

Virtuous lies share with luxury beliefs both a commitment to emancipatory political programs and a concern to signal moral goodness. However, as Rob Henderson's example of "defund" suggests, luxury beliefs are normative. They depict a prescribed course of action. Virtuous lies, in contrast, are purely descriptive. They purport to represent states of affairs as they exist in the world, for example, "police hunt and kill Black people,"[35] or "Black lives are systematically and intentionally targeted for demise."[36] Virtuous lies like these provide the "factual" basis for normative luxury beliefs like "defund the police."

Terminology

Why call virtuous lies "lies"? A lie is, by definition, a false claim that is asserted despite its known falsity. A lie involves intent to deceive. I would not pretend to know that everyone who utters what I have called a virtuous lie knows that it is false (or at least highly questionable) and intends to deceive. Surely some do, but I imagine that many or even most who repeat virtuous lies do so sincerely, because they know no better.

Why might so many know no better? The term "lie" seems especially fitting in light of the fact that unlike the unwitting laypeople who repeat them, those who invent and promulgate these untruths, including activists, media companies, and law professors, are in a good position to know better and have an epistemic obligation to the truth that should give them pause.

There is something gratuitous about virtuous lies, even when they are uttered unwittingly and sincerely. Respected law school professors who specialize in race and major media companies whose own data scientists have attempted to alert them to the truth have no excuse, of course. But neither do laypeople, really. The information that problematizes or even debunks them is not kept locked away. Anyone who even halfway cares about what the world was like before 1492, whether slavery was central to the young United States' economic surge, whether there is an epidemic of racist cops murdering Black people, or whether implicit bias is a well-defined construct that has a clear effect on behavior can find the truth, or at least vigorous debate that would cause one to back off of strong claims, with the click of a mouse.

Those given to whataboutery will have been champing at the bit to utter one word in response to my theory: Trump. The man is, after all, a liar of world-historic proportions. One of his most vicious lies is that the 2020 election was stolen. Indeed, according to a recent CNN poll, 63% of Republicans still believe that Biden "did not legitimately win enough votes to win the presidency."[37] But Trumpian lies, and rightwing lies more generally, are manifestly not virtuous. They make no pretense of serving an emancipatory project. They serve a project of acquiring political power and they do so nakedly. In a sense, this nakedness is refreshing. After all, virtuous lies, too, are promulgated in pursuit of political power, but under cover of the pretense of *fighting* it.

Some Consequences of Virtuous Lies

Why not just roll with virtuous lies? After all, they promise to inspire the activism and political will needed to address some of our most urgent problems. The answer is that theirs is a false promise. Let me say why.

First, the internet has put any citizen with even a modicum of interest and a free Sunday afternoon in a position to adjudicate these claims for herself. We are in an era in which you simply cannot keep information from people anymore, and you cannot lie to them.

Second, the lies will alienate at least as many people as they inspire. The virtuous lie is not a reliable formula for any political change apart from greater polarization. That is to say, a commitment to these lies on the part of the media and our "knowledge-producing" class more broadly means that there will always be a number of Americans who embrace the lies out of ignorance or tribal loyalty. However, there will also be a growing number of Americans who, as I have already suggested, will figure out that they are being lied to. This will create, or is already creating, a division in which a side consisting of tribally committed virtuous liars faces off against a side consisting of people who resent being lied to. This division is and will be toxic to our politics and hence to our democracy. It will only promote the rise of more Trump and DeSantis-like figures, who feed on and exacerbate the resentment of voters who dislike being lied to.

Let's take just one of the virtuous lies discussed above, the lie about racist murders by police, and play it out. Some might say, sure, perhaps it is not *quite* true that the police go out hunting for Black people. But this fib is innocent because it has beneficial effects. The proof is right before us: after all, it has spurred a massive nationwide and even worldwide movement for change. What could be bad about such a lie?

I would answer that the lie is not worth it.

The cost of the lie is paid as a psychological toll on all Americans but on Black Americans especially: the needless psychological suffering that results from hearing that you are being "hunted" by agents of the state in your own country. As Musa al-Gharbi put it, speaking of such narratives broadly:[38]

> For people of color, getting 'educated' in America is to be cudgeled relentlessly with messages about how oppressed, exploited, and powerless we are, and how *white people* need to 'get it together' to change this (but probably never will). Narratives like these grew especially pronounced during the post-2011 'Great Awakening.' The internalization of these messages may contribute to the observed ideological gaps in psychic distress among women and people of color.

The cost of the lie is paid as damage to our perceptions of Black and White race relations. Gallup has polled Americans on this almost every year since 2001.[39] In 2001, 70% of Black Americans said race relations were good. In 2021, not even half as many, 33%, could make that affirmation. The drop-off began in earnest in 2013, right around when use of terms like "racism" began to rise spectacularly in the media[40 41] and the newly formed Black Lives Matter began its messaging campaign.

The cost of the lie is not only ill-conceived campaigns to "defund"[42] but also the destruction of trust between communities and police, especially Black communities, whose disproportionate victimization by criminals shows they need policing, *good* policing, the most.[43] The cost of the lie is Black Americans' sense of alienation within their own country. The cost of the lie is the creation of preconditions for destructive rioting the next time a cop is caught on camera killing a Black person, whether under legally justifiable circumstances or not.[44]

So, the virtuous lie that police hunt Black people is not worth it, because it carries too many costs. There is a final cost to be reckoned with. Police killings do not ultimately constitute a distinctly "Black" issue, and a narrative that casts it as such has inherent limitations. First, the narrative's framing is divisive: there are "Black" issues and there are "White" issues but there are no "American" issues that affect us all. This framing requires activists to leverage enough guilt or empathy among Americans who are not Black to enact a "Black" agenda of reform. Moreover, the "hunting Black people" narrative is impotent to make common cause with those seeking justice for unjustified police killings of people of other races. (Almost half of the people killed by police are White.[45]) This impotence undermines the possibility of a broad-based, nonpartisan movement for reform.

For example, when police (both as it happens, Latino) in Fresno, CA, killed an unarmed White teenager, Dylan Noble, in 2016, and the killing was caught on video,[46] Noble's friends, family, and sympathizers initiated months of protests. But when protesters displayed "White Lives Matter" placards, perhaps inspired by Black Lives Matter, but finding no place in the movement for a White killing, they were predictably decried as "racist."[47] What if there had been a movement for police reform not based on identity politics with which Dylan Noble's family and supporters could have made common cause? Later, a young Black man, a rapper, Justice Medina, organized a protest in Fresno for *all* the lives lost to police violence, including that of Dylan Noble. He named Dylan Noble in one of his songs, and he sought to distance himself from BLM: "I'm out here for the human race," he said.[48]

Medina is precisely right: police reform is not well addressed through identity politics, in which one group's grievances are pitted against another group's perceived sins, biases, and privileges. The issue of police violence falls instead within the broader purview of *American* identity, which emphasizes our mutual bond and shared interests as citizens. Writing of the killing of a White woman, Hannah Fizer, by a police officer in June 2020, Adam Rothman and Barbara Fields point out that "a successful national political movement must appeal to the self-interest of White Americans" and advise that "those seeking genuine democracy must fight like hell to convince White Americans that what is good for Black people is also good for them." Only in this way will we find "the basis for a successful political coalition rooted in the real conditions of American life."[49]

The upshot is that virtuous lies, whether about the police or about any other matter of concern, will get us nowhere. Only if the media and knowledge-producing classes eschew such lies and hew closer to the truth can we hope to depolarize our discourse, restore faith in our information-generating institutions, and bring together a broad swath of the country in solidarity to confront the challenges that face all of us as citizens.

CHAPTER 29
Universities Must Choose One Telos[1]

By Jonathan Haidt

Aristotle often evaluated a thing with respect to its "telos"—its purpose, end, or goal. The telos of a knife is to cut. The telos of a physician is health or healing. What is the telos of a university?

The most obvious answer is "truth"—the word appears on so many university crests. But increasingly, many of America's top universities are embracing social justice as their telos, or as a second and equal telos. But can any institution or profession have two teloses (or *teloi*)? What happens if they conflict?

As a social psychologist who studies morality, I have watched these two teloses come into conflict increasingly often during my 30 years in the academy. The conflicts seemed manageable in the 1990s. But the intensity of conflict has grown since then, at the same time as the political diversity of the professoriate was plummeting, and at the same time as American cross-partisan hostility was rising. I believe the conflict reached its boiling point in the fall of 2015 when student protesters at 80 universities demanded that their universities make much greater and more explicit commitments to social justice, often including mandatory courses and training for everyone in social justice perspectives and content.

Now that many university presidents have agreed to implement many of the demands, I believe that the conflict between truth and social justice is likely to become unmanageable. Universities will have to choose, and be explicit about their choice, so that potential students and faculty recruits can make an informed choice. Universities that try to honor both will face increasing incoherence and internal conflict.

I am not saying that an individual student cannot pursue both goals. I urge students to embrace truth as the only way that they can pursue activism that will effectively enhance social justice. But an institution such as a university must have one and only one highest and inviolable good.

I am also not denying that many students encounter indignities, insults, and systemic obstacles because of their race, gender, or sexual identity. They do, and I favor some sort of norm setting or preparation for diversity for incoming students and faculty. But as I have argued elsewhere,[2] many of the most common demands the protesters have made are likely to backfire and make experiences of marginalization more frequent and painful, not less. Why? Because they are not based on evidence of effectiveness; the demands are not constrained by an absolute commitment to truth.

As I watched events unfold on campus over the past year, I began formulating an account of what has been happening, told from the perspective of moral and social psychology. I was invited to give several talks on campus this fall, and I took those invitations as opportunities to tell the story to current college students at Wellesley, SUNY New Paltz, and Duke. By the time of the Duke talk I think I got the story worked out well enough to send it out into the world, in the hope that it will be shown on many college campuses.[3] There are many pieces to the puzzle, and I had to present each one in order.

Outline of the Talk

Introduction

I begin with two quotations:

> The philosophers have only interpreted the world, in various ways; the point is to change it.
> — Karl Marx, 1845.

> He who knows only his own side of the case knows little of that. His reasons may be good, and no one may have been able to refute them. But if he is equally unable to refute the reasons on the opposite side, if he does not so much as know what they are, he has no ground for preferring either opinion.
> — John Stuart Mill, 1859.

Marx is the patron saint of what I'll call "Social Justice U," which is oriented around changing the world in part by overthrowing power structures and privilege. It sees political diversity as an obstacle to action. Mill is the patron saint of what I'll call "Truth U," which sees truth as a process in which flawed individuals challenge each other's biased and incomplete reasoning. In the process, all become smarter. Truth U dies when it becomes intellectually uniform or politically orthodox.

1. Telos

Each profession or field has a telos. Fields interact constructively when members of one field use their skills to help members of another field achieve their telos. Example: Amazon, Google, and Apple are businesses that I love because they help me achieve my telos (finding truth) as a scholar. But fields can also interact destructively when they inject their telos into other fields. Example: Business infects medicine when doctors become businesspeople who view patients as opportunities for profit. I will argue that social justice sometimes injects its telos of achieving racial equality (and other kinds) into other professions, and when it does, those professionals betray their telos.

2. Motivated Reasoning

A consistent finding about human reasoning: If we WANT to believe X, we ask ourselves: *"Can-I-Believe-It?"* But when we DON'T want to believe a proposition, we ask: *"Must-I-Believe-It?"* This holds for scholars too, with these results:

- Scholarship undertaken to support a political agenda almost always "succeeds."
- A scholar rarely believes she was biased
- Motivated scholarship often propagates pleasing falsehoods that cannot be removed from circulation, even after they are debunked.
- Damage is contained if we can count on "institutionalized disconfirmation"—the certainty that other scholars, who do not share our motives, will do us the favor of trying to disconfirm our claims.

But we can't count on "institutionalized disconfirmation" anymore because there are hardly any more conservatives or libertarians in the humanities and social sciences (with the exception of economics, which has merely a 3-to-1 left-right ratio).[4] This is why Heterodox Academy[5] was founded—to call for the kind of diversity that would most improve the quality of scholarship (at least, if you embrace Mill rather than Marx).

3. Sacredness

Humanity evolved for tribal conflict. Along the way we evolved a neat trick: Our ability to forge a team by circling around sacred objects and principles. In the academy we traditionally circled around truth (at least in the 20th century, and not perfectly). But in the 21st century we increasingly circle around a few victim groups. We want to protect them and help them and wipe out prejudice against them. We want to change the world with our scholarship. This is an admirable goal, but this new secular form of "worship" of victims has intersected with other sociological trends to give rise to a "culture of victimhood" on many campuses, particularly those that are the most egalitarian and politically uniform. Victimhood culture breeds "moral dependency" in the very students it is trying to help—

students learn to appeal to third parties (administrators) to resolve their conflicts rather than learning to handle conflicts on their own.

4. Anti-Fragility

"What doesn't kill me makes me stronger." Nietzsche was right, and Nasim Taleb's book *Antifragile*[6] explains why. Kids need thousands of hours of unsupervised play, and thousands of conflicts and challenges that they resolve without adult help, in order to become independently functioning adults. But because of changes in American childrearing that began in the 1980s, and especially because of the helicopter parenting that took off in the 1990s for middle class and wealthy kids, they no longer get those experiences.

Instead, they are enmeshed in a "safety culture" that begins when they are young and that is now carried all the way through college. Books and words and visiting speakers are seen as "dangerous" and even as forms of "violence." Trigger warnings and safe spaces are necessary to protect fragile young people from danger and violence. But such a culture is incompatible with political diversity, since many conservative ideas and speakers are labeled as threatening and banned from campus and the curriculum. Students who question the dominant political ethos are worn down by hostile reactions in the classroom. This is one of the core reasons why universities must choose one telos. Any institution that embraces safety culture cannot have the kind of viewpoint diversity that Mill advocated as essential in the search for truth.

5. Blasphemy

At Truth U, there is no such thing as blasphemy. Bad ideas get refuted, not punished. But at SJU, there are many blasphemy laws—there are ideas, theories, facts, and authors that one cannot use. This makes it difficult to do good social science about controversial topics. Social science is hard enough as it is, with big, complicated problems resulting from many interacting causal forces. But at SJU, many of the most powerful explanatory tools are simply banned.

6. Correlation

All social scientists know that correlation does not imply causation. But what if there is a correlation between a demographic category (e.g., race or gender) and a real-world outcome (e.g., employment in tech companies, or on the faculty of STEM departments)? At SJU, they teach you to infer causality: systemic racism or sexism. I show an example in which this teaching leads to demonstrably erroneous conclusions. At Truth U, in contrast, they teach you that "disparate outcomes do not imply disparate treatment" (Disparate outcomes are an invitation to look closely for disparate treatment, which is sometimes the cause of the disparity, sometimes not).

7. Justice

There seem to be two major kinds of justice that activists are seeking: finding and eradicating disparate *treatment* (which is always a good thing to do, and which never conflicts with truth), and finding and eradicating disparate *outcomes*, without regard for disparate inputs or third variables. It is this latter part which causes all of the problems, all of the conflicts with truth. In the real world, there are many disparities of inputs, but anyone who mentions such disparities on campus is guilty of blasphemy and must be punished. I work through an example of how the attempt to eliminate outcome disparities can force people to disregard both truth and justice. This is no way to run a university.

8. Schism

Given the arguments made in sections 1-7, I think it is clear that no university can have Truth and Social Justice as dual teloses. Each university must pick one. I show that Brown University has staked out the leadership position for SJU, and the University of Chicago has staked out the leadership position for Truth U— this has been confirmed by their rankings in the new Heterodox Academy Guide to Colleges.[7]

I close by urging students on every campus in America to raise the question among themselves: which way do we want our university to go? I offer a specific tool to raise the question: the Heterodox University Initiative.[8] If students on every campus would propose these three specific resolutions to their student government, perhaps as the basis of a campus-wide referendum, then students could make their choice known to the faculty and administration. The students would send a clear signal as to whether they want more or less viewpoint diversity on campus. At very least, a campus-wide discussion of Marx versus Mill would be a constructive conversation to have.

CHAPTER 30
Defining "Wokeness"[1]

By Cathy Young

In the culture-war discourse of the past decade, a variety of terms have been used to refer to the ideology of the socially progressive left: "political correctness" (first coined during an earlier phase of the culture wars, in the late 1980s/early 1990s), "social justice," "identity politics," and more recently, "wokeness" or "wokeism" (and occasionally, "cancel culture"). These shifting terms invariably become targets of left-wing ridicule as well as right-wing misuse (so that, for instance, any condemnation of actual bigotry is mocked as "political correctness," "social justice warrior-ism," etc.). Meanwhile, critics on the left dismiss the idea of a "woke" or "social justice" ideology as a right-wing myth. One such sarcastic dismissal comes from Vox writer Ian Millhiser who wrote on Twitter: "Have any of the writers who use the term 'wokeness' or 'wokeism' as if it is an ideology actually bothered to define the term?"[2] The supportive replies are typical: It's just "making an effort not be racist or sexist," or "a meaningless epithet whose unironic use is pure cringe."

But in fact, the ideology denoted by "wokeness" and "wokeism"—sarcastic riffs on "woke," a term from African-American vernacular that means being awake to social injustice—does exist (Writer Wesley Yang has also dubbed it "the successor ideology" to convey its succession to old-style liberalism).[3] To avoid the pejorative overtones, I will mostly use "Social Justice," since that term is embraced by many activists themselves.

Its basic tenets can be summed up as follows:

Modern Western societies are built on pervasive "systems of oppression," particularly race- and gender-based. All social structures and dynamics are a matrix of interlocking oppressions, designed to perpetuate some people's power and privilege while keeping others "marginalized" on the basis of inherent identities: race or ethnicity; sex/gender identity/sexuality; religion and national origin; physical and mental health (Class also factors into it, but tends to be the stepchild of Social Justice discourse). Individuals and their interactions are almost completely defined and shaped by those "systems" and by hierarchies of power and privilege. The only right way to understand social and human relations is to view them through the lens of oppression and power.

Everyone who belongs to a non-oppressed category in some core aspect of identity (White, male, heterosexual, cisgender, able-bodied, Christian, non-immigrant) possesses "privilege," enjoys unearned benefits at the expense of the oppressed, and is implicated in oppression. Thus, social justice advocacy must focus not only on the problems faced by the disadvantaged but on the unfair advantages of the "privileged."

Because various oppressions are so deeply embedded in everything around us, all actions that do not actively challenge it actively perpetuate it. Writer, scholar, and MacArthur Genius Grant winner Ibram X. Kendi, whose 2019 book *How to Be an Antiracist* has made him an intellectual star of the Great Awakening, puts it most succinctly: everything is either racist or antiracist, with no possibility of anything in between.

Challenging oppression and inequality requires not only combating injustices and reforming or dismantling oppressive institutions, but eradicating the unconscious biases we have all learned. A tweet from academic and TV commentator Mark Lamont Hill last July sums it up:

> In a racist, sexist, and homophobic world, the powerful and privileged must do the lifelong work of unlearning racism, sexism, and homophobia. None of us have clean hands. Instead of being indignant or self-righteous, let's actually do the work of self-critique and reflection.[4]

Again, the "powerful and privileged" here includes anyone who belongs to any non-oppressed category; but it is often argued that even the oppressed need to combat their internalized bigotry against their own group.

Language plays a key role in perpetuating oppression and must be reformed and controlled to achieve equality. Speech as well as writing, art, entertainment, and other forms of expression constantly "reinscribe" values, attitudes, and beliefs that validate or support oppressive systems and marginalize oppressed groups; thus, they must be constantly "interrogated," and even the most innocent verbal transgression can cause serious harm.

Social justice advocacy must be intersectional—that is, must support all movement-approved forms of advocacy for oppressed identities. Note, for example, the excommunication of famous novelist J. K. Rowling, a strong supporter of Black Lives Matter,[5] at the height of the antiracist "reckoning" last year over her "problematic" opinions on transgender issues.[6] Kendi provides an ingenious justification for intersectionality as an essential requirement for antiracism: You're not truly antiracist if you don't oppose (broadly defined) sexism, homophobia, and transphobia, because that means you don't oppose specific forms of racism directed at Black women and Black LBGT people.

Moral judgments of virtually any situation should be based primarily on where the people involved stand in the power/privilege hierarchy. As David Frum wrote in 2015, discussing many leftists' rush to blame the victims after Islamist gunmen attacked the offices of the French satirical journal *Charlie Hebdo* in retaliation for cartoons poking fun at Islam, killing 11 people and wounding 11 more, this moral theory can be summed up as: "1. Identify the bearer of privilege. 2. Hold the privilege-bearer responsible."[7]

These are the core foundational concepts; but there are other important tenets, spoken or unspoken. For instance:

All claims and accounts of identity-based oppression, abuse, or prejudice must be accorded the presumption of belief; to challenge or deny them without compelling evidence of their falsity is oppressive. Above all, a privileged person accused of causing harm to a marginalized person must listen, learn, and show contrition; to protest innocence is to show "fragility" and is itself an act of harm.

The privileged can easily harm people with marginalized identities by "appropriating" their voices or aspects of their culture such as dress or food. Offenses can range from a story, novel, or poem in the voice of a marginalized person to an ethnic Halloween costume.

Institutions and cultural products are irrevocably tainted by historical connections to oppressive practices or bigoted beliefs, whose effects remain deeply embedded. Thus, (inaccurate) claims that American policing had its origins in slave patrols have been used as proof of systemic police racism.[8] An author's or artist's racist or sexist views, even if normal for his/her time, are presumed to infect the work. Recent critiques of Dr. Seuss, for instance, argue that *The Cat in the Hat* subtly perpetuates "racist ideologies" because the Cat's appearance and mischievous behavior may have drawn on some tropes from Black minstrelsy (No, seriously).[9]

Western civilization (loosely defined as Europe and the "Anglosphere" of North America and Australia) is uniquely brutal and oppressive. The Social Justice critique of "systems of oppression" focuses entirely on Western societies, modern and historical. While this does not presume non-Western innocence, both the exclusive focus on Western wrongdoings and the frequent assumption that non-Western countries are victims of Western colonialism serve to promote the idea that the West is the world's primary driver of evil. The Social Justice movement's lack of interest in historical and even present-day slavery outside the West is a striking example of such double standards. Attitudes toward misogyny and homophobia in Muslim cultures are another. Thus, in 2015, feminist and LGBT groups at Goldsmiths College, University of London joined in solidarity with the Islamic Society when it tried to deplatform Iranian-born feminist Maryam Namazie on the grounds that her talk would make the campus less of a "safe space" for Muslim students.[10]

* * * * *

One reason "wokeness" or "social justice" has fairly wide appeal, at least in its more moderate guises, is that many of its ideas contain partial truths. Racism, sexism, and other bigotries have an ugly history and are still with us and we should strive to overcome them. If you advocate for a minority group, you should also favor human rights for other groups. Small indignities based on membership in a traditionally disadvantaged group can have a damaging effect, especially if they accumulate. Entertainment, literature, and everyday language can normalize insidious biases, accidentally or not. Humor that feels innocuous when directed at the majority ("All these White girls look alike!") can become odiously bigoted when it "punches down" at a minority that has been the target of prejudice and discrimination.

However, Social Justice takes such ideas to bizarre extremes increasingly detached from common sense and reality.

It's one thing to say that racism, sexism, and other prejudices are still a problem; it's another to claim that White supremacy and misogyny are omnipresent and life must be a constant struggle session to escape their clutches. It's one thing to say that we should avoid racial slights; it's another to demand constant vigilance against inadvertent "microaggressions" (like asking an immigrant, "Where are you from"?) and aggressive scrutiny of language for hidden offenses (like "sell someone down the river," which originally referred to selling slaves). It's one thing to acknowledge that *Gone with the Wind* is a hideously racist book, another to condemn a book because of a character's racist thoughts.[11] It's one thing to say that mocking someone's tweet as "typical White bullshit" is not as bad as tweeting anti-Black invective; it's another to normalize White-bashing as mere rhetorical attacks on White supremacy.

Social Justice in its current iteration has many troubling aspects that ultimately undermine the cause of equity. Its discourse of "White supremacy" and "patriarchy" provides an absurdly simplistic, reductionist picture of a multiracial, multiethnic society with a great diversity of cultural attitudes and norms. Its shift of language from race-based disadvantages faced by Blacks and other minorities to "White privilege" and "Whiteness" is in essence a shift of focus from improving the situation of minorities to stigmatizing Whites.

What's more, there is something uniquely pernicious about a concept of "privilege"—"White," "male," "straight," or any other kind—that equates *not* being mistreated with unfair advantage. It subverts one of liberalism's core principles: the existence of fundamental, inalienable human and civil rights. It also tends to erase bigotry against minority groups that are not readily defined as disadvantaged, such as American Jews and Asian Americans (who are sometimes classed as "White adjacent").

While "intersectionality" theoretically introduces more nuance into the discussion of privilege (since the same person can be privileged in some ways or contexts and disadvantaged in others), in practice it tends to turn into "oppression Olympics" in which one "marginalized identity" trumps all others and the others' unique concerns are cast aside.

Thus, discussions of sexual assault and "believing women" tend to entirely ignore the fraught history of false rape charges against Black men in America and the fact that nonwhite college students appear more likely to face dubious disciplinary charges of sexual misconduct.[12] Conversely, Social Justice discourse about White women weaponizing tears to deflect accusations of racism often parrots classic misogynistic tropes. Often-hyperbolic rhetoric about the constant danger to women from male violence is suddenly muted when it comes to concerns about opening women's single-sex spaces to any person declaring a female identity. And for all the talk of cultural sensitivity, feminist and queer activists' embrace of the gender-neutral "Latinx"—now firmly entrenched in mainstream media—overrules actual Hispanics, who overwhelmingly reject the term.[13]

Class is so "marginalized" (as it were) in Social Justice progressivism that a highly successful Indian American journalist can mock struggling White agricultural workers as "whiny assholes" and still feel she is "punching up."[14] When a 2019 study found[15] that a brief reading and discussion on "White privilege" made White liberals react less sympathetically to a (fictional) news article about a poor, unemployed, unskilled White man, the results received virtually no coverage outside publications critical of Social Justice.

But perhaps the most alarming aspect of Social Justice, as far as its effect on a liberal society, is the extent to which this ideology provides a justification for pervasive, quasi-totalitarian policing of speech, thought, and private behavior.

The language seems hyperbolic, since "wokists" are not throwing anyone in the gulag. But Social Justice is totalitarian in spirit in the same way that Trumpism is authoritarian: at least for now, both, fortunately, lack the power to enforce their will.

For one thing, Social Justice demands *de facto* banishment of "wrongthink" from the public square. Plenty of political movements seek to silence critics and dissenters; but Social Justice makes such silencing a moral imperative, since "bad" ideas and words are seen as inflicting "harm" or "violence." For instance, during the 2020 controversy over the "Letter on Justice and Open Debate" published in *Harper's* magazine,[16] Vox's Zack Beauchamp essentially argued[17] that views such as Rowling's are too detrimental to transgender people to be allowed in mainstream venues (Rowling has written that while transgender people should have full respect and equality, the reality of biological sex should not be denied and debate on difficult issues—from access to single-sex spaces to transition for minor children—should not be suppressed).[18]

The Social Justice view of the harms of speech was even more starkly stated three years ago by activists who tried to shut down an event with Christina Hoff Sommers, a feminist who critiques feminist claims about "rape culture" and the wage gap, at Lewis & Clark Law School in Portland, Oregon. In their statement, the activist students wrote with the certitude of zealots who have found Truth:

> We now understand how language works, and how it can be used to reproduce the systems of oppression we know we must resist at all costs. . . Free speech is certainly an important tenet to a free, healthy society, but that freedom stops when it has a negative and violent impact on other individuals. There is no debate here.[19]

Notably, the speech-policing is by no means reserved for ideological foes. For instance, books targeted by "woke" mobs are usually ones that promote the values of antiracism and inclusion but inadvertently violate identity taboos—whether it's the young adult novels *The Black Witch* by Laurie Forest (2017) and *American Heart* by Laura Moriarty (2018) or the 2020 mass-market novel *American Dirt* by Jeanine Cummins. Charges range from "White saviorism" to "cultural appropriation" to characters having prejudiced thoughts before being enlightened (The consequences have gone far beyond mere criticism: *American Heart* lost its initial positive review and "starred" status at the prestigious *Kirkus Reviews*, while *American Dirt* had its book tour canceled). Artist Dana Schutz experienced a vicious backlash for painting a lynching victim while White: when her work depicting Emmett Till was exhibited at the 2017 Whitney Biennial, there were calls for it to be not only removed but destroyed, and Schutz was slammed for "profiting off of Black murder."[20]

This is not about criticizing or countering speech with speech; the goal is to express collective condemnation, exact repentance, and either ostracize or enforce compliance.

The totalitarian tendencies of Social Justice are even more evident in its demands for the submission of everything to ideological *diktat*, from everyday language to personal life. This ranges from calls to purge idioms that supposedly demean people with disabilities ("that's crazy," "blind spot," "fell on deaf ears") to claims that an overly dark tan can be a form of Blackface. One could say this is "nutpicking," or cherry-picking of rare extreme views; but such extremism rarely encounters pushback in the "woke" community.

Family, friendship, and romance are not exempt, either. Shortly after the murder of George Floyd, *The New York Times* ran an op-ed suggesting White people should cut off relatives and friends "until they take significant action in supporting Black lives."[21] The "problematizing" of interracial relationships is an increasingly visible trend. Meanwhile, transgender advocates have argued that straight men and lesbians need to "work through" prejudices against sex with penis-having trans women.

A serious attempt to remake society in accordance with Social Justice dogma would require mass coercion on the scale of China's Cultural Revolution—which, thankfully, is as unrealistic a prospect as the alternative right's quest for a "White ethnostate" in America. But a more limited crusade toward utopian goals can still do considerable damage (especially since there's no telling what identities and goals the social justice movement could embrace next: if polyamorists become the next oppressed group *du jour*, disapproval of non-monogamy will make you a vile bigot).

Totalitarian tendencies in a political movement can be dangerous even when that movement does not run a dictatorship (As George Orwell noted in his classic 1946 essay "The Prevention of Literature," freedom of thought is not only doomed under totalitarian regimes but imperiled when intellectuals in free countries adopt a "totalitarian outlook").[22] This is especially true when that movement wields massive influence in the media and the educational system and is embraced by numerous public institutions and corporations. When your job includes seminars on "Interrupting Internalized Racial Superiority and Whiteness,"[23] or memos directing people to state their pronouns when introducing themselves,[24] it's hardly a stretch to see some resemblance to mandatory "political education" at Soviet workplaces.

What's more, many if not most "wokists" clearly favor the use of state power to promote their agenda. In a 2019 Politico forum on "How to Fix Inequality," Kendi proposed an "anti-racism amendment to the U.S. Constitution" and a permanent "Department of Anti-racism" staffed by "formally trained experts" (like himself), which would not only monitor public policies and even private businesses to stamp out "racial inequity," but "monitor public officials for expressions of racist ideas."[25] Kendi's definition of "racist ideas," it should be noted, is broad enough to include his own high school talk[26] arguing that Black youths are often held back by cultural attitudes that place a low priority on education, as well as Barack Obama's 2008 Father's Day speech noting that father absence is a particularly serious problem in the Black community.[27]

That's hardly the only example of the authoritarian dreams of social justice. Last year, as Canada went into lockdown due to COVID-19, *Toronto Star* "race and gender" columnist Shree Paradkar touted the drastic measures as evidence that "radical change" can happen with enough motivation.[28] Paradkar wrote approvingly that "[p]eople along various points on the political and social spectrum," including anti-racism activists, "are getting an unexpected glimpse into what an actual enforcement of their demands would look like."

* * * * *

Many will say that it's frivolous to focus on the "woke left" when we face an authoritarian menace from the Trumpian right. But you can be against two forms of illiberalism at the same time—especially when they reinforce each other. If nothing else, the fact that the social justice left demonizes Western liberalism as a cover for racism at the very time that liberalism is under attack from the equally grievance-obsessed populist right should give us pause.

CHAPTER 31
Ideology and the Social Sciences[1]

By Carl Bankston III

Because the character of the just society is a legitimate topic of debate and not a self-evident truth, an organization devoted to social justice requires its members to assume answers rather than asking questions and stifles freedom of thought.

My own discipline, sociology, can illustrate the institutionalization of ideology. Some may see sociology as a particularly egregious example. I think Christian Smith is correct that a sacred, moralistic vision has historically animated and bi-ased sociology.[2] Others, such as Irving Louis Horowitz[3] and several of the authors in Stephen Cole's edited book *What's Wrong with Sociology?*[4] have argued that so-ciology has suffered from heavy ideological bias in recent decades. Sociology has traditionally leaned left and this has led to attempts to impose intellectual conformity through organizational power. In an especially shameful episode, in 1976 the president of the American Sociological Association, Alfred McClung Lee, led a movement to expel prominent researcher James S. Coleman from the association because Coleman had dared to draw the ideologically unacceptable conclusion from research data that busing and other means of forcible school desegregation were actually exacerbating segregation by intensifying White flight. To the ASA's credit, the expulsion effort failed, but only after many attacks on Coleman's character and motivations.

As the sociologist Mathieu Deflem has noted,[5] during the 1990s, sociology went through a period of relative professionalization, during which most sociologists continued to be left-leaning in their personal beliefs, but the discipline stepped back from presenting the field itself as a socio-political program. As the twenty-first century opened, though, both the ASA and sociology in general swung back toward an institutionalized ideological program. In 2000, the newly elected president of the American Sociological Association, Joe R. Feagin, chose as his meeting theme "Oppression, Domination, and Liberation." In his presidential address he called for a decidedly radical "liberation sociology."

In 2003, following the U.S. invasion of Iraq, the ASA passed a resolution condemning the war and calling for its end. A minority of sociologists submitted a response arguing that the organization had violated its own code of professional ethics by using organizational means to advance political and moral causes. When ASA President Michael Burawoy announced "Public Sociology" as the theme of the 2004 meetings, supporters and critics of the theme had different takes on its meaning. For some, it meant simply that the discipline should seek to reach a wide public audience and address issues of public interest. For others, it meant the identification of sociology with a program of left-wing political activism. When Burawoy published an article in 2005 in the journal *Critical Sociology*, arguing that public sociology could have a "progressive impact" by promoting a vision of democratic socialism, he gave evidence that public sociology was indeed an institutional ideological program.

Frances Fox Piven, elected ASA president in 2006, made the ideological nature of public sociology even clearer. In a 2007 book chapter, Piven considered what kind of politics public sociology should encourage and proclaimed that the field should produce "a politicized sociology that is unashamed of the left." Piven's message to her academic colleagues was clear: get with my political program or get out.

Any review of the themes in the online meeting catalogues of the regional sociological societies will establish that the national organization is not alone in promoting progressive political activism as a central tenet of the profession. To attend a conference these days can feel like taking part in a rally of true believers. These associations are not government entities, one may argue, and they are entitled to become exclusive clubs of the committed. The problem is that the embedded ideologies of academic professional organizations are bound up with the embedded ideologies of universities. When we hire new faculty members or when we tenure or promote professors, one of the points we consider is whether the individuals concerned have been active in professional associations, especially the national association. Because the associations so strongly push political perspectives, universities implicitly encourage professors to hold and express the "correct" socio-political orientation.

Although I have used the national professional organization in sociology as my main example of institutionalized ideology in academia, one can easily find the same trend in other disciplines, such as American studies or anthropology. Universities, moreover, do not institutionalize ideology only through professional organizations. By defining debatable positions on policy issues as "core values"— the moral common sense that is expected of faculty and students—contemporary colleges and universities limit inquiry and build intellectual conformity into their everyday patterns.

Social Justice as Institutional Ideology

When an organization adopts a socio-political vision as part of its program, it takes decision-making away from individuals and substitutes officially approved assumptions for reasoning. The perspective known as "social justice" is clearly the dominant socio-political vision of higher education. It does not express only the opinions held by majorities on our campuses. Centers for social justice, administratively sponsored social justice conferences, and statements of allegiance to social justice in the mission statements of departments and schools set this vision into the structure of much of higher education.

What does "social justice" mean, though? For many students and some faculty on contemporary campuses, the assumptions have become so deeply entrenched that they do not even ask this question. It just means the obviously correct set of preconceptions, attitudes, and behaviors. Catholic teachings long ago defined social justice as "the conditions that allow associations or individuals to achieve what is their due, according to their nature and their vocation." Without theological premises about the nature of people and groups, though, it is difficult to say exactly what this means.

As I've argued elsewhere, the prevalent view of social justice on contemporary campuses (including Catholic campuses) derives not from religious concepts of the proper ordering of society, but from popularized versions of ideas associated with philosopher John Rawls. Rawls essentially argued that the just society is one that we would choose if we did not know what position we would occupy in it. He maintained that the rational person would choose the society in which she would be as well off as possible if she happened to land at the society's least advantaged place. Thus, societies and social policies are to be judged by the extent to which they maximize benefits to their most disadvantaged members.

The Rawlsian emphasis on disadvantage has combined with post-Civil Rights Era identity politics so that the disadvantaged have come to refer mainly to people in disadvantaged categories according to the trinity of race, class, and gender. "Intersectionality," or falling into multiple categories of disadvantage, gives people the greatest claims to be the measures of justice and the rightful beneficiaries of social justice. As an argument, this version of social justice may be defended or criticized. It offers a reasonable set of points for debate about social ethics and policy. But it is more than an argument in contemporary education. In establishing social justice centers and placing social justice in mission statements, universities have made it what Jonathan Haidt refers to as a *telos*,[6] or what I describe as an institutionalized ideology.

By setting up the neo-Rawlsian race-class-gender model of justice as the program endorsed by higher education, it defines all questions about this model as unjust and even as unethical. It bends research toward confirmation bias, since any findings of negative or even mixed consequences of, say, affirmative action for the sake of ethnic diversity are defined as inconsistent with the core values of the institution. When a university or college defines a socio-political viewpoint as officially just and virtuous, it is not necessary to engage in overt censorship or punish dissenters to encourage everyone on campus to fall into line.

In the case of sociology, most practitioners of the discipline would be left of center even if its professional organizations and leaders did not define it as political movement. But if we would treat socio-political beliefs as the property of individuals, and not as part of the discipline's identity, then sociology would not only have greater tolerance for intellectual diversity but left-wing sociologists would deepen their understandings of their perspectives by thinking seriously and respectfully about alternative views. Similarly, if colleges and universities did not take a particular version of social justice as an institutional goal, many professors and students would still advocate a Rawlsian approach to social justice. But this would be their view, to be tested against reason and evidence with an openness to debate and discourse, rather than a doctrine imposed by institutions.

CHAPTER 32
Attacks on Reality from the Left

Featuring
Jacob L. Mackey and Lawrence M. Eppard

The following is a conversation between Shippensburg University sociologist Lawrence M. Eppard and Occidental College classicist Jacob L. Mackey that took place in March 2023.

* * * * *

Lawrence M. Eppard (LE): Unfortunately, we live in a time when objective facts are becoming less influential in shaping public opinion than appeals to emotion and personal belief.

I have spent a lot of time focusing on how American conservatives are regularly lied to by Fox News, Newsmax, and OAN about a variety of issues, whether it's supposedly stolen elections, or climate change, or immigration, or any number of topics. But in this conversation, Jacob and I want to turn a critical eye toward those who feed American *liberals* misleading information.

Many in the left-wing bubble tell "virtuous lies," a concept that was coined by Jacob Mackey. These are seemingly authoritative yet flawed claims (those who make them present the empirical work behind them as stronger than it is)—made by some academics and others on the left—that further a social justice agenda. People make these claims without realizing or acknowledging the weak, unsettled, and even sometimes non-existent empirical support behind their assertions. Often research on a subject is in its infancy, but some on the left will nonetheless interpret it in a manner most ideologically aligned with their worldview and present that particular flawed interpretation as empirically sound.

Liberal audiences believe these claims because, while they haven't vetted them personally (because they do not have the time, desire, or expertise to do so), the claims come from credentialed people who they trust to have vetted them properly. They also believe these claims because they fit their worldview and make them feel good.

Additionally, for a liberal to oppose a virtuous lie would be to align oneself with supposedly bad people on the other side—supposed bigots, know-nothings, etc. To correct a virtuous lie is to oppose the noble goals of one's tribe and/or to signal that one does not take the problem seriously.

The left tells many virtuous lies, particularly about issues related to race and gender, including claims regarding the gender pay gap, gender identity, microaggressions, and implicit bias, to name but a few.

This of course doesn't mean that everything the left says about these topics is false—it doesn't even mean that most of the things they say about these topics are false. But many claims made by academics and partisans on the left about social justice issues are biased and incomplete explanations of important topics—yet they're often presented as if they are the authoritative consensus.

We are bombarded with this misleading information frequently, and this contributes to feelings and beliefs becoming more important than facts for millions of people, people becoming increasingly comfortable bending reality to their beliefs instead of bending beliefs to reality, and millions of Americans losing faith in notions of facts, expertise, and reality altogether.

A big fear that I have, Jacob, is that this is really undermining institutions of knowledge production—in universities in terms of not only what we are teaching students but in the knowledge claims that scholars are making in their scholarship.

Jacob L. Mackey (JM): It's definitely had an impact. There has been an extreme tilt to the left in universities—which you can clearly document statistically—in terms of the number of professors in various fields that identify as being on the left or the far left. It's changed the starting principles from which people begin their inquiry. This is one of the core ways in which this shift to the left has changed knowledge production in the academy. It changes the core "givens," their *a prioris* that inspire them to ask questions that are driven by underlying premises that not everyone would agree with.

The academy has become so tilted to the left that it has simply ignored an entire range of questions and attitudes toward inquiry that you could get if you had more intellectual diversity.

LE: If the problem was just the crowding out of certain questions and even eliminating the possibility that we would think to formulate certain questions, that would be bad enough. But I also believe that the standards of evidence in many fields in the social sciences are really low. Empirically weak claims are regularly making their way into our academic journals, and then they make their way into the public discourse and into policies across the country.

Take microaggressions as just one example, but an illustrative one. I'm not making any claims about what they are specifically, how often they occur, and how damaging they are. This is all for qualified researchers to sort out with rigorous studies. But instead of admitting that the research in this area is in its infancy and is really unsettled and unclear, many on the left have moved full speed ahead in defining microaggressions as something specific that we haven't empirically demonstrated yet, claiming harm that has not been conclusively demonstrated, and developing policies based upon all of this new, empirically unsettled, and preliminary work.

JM: I agree completely. Something like microaggressions, it was an interesting idea that someone dreamed up. There were anecdotes from Derald Wing Sue's personal subjective experience to suggest that there might be something there. But from that personal subjective experience people created a whole program that was not subjected to proper empirical testing. It would be fine if it was just people speculating in journal articles about microaggressions. But that thing then went from just being a critique of what happens in some social interactions to generating an entire quasi-scientific worldview. And then that paradigm got institutionalized in regimes. There are whole offices that actually have physical addresses and that hire people, pay millions of dollars a year for staff, and it's all based on the construct of the microaggression.

So because the professorate has certain *a prioris* and certain cultural left premises that it does not question, it privileges certain kinds of research even when there has not been due diligence done. We're in a golden age of creating constructs for which you do not have to provide proper empirical evidence. Then, even though the claim hasn't been clearly demonstrated, it gets adopted and turned from a paradigm into a regime with offices. It's incredibly distorting—not only the knowledge the academy produces but it actually distorts the institution in its very structure.

Once you've gone from faulty knowledge production to institutional offices dedicated to combating the microaggression, you've created institutional structures with coercive power that begin to interfere in the lives of individual actors. It's far more than just our knowledge, we are now intervening in the interpersonal interactions of young people.

What are going to be the downstream effects for these students of having been brought up on a coercive regime of microaggression policing? I don't think we know what this is going to do to society yet. We don't know what the systemic social consequences of our faulty knowledge production are yet, but I think we have reason to think it's not going to be good. We do know that it causes minority students to perceive ambiguous interactions as harmful more than they would if they had not been sensitized.

LE: Let's be clear—it's not wrong to suggest a new concept or area of inquiry. What is wrong is to disseminate information to the public about this concept or area as if it has been clearly demonstrated, give it the symbolic credibility of having been peer reviewed and therefore assumed to be empirically rigorous, and then have people develop policies based on what they believe are authoritative and evidence-based claims, when in fact the empirical work on it has just begun and is highly unsettled. That's something totally different from just us having academic conversations about plausible concepts.

JM: I'm glad you said that. The whole point of being a researcher in the academy is to dream up hypotheses and concepts and notions and ideas and then figure out how to empirically test them and falsify them. The theory of microaggressions absolutely should have been dreamed up.

In fact, I say that as someone who has been subject to microaggressions his whole life. I'm missing my left arm from below the elbow, I was born that way. I've always had a very noticeably different body. For my whole life, as long as I can remember, I was subject to both outright attacks—like kids who would physically attack me because of my arm—or they would verbally attack me, insult me, abuse me, etc. But also through that whole time I experienced what I now know to call microaggressions, these unintended slights. For me it has been a lifelong thing.

So when I first learned of the theory, it clicked. I was like, "Oh, that's what that is. That's this thing that happens to me once a week where someone does something, without intending to, to sort of diminish me a little bit or slight me or insult me just a little."

So absolutely these are important things to investigate.

It's hard to argue a counterfactual, but I think if someone told me when I was a child that the microaggression literature tells you that microaggressions are harmful, I cannot imagine what the consequences for my psychological and emotional development would've been.

LE: It seems that some of the big claims have just not yet been supported with nearly enough evidence—both in terms of the intent behind the microaggression and the harm that it supposedly causes. In fact, it seems the word "harm" has been a victim of concept creep here in much the same way that other words have fallen prey, like "trauma."

JM: An explicit part of this new ideology—call it wokeness or whatever you like— is that you do not have to demonstrate it. In fact, it's yet another aggression to ask someone to demonstrate harm. I just have to take your word for it.

LE: In addition to low standards of evidence for claims—as long as they align with social justice goals—is the problem of cancel culture.

By cancel culture, I am not referring to people who bring bad faith arguments into this discussion. I am talking about the numerous incidents where people have voiced legitimate, good faith criticisms of things like microaggressions and implicit bias and other social science concepts and these critics have been labeled as bigots and been personally attacked for not conforming to the prevailing orthodoxy. I think the left is really blind to how much of a problem this is.

Take the really controversial example of gender identity. Now, there are plenty of people who make bad faith arguments about gender identity and who really want to hurt trans people. I'm not talking about those people, those people deserve the negative reaction they get for wanting to hurt another human being. But there are good faith arguments to be had both in support of prevailing notions of gender identity as well as in critiquing those notions. Good faith critiques are necessary, appropriate, and should not just be shut down and the messenger attacked.

People should not just say things like "You're denying my right to exist" or "You are committing violence against me" because somebody, in good faith, does not agree with their particular view of gender identity. In my opinion, this is not an appropriate response to a good faith critique of a scientific issue that is unsettled.

JM: You're denying my existence—it's this claim to the ultimate harm, right? It's more than just a microaggression or something like that, you're actually erasing me, you're killing me. The power of this claim to harm has been so weaponized to bully people into submission and to end conversations.

These gender questions are some of the most complicated questions that there are right now. The idea that we can't talk about it because talking might be harmful to you, that's a non-starter for me.

LE: I want to be clear that I do not deny that there are plenty of people in the world who want to hurt trans individuals. I am vehemently against that; I believe that should be something that's out of bounds. But I think it is highly inappropriate to claim that any good faith disagreement with a particular view of gender identity is "genocide" or is "erasing somebody" or "harming" them, or that it makes you a bigot or on the "other team."

Jacob, there's a concept you've coined called the "virtuous lie," which refers to claims that stand on shaky empirical ground but, since they further a social justice agenda, their empirical weakness is ignored or downplayed. If the claim furthers a particular agenda—in the example we just discussed, a particular view of gender identity for instance—then the claim does not get as rigorously critiqued as it should by the left. And to question it would signal to everybody that you are really "playing for the other team."

JM: They are not always outright lies, oftentimes they are just highly questionable claims. This idea of the virtuous lie is that sometimes we actually know, given the preponderance of the evidence, that the claim is either false, badly evidenced, or highly speculative. But it's morally good to pretend that the claim is true and has significant empirical backing. It becomes morally good to affirm them rather than to question them. This is necessary for us to maintain our standing as good moral people.

LE: And the problem is not in suggesting concepts for further examination. The problem is when social justice or "woke" ideology short circuits the disconfirming responsibilities and mechanisms of the epistemic system.

JM: Absolutely. It's an intervention of morality in what should be an epistemological process. When you make a claim, it's an epistemological problem to figure out whether that's correct and whether we've got it right. But sometimes a moral concern comes in and short circuits the epistemological concern and just says, "To ask about the truth or falsity of this claim is a form of violence." You can't do the epistemological work because there's a moral reason not to. We're killing epistemology in the name of morality.

LE: There are a variety of reasons why I care about these things. Number one is because that is the business we are in: figuring out the truth, verifying claims. And we should be doing that regardless of how painful the claims are. This is the work that we are doing, that is the number one priority for me.

But in addition to that, one of the things that I'm concerned about is the pedagogical aspects of this. We have to be concerned with how people are going to hear our message if we want our message to win the day and to help influence positive social change. One way to clearly *not* have people hear your message is for them to become aware of ways in which you have distorted the truth. Ways in which you have disregarded the scientific method and used less-than-rigorous standards of evidence.

So I care about this first and foremost because I care about the truth. But I also care about helping to make society better, and you cannot do that if (a) you are wasting time and energy on methods that are not actually helping and (b) you are repelling people you need to hear your message because you are contributing to their mistrust of you. You are going to have to get people on board who are resistant to your ideas, and bending the truth will not help—in fact, it will probably cause them to be more resistant.

JM: There is a decline in trust in all institutions right now, including academic institutions. I think it's for precisely the reason you put your finger on. People are not stupid. They can see that the academy is bending the truth, to put it mildly, and often tells virtuous lies. It is often affirming things because it seems politically correct rather than what the most rigorous research shows.

This is really bad—not just for us and our credibility and the credibility of our institutions—but if we do care about social problems, it's only the honesty and credibility of the institutions tasked with investigating those problems that's going allow us to come together broadly a society.

LE: When I talk about this with colleagues, they often respond, "Yeah but the other side is way worse." That is one of the ways that I find this debate often grinds to a halt. I am not saying they are equal, I don't personally know how'd I'd measure that. And I agree that Fox News is one of the worst purveyors of misinformation and disinformation in our society.

But both sides are contributing to the amount of bad information Americans are exposed to, and I don't think there is any hope of reaching across the aisle and convincing conservatives to ignore bad information if the left isn't following its own advice. I don't think the left realizes just how much they're also in an ideological silo.

JM: They're co-creating the problem. They're responding to each other just as when you dance a tango, you respond to your partner's moves. That's what they're doing. But each side thinks the other side is the sole transgressor.

LE: Denying that Joe Biden won the 2020 presidential election, denying the major findings in climate change research, those things are legitimately ludicrous. And I'm not absolving the right when it comes to that stuff, I'm very, very concerned about that. I'm very concerned about the hyperpartisan misinformation and disinformation coming from places like Fox News.

But the right seems to be more self-aware about what they are doing. They are aware that they are creating their own institutions to get "their side of the story" into the public square and into the minds of Americans. The left I think is more oblivious to the ways in which they distort reality to fit their agenda.

JM: The right very consciously said that they needed to just start their own institutions. Big money began to fund alternative streams of knowledge production to counter what they saw as the distorted knowledge production coming out of the legacy institutions. They said, "We've lost the legacy institutions, it's time to create our own ecosystem, our own institutions." And by the time Rush Limbaugh comes along, that's well underway and he knows exactly what he's doing.

But if you're a professor at Harvard, you just take for granted that you're a part of the community of the good, that you've been tasked with pronouncing the truth to the masses.

LE: Now, I certainly hope people would not read our conversation and think we are joining forces with equally bad or worse actors on the other side, like Christopher Rufo.

You cannot fix a problem with a problem. If I am at the beach and I see somebody drowning in the water, I am not going to throw them a shark as a life preserver, or an anvil.

JM: Just imagine one of our most tribal colleagues. They might say, "You know what? You're right. There have been excesses on our side. We have been a little shrill on our side. We have overstated things on our side. We have overdone it. However, it's still our side. You're going over to the enemy by raising these concerns. You're aiding and abetting the enemy. You have to circle the wagons and defend our side."

To me, that's actually a form of self-destruction. When I criticize academia, I'm actually trying to save the thing.

LE: Right. I am not joining "their side" by questioning the standards of my own discipline. People like Christopher Rufo are not acting in good faith. Rufo said publicly on Twitter that he wanted to brand anything he disagreed with as "woke" or as "Critical Race Theory" in order to discredit anything he doesn't like, to make it a toxic brand. That's not honest, good faith discourse. His "fixes" not only wouldn't help the parts of the epistemic system which are malfunctioning, they would probably corrupt the larger epistemic system—the majority of which is working extremely well—with his nonsense.

JM: He wanted to create a situation in which the average American, the second they hear anything of a certain sort—critical of the country on race, for instance—the second they heard that, they would wrap it up in a ball with concepts that he has helped make toxic. He wanted to make certain things just toxic.

LE: The people I've observed in academia who make really empirically weak claims, I don't know that they're aware they're doing it. I think they are making the claims in good faith, they believe them to be true and are just suffering from motivated reasoning like the rest of us. They honestly believe they're developing their research questions correctly, constructing their variables appropriately, interpreting the data accurately. I think they truly believe it and I can back that up with "receipts" as young people say.

JM: What I come away from interactions with colleagues with more than anything is a sense of, "I cannot believe you don't know this." Their starting premises are either demonstrably known to be false or, at best, they're often just incredibly tendentious and contested. Yet my colleagues just complacently accept them as settled fact. And it's because they're in an environment in which they never have to question them. All of the rewards are in the direction of just accepting them.

CHAPTER 33
Bad Behavioral Science Exposed[1]

By Terence Hines

There is probably no other scientific discipline in which fads come and go so quickly, and with so much hype, as psychology. In his book, *Quick Fix*, Jesse Singal discusses eight different psychological ideas that have been promoted as quick fixes for different social problems.[2] He refers to these as "half-baked" ideas—"ideas that may not be 100 percent bunk but which are severely overhyped" (p. 6).

The Self-Esteem Movement

The first chapter concerns the self-esteem movement, which began in 1990 with a report from the State of California titled *Toward a State of Esteem*. The report argued that increasing a person's self-esteem, especially for children and adolescents, would improve nearly everything from social behavior to academic performance. The questionable origins of this report have, to my knowledge, not been previously described. Due to pressure from a "very eccentric California politician" (p. 13) named John Vasconcellos, major findings that called into question the utility of increasing self-esteem were suppressed from the report. This, in turn, led to all sorts of dingbat programs for improving self-esteem. The chapter provides many illuminating examples, such as banning games with winners in elementary schools. Self-esteem improvement programs do seem to make people score higher on subjective measures such as happiness, which is important. But they have little effect on more objective measures of behavior. The cottage industry of self-esteem therapists is doing little to improve objective measures.

"Superpredators"

The concept of the "superpredator" (Chapter 2), the (usually Black) teenager who ran wild killing, raping, and pillaging, became a popular stereotype in the 1990s. It generated a rush of legislation that meted out much harsher punishment for teenage criminals. The claim was that these teens were destined to become career criminals because of genetic faults, poor upbringing, or both. Since birth rates were increasing, the fear was that there would be a dramatic increase in the coming years of such wilding teens, thus posing a severe threat to society. The idea was advanced by some criminologists and picked up by politicians of both conservative and liberal persuasions. Prominent among the criminologists who advanced the superpredator idea was John Dilulio, "a careful academic in other respects" (p. 72). Singal notes that Dilulio did not put forth this idea in peer-reviewed publications, and thus the idea was not subject to the criticisms that it would have generated due to lack of evidence and sloppy conceptualization. In 2001, Dilulio "acknowledged. . . that he had simply been wrong" (p. 72) but rejected the idea that he was the cause of so many kids going to jail.

Power Posing

Remember how your mother would tell you to "sit up straight and have a good posture?" Well, in 2010 that advice was reshaped into a sure-fire method of empowerment, especially for women, in the form of "power posing." The idea was that if you sat up straight, leaned forward, sort of took possession of the space around you. . . all kinds of good things would happen. The original paper reported that assuming such a pose increased feelings of power and people's willingness to take a financial risk. It even increased testosterone levels compared to what was defined as more submissive or passive poses. This led to the expected outbreak of self-help books, TED talks, and general hype. The trouble was that none of it was true. In 2016 the lead author of the study, Dana Carney, posted on her UC-Berkeley webpage that "I do not believe that 'power pose' effects are real" (p. 82), although she has never formally had the paper retracted. The problem was a statistical manipulation (called p-hacking) that led to finding differences between the power and passive pose conditions where none existed.

One of the goals of the power pose movement was a legitimate one—to help women overcome sex/gender discrimination in hiring and salaries. Singal makes an important point here and throughout the book: it would be better to direct attention to the root causes of these problems rather than fall back on "half-baked" fad psychology quick fixes that don't fix much of anything.

Positive Psychology

"Positive psychology," the focus of Chapter 4, is a kind of successor to humanistic psychology, but without the high psychobabble content of the former and more interest in empirical verification. Positive psychology emphasizes finding ways to make already psychologically healthy people happier and more satisfied with their lives rather than dwell on psychopathology. This is a laudable goal, but positive psychology has had major problems empirically verifying its interventions.

One of the founders of positive psychology is Martin Seligman, a professor at the University of Pennsylvania. Seligman is famous for trying to apply the principles of positive psychology on a mass basis through various interventions. However, these interventions have proven to be of questionable effect. "On multiple occasions, Seligman and his center [Positive Psychology Center] have made impressive claims about interventions that outpace the available evidence" (p. 108). One program, the Strath Haven Positive Psychology Curriculum, is aimed at increasing the "strength of character" of elementary school students. On his university website, Seligman claimed that the program "builds character strengths, relationships, and meaning, as well as raises positive emotions and reduces negative emotions" (p. 109). But in a peer-reviewed journal paper, he said precisely the opposite; specifically, that the "positive psychology program did not improve. . . character strengths" nor several other outcome measures. That report is vague about the overall effects of the program, and Singal notes that, while the study was funded by a grant worth almost $3 million, no complete report of the results has ever been published.

Despite the questionable effectiveness of Seligman's programs, in 2008 the United States Army reached out to him to devise an intervention to deal with a significant problem—PTSD among soldiers. The result was the Comprehensive Soldier Fitness (CSF) program which incorporated modifications of an earlier intervention called the Penn Resilience Program (PRP). The PRP was "delivered to (mostly) healthy students by laypeople who can be quickly trained for the task" (p. 114). The intervention was done in groups and, not surprisingly, didn't have much effect on students. Promoting it as an effective treatment for adults who had suffered severe trauma was, to put it mildly, a stretch. Nonetheless, the Army gave Seligman's group a $31 million contract. As expected, the program had little effect.

The CSF program was approved and mandated by a single person, the then Army Chief of Staff, General George Casey. Casey, a fine general that he might have been, had no experience evaluating psychological intervention programs. Singal cites this as an example of what he terms "unskilled intuition," which is when a decision maker thinks they have the skills and knowledge to make a decision but do not. This is a case of the Dunning Kruger Effect, a cognitive bias whereby people with limited knowledge or competence in a given intellectual or social domain vastly overestimate their knowledge or competence relative to objective criteria or performance of their peers or people in general. By falling for the sales pitch from Seligman et al., the Army passed up the opportunity to implement more effective programs to treat PTSD.

Grit

The concept of "grit," (Chapter 5) pretty much the same as stick-to-it-iveness, is another spawn of positive psychology. Grit was marketed to American schools by Angela Duckworth in her 2016 book *Grit: The Power of Passion and Perseverance*. The text mainly consisted of success stories of people with, you guessed it, real grit. But as Singal correctly notes, this was cherry picking. Reports of students who clearly had grit but didn't succeed were largely left out. And such people indeed do exist, as documented in Linda Nathan's 2017 book *When Grit Isn't Enough*.

Grit is said to be able to predict success in various situations better than older, well-established measures such as consciousness. For example, a short ten-item grit scale was said to make valuable predictions about whether West Point cadets would make it through a challenging seven-week training course. And so it did. . . But not really. Ninety-eight percent of cadets scoring high on this scale completed the course. But 95% of *all* cadets complete the course, so the grit scale didn't *really* add much. Some schools have jumped on a grit bandwagon with the hope that it is possible to increase grit levels and thus student success. This harkens back to the self-esteem movement in many ways.

Similarly, since grit doesn't correlate very highly with measures of student success, and there is little evidence that interventions can change grit, such programs are ill-conceived. As was the case with the Comprehensive Soldier Fitness program to combat PTSD, there are much better and proven ways of improving student success, such as teaching best study habits and nurturing skills that require class attendance and time management. Grit was just the fancy new kid on the block who got all the attention.

An appealing marketing ploy for grit was to claim that increasing grit would be especially helpful in decreasing the inequality between wealthy and poor children in school achievement. The failure of grit to improve much of anything, or to predict much of anything, belies this hope. Grit was another attempt to avoid making the major changes in the American educational system that would be needed to really address social inequalities. It was just another failed, quick fix.

The IAT

In Chapter 6, Singal discusses the Implicit Attitude Test (IAT), commonly known as the "bias test," arguably the most controversial topic in social psychology. There are numerous different varieties of this test, first developed in 1998. "Implicit," as used here, means "unconscious." The test is said to measure implicit or unconscious bias against a given racial or ethnic group by using a reaction time measure. Bias is found when "someone is quicker to connect positive concepts with white people and negative concepts with black people" (p. 186). The controversial finding is that people who show no racial or ethnic biases in behavior or explicit attitudes are scored as highly biased by the IAT. The test has become a mainstay of diversity training programs. The basic idea is to identify people who hold implicit biases and then train these biases out of them.

There are serious problems with this approach. The IAT is a test and, like any other test, must meet two fundamental criteria before it can be ethically used to guide any decision making. First, a test claimed to measure some stable characteristic must be reliable. Reliability means that a test must give close to the same results on repeated testing. If the Hines Test of Baseball Skill (HTBS) generates widely different scores when given two weeks apart, it isn't reliable. A test must also be valid—there must be independent evidence that it measures what it claims to measure. If the HTBS is very reliable, but HTBS scores do not correlate highly with some real-world measure of baseball skill, it is not valid. The IAT is not reliable. The correlations obtained when reliability is measured "have ranged from $r = 0.32$ to $r = 0.65$" (p. 182). "By the normal standards of psychology," these figures put "the IAT well below the threshold of usefulness in real-world settings" (p. 181). What Singal does not point out, unfortunately, is that if a test is not reliable, it cannot be valid. That is, if the scores are bouncing around, they can't be telling us anything about the stable trait the test is advertised as measuring. Indeed, it is clear that the IAT is not valid based on several meta-analyses described by Singal.

A related problem exists: "it has never been clearly stated what it [the IAT] measures" (p. 186) but simply tautologically assumed that having a particular score on the IAT meant that the person had implicit bias "without that score implying a connection to real-world behavior" (p. 187). The meta-analyses referred to above show that "the evidence is simply too lacking for the test to be used to predict individual behavior" (p. 184). Still, people do show a wide range of scores on these tests—these differences must be due to something. One possibility, of course, is some sort of bias. But Singal reviews "a significant amount of evidence that the IAT measures a variety of things apart from implicit bias itself" (p. 188). Given this, it's certainly odd that the IAT is accepted when the "psychological establishment. . . would surely reject a similarly noisy and arguably misleading test of depression or anxiety" (p. 188).

The general lack of validity of the IAT makes it highly problematic as a tool for changing behavior, although it has become an established tool in antiracism and diversity training. Singal devotes much discussion at the end of Chapter 6 to the idea that it would be better to recognize that the most serious problem facing minority groups is not implicit cognitions that may never express themselves in overt behavior but in the structure of a society that oppresses minorities. This point is similar to the one made regarding self-esteem and grit in previous chapters. It's a lot easier to focus on "even more microscopic examinations of white people's behavior and attitudes and etiquette" than to change the structure of the system that so disadvantages minorities. None of this is to say that implicit bias doesn't exist, an important point made by Singal. It does. The question is whether the IAT: (1) measures it; and (2) whether training programs based on the IAT have any real beneficial effects in mitigating it. The answer to both these questions appears to be "no."

Psychology's Replication Crisis

The crisis of replication in psychology in general and the claims for "social priming" in particular are the topics of Chapter 7. Social priming refers to the idea that subtle environmental cues can have large effects on behavior. Two such claims are illustrative.

In one study, one group of college students processed words that suggested elderliness (i.e., frail, old, Florida, etc.) while a control group processed age-neutral words. The supposed finding was that those who processed the "geezer" words took more time to walk down a corridor than the control group. In another study, looking at a picture of Rodan's *The Thinker* reduced viewers' religiosity compared to a control group. Studies like these exploded in the early 21st century.

Then along came Daryl Bem and his (in)famous study of psi in which he claimed to have shown real psi effects. Since his paper was published in what was considered the leading journal of social psychology, it attracted a great deal of attention from other psychologists and the popular media. Singal discusses the fact, noted previously by many other commentators, that Bem's study was the straw that broke the camel's back in terms of accepting the standard way that statistical analyses of psychological research had been done. This was because the results of Bem's experiments were so inherently implausible. That the usual statistical analyses seemed to yield evidence in favor of parapsychological phenomena suggested something badly amiss in how those analyses operated. These included using multiple statistical tests and then reporting only those that seemed to confirm the initial hypothesis. There was also the practice of changing the study's hypothesis after the fact to conform with the obtained results, among other issues. A broader problem was calculating levels of statistical significance and reporting them as traditional p-values where 0.05 or less was taken as showing that the effect was real. To be clear—all that the 0.05 means is that the result is *unlikely*; that is, it would have occurred by chance five times or less out of 100. It does not mean that it could not have occurred by chance.

The replication crisis refers to the finding that many of the much-ballyhooed study results in social psychology do not replicate when other researchers repeat the experiments. This, too, became clear when Bem's results did not replicate in the hands of those who tried. To make matters worse, even the journal that published Bem's paper refused, initially, to publish failures to replicate his findings, not even sending the paper reporting the failures out for peer review. Most journals never published studies reporting attempts to replicate previous findings, whether the replications succeed or not. Thus, results due to chance or statistical manipulation continued to be accepted as real. When this was realized, attempts began to replicate many of the "sexy" findings in social priming. Most failed to replicate, including the priming studies noted above.

The positive response to this methodological embarrassment is that some journals now require more rigorous standards for publication. Some even require that researchers submit a sort of "letter of intent" detailing the exact hypotheses to be tested, methodology, and statistical analysis to be used before the study is even begun. More researchers are using Bayesian approaches to statistical analysis. This approach can be best summed up by the phrase well known to skeptics: "extraordinary claims demand extraordinary proof." In other words, if your claim is highly unlikely to be true before the study (i.e., looking at *The Thinker* makes people less religious), you'd better have more than one lone result of $p < 0.05$ to support it.

Oddly, Singal hardly mentions that the same replication crisis is found in many medical studies and does not cite Ioannidis's 2005 *PLoS Medicine* paper that brought this problem to the fore, well before Bem's paper appeared. The chapter seemed a bit out of place in the book because, popular as social priming was, the enthusiasm about it never reached the level of claiming that priming was a way to cure various social ills, as was the case for the topics of the other chapters.

Nudging

The final chapter with a specific program or concept as its subject, Chapter 8, is about "nudging." Nudging is a way of arranging the environment to make it easier for people to behave in a desired way, as opposed to strong-arm tactics such as regulations or legislation. This technique for changing behavior "has a fair bit of genuine empirical heft behind it" (p. 263).

The chapter starts with a great example. Before 2015 or so, New Yorkers who committed minor violations were given a carbon copy of the ticket the office wrote. Buried in the small print on the ticket was the requirement that the defendant appear in court at a particular date, place, and time. An unacceptable number of people didn't show up for their court dates. To solve this problem, the design of the ticket copy was changed to make the requirements much more obvious. This is a beautiful example of using human factors design to solve a problem.

Given this example, I expected the rest of the chapter to be about how the human factors approach to designing such things as forms, signs, roadways, kitchen appliances, and even buildings can be extremely useful in producing desired behavior. But right away, the chapter took a bizarre turn. It veered off into decision-making research and the work of Kahneman and Tversky on how mental shortcuts ("heuristics") result in poor decision making. This goes on for a few pages, and then we're back to nudging. There's an interesting example of how the Obama administration arranged for stimulus money to be distributed to individuals in increments rather than as one lump sum. The goal of the stimulus money was to get people to spend more. Had it been delivered in one lump sum, people would have been more likely to put it away in savings. Multiple smaller individual payments were more likely to be spent. The chapter, which seems more disjointed than the others, ends with the important observation that nudges don't always work and that by focusing on them, more serious institutional problems can be overlooked.

Why We Fall for Quick Fixes

In the book's final chapter, Singal covers the reasons for the wide acceptance of quick fixes and the problems with such acceptance. The reasons are rather obvious—quick fixes are easy to understand and thus gain popularity, especially when their creators promote them through TED talks and public media. As mentioned previously, unskilled intuition also plays a role. Quick fixes get other rewards—academic promotions, consulting gigs, book royalties, etc. Nothing too surprising there.

What is more revealing is how the acceptance of quick fixes may do harm—more harm than just not solving the problems very well. To the extent that quick fixes don't work particularly well, the groups at which they were directed will not benefit very much. There is then a danger that these groups will be blamed for their failures. If all it takes for disadvantaged children to succeed in school is more grit, then when they get all gritty and still don't excel, well, it must be their fault. And this can, in turn, breed disappointment and hostility.

Singal's book is an excellent contribution to the skeptical evaluation of social programs where the claims go far beyond reality. It will be eye-opening to many unfamiliar with the actual success rates of the programs discussed. The text is never heavy with academic jargon and clearly explains the many, sometimes complex, ideas. It is well referenced and not without a pleasing bit of wit.

* * * * *

Note: After this review was first published, Martin Seligman objected that neither the book nor my review noted that studies not included in the book support the effectiveness of some positive psychology interventions. He referenced Carr et. al.'s 2021 article in The Journal of Positive Psychology, "Effectiveness of Positive Psychology Interventions: A Systematic Review and Meta-Analysis." However, that review stated that "almost half of the studies (47%) included in our meta-analysis were rated as poor quality."[3]

CHAPTER 34
The Questionable Science of Microaggressions[1]

By Lee Jussim

Microaggressions have received a lot of attention recently from academics, activists, administrators in various organizations, and progressively-oriented laypeople. A "microaggression" has been defined as an act that conveys subtle animus or bias against someone in a traditionally marginalized group, with research in this area typically focusing on those directed toward racial minorities. Microaggression researchers claim to be able to detect hidden evils present in the everyday social interactions of Americans which help to perpetuate racial inequality. These claims align with a central tenet of critical race theory (CRT), that the contours of culture are saturated with hidden or subtle racism. These researchers believe that their findings can help to change society for the better.

If one were to read much of the psychological literature uncritically, one would come away with the conclusion that microaggressions are a serious problem. For example, prominent microaggression researcher Monnica Williams recently declared, "Data from academic institutions and the general public highly suggests that microaggressions are common."[2] Such a claim is common, but a closer look at the evidence on which such claims are made paints a different picture, revealing extreme methodological shortcomings.

While diversity scholars and administrators regularly promote lists of alleged microaggressions that they claim reflect unconscious racial bias, the scientific legitimacy of their claims is highly questionable. As my colleague Edward Cantu and I have argued:

> Microaggression research provides a veneer of scientific credibility to vested critical premises, as those studies have statistics, p-values,

and reliability coefficients, all useful for creating the appearance of scientific foundations for assumptions, so long as one does not examine the methodological details of the studies too closely.[3]

All across the U.S. there are educators, scholars, and administrators who have accepted the prevailing microaggression research as valid. I do not deny that microaggressions happen—the concept has some validity and describes a real phenomenon. The problem is that psychologists have made several big claims about microaggressions that go far beyond what the empirical research supports:

> Microaggression researchers' fundamental challenge is one they so far have failed to meet: they have not provided sound scientific bases for labeling as microaggressions most of the items they so label. This failing is the result of a problematic, yet necessary, aspect of their construct: in determining what acts count as microaggressions, researchers depend fundamentally on a metaphysical ascription of racist meaning to often facially innocuous acts and language.[4]

As the late psychologist and microaggression critic Scott Lilienfeld argued, while microaggression researchers have "generated a plethora of theoretically and socially significant questions that merit thoughtful examination in coming decades," their findings are "not close to being ready for widespread real-world application."[5] The question is not whether many microaggression research claims are *plausible*, but whether they have been *sufficiently demonstrated* yet. For many of the biggest claims, the answer is they have not.

There are multiple plausible reasons why such flawed claims have gained widespread acceptance. Among researchers, it could be sloppy research and/or confirmation bias. For non-psychologists, it could be that they assume that microaggression research is legitimate because of the support it has received from experts.

When Is Bad Treatment a Microaggression?

A microaggression is some sort of subtle racial insult, plausibly deniable as not racist. But people are treated badly all the time. The day I wrote this, I had to wait for a ridiculous amount of time to pay $13 for a small, desiccated hamburger at an airport. Interestingly, this is exactly the type of incident that leading microaggression researcher Derald Wing Sue and his colleagues highlighted as an example of a microaggression: "When a Latino couple is given poor service at a restaurant."[6] Psychologist Kevin Nadal used this item to assess people's experiences with microaggressions: "I received substandard service in stores compared to customers of other racial groups."[7]

As per Nadal, if I believed customers of other races were given better service, I should consider this a microaggression. Nonetheless, I am pretty sure my long wait for a bad burger was not a microaggression. And I am pretty sure it would not have been a microaggression if the burger shop provided the same overpriced, undersized, desiccated burger to a person of color (POC), notwithstanding Sue's analysis or Nadal's implication that if I attributed it to race it would be a micro-aggression.

What makes some sort of bad treatment a microaggression versus just another form of people treating each other badly sometimes? The treatment needs to be motivated by, express, and reinforce racism. Long waits for bad burgers could be a microaggression—if, say, the burger joint made POC wait longer to order. But if everyone has a long wait for bad overpriced burgers, there is no racism involved, so no microaggression.

How can one tell whether any particular insult or mean-spirited act or state-ment is a microaggression or just a person acting badly that has nothing to do with race (or any other identity)? One definition of microaggressions is "[B]rief and commonplace daily verbal, behavioral, or environmental indignities, whether intentional or unintentional, that communicate hostile, derogatory, or negative racial slights and insults toward people of color."[8] Did they literally mean "daily," or is it just a figure of speech? Sue and his colleagues clarify: minorities don't "just *occasionally* experience racial microaggressions. Rather, they are a constant, continuing, and cumulative experience" in their lives.[9] They are, supposedly, dis-turbingly common racial slights. Another more recent definition is that these are "deniable acts of racism that reinforce pathological stereotypes and inequitable social norms."[10]

As a *political* statement, this is fine. In politics, anything one says to advance one's agenda is fair game. But Williams' statement was published in a *scientific* psy-chology journal. As a scientific statement, it's a doozy. It states that microaggres-sions are racist, but deniable as not racist. They have clear causal effects—rein-forcing pathological stereotypes and inequitable social norms. This would seem to require researchers to do the following:

1. Establish that an insult/slight is motivated by racism.

2. Identify stereotypes that the insult/slight reinforces.

3. Empirically establish the "pathology" of the stereotype. Many stereo-types are simply accurate—on average, men are taller than women, Asian Americans have higher academic achievement than other groups, liberals are more likely to support abortion rights than are conservatives, etc. Even wrong stereotypes are not necessarily pathological—one sur-vey found that most liberals believe that the police kill at least 100 un-armed Black people per year and almost 40% believe the number is 1000 or more[11] (the real number in recent years is about 20, depending on how one counts and the year). This level of inaccuracy may be colloquially described as "nuts," but it is not "pathological" in any serious psycho-

logical sense. If not all stereotypes are pathological, one cannot presume pathology in any particular stereotype; it requires evidence.

4. Show that the microaggression actually strengthens those particular pathological stereotypes.

5. Identify relevant inequitable social norms.

6. Show that the microaggression reinforces those norms.

Given that all of this is in Williams's definition of microaggressions, to take this seriously scientifically, one would expect all of this to be empirically established for a particular slight before it would be labeled a microaggression. Instead, the reverse occurs—some act is labeled a "microaggression" by one or more scholars, then all of the ills attributed to microaggressions are presumed rather than demonstrated. Then the act is triumphantly paraded as scientific evidence of a microaggression.

The academic legerdemain by which the ills of microaggressions are implicitly imported or declared by fiat rather than empirically demonstrated has been exposed in each of the following articles:

- Kenneth R. Thomas, "Macrononsense in Multiculturalism," *American Psychologist* 63, no. 4 (2008): 274-275.
- Scott O. Lilienfeld, "Microaggressions: Strong Claims, Inadequate Evidence," *Perspectives on Psychological Science* 12, no. 1 (2017): 138-169.
- Edward Cantu and Lee Jussim, "Microaggressions, Questionable Science, and Free Speech," *Texas Review of Law & Politics* 26, no. 1 (2021): 217-267.

For example, Scott Lilienfeld[12] concluded that there is insufficient evidence to support any of these major claims by microaggression advocates:

1. They are operationalized with sufficient clarity and consensus to afford rigorous scientific investigation.

2. They are interpreted negatively by most or all minority group members.

3. They reflect implicitly prejudicial and implicitly aggressive motives.

4. They can be validly assessed using only respondents' subjective reports.

5. They exert an adverse impact on recipients' mental health.

The "Best" Studies

Some of the "best" studies often held up by microaggression advocates as establishing the validity of these main claims fail to do so. For example, in defending the microaggression concept in light of Lilienfeld's critique, Williams[13] invoked a study by Kanter et. al.[14]: it provides "important empirical support for something that diversity researchers knew all along—microaggressive acts are rooted in racist beliefs." This was a small-scale study, including only 33 Black and 118 White students, all from a single university. These numbers are so small and so unrepresentative of any population that the entire study should be viewed as little more than question-raising, regardless of other limitations, of which there are many, as I have elucidated previously.[15]

Williams[16] also extolled "Another important measure of microaggression frequency—the Racial and Ethnic Microaggressions Scale, which was validated with a large sample of African Americans, Hispanic Americans, Asian Americans, and multiracial participants."[17] Whether anyone should take Nadal's scale seriously, given its numerous limitations, is, however, another issue. For example. consider the item "[S]omeone avoided walking near me on the street because of my race." This requires mindreading.

However, one does not need to criticize the methods to understand how damaging Nadal's study was for claims extolling the frequency with which POC experience microaggressions. Respondents were provided with supposed examples of microaggressions and were then asked how frequently they had experienced such discrimination in the prior six months. For a vast majority of the items, most respondents reported that they either had not experienced the supposed microaggression in the past six months at all or, if they had, did so one to three times. In light of this result, it's difficult to characterize microaggressions as constituting a major social ailment. And that comes from taking his results at face value, which is probably not warranted.

Perhaps because my colleague Edward Cantu and I highlighted the strange state of affairs whereby an article extolled as testifying to the importance of microaggressions actually found just the opposite,[18] Williams recently[19] highlighted a study[20] as demonstrating that microaggressions are experienced very frequently by medical students. That is indeed what the authors claimed to have found: "Our first major finding was that medical students frequently experience microaggressions."[21] Unfortunately, the authors' claims notwithstanding, they did not assess "microaggressions." They assessed variations on "How often do you think has someone been mean to you?" Items included "People trivialize my ideas in classroom discussions" and "I am made to feel unwelcome in a group." There is nothing about race or racism here (or in their other questions). These types of experiences have probably happened to everyone. To be sure, though, I have no doubt that people are subject to subtle insults, and that *sometimes*, these are racially motivated. But if one wishes to know how often one cannot possibly obtain much of an answer from even the supposedly best published psychological science on the topic.

And that, gentle reader, is how peer-reviewed social science creates myths (much as it has about stereotype threat and implicit bias) about the power of problems that it has not actually established to exist to any substantial degree.

Major Flaws in Microaggression Research

For a deeper dive into the flaws with leading microaggression studies, see my 2021 article with coauthor Edward Cantu in the *Texas Review of Law & Politics* titled, "Microaggressions, Questionable Science, and Free Speech."[22] But the following represent what I consider to be some of the most important flaws in much of the leading microaggression research:

- Researchers state that several acts are microaggressions simply by claiming them to be so, without a proper scientific basis.
- No scientifically rigorous method exists for identifying whether many microaggressions have or have not occurred. Proof that a microaggression has occurred often largely depends on the subjective experience of the recipient, leaving the researcher (a) no way to verify what took place and (b) no way to verify the intent of the perpetrator.[23] Much of what researchers claim is not measurable or verifiable.
- Microaggression researchers argue that microaggressions cause harm, but in many instances this has not been empirically demonstrated.
- There is little evidence that most racial minorities consistently consider several microaggressions to be offensive.
- No demonstrated link exists between many microaggressions and racial bias on the part of the perpetrator[24] (see our particularly damning discussion of one study's microaggression scale in our aforementioned article).[25]
- For some microaggressions identified by researchers, it is claimed that even if the person who committed the act did not intend harm, and even if the recipient did not perceive the act in a negative manner, the microaggression itself was designed by somebody else with the intent of doing harm and/or upholding racial inequality:[26] "[T]he legitimacy of lists of microaggressions depends on researchers being able to divine objectively racist meaning in facially innocuous acts that others cannot detect."[27] These researchers argue that microaggressions are a "manifestation of the aggressive goals of the dominant group, taught to unwitting actors through. . . social mechanisms."[28] Yet these same researchers have not provided empirical support for these claims.
- No demonstrated link between many alleged microaggressions and reinforcement of racism/racial inequality.
- Many supposed microaggressions have multiple interpretations but are determined to be microaggressions by researchers because the researchers themselves privilege a particular interpretation.
    - ◊ If a person were to say things like "America is a melting pot" or

"I believe the most qualified person should get the job," for instance, there are multiple reasons why they might say this, some of which are motivated by prejudice and some of which are not.

◊ In fact, some microaggression researchers declare statements that reflect reasonable moral, political, and scientific disagreements as microaggressions because they are not aligned with a specific social justice perspective shared by those researchers.[29]

- Some researchers claim that microaggressions occur with a frequency that they have not empirically demonstrated.[30]

- Much of the microaggression research depends on small or unrepresentative samples and/or has not been replicated.

- Some microaggression researchers argue that "overt expressions of White racial superiority. . . [have] evolved into more subtle, ambiguous, and unintentional manifestations in American social, political, and economic life"[31] without providing empirical support for this claim.

- The term "microaggression" itself seems to be an example of concept creep.[32] To the layperson, "aggression" suggests hostility and intentionality, but microaggression researchers maintain that hostility and intentionality are not required for something to be categorized as a microaggression.

  ◊ The use of other concepts like "harm" and "discrimination" in this research might be considered examples of concept creep as well.

- Priming people to look for microaggressions in every social interaction could plausibly (a) be more damaging to racial minorities and socially corrosive to society than the infrequent experience of microaggressions in the first place and/or (b) not achieve any meaningful reduction in racial inequality in America.

- Microaggression research has gone through "idea laundering":

  1. Peer review processes are captured by ideologues,

  2. They allow flawed claims to be published in academic journals and books,

  3. Lack of awareness and/or confirmation bias causes other researchers with similar beliefs to cite and amplify those claims,

  4. As citations grow and grow, so does the alleged credibility of the original claim, as the number of citations can be used as proof of the concept's strength,

  5. The false impression is then created that ideologically and/or rhetorically useful claims have scientific credibility.[33]

At times, leading microaggression researchers have responded to reasonable and professional challenges to their work with pointed charges of implicit racism and accusations that critics have committed microaggressions by merely raising good faith scientific objections. Derald Wing Sue, for instance, responded to one critic by saying that:

> As a privileged [w]hite male, Thomas [a scholarly critic] failed to understand how European Americans have historically had the power to impose their own reality and define the reality of those with lesser power. That is perhaps one of the reasons why Thomas tried to impose his own reality so freely in his response.[34]

Similarly, Monnica Williams responded to a reasonable critique by saying that her critic's "research framework could itself constitute a microaggression."[35] Such charges could stigmatize and perhaps silence those who do not share the ideological assumptions of microaggression researchers,[36] and insulate microaggression research from healthy challenge. Scientists must address good-faith criticisms of their work on the merits, not simply by deflection with ad hominem impugnment of the integrity or decency of the critic.

I believe that much of microaggression research represents a form of activism which aims to advance a CRT narrative of social reality, even if it means using questionable research methods. As I have argued elsewhere:

> This methodological activism serves the primary role of bridging empirical gulfs in the research. Researchers invoke the 'experiential reality' of *some* POC as being somehow scientifically authoritative, or they reject calls for greater empirical support with the charge that such demands represent epistemological imperialism by critics seeking to, as white males, hold on to their 'power to define reality.'[37]

As I noted previously, the microaggression concept has gone through "idea laundering"—that is, despite resting on a weak empirical foundation, articles on the topic are allowed to be published in peer-reviewed academic journals by ideological peer reviewers and journal editors, they are then cited in other peer-reviewed work, and on and on with citation after citation in legitimate scientific venues. The concept ricochets through psychology scholarship and the broader culture, growing to a mass of citations that looks impressive and obscures the original weak claim, giving it unearned scientific credibility. To know better would require a deep dive into primary sources that most people lack the desire, time, and/or skills to undertake. Many people outside the field of psychology can be forgiven for not knowing this and making the mistake of assuming that peer-reviewed publication of a social science idea means the idea has by definition been thoroughly vetted scientifically. This *should* be the case, but unfortunately this cannot be assumed.

* * * * *

After reviewing scholarship in which psychologists attempt to confirm the legitimacy of prevailing microaggression research assumptions, and in which they debate the issue with dissenting psychologists, I conclude that the research is in its infancy and that the current operationalization of the concept in scholarship, social justice discourse, and education administration is significantly unwarranted:[38]

> When scientists speak, people listen, even if the science is unscientific. If scientists are going to declare a broad and indeterminate number of acts inherently subtly racist, and a critical mass of those in positions of power and influence are ideologically inclined to believe them, it is imperative that the claims not be grossly exaggerated. Instead, they must be grounded in solid scientific methodology. The [prevailing microaggression research] fails in this regard. After critical analysis, the [prevailing research] appears to be a project in attempting to retroactively validate initial ideological hunches, or, at best, to give voice to [racial minorities] by substituting the scientific method for the perceptions of *some* of them. Whichever it may be, it is clear that at this point, nobody—neither diversity administrators, academics, or journalists—should take currently propagated lists of microaggressions as representative of anything meaningful.[39]

I am also concerned about how the current propagation of the prevailing research assumptions, given its lack of adequate bases and therefore its limited utility, might have the primary effect of proving socially caustic—and therefore counterproductive in the quest for social justice—without countervailing benefits. It is hard to see how conditioning people to be paranoid in everyday social interactions is good for society if the social benefits are not demonstrable and significant.

Therefore, I recommend that scholars and administrators—and everyone else for that matter—generally refrain from relying on commonly propagated lists of microaggressions as reflecting anything meaningful, at least until psychologists perform the significant amount of empirical work left to be done to render the current microaggression paradigm as scientifically valid and useful.

CHAPTER 35
Problems with the IAT[1]

By Carol Tavris

WHAT DOES IT MEAN to be a racist?

- A person who thinks their "race" or ethnic group is better than everyone else's by virtue of genetic superiority, religion, customs, food, way of life, or beliefs.
- A person who fails to hire an applicant with the best qualifications if that person is from a different ethnic or religious group from the employer's.
- A person who is part of an institution that requires him or her to systematically target and discriminate against African Americans or other minorities.
- A person of any race, ethnicity, or religion who feels more comfortable with others who are like themselves.

or:

- A person whose score on the Implicit Association Test (IAT) reveals that he or she is unconsciously biased against Black people.

Some of the above? All of the above?

* * * * *

Throughout the first decade of this century, surveys repeatedly found that prejudiced attitudes—notably the once-common beliefs that Blacks were inferior to

Whites, women inferior to men, gay men and lesbians inferior to straights—had declined sharply, especially among young people. Surveys, of course, supposedly assess what you think. But what if they assess what you think *others* think you should think? What if they simply reflect your awareness that it isn't cool to reveal your actual negative feelings about another group? Self-reported data is inherently plagued with this problem. Thus, most social psychologists who study prejudice and discrimination focus on what people do, not what they *say* they *might* do. For example, when researchers have sent identical résumés to potential employers, varying only a name that indicates gender, or implies race (a Black-sounding name or membership in an African American organization), or mentions religious affiliation, many employers have revealed a bias in whom they choose to call for an interview.[2]

Of course, whether or not you choose to tell an interviewer that you would never willingly hire a [fill in the target person], you know what you feel about "those people." But some researchers have set their sights on capturing the prejudices that they believe lurk below awareness, hoping to identify *implicit*, unconscious negative feelings—not only in people who know they are prejudiced but don't want to admit it, but also among people who believe they are unprejudiced.

Nearly twenty years ago, a team of eminent psychological scientists, including Anthony Greenwald and Mahzarin Banaji, developed the Implicit Association Test, which measures the speed of people's positive and negative associations to a target group.[3] You sit at a console or your computer and are shown a series of faces you must sort as quickly as you can—pressing a left key for a Black face, say, and a right key for a White face. Now you have to do the same for a series of positive or negative words—press the left key for positive words (such as *triumph, joy, honest)* and the right key for negative words (such as *devil, maggot, failure*). Once you've mastered these sorting tasks, the faces and words are combined: Now, as quickly as possible, you must press the left key when you see a Black face or a positive word and the right key when you see a White face or a negative word. You are given a rapid set of combinations: *Black + triumph, Black + poison, White + peace, White + hatred*. The pairings get harder as you go along. Many people respond more quickly when White faces are paired with positive words and when Black faces are paired with negative words. That speed difference is said to be a measure of their implicitly racist attitudes toward African Americans because it's harder for their unconscious minds to link African Americans with positive words.

When the research first appeared all those years ago, my colleague Carole Wade and I were disinclined to report it in our introductory psychology textbook. It was unclear what those microsecond "associations" meant; it seemed a leap to call it a measure of prejudice; at best it seemed simply to be capturing a familiar cultural association or stereotype, in the same way that people would be quicker to pair *bread + butter* than *bread + avocado*. A person of any age might be aware of negative associations between old people and mental decline without being prejudiced against old people in general. One team got an IAT effect by matching target faces with nonsense words and neutral words that had no evaluative connotations at all. They concluded that the IAT does not measure emotional evaluations of the target but rather the *salience* of the word associated with it—how much it stands out—and negative words attract more attention. When they corrected for these factors, the presumed unconscious prejudice faded away.[4]

So Carole and I figured that the IAT would travel the route of other hot ideas that cooled off in the face of failed replications or more plausible interpretations. Indeed, had the measure's originators simply said they had found a modest but interesting association between various groups and words culturally linked with them, that might have been that. Instead, over the years, the success of the IAT grew so rapidly, spilling into the public arena with such an enormous splash, that textbook authors (let alone the public, college administrators, and politicians) could no longer avoid it. To date, more than 17 million people have taken the test online (at "Project Implicit"),[5] and it has also been given to students, business managers, employees, and countless others to identify their alleged prejudices toward Blacks, Asians, women, old people, people with disabilities, and other groups. I asked a young friend, one of the least prejudiced and most open-minded humans on the planet, if he knew about the IAT, and he said yes, he'd taken it online. "What in the world for?" I asked. "To see if I have an unconscious bias," he said.

Carole and I were awakened from our somnambulance by Malcolm Gladwell, who set off our skeptical buzzers on high alert. Gladwell, who is biracial, took the IAT and learned that he was prejudiced against Black people. In an interview with Oprah Winfrey, he said: "The person in my life [his mother] who I love more than almost anyone else, is Black, and here I was taking a test, which said, frankly, I wasn't too crazy about Black people, you know?" A gay activist said she was stunned to learn that "her own mind contained stronger gay = bad associations than gay = good associations." But the *pièce de résistance* was that one of the developers of the IAT, Mahzarin Banaji, a woman of color who was born and raised in India, reported that she herself "failed" the racial IAT, revealing antiblack associations that she consciously repudiates.[6]

Now this is curious. Why jump to indict oneself instead of saying, "Uh oh, maybe something's wrong with the test?" Banaji and Greenwald might have considered the possibility that they got too enthusiastic too soon, claiming more for their test than it warranted. However, by the time their 2013 book for the public appeared, *Blindspot: The Hidden Biases of Good People*,[7] they had much invested in the IAT; and, in their admirable zeal to educate people about the persistence of prejudice, they began claiming more and more about the test's significance and relevance. For their part, many laypeople accepted the IAT's findings because of the great power attributed to methods that purport to uncover what our brains are doing without our knowledge. How do I know what my unconscious is thinking? By definition, it's unconscious! Clearly, the test knows more than I do, even if I do love my mother!

If the IAT were being used solely as an instrument to generate discussions of what prejudice is and is not, few would object. Having a "hidden bias" is not, in and of itself, a sign of prejudice; it's a sign of having a human brain. What social psychologists call the "in-group bias"—a feeling of comfort with, and preference for, people who are like us—is a universal phenomenon, undoubtedly one that evolved to aid human survival by binding us to our groups. But it does not inevitably produce "out-group hostility" or discrimination against those who are unlike us.

Unfortunately, as the IAT's reputation grew, claims about what this test was revealing began to outstrip the data. The IAT was no longer said to be capturing an "association"; not even merely a "bias"; but a prejudice —especially racism. And not just racism, but *discrimination*—the willingness to act on that prejudice. The Project Implicit website warns: "When we relax our active efforts to be egalitarian, our implicit biases can lead to discriminatory behavior, so it is critical to be mindful of this possibility if we want to avoid prejudice and discrimination."[8]

And so we come to the crux of the matter: does the IAT really capture unconscious prejudices? Can the test predict whether people will actually behave in a biased or discriminatory way? The evidence is now pretty clear that the answers to both are "no."[9] When people are asked to predict their responses toward different groups on the IAT, they are highly accurate— regardless of whether they were told that implicit attitudes are true prejudices or culturally learned associations. People's scores aren't reliable, either; they might score "highly biased" one week and get a different result two weeks later. And as for the IAT's ability to predict behavior—the ultimate measure of any test's scientific validity—meta-analyses of hundreds of studies on many thousands of people find that the evidence linking IAT scores with behavior is weak to nonexistent. "The IAT provides little insight into who will discriminate against whom," wrote Frederick Oswald and his colleagues in a 2013 meta-analysis, and it provides no more information than just asking people if they are biased.[10] They concluded that the correlation between people's IAT scores and their behavior is so small as to be trivial. Greenwald and Banaji countered that statistically small effects can have "societally large effects."[11]

In the final analysis, I think what is most problematic about the IAT is that it directs people's attention to their supposed unconscious feelings, leaving many puzzled and worried that they might be awful racists without knowing it, and without knowing what they are supposed to do about it. It confuses normal cognitive biases with bigotry. And it locates the problem of discrimination in people's unconscious minds, not in the systemic patterns of racism that deserve our far greater attention and search for remedies.

In his meticulous investigation of the IAT, Jesse Singal concluded that:

> [A]fter almost 20 years and millions of dollars' worth of IAT research, the test has a markedly unimpressive track record relative to the attention and acclaim it has garnered. Leading IAT researchers haven't produced interventions that can reduce racism or blunt

its impact. They haven't told a clear, credible story of how implicit bias, as measured by the IAT, affects the real world. They have flip-flopped on important, baseline questions about what their test is or isn't measuring. And because the IAT and the study of implicit bias have become so tightly coupled, the test's weaknesses have caused collateral damage to public and academic understanding of the broader concept itself. . . [S]crutinizing the IAT and holding it to the same standards as any other psychological instrument isn't a sign that someone doesn't take racism seriously: It's exactly the opposite.[12]

How ironic that this well-intended effort to illuminate a dark side of our natures now obfuscates the very thing we're trying to understand. And it's a story with an all-too-familiar lesson for scientists and other skeptics: we can't let our wish for a method or a finding to be right block our ability to evaluate it critically, and to change our minds when the evidence dictates.

CHAPTER 36
The Gender Identity Debate[1]

By Lisa Selin Davis

Among the most contentious topics in America today is that of kids who identify as transgender: how to understand them, treat them, and make policy based on them. The number of kids with gender dysphoria (GD)—marked distress at an incongruence between gender identity and biological sex—has risen exponentially in the past decade.[2] So has the demand for what have come to be known as "gender-affirming" medical interventions: puberty blockers, often followed by cross-sex hormones and sometimes "gender-affirming" surgeries, including the irreversible "top surgery" (in one study, a 13-year-old received a double mastectomy for gender dysphoria)[3] and sometimes "bottom surgery" such as vaginoplasty.[45]

This medical model, originated in The Netherlands and known as the "Dutch protocol," was restricted to kids who had "suffered from lifelong extreme gender dysphoria, are psychologically stable and live in a supportive environment."[6] The protocol was adopted and adapted in the United States beginning in 2007, when the first pediatric gender clinic opened in Boston.[7] For years, it was challenging for anyone to access this treatment: The practitioners were few, the stigma enormous. But now, perhaps with increasing acceptance and perhaps lured by the glow of financial opportunities,[8] the number of gender clinics has exploded.[9] Some of these new practitioners don't follow the Dutch protocol, opting for the affirmative model, in which young children are sometimes socially transitioned and subsequently allowed to medically and surgically transition using the informed consent model now common for adults—less evaluation, more affirmation. The model aims "to listen to the child and decipher with the help of parents or caregivers what the child is communicating about both gender identity and gender expressions."[10]

Many sources of mainstream media, most notably those with a political bent, present this issue as a left/right battle. They portray liberals as supporting trans kids and their access to medical interventions in order to save their lives.[11] They present anyone who objects to these treatments as conservative, transphobic bigots, who call these treatments experimental and dangerous[12] and want to ban all medical interventions.[13] The two tweets in Figure 36.1 capture the sentiments of these polarizing sides. What was just a few years ago a topic of debate is now a test of loyalty.[14]

Figure 36.1 Example of Polarization in Gender Identity Debate.
Lisa Selin Davis, "Trans Matters: An Overview of the Debate, Research, and Policies," *Skeptic Magazine*, May 25, 2022, https://www.skeptic.com/reading_room/trans-matters-overview-debate-research-policies/.

This binary framing politicizes the scientific research and makes it hard for both laypeople and medical and psychological practitioners to ask questions and find answers about how GD develops; how to treat it; its relation to transgender identity; and how safe and effective the treatments are. How should the *primum non nocere* principle be applied in these cases? Is "do no harm" postponing hormones and surgery until adulthood, or is it easing present suffering through starting medical treatment in adolescence or younger?

In fact, there are many viewpoints on how to answer those questions, including those of liberals and trans people with concerns about the medical model and conservatives who embrace it. Meanwhile, some of the most experienced practitioners don't want to ban medical interventions, but they do believe there are abuses and misuses of them.[15]

Some young people are helped by medical interventions, at least in the short term,[16] since we have little long-term data on those treated since 2007; others are deeply harmed by them.[17] Some people look at the growth of gender-affirming care and see transgender people finally getting the treatments they want or need. Others see a medical scandal of epic proportions. Some believe medicalizing gender dysphoric youth is child abuse; others think withholding it is child abuse. Somewhere in between are the multiple and competing narratives that most of the mainstream media has ignored. Here are just a few of them.

Being Trans and Having Gender Dysphoria Are Not Interchangeable

One of the biggest challenges with even talking about these issues comes from the lack of common language. Gender, for instance, can be a synonym for biological sex, or it can mean expectations and norms based on biological sex, or an internal sense of self, separate from biological sex: that is, gender identity.

Trans or transgender is an umbrella term that can include anyone defying gender norms or people formerly known as transsexuals, who change their bodies to appear as the opposite sex (or, increasingly, some people who identify as non-binary and change their bodies to appear ambiguously sexed).

It's commonly accepted that not all trans people have gender dysphoria. Less accepted is the idea that someone with gender dysphoria isn't necessarily trans, or that identifying as trans, or having gender dysphoria, may not persist. But as the following research shows, the latter has often been the case.

A New and Growing Cohort

In much of the developed world, referrals to gender clinics and diagnoses of gender dysphoria have been on a steep incline in a short period of time.

A study of youth referred for puberty blockers and hormones in Canada showed a tiny number of young people—the majority male—sought care until 2007 at a gender clinic in British Columbia (see Figure 36.2).[18] Since then, the number of referrals has grown more than tenfold, and the majority are now female. The Netherlands saw a similar trend.[19] The U.K.'s Gender Identity Development Service reports an almost 4,000% increase in ten years,[20] also shifting from majority males to females, the great bulk of them teenagers. In the past, the majority of referrals were young children or adult males.[21]

Many of these teens have co-occurring mental health issues,[22] like depression, anxiety, trauma,[23] or eating disorders, or are neuro-diverse (for example, ADHD, dyslexia, or on the autism spectrum), and they appear to differ from prior cohorts, who had childhood-onset GD. There is almost no research on this population, which has prompted some people to ask if it is ethical or safe to apply a medical protocol designed for a different kind of patient to them.[24]

What accounts for this demographic shift? Some argue it is increasing awareness and acceptance of trans people, and access to language and information; perhaps gender dysphoria and transgender identities were far more common than people knew. Others say it is the influence of social media, popular culture, and social contagion, leading some struggling people to self-diagnose with gender dysphoria and land on transition as the answer. A doctor and public health researcher, Lisa Littman, conducted an exploratory study based on parental reports[25] (a common method) and found entire peer groups declaring transgender identities after social media immersion. She coined the term "rapid-onset gender dysphoria" (ROGD) to describe the phenomenon of this new population in a dispassionate, descriptive way.

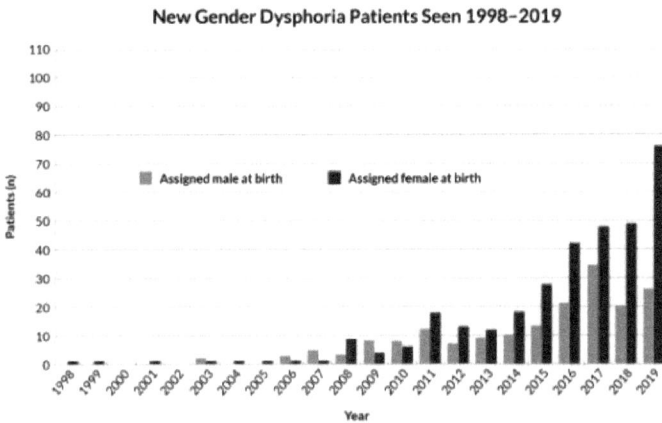

New Gender Dysphoria Patients Seen 1998–2019

Figure 36.2 Gender Dysphoria Over Time.
Lisa Selin Davis, "Trans Matters: An Overview of the Debate, Research, and Policies," *Skeptic Magazine*, May 25, 2022, https://www.skeptic.com/reading_room/trans-matters-overview-debate-research-policies/.

Many object to the term and its implications, categorizing ROGD as a fake diagnosis invented by the right wing to undermine teens' transitions.[26] Some papers[27] and groups say data do not support ROGD and suggest not using the term because it can be employed to deter people and politicians from supporting gender-affirming medical care. Some clinicians I've talked to don't want to use the term ROGD because of its political baggage but may acknowledge that this is a new and complex population that's much harder to treat. Still others don't want there to be any research into why someone identifies as trans, because they feel it presents being trans as a pathology, a problem that needs solving, instead of presenting trans identities as variations, not deviations.

The Unspoken Relationship Between Gender and Sexuality

Under the current zeitgeist, gender is often defined as an internal sense of self, unrelated to sexuality. But decades of psychological and anthropological research suggest that gender and sexuality are often deeply intertwined.[28]

There is, for example, which sex you identify as and which sex you are attracted to. But it's even more complicated than that. So called "third genders"[29] like the *muxes* of Mexico, the Samoan *fa'afafine*, Brazil's *travesti*, or the *hijra* of India are androphilic (that is: attracted to men), traditionally feminine males.[30] These alternative categories seem to protect feminine androphilic males in places where open homosexuality is either illegal or not tolerated, but gender nonconformity is. Some of Samoa's masculine, gynephilic (attracted to women) females, who may be referred to as butch lesbians elsewhere, have referred to themselves as trans men; they seem to have less acceptance than *fa'afafine*.

In Europe and North America, some psychologists and sexologists working in gender clinics in the 1980s and 1990s divided those seeking sex reassignment into two main categories[31] of patients: "homosexual transsexuals" and "non-homosexual transsexuals." The former group tended to include traditionally feminine boys and traditionally masculine girls, who were so from a very young age, and were later attracted to members of their own sex. In several long-term studies, most prepubescent children referred to clinics, for what was then known as gender identity disorder, "desisted;" that is, the majority were gay, not trans.[32]

The latter cohort, "non-homosexual transsexuals," often didn't present until puberty or much later, and rarely had a history of childhood gender nonconformity, cross-sex identity, or dysphoria. Most got an erotic charge from imagining themselves as women, which manifested in everything from wanting to wear women's clothes to masturbating to the idea of themselves lactating or menstruating. Sexologist and psychologist Ray Blanchard called this "autogynephilia," or "love of oneself as a woman" (Many trans women object to the idea of autogynephilia and feel it paints them as perverted, though Blanchard meant it only as a descriptor and not a moral judgment.[33] Some autogynephiles, however, embrace it).[34]

There are many more than two types of trans people now, including today's cohort of young people who tend to have much more complex mental health issues. But today's youth are also generally taught that gender and sexuality are not linked, when past research shows transgender identity or gender dysphoria were often related in some way to sexuality. There can be a connection of some kind, but no causation.

High Desistance Rates in Older Research

As noted, in past studies the vast majority of kids with early-onset (prepubertal) gender dysphoria desisted,[35] and many grew up to be gay. In a recently published 15-year follow-up study of boys referred to a gender clinic for what was then called gender identity disorder, 88% of them desisted, and 63.6% were later same-sex attracted.[36]

But those kids were not socially transitioned to live as the opposite sex or another social category, as many children are today. Some clinicians believe that social transition will increase the chances of more severe dysphoria at puberty, therefore creating medicalized trans children who would otherwise have been gay.[37] One study noted an association between persistence and social transition.[38] Some more recent research shows much higher rates of persistence—96% in one case—which likely includes socially transitioned kids. And the older desistance research has been critiqued for a number of reasons, including that it is "built upon bad statistics, bad science, homophobia and transphobia."[39]

While some research notes that it appears that "the persistence, insistence, and consistency of statements, and behaviours in childhood"[40] helps predict whether GD will continue or not, no clinician, child, or parent can know *for certain* how to forecast from childhood GD or from gender nonconformity. There is no clinical test.

The proposed eighth edition of the Standards of Care for how to treat trans and gender-diverse people, created by the World Professional Association of Transgender Health, notes that childhood gender diversity is normal. WPATH writes: "Diverse gender expressions in children cannot always be assumed to reflect a transgender identity or gender incongruence."[41] However, they do not mention desistance.

It used to be thought that the older a young person came out as transgender or experienced gender dysphoria, the more likely they'd persist, but that was perhaps because some of those studied were autogynephilic men whose sexual orientation was intertwined with gender, and sexuality is generally considered to be difficult to change. But today, as more teens come out, the majority girls, that research does not necessarily apply.

Other Countries are Rethinking Medical Approaches—Not for Political Reasons

Several countries, or major medical centers in those countries, are banning or limiting puberty blockers, cross-sex hormones, and gender-affirming surgeries for children. Finland has severely restricted the practice,[42] and in at least one pediatric gender clinic in Western Australia a patient now needs a court order to medically transition.[43]

The Royal Australian and New Zealand College of Psychiatrists (RANZCP) changed its position in 2021 to promote thorough mental health evaluation before proceeding medically. The move doesn't come from politics but a review of the evidence. Their guidance states that, "There is a paucity of quality evidence on the outcomes of those presenting with gender dysphoria. In particular, there is a need for better evidence in relation to outcomes for children and young people."[44]

Sweden's Karolinska Hospital and several other Swedish hospitals have stopped providing gender-affirming medical treatment for kids under 18, except in clinical trials.[45] The reason? Several kids were severely harmed in what they called "healthcare-related injuries," including a teenager with osteoporosis, who stopped growing. Per *Medscape*, "This decision comes amid growing unease in some quarters regarding the speed at which hormonal treatment of children with gender dysphoria has become accepted as the norm in many countries, despite what critics say is a lack of evidence of any benefit, plus known harms, of treatment." A young woman named Keira Bell successfully won a case against the U.K.'s gender identity development service for facilitating the transition she came to regret,[46] arguing that children could not understand what they were consenting to. Medical interventions for under-16s were briefly stopped, save for those with court orders. But the ruling was overturned; the court said "it was for clinicians rather than the court to decide on competence [to consent]."[47]

As a 2015 article in the *Journal of Adolescent Health* noted, "no consensus exists whether to use these early medical interventions."[48]

Trans, Suicide, and Mental Health: Confounding Variables

A paper in *Pediatrics* suggested an "inverse association between treatment with pubertal suppression during adolescence and lifetime suicidal ideation among transgender adults who ever wanted this treatment,"[49] though some have noted the data came from a "low-quality survey,"[50] and were based on a convenience, not representative, sample of self-selected participants (the same reason the ROGD survey is often critiqued). As the paper's author noted, "Limitations include the study's cross-sectional design, which does not allow for determination of causation." Other criticisms were that the paper didn't establish that people had actually received the treatment, since many claimed to be over 18 when receiving the treatment.

Still, the finding is not surprising considering many young people have been told these drugs will make them feel better and they desperately want them, so a placebo effect may account for those provisional outcomes.

A recent study in the *Journal of Adolescent Health* examined "associations among access to GAHT [Gender Affirming Hormone Therapy] with depression, thoughts of suicide, and attempted suicide among a large sample of transgender and nonbinary youth."[51] The authors found that those who wanted puberty blockers and didn't get them had worse mental health than those who wanted them and got them. This, too, was a convenience sample. However, the participants' mental health scores were low, all around. Some 44% of those who received puberty blockers (PBs) seriously considered suicide in the past year, versus 57% of those who didn't receive them. Fifteen percent of those who received PBs attempted suicide, versus 23% of those who didn't. Another and more likely explanation is the increasing number of trans youth with co-occurring mental health issues, so the trans variable may be confounding, not causal.

Many people believe that youth are at risk if their pronouns aren't respected. The Trevor Project reported that "Transgender and nonbinary youth who reported having pronouns respected by all of the people they lived with attempted suicide at half the rate of those who did not have their pronouns respected by anyone with whom they lived."[52] Almost every media outlet notes that trans and gender dysphoric kids have a higher rate of suicidal ideation, and one study found an attempted suicide rate of over 50% for female-to-male adolescents.[53] Another study found that gender-referred children were 8.6 times more likely than non-referred children to self-harm or attempt suicide.[54] These rates, however, are similar to those of children with other mental health struggles.[55] So, again, transgender identity, or gender dysphoria, could be confounder variables, not causal.

These studies do not establish *causation* between transition and preventing suicide, only correlation. The research on suicide is in no way conclusive, and some parents have reported that clinicians told children that if they didn't transition, they'd be at risk for suicide; self-fulfilling prophecy may be at work considering how contagious suicidal ideation is among young people. Most recent studies are not long term enough to know lasting effects of medical intervention on suicidal ideation, depression, or dysphoria.

As well, even the findings linking trans identities to suicide are not always replicated. One Swedish study of over 6,000 people with GD found only 0.6%, or 0.006, had died by suicide, and notes that "people with different psychiatric conditions generally have even higher risks of suicide than people with gender dysphoria."[56] The U.K.'s Gender Identity Development Service notes suicide is "extremely rare."[57]

One recent study found both positive and negative psychological changes correlated to puberty blockers.[58] A study of adults (albeit with research from 1973 through 2003, when there was less cultural understanding of trans issues), showed "mortality for sex-reassigned persons was higher during follow-up," post-surgical transition and that "Sex-reassigned persons also had an increased risk for suicide attempts."[59]

Why the Dutch Protocol Does Not Apply to Today's Demographic

We're often told that medical interventions alleviate gender dysphoria and that regret is rare. In a 2014 study of kids medically transitioned using the Dutch protocol, most found their gender dysphoria improved and their psychosocial functioning was akin to their gender conforming peers, at least in the early assessments[60] (There is, though, a critique of the study's methodology).[61]

These kids, however, were all carefully assessed and thoroughly informed—and excluded if they had other serious mental health issues. Most had childhood onset GD and were not socially transitioned.[62] The way some clinics operate today is much different, assuming that any child who says they are trans is so. As Thomas

Steensma of the Center of Expertise on Gender Dysphoria at Amsterdam UMC, an expert in the Dutch protocol, told a Dutch newspaper in 2021: "the rest of the world is blindly adopting our research."[63]

Children in the U.S. may still need support letters from therapists or doctors to access hormones or surgeries, but the practitioners may not be carefully evaluating children or directing those with co-occurring mental health issues or trauma, who may not appear to be good candidates for medical transition, toward non-medical options.

Unclear Long-term Physical Effects of Medical Transition

Puberty blockers are often discussed as a way to "hit the pause button" on puberty and give kids time to decide if they want to proceed medically. But they are largely the first step in medicalization. In one study, 98% of kids went from puberty blockers to cross-sex hormones.[64] Though puberty blockers are often discussed as reversible—meaning a child will go through their endogenous puberty if he or she goes off them—the long-term effects are either unknown or negative, impacting bone density[65] and fertility.[66] Little is known about lasting effects on brain development or cardiovascular health.

The safety of and satisfaction with hormonal and surgical transition for children is largely unknown, and wildly variant for adults. Many participants in studies were lost to follow up,[67] which can skew conclusions and outcomes. One study "found insufficient evidence to determine the efficacy or safety of hormonal treatment approaches for transgender women in transition."[68] Medical transition has been linked to reduced sexual function,[69] corrective surgery,[70] incontinence,[71] and heart attacks.[72]

That doesn't mean some transsexual adults (those who have had medical interventions) don't find the complications worth it; some studies show improved happiness post-medical transition.[73] The question of whether children can understand and consent to these complications and lifelong changes is hotly debated.

No One Knows the Rates of Regret, But the Number of Detransitioners is Rising

The dominant narrative is that regret and detransition—returning to living as one's biological sex, post medical transition—are rare. One review of studies claimed that less than one percent of those who'd had gender-affirming surgeries regretted them[74] (A rebuttal to the study called it erroneous, inflated, and miscalculated).[75]

Most (but not all) of those study subjects were carefully evaluated, sometimes forced to participate in the "real life test," living as the opposite sex before being allowed by therapists and doctors to transition, to try to establish that it is what they really wanted. If they detransitioned later, it was sometimes attributed to stigma, access to care, or financial problems—external, not internal, issues.

But the number of people detransitioning because of internal regrets is grow-ing. They are speaking out on social media and forming networks and groups. A new study in the *Journal of Analytical Psychology*,[76] as well as a new study on 100 detransitioners by Lisa Littman in the *Archives of Sexual Behavior*,[77] find that more people are detransitioning because they realized that they never should have al-tered their bodies in the first place. Littman found that 71% of respondents said that they believed that medical transition was the only path toward feeling better; did not want to be associated with their natal sex; or said their body felt wrong. They understood transition as the way to "become their true selves."

Participants said they experienced pressure to transition; therapists presented transition as a panacea; doctors pushed hard for drugs and surgery; and friends told them they should transition. Some 60% of detransitioners returned to identi-fying as their biological sex once they understood that the biological categories of male and female could accommodate them. More than half of respondents said they had not been properly evaluated by doctors or therapists, and 65.3% said their evaluations did not investigate whether trauma played a role in their desire to transition. Almost three-quarters did not report their regret to their doctors or therapists.

We are not keeping careful statistics on detransition or regret—or satisfac-tion—so we don't know how common or rare it is. Littman's study, like many in this field, is based on a convenience sample, so while it offers some glimpses into this phenomenon, it is not conclusive. She advises: "More research is needed to understand this population, determine the prevalence of detransition as an out-come of transition, meet the medical and psychological needs of this population, and better inform the process of evaluation and counseling prior to transition."

Exploratory Therapy Is Not Conversion Therapy

Conversion therapy—trying to reprogram sexuality— has been clearly shown to be ineffective and harmful for gay people and is considered unethical.[78] Some people claim that providing therapy for kids who identify as transgender is akin to conversion therapy—exploring rather than accepting, they say, assumes it's worse to be transgender than cisgender (meaning having a gender identity that aligns with biological sex). At least 25 states have some kind of ban on conversion thera-py, though the term is ill-defined.[79]

But others argue that conversion therapy for sexuality is very different than exploratory therapy to examine the source of gender dysphoria since, as outlined above, there are many different sources, and many people do not suffer from it persistently.[80] And accepting oneself as gay requires no permanent medical inter-vention. Some therapists who practice exploratory therapy are afraid to identify themselves, lest they be labeled transphobic. The newly formed Gender Explor-atory Therapy Association helps connect kids suffering from gender dysphoria with a therapist who will neither affirm nor convert.[81]

Supporting children who identify as transgender, or who are gender dysphoric, is correlated with improved mental health outcomes.[82] But support is not synonymous with affirmation, nor does it imply lack of careful evaluation and/or exploratory therapy. As schools sometimes facilitate secret social transitions without informing parents, and some activists advocate for family abolition—believing families are standing in the way of children's transition and mental health—some families are divided when a child comes out, much the way the country is. The more the debate is presented as right versus left, or transphobia versus trans rights activism, rather than science versus belief, the more harm will be done to families and kids, who deserve the right to know all the information in order to make an educated decision.

What's clear about the evidence is that it's not very clear at all.

CHAPTER 37
The Alt-Left and Moral Righteousness[1]

By Kevin McCaffree

> The surest way to work up a crusade in favor of some good cause is to promise people they will have a chance of maltreating someone. To be able to destroy with good conscience, to be able to behave badly and call your bad behavior 'righteous indignation'—this is the height of psychological luxury, the most delicious of moral treats.
> —Aldous Huxley[2]

The Alt-Left and the Alt-Right are secular religious ideologies. For both, if only the right group is subjugated and the government purged of their influence, history will take a new turn toward righteousness. The similarities between the two ideologies are troubling. The Alt-Left and Alt-Right are two panicked grasps for power, sharing a seething distrust of people, government, and society. I will endeavor to explain these dynamics as I see them.

The Ideology of the Alt-Left

The Alt-Left's essential axioms originate in the righteous fervor for universal equality which animated the French Revolution and that has probably animated many more revolutions lost to historical description. Subsequently, the Alt-Left has been tinged with large doses of the Marxist view that history is a dialectic between the economic oppressor and the economically oppressed, and of Jacques Derrida's view that a proper deconstruction of culture reveals oppression as multi-dimensional (and culturally ubiquitous), not merely class-based. Michele Foucault's insistence on how dominant groups subtly and clandestinely institutionalize their power and control underwrites the Alt-Left's claims of systemic oppression. Underlying all of this is a Nietzschean view that life is merely a ruthless struggle for power enmeshing all people. The Frankfurt School, Critical Race Theory, and Feminist Theory have been very influential in laundering this combination of cynical philosophies into university social science and humanity departments.

Allow me to give some more context.

The German Frankfurt School entered the American public conscience in the 1960s. As regards the Alt-Left, Theodor Adorno and Herbert Marcuse are probably the most influential figures. For Adorno,[3] capitalism failed spectacularly to address the most important human needs; instead of selling community and self-actualization, Western markets sold mass produced cars, clothes, and TVs. Satiated with their shiny objects and their sanitized media, the masses were forever at risk of being suddenly mobilized by future fascists. Adorno had observed World War II carefully and, to his mind, the civilizational soil was again fertile for more mass bloodshed, and the capitalist economy had made this so.

To prevent this imminent return of fascism, Adorno and his colleagues pioneered the use of statistics in personality studies to develop the "California Fascist Scale," a questionnaire used to spot such dangerous individuals. In Adorno's mind, fascists were an intrinsic outgrowth of the Right's desire for power and dominance—the ever-innocent Left had no choice but to identify and purge them from society.

Herbert Marcuse also shaped Alt-Left ideology, specifically its need to deny public platforms to those regarded as fascists. In an essay dedicated to his students at Brandeis, "Repressive Tolerance," Marcuse implores the Left not to allow any public platforms to non-Leftists, "because they are impeding, if not destroying, the chances of creating an existence without fear and misery." Until the wrongs of history are righted, true justice requires marginalizing and suppressing anyone not aggressively advocating for revolutionary retribution. In Marcuse's words:

> [The oppressed's] continued existence is more important than the preservation of abused rights and liberties which grant constitutional powers to those who oppress these minorities. It should be evident by now that the exercise of civil rights by those who don't have them presupposes the withdrawal of civil rights from those who prevent their exercise, and that liberation of the Damned of the Earth presupposes suppression not only of their old but also of their new masters.[4]

Critical theories and the Alt-Left they help constitute contain kernels of truth in the form of empirical observations. The Alt-Right does as well. The problem is in how these ideologies interpret those empirical observations. And both will do so hopelessly, cynically, fatuously.

For example, critical theorists will point to U.S. Census[5] data that show median Black household wealth (not income) in the U.S. is only about 6% ($7,113) of median White household wealth ($111,146) and that median Latino household wealth is only 7.5% ($8,348) of median White household wealth. Regarding gender,[6] the wealth of a median single woman aged 18-64 in the U.S. is 31.6% ($3,210) that of the median man's ($10,150). Worse, the median Black woman owns only 0.007% ($200) of the wealth of the median White man ($28,900). These disparities, they argue, have countless downstream consequences for educational, political, and occupational access. These disparities are also intergenerational, passed on from parents to children through inheritance and social contacts.

The violence and suffering that maintained such disparities for centuries haunts women and minorities in ways scarcely imaginable to the privileged, White, heterosexual man. Columbia Law School professor Kimberlé Williams Crenshaw is credited with developing the concept of "intersectionality," the idea that peoples' identities can render them susceptible to varying, continuous, interlocking systems of oppression.

Crenshaw provided legal counsel in the early 1990s for Anita Hill, the woman who accused Clarence Thomas, a nominee for the Supreme Court at the time, of sexual harassment.[7] During this hearing, Crenshaw noticed how Hill's womanhood was acknowledged as relevant, while her Blackness was ignored. Crenshaw felt that the legal system wasn't prepared to grapple with the full context of the situation; this was not only a woman accusing a powerful man of harassment, but also a Black woman who was challenging taboos about harassment within the Black community. These forms of oppression—being a woman and being a Black woman—thus "intersected" or "interlocked" in a way that obscured the true seriousness and inequity of the situation. Thomas was, of course, subsequently appointed to the Supreme Court, which Crenshaw regarded as clear evidence that the legal system either didn't detect or didn't care about intersectional oppression.

In the meantime, other legal scholars such as Derrick Bell[8] and Richard Delgado[9] made general accusations about Western history and about the moral impotence of Western institutions. Delgado, for example, argued the West's very concept of "morality" was merely a tool to engineer self-perpetuating systems of White supremacy. Moral justifications had been provided for slavery and colonization, and we have subliminally inherited these presuppositions about superiority, difference, and naturalized disadvantage. Other scholars in this area take aim at the criminal justice system, claiming that mass incarceration of non-violent drug offenses is intended by those in power to decimate Black and Hispanic communities both economically and socially.[10]

Patricia Hill Collins,[11] Peggy McIntosh,[12] and many others have carried these views about intersectionality and Western moral destitution into sociology and social science more broadly. Collins, for example, regards race, class, gender, sexuality, ethnicity/nation, ability, and age as interlocking identities that subject people to varying levels of financial, political, and social oppression. Redressing all of these indignities of Western society requires a veritable undoing of the social order, an untying of countless knots of oppression. In the words of Alt-Left hero Susan Sontag: "The white race is the cancer of human history."[13]

Since the 1960s, students all across the U.S. in social science and humanities programs have been reliably presented with an "Alt-Left" view of the world. This ideology manages to fill many of the gaps left by the recession of Christianity and manages to direct anger and shame toward a seemingly legitimate target. White, male, heterosexual privilege is unconscionable evil while true moral wisdom, reluctantly gleaned from the indignities of oppression, is salvation.

* * * * *

In a later chapter in this book I explain what I perceive to be the causes of both the Alt-Left and the Alt-Right. The answer, in brief, is that secularization, increasing income and wealth inequality, along with declining trust and civic engagement, are giving rise to charismatic authorities with dark utopian dreams on both the Left and the Right.

IV. I DON'T KNOW — THEREFORE, ALIENS

CHAPTER 38
Common Traits of Conspiracy Thinkers[1]

By Joshua Hart

Conspiracy theories have been cooked up for ages, but for the first time in history, we have a president who has regularly endorsed them. Assuming that President Donald Trump's preoccupation is genuine, he shares it with many fellow Americans. What explains it?

I'm a psychologist who studies, among other things, people's worldviews and belief systems. I wanted to figure out why some people gobble up conspiratorial explanations while others dismiss them as the raving of lunatics.

Consistency in Views

By and large, people gravitate toward conspiracy theories that seem to affirm or validate their political views. Republicans are vastly more likely than Democrats to believe the Obama "birther" theory or that climate change is a hoax. Democrats are more likely to believe that Trump's campaign "colluded" with the Russians.

But some people are habitual conspiracists who entertain a variety of generic conspiracy theories. For example, they believe that world politics are controlled by a cabal instead of governments, or that scientists systematically deceive the public. This indicates that personality or other individual differences might be at play.

In fact, some people seem to be downright devoted to conspiracy theories. When conspiracy maven Alex Jones' content was recently banned from several social media websites, the popularity of his InfoWars app skyrocketed.

Scientific research examining the nature of the "conspiratorial disposition" is abundant, but scattershot. So in a pair of new studies, and with help from my student Molly Graether, I tried to build on previous research to piece together a more comprehensive profile of the typical conspiracy theory believer, and for that matter, the typical non-believer.

Common Traits

We asked more than 1,200 American adults to provide extensive information about themselves and whether they agreed with generic conspiratorial statements. We tried to measure as many personal factors as possible that had been previously linked to conspiracy belief. Looking at many traits simultaneously would allow us to determine, all else being equal, which ones were most important.

Consistent with previous research, we found that one major predictor of conspiracy belief was "schizotypy." That's a constellation of traits that include a tendency to be relatively untrusting, ideologically eccentric, and prone to having unusual perceptual experiences (e.g., sensing stimuli that are not actually present). The trait borrows its name from schizophrenia, but it does not imply a clinical diagnosis.

Schizotypy is the strongest predictor of conspiracy belief. In addition to experiencing the world in unusual ways, we found that people higher in schizotypy have an elevated need to feel unique, which has previously been linked with conspiracism. Why? Probably because believing in non-mainstream ideas allows people to stand out from their peers, but at the same time take refuge in a community of like-minded believers.

In our studies, conspiracy believers were also disproportionately concerned that the world is a dangerous place. For example, they were more likely to agree that "all the signs" are pointing to imminent chaos.

Finally, conspiracists had distinct cognitive tendencies: They were more likely than nonbelievers to judge nonsensical statements as profound—for example, "wholeness quiets infinite phenomena"—a tendency cheekily known as "bullshit receptivity."

They were also more likely to say that nonhuman objects—triangle shapes moving around on a computer screen—were acting intentionally, as though they were capable of having thoughts and goals they were trying to accomplish. In other words, they inferred meaning and motive where others did not.

Is Trump a Conspiracy Thinker?

Although we can't know how he would score on our questionnaires, President Trump's public statements and behavior suggest that he fits the profile fairly well.

First, he does display some schizotypal characteristics. He is famously untrusting of others. Donald Trump Jr. has described how his father used to admonish him in kindergarten not to trust anyone under any circumstances. The elder Trump is also relatively eccentric. He is a unique politician who doesn't hew consistently to party lines or political norms. He has espoused unusual ideas, including the theory that people have a limited lifetime reservoir of energy that physical exercise depletes.

President Trump also seems to see the world as a dangerous place. His campaign speeches warned about murderous rapist immigrants flooding across the border and Black communities being in "the worst shape" they've ever been. His inauguration address described a hellish landscape of "American carnage."

Chaos Needs Comfort

The dismal nature of most conspiracy theories presents a puzzle to psychologists who study beliefs, because most belief systems—think religion—are fundamentally optimistic and uplifting. Psychologists have found that people tend to adopt such beliefs in part because they fulfill emotional goals, such as the need to feel good about oneself and the world. Conspiracy theories don't seem to fit this mold.

Then again, if you are a person who looks at the world and sees chaos and malevolence, perhaps there is comfort in the notion that there is someone to blame. If "there's something going on," then there is something that could be done about it. Perhaps, then, even the darkest and most bizarre conspiracy theories offer a glint of hope for some people.

Take the "QAnon" theory that has recently received a flurry of media attention. This theory features a nightmare of pedophile rings and satanic cults. But some adherents have adopted a version of the theory that President Trump has it all under control.

If our research advances the understanding of why some people are more attracted to conspiracy theories than others, it is important to note that it says nothing about whether or not conspiracy theories are true. After the Watergate scandal brought down a president for participating in a criminal conspiracy, the American public learned that seemingly outlandish speculation about the machinations of powerful actors is sometimes right on the money.

And when a conspiracy is real, people with a conspiracist mindset may be among the first to pick up on it—while others get duped. The rub is that the rest of the time, they might be duping themselves.

CHAPTER 39
Flat Earthers and Disinformation[1]

By Carlos Diaz Ruiz

Around the world, and against all scientific evidence, a segment of the population believes that Earth's round shape is either an unproven theory or an elaborate hoax. Recent polling found that as many as 11% of Americans believe the Earth might be flat.[2]

While it is tempting to dismiss "flat Earthers" as mildly amusing, we ignore their arguments at our peril. Polling shows that there is an overlap between conspiracy theories,[3] some of which can act as gateways for radicalization. QAnon and the great replacement theory, for example, have proved deadly more than once.

By studying how flat Earthers talk about their beliefs, we can learn how they make their arguments engaging to their audience, and in turn, learn what makes disinformation spread online.

In a recent study,[4] my colleague Tomas Nilsson at Linnaeus University and I analyzed hundreds of YouTube videos in which people argue that the Earth is flat. We paid attention to their debating techniques to understand the structure of their arguments and how they make them appear rational.

One strategy they use is to take sides in existing debates. People who are deeply attached to one side of a culture war are likely to wield any and all arguments (including truths, half-truths, and opinions) if it helps them win. People invest their identity into the group and are more willing to believe fellow allies rather than perceived opponents—a phenomenon that sociologists call neo-tribalism.

The problem arises when people internalize disinformation as part of their identity. While news articles can be fact-checked, personal beliefs cannot. When conspiracy theories are part of someone's value system or worldview, it is difficult to challenge them.

The Three Themes of the Flat-Earth Theory

In analyzing these videos, we observed that flat Earthers take advantage of ongoing culture wars by inserting their own arguments into the logic of, primarily, three main debates. These debates are longstanding and can be very personal for participants on either side.

First is the debate about the existence of God, which goes back to antiquity, and is built on reason rather than observation. People already debate atheism versus faith, evolution versus creationism, and the Big Bang versus intelligent design. What flat Earthers do is set up their argument within the longstanding struggle of the Christian right by arguing that atheists use pseudoscience—evolution, the Big Bang, and round Earth—to sway people away from God.

A common flat Earther refrain that taps into religious beliefs is that God can inhabit the heavens above us physically only in a flat plane, not a sphere. As one flat Earther put it:

> They invented the Big Bang to deny that God created everything, and they invented evolution to convince you that He cares more about monkeys than about you. . . [T]hey invented the round Earth because God cannot be above you if He is also below you, and they invented an infinite universe to make you believe that God is far away from you.[5]

The second theme is a conspiracy theory that sees ordinary people stand against a ruling elite of corrupt politicians and celebrities. Knowledge is power, and this theory argues that those in power conspire to keep knowledge for themselves by distorting the basic nature of reality. The message is that people are easily controlled if they believe what they are told rather than their own eyes. Indeed, the Earth does appear flat to the naked eye. Flat Earthers see themselves as part of a community of unsung heroes, fighting against the tyranny of an elite who make the public disbelieve what they see.

The third theme is based on the "freethinking" argument, which dates back to the spirited debate about the presence or absence of God in the text of the U.S. Constitution. This secularist view argues that rational people should not believe authority or dogma—instead, they should trust only their own reason and experience. Freethinkers distrust experts who use "book knowledge" or "nonsense math" that laypeople cannot replicate. Flat Earthers often use personal observations to test whether the Earth is round, especially through homemade experiments. They see themselves as the visionaries and scientists of yesteryear, like a modern-day Galileo.

Possible Counterarguments

Countering disinformation on social media is difficult when people internalize it as a personal belief. Fact-checking can be ineffective and backfire, because disinformation becomes a personal opinion or value.

Responding to flat Earthers (or other conspiracy theorists) requires understanding the logic that makes their arguments persuasive. For example, if you know that they find arguments from authority unconvincing, then selecting a government scientist as a spokesperson for a counterargument may be ineffective. Instead, it may be more appealing to propose a homemade experiment that anyone can replicate.

If you can identify the rationality behind their specific beliefs, then a counterargument can engage that logic. Insiders of the group are often key to this—only a spokesperson with impeccable credentials as a devout Christian can say that you do not need the flat-Earth beliefs to remain true to your faith.

Overall, beliefs like flat-Earth theory, QAnon, and the great replacement theory grow because they appeal to a sense of group identity under attack. Even far-fetched misinformation and conspiracies can seem rational if they fit into existing grievances. Since debates on social media require only posting content, participants create a feedback loop that solidifies disinformation as points of view that cannot be fact-checked.

CHAPTER 40
QAnon, Descartes, and Brains in Vats[1]

By Guy Elgat

Recently, CNN sent their reporter to cover yet another Trump rally (in Pennsylvania), but this time reporter Gary Tuchman was assigned the more specific task of interviewing Trump supporters who were carrying signs or large cardboard cut-outs of the letter "Q" and wearing T-shirts proclaiming "We are Q".[2] These Trump supporters were professing their belief in the existence of a person known as Q or QAnon who is supposed to be an anonymous, high-level activist who works from inside the administration with the goal of supporting Trump's agenda by squashing "deep-state" anti-Trump forces and removing any other obstacle that might stand in the way of consummating the President's revolutionary vision.

At one point in the interview, in his attempt to probe the beliefs of the Q-ers, as I shall call them, Gary Tuchman challenged one of them and said: "So you don't have any proof [that Q exists] but that's what you're guessing," in response to which the interviewee said "and you don't have any proof there isn't." In another exchange, Tuchman again tried to interrogate a Q-er about her beliefs, saying "Maybe it is not true [that Q exists] because there is no evidence of it," in response to which the interviewee shot back: "There hasn't been any *non-evidence* yet."

Upon hearing these retorts many might react with a baffled scoff and dismiss them as not worthy of taking seriously. But though this reaction is at the end of the day warranted—or so I shall argue—it is hard, though important, to explain exactly what is wrong with the Q-ers' response and why Q-ers might think that it serves their purpose and is thus perfectly legitimate. As we shall see, once we start to reflect on these questions, we will find ourselves pretty quickly knee-deep in philosophy.

We can start with the observation that the response which says, "You cannot prove that I am wrong either," crops up on occasion in a different context, namely, in religious debates between atheists and believers. Here those who hold religious beliefs protest in response to the charge that there is no proof for God's existence with the counter-charge that their atheistic interlocutors cannot prove that God does *not* exist either. What is the point of this retort? The immediate aim is of course to neutralize the criticism which seeks to show that belief in God, since not based on evidence, is irrational. By responding that there is no proof that God does *not* exist, the believer can be interpreted as aiming to level the epistemological playing field as it were, as if saying, "Your atheistic view is not more rational than my theistic view, so you are in no position to criticize me." A similar idea is at play in the case of the Q-ers: by responding that there is no proof that QAnon is not real, the Q-er aims to disarm the interviewer's rebuke and knock such non-believers off their high horse and back to their rightful place.

There are, however, less immediate or secondary effects that such responses can be seen to have. First, as we can learn from our own reaction to the broadcast interview, by challenging the non-believer to cite evidence that shows that QAnon is *not* real, the Q-er can achieve a dumbfounding effect that can leave the interlocutor, and us, at a loss for words, without the ability to respond, at least temporarily. This can generate the appearance that the Q-er has won the day (or at least has not lost) and can moreover give rise to epistemological *confusion* or *disorientation*, where, at least for a moment, we lose our cognitive bearings. Second and relatedly, the response, if successful, can *shut down discussion* for it gives the impression that nothing more can be said in defense or in criticism of either view. Put differently, such responses can help create or further buttress the proverbial "echo-chambers" in which we have come to see ourselves as trapped.

Finally, and perhaps most importantly, the Q-er seems to believe that defusing the interlocutor's challenge *legitimizes his or her own view:* the response "prove that I am wrong" not only silences the objector but also gives the Q-er the impression of being entitled to his or her own belief. The implicit thought here seems to be this: since I cannot show you I am right and you cannot prove me wrong, I am perfectly within my rights, so to speak, to continue to believe in whatever I choose to believe. In other words, if the epistemological playing field is levelled and there is just as much or just as little evidence in favor of one belief as there is in favor of its contrary, it is a free-for-all and you are rationally allowed to seize upon either one, per your heart's desire.

The principle articulated here, however, is false. If it is indeed the case that the scales are in a state of perfect equilibrium, the rationally warranted response is to suspend judgment and adopt *neither* option; it is to withhold one's assent both from the belief that QAnon is real as well as from the belief that he is not. But this is precisely what the Q-er does not proceed to do; he or she rather continues to manifest and act on the belief that QAnon is real by wearing QAnon shirts, waving QAnon posters, and encouraging him to keep up the good work he's been doing.

I have so far proceeded on the assumption that the Q-er has indeed shown, by making us acknowledge that we cannot prove that QAnon does not exist, that we are indeed in an epistemological stand-off. But is this in fact the case? I would now like to argue that this would already be conceding too much ground to the Q-er and that we non-believers can do better than that: we are in fact in a better epistemological position than mere doubt, and are consequently in a better position than the person who proclaims allegiance to Q. To see this it would be helpful to look at a similar case, one from the history of philosophy.

In his *Meditations on First Philosophy* from 1641,[3] the French philosopher René Descartes employs the method of radical doubt and introduces a number of highly skeptical arguments that he hopes will help him call into question all of his opinions. This he does in an effort to free his mind of all prejudice and error so that at the end of the day he will be able to reconstruct the edifice of knowledge anew, but this time on secure and certain foundations. One skeptical argument Descartes employs at the end of the first chapter of the work concerns the possibility of there being an evil spirit or malicious demon. The argument can be interpreted as saying that given that we cannot know whether there is or there is not a malicious demon who "is supremely powerful and intelligent and does his utmost to deceive" us,[4] then we cannot claim to know anything at all and should suspend our judgment—be in a state of doubt—with respect to all of our beliefs.

If talk of a malicious demon seems quaint and unpersuasive, then we can think instead in terms of the more high-tech possibility that we are all brains in vats filled with nutrients and are hooked up to super-computers that perfectly simulate our everyday reality. Since we cannot know whether we are brains in vats or not—the argument goes—we cannot claim to know anything and should suspend our judgment. Outraged and befuddled we might respond that there is, after all, no proof that we *are* brains in vats, so why worry? But here our skeptic rival, playing the QAnon card, will grinningly retort: "but you don't have any proof that you aren't."

Should we then suspend our judgment and neither affirm nor deny the belief that we are brains in vats? Is it the most that we can hope for? It is easy to see that this way madness lies, for then we will also have to suspend judgment over an infinite number of equal or worse absurdities. We would thus have to admit that we can't really say whether unicorns are real or not, whether there is or there is not a troupe of invisible leprechauns dancing the hora behind our backs, or whether or not we are professional assassins whose incriminating memories are erased by our employers, the undetectable aliens from planet Xanadu. This would be utter epistemological bankruptcy.

One way out of this horrific predicament, which, as we can now see, is not a mere intellectual game but has real-life political consequences, involves noticing that in all such cases we are challenged by the skeptic to prove that a certain absurd possibility does *not* obtain. But then, we should ask, what evidence that we are not brains in vats (say) could there possibly be that *would* satisfy the skeptic? Once we start to reflect seriously on this question we will see that the answer is not obvious at all. Indeed, I believe that at the end of the day there is no possible fact to be unearthed that would give us reason to believe that we are not brains in vats. This impossibility of evidence is common, I think, to many cases in which what is at stake is the non-existence of something. This means that when we are challenged to show that something is not real we are in effect confronted by a demand that is impossible (or nearly impossible) to meet. But failure to meet an impossible demand is no failure at all. And while the possibility of unearthing evidence that we *are* brains in vats is not an easy feat to accomplish, it is, I believe, readily more intelligible. Thus, if I discover tomorrow that the technology to hook up brains to computers is available and has been already applied to thousands of people who are, for all we know, absolutely oblivious of their sorry predicament, I *will* scratch my head and start to entertain the possibility that maybe I too am one of those unlucky brains; I will thus start to move from non-belief in the direction of belief. What all of this means in my view is that we should not suspend judgment about whether or not we are brains in vats, and that we are justified in believing we are not: the epistemological credit we possess insofar as we have no evidence for the belief that we are brains in vats is *not* counterbalanced by our failure to cite evidence that we are not, for, to repeat, this is not a failure at all.

It thus follows that we are in a better epistemological position vis-à-vis our skeptic opponent, and this assessment holds, *mutatis mutandis,* with respect to our Q-ers. Our demand of them that they provide evidence that QAnon is real is not cancelled out by the demand that they present to us, since the latter is almost practically impossible to meet. We should therefore counter the "prove that I am wrong" challenge with "that's a ridiculous demand!"

Despite, however, such errors in thinking, the Q-ers' behavior is perhaps understandable: it is the behavior of someone who, even though he or she lacks all evidence, believes that the situation is so dire that it requires *some* action. It can then be likened to the desperate passenger frantically pushing all the buttons in an elevator in a state of free fall, thinking there is no evidence that it is *not* going to work.

CHAPTER 41
Anatomy of a Viral Conspiracy Theory[1]

By Jim Swift

Just north of Orlando lies Florida's 7th Congressional District—at least for now. The Sunshine State is set to gain a new seat due to redistricting, and Florida hasn't yet finalized its new map. For more than two decades, the seat was held by Rep. John Mica, who came in with the mini-wave of 1992 when the GOP netted nine House seats, two years before the huge wave of the Republican Revolution. Florida's congressional map was redrawn in 2015 due to a court order, as groups sued to ensure compliance with a law meant to curb gerrymandering. Mica's district hadn't been as gerrymandered as others in the state, but it was redrawn, and in 2016, a year that was generally good for Republican candidates, Mica lost in a squeaker to Democrat Stephanie Murphy.

In late 2021, Rep. Murphy, a centrist Blue Dog who serves on the House January 6th Committee, announced that she won't be seeking a fourth term. Nine Republicans have already thrown their hats in the ring but only one Democrat has so far, newcomer Allek Pastrana. Pastrana had planned on running against Rep. Val Demings in the primary for Florida's 2022 Senate race, hoping to unseat Marco Rubio, but instead opted to be the first Democrat in for the fightin' 7th.

As with any open seat, there are a few no-names running. Then, as you might expect of a Republican primary, there's your typical conservative businessman, your small businesswoman, your retired Navy captain, and, uh, your Navy SEAL sniper-turned-Christian minister.

But then there are your crazies—like your Trump-loving veteran who wants to "stop the steal," your gun-loving veteran who is part of the Three Percenters militia who wants to add Republicans as a federally protected class because of the gays, and your state representative who tweets out things like "Fauci should spend the rest of his life rotting away in a federal prison"[2] and who is pals with Laura Loomer, the far-right fringe conspiracy theorist best known for chaining herself to Twitter headquarters after being banned from the platform.

And while the primary is still nearly seven months away, the crazies are getting an early start in stirring things up. Over the weekend, a handful of Floridians protested outside an extended-stay hotel in Maitland, Florida (just outside Orlando) that they believed to be occupied by masses of unauthorized immigrants brought there by President Biden on buses.

Why? Because Loomer filmed a video of the men in question getting off the buses.[3] The video was amplified on far-right social media sites by the likes of Roger Stone. On Twitter, a failed inventor who goes by the name J. Hutton Pulitzer shared the video (Pulitzer was last in the headlines for helping the Cyber Ninjas—remember them?—look for bamboo in supposedly fraudulent ballots).

This came to the attention of Anthony Sabatini, the state representative vying for the 7th District congressional seat. Sabatini promoted Pulitzer's post of Loomer's video,[4] apparently without doing any research of his own (You can always rely on those big-brained Claremont types—Sabatini was a Claremont Institute fellow last year—to see an internet video and immediately know all of the answers. Or maybe Loomer's word was good enough for him).

Sabatini then took a potshot at Florida House Speaker Chris Sprowls, whom he called Speaker "Strawberry Shortcake," wondering why nothing had been done about the "hundreds of illegals" being "shipped" into the district.[5] He then encouraged followers to sign his campaign's petition calling for Florida to deport unauthorized immigrants under powers he believes the Tenth Amendment leaves to the states.[6] Jeremy Liggett, the Three Percenter militia candidate in the 7th District race, also promoted the claims about the "hundreds of illegal immigrants" that "Joe Biden dumped" in the district and encouraged people to protest outside of the hotel.[7]

One problem with all this: The supposed unauthorized immigrants staying at the hotel are actually in the United States legally on H-2A visas.[8] We know this thanks to Christopher Heath, a reporter from WFTV, who did some actual reporting. Heath attended the protest and talked to those who seriously believed that President Biden would fill up buses with unauthorized immigrants and put them up at an extended-stay in Maitland. Some of their responses and their signs are almost beyond parody, but then again, this is Florida.

I was curious to hear if Sabatini was there at the protest and, since his claims had been debunked, if he cared to comment—especially since, again, he had chastised the speaker of the Florida House for not responding.[9] When I emailed Sabatini's campaign for comment, I received the following odd reply: "The situation is still being investigated. Florida has over 1 million illegal aliens—if it's the case that these individuals were legally present, that would be a rare occurrence."

It's unclear who, if anyone, is "investigating" the hotel's residents. The company, Dewar Nurseries, that employs the workers who were at the hotel has confirmed that these are legal workers with H-2A visas. Legal immigrants. Hundreds of thousands of people are working the fields of America under this highly re-stricted program.[10] The companies that participate in the program are all in the public record. Isn't that what we hear Republicans always saying they support—legal immigration, people who jump through the appropriate hoops? Alas, Laura Loomer saw a bus full of men with brown skin, and of course, there must be a nefarious conspiracy afoot.

A final irony: Sabatini wasn't at the protest because, according to his social me-dia, he was apparently busy hobnobbing with "Florida legend" Alfie Oakes, who endorsed him. Oakes is known not only for Seed to Table, his store/restaurant in Naples, Florida, but also for his hatred of mask mandates and of vaccines, and for being part of the Jan. 6th insurrection. Oakes sent two buses full of people to Washington for Jan. 6th (but went by private jet himself).[11]

But get this: Oakes has been busted for using illegal labor before, telling CBS: "Forty to 80 percent can be undocumented on any given day, and I can tell you, if we were to lose 40 to 80 percent of our workforce, we would be crippled here."[12]

So Sabatini would rather shake that guy's hand than join the brigade protesting with threatening signs outside of a hotel housing legal immigrant farm workers.

Allek Pastrana, the lone Democrat in the race for the 7th District seat (so far), offered this comment on the viral lies and overall nuttiness:

> I'm for immigration reform, what I'm not for is political candidates jumping the gun without facts, posting false information to social media, just to push a xenophobic narrative. These workers are here legally on H-2A visas thus making these individuals legal to work in our country.

If other competitive Republican primaries around the country are any guide, the craziness is bound to get worse as the primary election approaches. Buckle up.

CHAPTER 42
Fighting Conspiracy Theories with Evidence[1]

By Adam G. Klein

One in four American millennials believe the Holocaust was exaggerated or entirely made up, according to a recent national survey that sought to find out what young adults know about the genocide of nearly 6 million Jews at the hands of Nazis some 80 years ago.[2]

That startling statistic was cited as one of the main reasons that Facebook CEO Mark Zuckerberg decided in October 2020 to finally ban Holocaust denial across the social network. Denying the Holocaust ever happened is an enduring form of anti-Semitic propaganda that attempts to deny or minimize the atrocities committed by the Nazis against the Jews during World War II.

Following Facebook's lead, Twitter announced it, too, would remove any posts that denied the history of the Holocaust, though CEO Jack Dorsey appeared to contradict that policy at a Senate hearing weeks later.

Holocaust deniers have continued to emerge in social media, and perhaps predictably, many have migrated to less restrictive sites like Parler, where hashtags like #HolocaustNeverHappened and #HolocaustIsALie are widespread. "If you want Holocaust denial, hey, Parler is going to be great for you," Bill Gates recently said of the social network.[3]

While some tech companies address the rise in Holocaust revisionism, and others leave the door open, social networks have played an unwitting role in helping to distort the memory of these horrific events. But as a scholar who studies online extremism, I believe that same community could do more to protect Holocaust remembrance by highlighting the digitized accounts of those who lived through it.

A Decades-Long Campaign

Holocaust denial has been a tool of anti-Semitic movements since the 1960s. Pseudo-academic groups like the Institute for Historical Review, for example, spent years working to distort the public's aging memory of the Holocaust, which took place between 1933 and 1945. They tried to cast doubt on the feasibility of the mass executions and even the existence of the gas chambers. They held annual conferences and gathered fellow deniers to share their beliefs that these events were conjured up by the Jewish people mostly as a means to justify the creation of the state of Israel in 1948.

For decades, most people quickly discarded those claims, because they had heard the firsthand accounts of the survivors who were sent to the camps and witnessed the daily operation of genocide and the murder of family members. The allegations of the deniers could also not withstand the accounts of soldiers who liberated the camps and made the terrible discoveries of body-filled crematoriums and mass graves.

But for deniers, Holocaust revision has little to do with history. Denialism is really a pretext for delivering anti-Semitism in the form of "scholarship," although few academics ever gave it such attention. So hate groups had to find other means of circulation. They found it online.

A Conspiracy Resurrected

When the internet took off in the late 1990s, Holocaust deniers and countless other conspiracy theorists saw an opportunity to spread their ideas to new audiences. Anti-Semitic groups could now publish their distortions in well-visited forums, and later in faux-informational websites like Metapedia and The Occidental Observer—extremist communities, in fact, that collectively receive some 350,000 visitors each month.

The internet also gave Holocaust deniers an opportunity to reach a much wider public through social media. As early as 2009, Facebook groups emerged that were dedicated to "debunking" the Holocaust, as #Holohoax became a popular hashtag on Twitter, which it continues to be today. Reddit also became a far-right haven for Holocaust deniers, one of whom gained national attention when he was the invited guest of a Florida congressman to the 2018 State of the Union address.

For deniers, the internet helped repackage their conspiracy into something less recognizable than hate. I've long studied this process, which I call information laundering, tracking illegitimate forms of information, like Holocaust denial, that flow through social networks, blogs, and search engines. There they intermix with mainstream ideas and slowly become washed of their radical origins.

This decades-long campaign has resulted in the current surveys that show nearly a quarter of young adults are misinformed or skeptical about the Holocaust. Only now, few survivors are left to correct the record. That makes it even more important to spread the truth. Perhaps the internet can help.

Eisenhower's Intuition

When Gen. Dwight Eisenhower visited the Buchenwald concentration camp in 1945 after its liberation by U.S. forces, he realized how impossible it might be for people to believe the scale of Nazi atrocities. He wrote powerfully of the experience and of his reasons for going to see it in person:

> The things I saw beggar description. . . In one room, where they were piled up twenty or thirty naked men, killed by starvation, George Patton would not even enter. . . I made the visit deliberately, in order to be in position to give first-hand evidence of these things if ever, in the near future, there develops a tendency to charge these allegations merely to 'propaganda.'[4]

Eisenhower's words are instructions for future generations. They underscore the need to be a witness to human cruelty in order to protect the memory of, and lessons learned from, these events from those who would try to distort them.

Back online, it may not be enough for social networks to ban Holocaust denial. Similar bans in Europe haven't limited the rise of anti-Semitism there. Instead, social networks could follow Eisenhower's example by answering the falsehoods of Holocaust deniers with the true stories of survivors.

The internet is already home to thousands of digitized survivor testimonies. They include oral histories that could be readily activated by social networks to refute those who deny the existence of the gas chambers with the accounts of those who stood inside them or witnessed them at work. Platforms like Facebook, Twitter, and Reddit might share firsthand stories wherever false claims arise to counter denials with facts.

In the spirit of that counternarrative, I will place my grandmother's story here. My grandmother, Cecilie Klein-Pollack, was a Holocaust survivor. She later wrote about her experiences in Auschwitz where, upon arrival, she and her sister were separated from their mother and her sister's son, never to see them again. There are millions of other experiences like hers, and survivors of other genocides whose stories must be retold as well, from Armenia to Rwanda.

Holocaust deniers have long waited for the time when there were no remaining survivors or witnesses to keep these histories alive. But the internet is a powerful archive. Social networks have an opportunity to combat hateful disinformation by posting the personal stories of these tragedies and end the so-called "debate" about whether the Holocaust ever happened.

As Eisenhower well understood, history needs protecting.

Figure 42.1 Holocaust Survivor Cecilie Klein-Pollack.
Adam G. Klein, "How To Fight Holocaust Denial in Social Media—With the Evidence of What Really Happened," *The Conversation*, December 3, 2020, https://theconversation.com/how-to-fight-holocaust-denial-in-social-media-with-the-evidence-of-what-really-happened-150719.

V. PARTING THOUGHTS

CHAPTER 43
In Defense of Merit in Science[1]

By Abbot et. al.[2]

We live in an incredible time of human history. As Barack Obama said:

> If you had to choose one moment in history in which you could be born, and you didn't know ahead of time who you were going to be—what nationality, what gender, what race, whether you'd be rich or poor, gay or straight, what faith you'd be born into . . . you would choose right now.

While the benefits of significant global progress and economic development have not been shared equally, the world as a whole has never been healthier, wealthier, better educated, and in many ways more tolerant and less violent, than it is today.[3]

How did we get here? Science provided solutions to such calamities as famine and plague, transforming them "from incomprehensible and uncontrollable forces of nature into manageable challenges."[4] By improving the world economy and increasing global wealth, scientific progress helped create a more peaceful and just world. Science eradicated smallpox, discovered penicillin, decoded the SARS-CoV2 virus in a weekend, helped to halve the maternal and child mortality rate globally, revolutionized agriculture, contributed to extending life expectancy in every country, and has generally granted humanity the gifts of life, health, wealth, knowledge, and freedom. By increasing literacy and communication, science has promoted empathy and rational problem-solving, contributing to a global decline in violence of all forms.[5]

Of course, serious problems continue to challenge us; poverty, inequality, wars, and violence persist. Climate change, biodiversity loss, antimicrobial resistance, and pandemic disease threaten global gains made over the past century. However, science continues to be the best tool humanity possesses to address these complex, collective challenges. Indeed, science holds the key to solving these problems—it provides the basis for renewable energy technologies, mitigating anthropogenic impact on the global climate, feeding the world's growing population, controlling pandemics, and eradicating debilitating diseases. Of course, science alone is not sufficient: science is but a tool that can be used for good and bad. It is our responsibility as a society to use it responsibly, ethically, and effectively.

Fulfilling this responsibility, however, is being hindered by a new, alarming clash between liberal epistemology and identity-based ideologies. Liberal epistemology prizes free and open inquiry, values vigorous discourse and debate, and determines the best scientific ideas by separating those that are true from those that are likely not. The statuses, identities, and demographics of scientists are irrelevant to this great sifting of valid versus invalid ideas.

In contrast, identity-based ideologies seek to replace these core liberal principles, essential for scientific and technological advances, with principles derived from postmodernism and Critical Social Justice (CSJ), which assert that modern science is "racist," "patriarchal," and "colonial," and a tool of oppression rather than a tool to promote human flourishing and global common good.[6]

In this perspective, we explain the differences between the two epistemologies and argue that meritocracy[7] (grounded in philosophical liberal epistemology), however imperfect, is the best and fairest way to conduct science. We endorse policies to mitigate existing inequalities of opportunities, but explain why CSJ-based policies are pernicious (CSJ differs from social justice as a concept).[8] Therefore, we offer a liberal, humanistic alternative that is compatible with maximizing scientific advances.

Merit-Based Science is Effective and Fair

Why science is an engine that propels societies to health, wealth, and prosperity—ultimately saving and improving lives worldwide—is well understood.[9] The cornerstone of science is the notion that objective truth exists and can be understood through observation, experiment, and iterative hypothesis generation. Because objective truth exists, ultimate consensus among truth-seeking actors—scientists—is possible.

The scientific method has proven an effective tool for revealing objective truths about the natural world. These truths are not final and immutable, but provisional—open to challenge and refinement as knowledge expands. For example, quantum mechanics has shown that the laws governing the motion of billiard balls and planets are not sufficient to describe the motion of nuclei and electrons. Yet, the Schrödinger equation does not invalidate Newton's Laws, which we continue to use to engineer cars, airplanes, and rockets. Rather, quantum mechanics expanded our understanding of reality by revealing that classical mechanics is limited to the macroscopic world. In much the same way, Einstein's theory of relativity did not negate Newton's law of universal gravitation—it extended it to include new phenomena such as black holes.

The scientific method is the core of liberal epistemology. In *The Constitution of Knowledge*,[10] Rauch addresses the current epistemological crisis by reaffirming the central tenets of liberal epistemology (developed by Popper, Albert, Weber, and others). Namely, that provisional truth is attainable and that a truth claim can be made only if it is testable and withstands attempts to debunk it (the Fallibilist Rule). He also emphasizes that no one has personal authority over a truth claim, nor can one claim authority by virtue of a personally or tribally privileged perspective (the Empirical Rule). Similarly, truth claims cannot be less valid by virtue of the claimant's membership in any particular group. Liberal epistemology implies that "positionality statements" (in which scientists disclose their demographic identity memberships and which are now being advocated throughout academia) have no value in evaluations of scientific claims,[11] since the validity of a truth claim cannot be evaluated by knowing the claimants' tribal or demographic affiliations.[12] In liberal epistemology, the validity of truth claims can only be evaluated by evidence and the logic of inferential processes linking that evidence to further conclusions.

However, evaluating the quality of that evidence or the validity of the inferential processes is itself a social process, a point upon which some liberal[13] and feminist[14] philosophers agree. In both Rauch's[15] and Longino's[16] perspective, no one has final say; scientific truths are determined by an ongoing social process that includes discussion, debate, and criticism until a broad consensus is reached (and which can be challenged by new evidence and arguments). Although both perspectives permit all members to participate in the social process of truth-seeking, in neither perspective is truth determined by the group-based identities of the claimant.

Further, reality-based scientific communities must be open to conceding and correcting errors. The ability of science to self correct—one reason that scientific truth claims are uniquely credible[17]—can be epistemically contrasted with conformity to religious and political dogmas, which are disturbingly closed to self correction. Self correction is facilitated by pluralism to maintain intellectual diversity and maximize the chances of uncovering provisional truths. Intellectual diversity ensures vigorous skeptical vetting of scientific claims by a critical mass of doubters who ultimately accept being bound by objective truths once they have been rigorously determined by extensive evidence.

These core principles, which have served us well for centuries, are under attack by ideologies originating in postmodernism and Critical Theory,[18] versions of which reject objective reality in favor of "multiple narratives" promulgated by different identity groups and "alternative ways of knowing." They engender "radical skepticism about whether objective knowledge or truth is obtainable" and "a commitment to cultural constructivism," which asserts that knowledge and reality are products of their cultural context.[19] When claims about lived experiences and subjectivism are proposed to constitute a better basis for understanding the world than empirical evidence and facts, the identity of participants in a discourse becomes more important than the substance of their arguments or the strength of the evidence, and objectively adjudicating claims becomes impossible.

These perspectives often view science as a tool of power, are hostile to the central liberal principle of free inquiry and open discussion, and are closed to calls to justify their claims on scientific grounds.[20]

Such ideologies suffer from at least two serious philosophical problems. The first is that their rejection of objectivity undermines their credibility. If there is no objectivity, then their claims are not objectively true. If their claims cannot possibly be objectively true, there is no reason for anyone to believe them. Their claims warrant serious consideration only if they might actually be true—which requires at least the possibility of objectivity.

The second is that these philosophies[21] conflict with a set of principles of modern science known as the Mertonian norms (see Figure 43.1).[22] Merton, a founder of sociology of science, formulated these principles based on his analysis of factors that enabled the scientific revolution and explained that they are dictated by the goals of science. Indeed, following these principles has served us well, and, as we argue below, a departure from these ideas has a long history of harming science.[23] Together, the Mertonian principles imply that merit must be the key metric to judge and evaluate scientific claims. The merit of an idea should be evaluated through scrutiny and organized skepticism, essential components of scientific discovery. The ultimate test of the merit of a claim is its ability to accurately predict the functioning of the universe as elucidated through replicable experiment and observation, not whether it feels right or comports with a particular worldview or

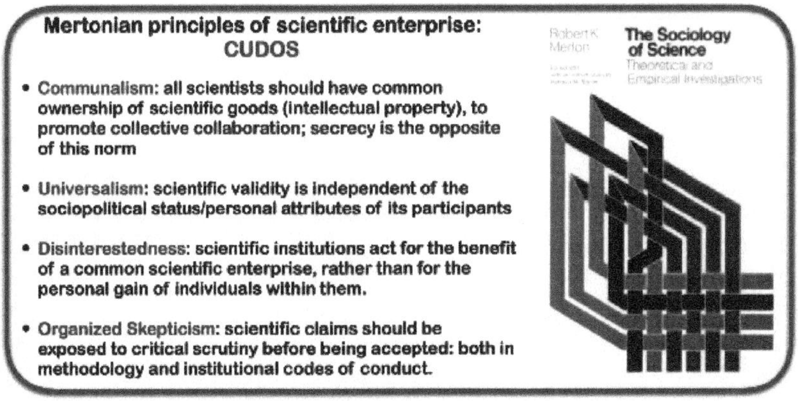

Mertonian principles of scientific enterprise: CUDOS

- Communalism: all scientists should have common ownership of scientific goods (intellectual property), to promote collective collaboration; secrecy is the opposite of this norm

- Universalism: scientific validity is independent of the sociopolitical status/personal attributes of its participants

- Disinterestedness: scientific institutions act for the benefit of a common scientific enterprise, rather than for the personal gain of individuals within them.

- Organized Skepticism: scientific claims should be exposed to critical scrutiny before being accepted: both in methodology and institutional codes of conduct.

Figure 43.1. The Mertonian Principles.
D. Abbot et. al., "In Defense of Merit in Science," *Journal of Controversial Ideas* 3, no. 1 (April 2023): 1-26.

group interest. Ideological orthodoxies deserve no place in science.

To ensure that the best scientific ideas are put forth, merit must also be applied to evaluate research proposals and prospective students and faculty. Here, merit comprises the scientific claims contained in the research plans, the quality of the proposed methods, and the expertise and academic track records of the individuals involved.

Scientific truths are universal and independent of the personal attributes of the scientist. Science knows no ethnicity, gender, or religion. Of course, by itself, universalism does not prevent the personal views of scientists, which are influenced by culture and society, from affecting the practice of science. Indeed, scientists have not always lived up to the ideals of fairness and impartiality in evaluating merit. In the past, scientific culture contributed to the exclusion of various groups from the scientific enterprise. For example, sexism limited women's entry into science, and those who helped raise awareness of such issues have done science a service. However, the shortcomings of individuals or the community should not be confused with the science itself. Whether sexism prevented Cecilia Payne-Gaposchkin from receiving credit for her conclusion that the Sun was made mostly of hydrogen is irrelevant to the fact that the Sun is made mostly of hydrogen. Although there are feminist critiques of how glaciologists have conducted themselves, there is no such thing as "feminist glaciology," just as there is no "queer chemistry," "Jewish physics," "White mathematics," "indigenous science," or "feminist astronomy."[24] Glacial, physical, genetic, or prehistoric phenomena are independent of the positionality of the scientist. By prioritizing the truth value of scientific research, personal influences of individual scientists are minimized.

Merit-based science is truly fair and inclusive. It provides a ladder of opportunity and a fair chance of success for those possessing the necessary skills or talents. Neither socioeconomic privilege nor elite education is necessary. Indeed, several coauthors of this perspective have built successful careers in science, despite being immigrants, coming from lower socioeconomic backgrounds, and not being products of "elite education." As an example of how the inclusiveness engendered by merit-based science benefits society, the first mRNA COVID19 vaccine was developed by scientists with an immigrant background (Hungarian and Turkish) who built successful careers in Germany. Likewise, the founder of Apple, Steve Jobs, came from a poor adoptive family and did not have access to regular education.

Merit is a vehicle for upward mobility.[25] Recruiting, developing, and promoting individuals based on their talent, skills, and achievements has enabled many who started life in disadvantaged conditions to realize their dreams and build better lives. Imperfections in a merit-based system are not grounds for dismantling or disrupting it. Changes to an effective system should occur only when the superiority of the alternative has been demonstrated. There is no evidence that CSJ produces better mathematics, physics, or chemistry, and it has already damaged medicine and psychiatry.[26] While some might argue that CSJ has improved science by disrupting the barriers to entry for marginalized groups, those barriers had been falling for decades, without any help from CSJ dogmas, and long before CSJ rose to prominence and power. For example, in 1970, women received about 10% of all doctoral degrees in the U.S.; by 2006, they were receiving the majority.[27]

In order to achieve a more fair and equitable scientific community, we should strengthen meritocratic practices. It would be unjust and pernicious not to identify and nurture talent—wherever it may be found. Prioritizing merit-based science does not preclude other actions to enhance inclusivity, an issue we return to later.

How to Apply Merit: Caveats, Pitfalls, and Good Practices

The primacy of merit-based scientific truth claims raises the following question: How can we apply merit consistently and effectively? Although it may be straightforward to rank chess players, ranking prospective students, job applicants, tenure candidates, and scientific proposals is more difficult. Judgment may be affected by personal preferences, blind spots, and biases. Yet there are established good practices that have been honed and refined over decades.

In assessing merit and scientific promise, quantitative metrics have benefits, despite their limitations.[28] While merit cannot be quantified by simplistic formulas (e.g., number of publications times impact factor), using numerical data to quantify scientific output is a useful component of the evaluation because it provides a quantitative measure of productivity. Good practices currently use a combination of quantitative metrics and qualitative assessment, e.g., letters from reviewers assessing how influential, original, and innovative the work is.

Although we view objective quantifiable metrics (such as publications) as one important dimension of merit, merit cannot be reduced to bean counting. Is one superb publication more valuable than four pretty good ones? This is a judgment call about which different people and institutions may honestly disagree. And what makes a published report "superb" will differ among fields and institutions. Although subjective judgments should play an important role in evaluations of merit, we recognize that they are also most vulnerable to biases.

How, then, can the potential for bias be mitigated so that even subjective judgments have a laser-like focus on merit? We suggest that two questions are central to the evaluation of scientific merit (see Figure 43.2): (1) How important is the finding? (2) How strongly does the evidence presented indicate that the main claims are true? Differences of opinion may exist regarding both of these dimensions. However, the key is that focusing on the importance of the finding and the strength of evidence can limit bias. Astronomers may value the discovery of a new exoplanet more than material scientists value improvements in ceramic tensile strength, but this is normal science and can be threshed out among scientists. The identity or positionality of the authors is irrelevant.

Merit also includes mentoring students. Again, numerical data related to the professional development of a candidate's mentees (papers published, conference presentations delivered, awards received, graduation rate, job placements, etc.) are helpful to build an overall assessment of merit. Academic promotion panels also consider teaching, professional and public service, and community engagement.

Many universities use quantitative indicators to compare individuals working in similar areas at similar career stages to detect deviations and create benchmarks of performance. It is recognized that quantitative metrics vary greatly among fields and depend on the nature of a position (e.g., teaching undergraduates versus graduate level research) and this is justifiably taken into consideration when appraising academic performance.

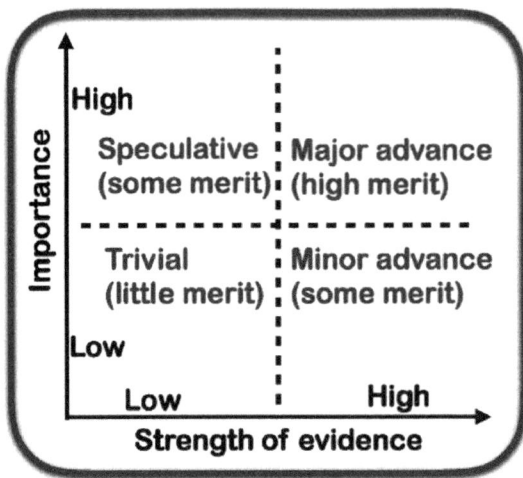

Figure 43.2 Guide for Evaluation of Merit.
D. Abbot et. al., "In Defense of Merit in Science," *Journal of Controversial Ideas* 3, no. 1 (April 2023): 1-26.

Qualitative and subjective judgments are also important. There may be genuine differences of opinion about whether mentoring one student who goes on to be an academic research star is a greater or lesser accomplishment than mentoring five students, four of whom go into industry and one who becomes an academic at a small liberal arts college. But the value of just counting, however imperfect, should be obvious: all else equal, mentoring one star is better than mentoring no stars; mentoring four students who go on to professional careers in industry is more of an accomplishment than mentoring none. Again, though, the identity or positionality of the mentor is irrelevant to the evaluation of merit when using these sorts of quantitative metrics.

The Perils of Replacing Merit with Social Engineering and Ideological Control

Lessons from History
The universalism of science does not preclude culture and politics from being involved in funding priorities. Funders, whether government or private, expect to receive a return on their investment. Yet politicians should not dictate how science is done, and political agendas should not replace Mertonian norms. History demonstrates the dangers of replacing merit-based science with ideological control and social engineering.[29] In the Soviet Union (USSR), the aberrations of Trofim Lysenko had catastrophic consequences for science and society.[30] An agronomist and

"people's scientist" who came from the "superior" class of poor peasants, Lysenko rejected Mendelian genetics because of its supposed inconsistency with Marxist ideology. Dissent from Lysenko's ideas was outlawed and his opponents were fired or prosecuted. Lysenko's ideologically infused agricultural ideas were put into practice in the USSR and China, where, in both countries, they led to decreased crop yields and famine.[31] Today, biology is again being subjugated to ideology— medical schools deny the biological basis of sex, biology courses avoid teaching the heritability of traits, and so on.[32] More examples of ideological subversion of science, relevant to physics and chemistry, were discussed in a recent viewpoint.[33]

Such analysis[34] is often dismissed with vague deflections such as "everything is political" and "everyone is biased." There is an element of truth to these declarations, which can help raise awareness of the potential of scientists to have biases, including biases on politicized topics, and help minimize such biases. However, those making these arguments often use them to impose their own ideological agendas on what can be studied and what kind of answers are permissible.[35] It is this sense of the politicization of science that we categorically oppose.

The Damage Inflicted by Today's Politicization of Science

The lessons from history are clear: ideological control of the scientific enterprise leads to its decline. The ongoing ideological subversion of STEMM (science, technology, engineering, mathematics, and medicine) education is particularly worrying. Ideological changes in the U.S., Canada, and New Zealand are already under way[36] and are quickly influencing other democracies.

The worst excesses of CSJ ideology are spreading to medicine, psychology, and global public health with worldwide implications.[37] For example, in global public health, the ideology manifests in the Decolonize Global Health movement, which calls for dismantling global health, questions research-based knowledge, emphasizes intergroup and international antagonisms, and challenges universalism as an ideal for global health, humanitarian aid, and development assistance.[38]

CSJ driven pedagogy can be pernicious, even when proposed innovations appear benign. For example, the proposed curriculum decolonization in pharmacology[39] involves teaching about drugs developed from folk remedies and focusing on the contributions of non-Europeans. While such topics might be appropriate for a history of medicine course, centering the curriculum around them, as has been proposed, would be detrimental to training health professionals. The vast majority of today's pharmacopeia is derived from the research and development efforts of the modern pharmaceutical industry; effective treatments derived from traditional medicine are rare, especially in the era of bio and immunotherapies. For example, of the over 150 anticancer drugs available today, only three are of natural origin (trabectedin, taxanes, and vinca-alkaloids).[40] Decolonizing pharmacology also contributes to the public's infatuation with traditional medicine, while health agencies report numerous therapeutic accidents involving herbal products not validated following "colonial" standards.[41] Such pedagogy also reinforces mistrust toward "White medicine," feeding conspiracy theories against the pharmaceutical industry, as exemplified by campaigns against COVID vaccines, which, sadly, disproportionately impacted minority groups.[42]

Scientific research requires dedication, intensive technical training, and a commitment to rigor and truth-seeking. Weakening merit-based admissions, created to identify and cultivate the best and brightest, will have long-lasting consequences for the scientific workforce, discouraging or preventing many promising students from entering the field. Signs of this are already evident. The weakening of the workforce in the U.S. has contributed to that country's recent fall from the position of world leader in science.[43] If the movement in North America to replace merit with ideology in funding[44] and faculty hiring[45] progresses, further deterioration in the ability to foster excellence in research in the U.S. is all but inevitable. This does not bode well for the future of science and society globally.

Enforcing identity-based hiring is discriminatory,[46] as it deprives some high-achieving individuals, including economically disadvantaged individuals who are not members of politically favored identity groups, of opportunities they have earned,[47] thereby potentially damaging morale and engagement. In the U.S., this has resulted in the unfair treatment of Asian American, Jewish, White, male, and foreign students.[48]

Ironically, replacing universalist principles with identity-based selection risks ultimately harming qualified underrepresented researchers by introducing doubt as to whether they merited their position or were hired for ideological reasons. Attempts to demonize, inflict reputational damage, or silence critics of social engineering practices by characterizing them as racists, White supremacists, or worse[49] is particularly detrimental to the open intellectual environment in which scientific inquiry into difficult social problems thrives. For every incident in which a scientist is targeted, thousands get the message and self-censor.[50]

Besides directly impacting the scientific enterprise, the ideological capture of scientific institutions[51] has broad consequences for society. Scientists and scientific institutions have a responsibility to enhance understanding and acceptance of the scientific consensus on matters of public importance. As seen with climate change and COVID19, once a scientific topic becomes politicized, trust in science diminishes, laying the groundwork for science denial, conspiracy theories, and political opportunism.[52] Research has consistently shown that public acceptance of a scientific consensus is driven not by scientific literacy (accepters are no more knowledgeable than deniers) but by political ideology and trust in scientific institutions.[53] When scientific institutions issue political position statements and adopt identity-based policies, they alienate and lose the trust of large dissenting segments of the public.[54] When prominent scientific journals promote these ideologies through editorials and perspective pieces, they magnify the alienation. Conflicting with the Mertonian principles of disinterestedness and universalism, these manifestos undermine the credibility of science as an objective, disinterested, and truth-seeking enterprise.[55]

The Genesis of the Current Attacks on Merit-based Science

The ideological basis of the current attacks on science emanates from certain veins of postmodernism and the identity-based ideologies they have spawned: various CSJ theories, including Critical Race Theory (CRT), related theories of structural racism, and postcolonial theory.[56]

These ideologies are increasingly finding their way into politics, culture, and education and are negatively affecting science, medicine, technology, psychology, and global health.[57] They are not imposed by totalitarian regimes, but spread by activists and abetted by university administrators and business leaders who fail to protect their institutions from these illiberal, regressive ideas.[58] The genesis of these ideologies is often obscure to the public or even to their bearers—e.g., administrators trained in Diversity, Equity, and Inclusion (DEI)—who are unlikely to have read Gramsci, Derrida, Foucault, Bell, Crenshaw, and Delgado. But just as a Soviet apparatchik need not have read Das Kapital to have been an agent ensuring conformity to Marxist doctrine, one need not be fully versed in postmodern or CRT-inspired scholarship to be implementing the ideology. The problems emerge from doctrinaire implementation, not from deep knowledge of the scholarship.

Critical Theory and CSJ conflict with the liberal Enlightenment. According to Delgado and Stefancic,[59] their characteristic elements include anti-rationalism; anti-enlightenment; rejection of equal treatment, philosophical liberalism, and neutrality in law; standpoint epistemology and subjectivism as the basis of knowledge; and intersectionality. Recently, ideas that emerged from Critical Theory have been aggressively disseminated to the public, notably in books by DiAngelo and Kendi,[60] now promoted as essential reading in many schools and universities. Critical Theories seek to fundamentally change the practice of science.[61] Figure 43.3 contrasts CSJ epistemology with the ideas of the liberal Enlightenment.

Liberal epistemology:	Critical Social Justice epistemology:
• Provisional truth is attainable; • Fallibilism: anyone can always be wrong; • Objectivity: a rejection of any theory that cannot be proven or disproven by reality; • Accountability: the openness to conceding and correcting errors; • Pluralism: the maintenance of intellectual diversity to maximize the chances of finding the truth.	• Denies existence of objective reality; • Replaces the concept of truth by "multiple narratives" and "alternative ways of knowing"; • States that claims to truth are merely claims to power; • Considers lived experience and subjectivism as the basis of knowledge; • Rejects that a theory can be proven or disproven by the empirical process; • Denies the legitimacy of other viewpoints; • Does not admit corrections from outside (closed system).

Figure 43.3. Liberal Enlightenment versus CSJ Epistemology.
D. Abbot et. al., "In Defense of Merit in Science," *Journal of Controversial Ideas* 3, no. 1 (April 2023): 1-26.

CSJ is not an empirical theory, because its tenets are maintained despite their being either demonstrably false or unfalsifiable.[62] The existence of objective reality, for example, which CSJ denies, is attested to by every successful engineering project, from bridges to satellites, from cell phones to electric cars, ever conducted. The fallibility of "lived experience" is attested to by a wealth of psychological research demonstrating errors and biases in self-reports.[63] Yet, CSJ has found its way into STEMM, evoking parallels with the ideological corruption of science of past totalitarian regimes.[64] As an illustration, *The Lancet* published a paper in 2020 titled "Adopting an Intersectionality Framework to Address Power and Equity in Medicine"[65]—a call to adopt CSJ ideology in medical education and practice. This is reminiscent of the ideological control of science[66] and medicine[67] in the USSR. In medicine, Marxist ideology manifested itself in "'workerizing'. . . [the] apparatus [of medical care]" (i.e., selecting future doctors from the working class, rather than the intelligentsia by means of class-based quotas) and prioritizing medical care for citizens based on class (the proletariat was to be given higher priority than the farm workers; the farm workers, higher priority than the intelligentsia; and so on).[68]

The CSJ view—that institutions of knowledge, art, and law perpetuate systemic racism and, therefore, must be dismantled, and that merit-based criteria in hiring, publishing, and funding must be replaced with CSJ criteria—has been aggressively advanced by many of our academic leadership—university administrators, executive bodies of professional societies, publishers, etc. A search for "racism" in the titles of papers published by the *Science* and *Nature* Publishing groups returns hundreds of hits such as "NIH Apologizes for 'Structural Racism,' Pledges Change,"[69] "Dismantling Systemic Racism in Science,"[70] and "Systemic Racism in Higher Education." This reflects the axiomatic ideological perspective of CSJ that systemic racism is indelibly etched into every Western institution. The perspective is taken as an article of faith, which is why some have argued that CSJ is more a secular religion than an evidence-based science.[71]

Below we discuss publications making unsupported claims of systemic injustices and attacking merit. Such publications rarely, if ever, provide evidence that observed disproportionalities in the race or gender distribution of a scientific field are the result of presentday structural or systemic racism. Whereas historical events, such as apartheid, slavery, and Jim Crow, are beyond dispute, the extent to which systemic racism influences STEMM or academia today is a contested question.[72] Its existence cannot be established by proclamation. In the absence of compelling evidence, these assertions are not scientific; they are dogma. In his book *Discrimination and Disparities*,[73] Sowell takes to task the central axiom of CSJ—that disparate outcomes for various social groups emerge as a result of discrimination—and presents ample evidence illustrating its fallacy. Sowell's arguments present compelling counterpoints to the standard set of arguments against meritocracy, such as those presented in *The Tyranny of Merit*[74] and *The Meritocracy Trap*.[75]

Space considerations do not permit a full evaluation of the arguments, many of which boil down to merit systems being imperfect; that is, that there are biases in judgments of merit, that they are not always implemented as promised, and that they risk creating hubris in the successful and despair among the unsuccessful. Our perspective is that, however valid these criticisms, merit-based systems are still immensely superior to alternatives that have either been tried before or are being proposed now.[76] Communist systems, for example, which are vastly more egalitarian, produced misery on an unimaginable scale.

Can newly proposed alternatives deliver better results? Let us consider an example. In *The Tyranny of Merit*,[77] Sandel proposes the following approach: identify some minimum standard that constitutes "qualified" for admission to Harvard or Stanford and use a lottery system to select among those. Specifically, he mentions cutoffs that would treat 50-75% of applicants as "qualified," which stops short of abandoning merit altogether. He justifies these cutoff points by using anecdotal data about athletes who were overlooked by professional teams in early draft rounds, but who went on to have highly successful careers in their sport. But examples of a few overlooked individuals do not imply that merit-based selection is ineffective—indeed, players drafted early are much more likely to go on to professional careers.[78] Sandel also seems to presume that identically capable college applicants will suffer if some end up attending lesser schools. However, in STEM (science, technology, engineering, and mathematics), where education provides objectively assessable technical skills, attendance at a top university provides little advantage in students' earnings potential. Measured 10 years postgraduation, a top-tier education provided no significant earnings advantage for science majors and at best a marginally significant one for engineering majors.[79] Moreover, Sandel seems to be unaware that his strategy, by nature of being based on a lottery, guarantees that many candidates will end up in lesser schools than their equally qualified counterparts, an outcome that a merit system, by its nature, aims to minimize.

Exhibits of the Intrusion of Ideology into Science and Attacks on Merit

In recent years, numerous statements issued by scientific societies and papers published in *Science*, *Nature*, the *New England Journal of Medicine*, *The Lancet*, and other respected journals have been advancing CSJ ideology and attacking science and liberal epistemology.[80] Journals now publish entire topical issues dedicated to CSJ subjects. For example, in 2022, *Science* published the topical issue "The Missing Physicists: How Physics Excludes Black Researchers";[81] *Chemical Education* published a virtual DEI collection comprising 67 papers exploring such topics as decolonization of the chemistry curriculum, chemistry and racism, and gender and sexual orientation identities in the chemistry classroom;[82] *Inorganic Chemistry* published an issue celebrating "LGBTQIAPN+ inorganic chemists";[83] *World Scientific* published the three-volume set *Porphyrin Science by Women*;[84] and *Nature* published an editorial, "Science Must Overcome Its Racist Legacy," announcing four forthcoming special issues dedicated to the topic[85] (the first issue was published in 2022).[86]

Below, we highlight selected examples of such publications, grouped according to recurring themes. Common among them is revolutionary destructivism, which calls for the established structures and practices of science to be replaced by CSJ-based practices. Words like "excellence," "impact," or "quality" rarely appear, or appear only to be problematized (which, according CSJ, can be done to anything).[87] Instead, we see ample mention of "White supremacy," "discrimination," "harassment," "race," "gender," "violence," "intersectionality," and "marginalization," typically without citation to supporting evidence, an egregious failure for journals purporting to be about science.

These pieces fail to acknowledge the progress that has been made and continues to be made toward equality, fairness, and justice throughout the Western world.[88] Instead, they attribute, generally without evidence, the underrepresentation of any group in any domain to systemic racism or sexism in the present and within the domain itself. This precludes an honest appraisal of the root causes of disparities and is likely to lead, therefore, to solutions that are ineffective, unjust, and damaging to science.[89]

The scientific community must come to the realization that such articles are not innocent expressions of well-meaning individuals. They are not exaggerations or outliers, but are true to the creed of the ideology that produced them.[90] The sheer volume of these publications illustrates the extent of the ideological intrusion into science.

Below we analyze three recurring themes in these papers: (1) science is White and colonial; (2) science is racist; and (3) merit-based policies should be replaced by identity-based policies.

Theme 1: Science is White and Colonial

For decades, Critical Theories had been confined to humanities and Studies departments of universities. But the ideas have spread to other disciplines and the outside world, where they have been picked up by activists and the press. Following the canons of CSJ, science is described as "White" and "colonial" and, therefore, should be dismantled. These ideas now routinely appear in some of the most influential scientific journals without citation to actual data supporting their claims. The apex journal *Nature* has created a "Decolonizing Science Toolkit,"[91] which includes articles such as "Institutions Must Acknowledge the Racist Roots in Science,"[92] "Decolonization Should Extend to Collaborations, Authorship and CoCreation of Knowledge,"[93] and "Seeding an Anti-Racist Culture at Scotland's Botanical Gardens."[94]

Decolonization is already a reality. For example, in New Zealand, decolonization of the sciences by adding the mythological content from Mātauranga Māori to the science curriculum is now actively pursued throughout schools and universities with the support of the government,[95] and any criticism to this is termed racist.[96]

The decolonization theme has been amplified, ironically, by institutions whose supposed telos is to support science. An article published in *Nature* attempting to justify the decolonization of science in South Africa states: "Decolonization is a movement to eliminate. . . the disproportionate legacy of white European thought and culture in education . . . dismantling the hegemony of European values and making way for the local philosophy and traditions that colonists had cast aside."[97] One might think, the article would identify how, for example, Newtonian physics or Darwin's biology went wrong and the errors were fixed by indigenous knowledge. It does nothing of the kind. Instead, it discusses the value of greater local involvement in science and having science education address local needs and interests. These laudable goals, which we hope succeed, have nothing to do with "the hegemony of European values." Indeed, the article acknowledges that "the meaning of decolonization is not well defined . . . " We doubt it can be because it is ideological rhetoric rather than a scientific statement with truth value.

In 2021, *The Lancet Global Health* invited and published the opinion piece "Says Who? Northern Ventriloquism, or Epistemic Disobedience in Global Health Scholarship," which purports to expose "epistemic violence" in the scientific literature.[98] The author calls for "epistemic resistance" to disrupt the accepted standards and practices in global health scholarship. She claims:

> Epistemic violence is the active oppression by powerful structures to displace the marginalized from socioeconomic and knowledge-creating institutions to suppress their political voices. This exclusion incessantly erases contributions from LMICs [Low and Middle Income Countries] to global knowledge creation.

She cites three sources to justify this alleged "incessant erasure"—all of which include a great deal of historical analysis but nothing recognizable as empirical evidence of said erasure in the present.

Papers calling for "decolonization" of practically every domain of STEMM are mushrooming in the literature, with little opposition. A rare exception[99] critiques the notion of decolonizing global health. The authors articulate the harms of the decolonization agenda, namely, that it undermines confidence in scientific knowledge, promotes intergroup and international antagonisms, disregards the possibility of progress, and, most importantly, closes the door to achievable change in an unequal world. Dismantling global health will not give us better treatments for debilitating diseases or tools to control the next pandemic.

Theme 2: Science is Racist
Race has become a central political and social issue in the U.S. and beyond. Learned societies and institutions, including the National Academy of Scienc-

es (NAS),[100] the National Academy of Engineering,[101] the National Academy of Medicine,[102] and the National Institutes of Health,[103] have issued statements asserting, without evidence, the existence of systemic racism among their ranks and pledging to combat it. The American Physical Society, the American Geophysical Union, the Geological Society of America, the Society for the Study of Evolution, the National Association of Geoscience Teachers, and their sister societies outside the U.S. have published similar statements. Numerous university science departments have followed suit. In the journal *Science*, chemist Holden Thorp claimed (ironically, without evidence) that "evidence of systemic racism in science pervades this nation [the U.S.]."[104] In an unsigned editorial, *Nature's* editors stated that "scientific institutions were—and remain—complicit in systemic racism" and pledged to "end anti-Black practices in research."[105] The American Chemical Society published an editorial signed by all senior editors alleging the existence of systemic racism in chemistry publishing. Among several action points, they pledged to include "diversity of journal contributors as an explicit measurement of Editor-in-Chief performance."[106]

A *Nature* editorial[107] in 2021 reaffirms this narrative: "Racism in science is endemic because the systems that produce and teach scientific knowledge have marginalized and ill-treated people of other skin colors and underrepresented groups for centuries"; organizations "must ensure that anti-racism is embedded in their... objectives and that such work wins recognition and promotion"; and "too often, conventional metrics—citations, publication, profits—reward those in positions of power, rather than helping to shift the balance of power." *Nature* continued this theme in a recent editorial, calling for the decolonization of science and arguing that past racism has left "an indelible mark on science." In 2022, the journal released a volume, titled "Racism,"[108] which includes personal accounts of several authors of perceived racism throughout STEMM, including artificial intelligence and computer science, genetics, plant biology, and medicine (citing oxygen-sensor inaccuracy in Black people), as well as more general contributions on how to confront "imperialism's long shadows" and its racist past.

In 2022, *Science* published the special issue "The Missing Physicists: How Physics Excludes Black Researchers" featuring an editorial "Dismantle Racism in Science"[109] and several pieces with titles such as "Can U.S. Physics Overcome Its Record of Exclusion?,"[110] "The Toll of White Privilege,"[111] and "Fix the System, Not the Students."[112] The recurring themes are that physics is racist and exclusionary, run by a "White priesthood," and based on "White privilege"; that existing programs do not serve women or minorities, who purportedly need a different educational approach; and that merit-based evaluations must be relaxed to increase diversity in science, and that this will benefit the field.

As is typical when viewed through the lens of Critical Theory, these assertions were not buttressed by actual evidence of systemic racism—the existence of quantitative disparities was the only evidence required.[113] This may be valid in a dogmatic ideological framework that attributes all inequality to "isms." But from a scientific perspective, assertions require evidence and correlation does not imply causation. In fact, the assertion that all inequality in the present is determined by discrimination in the present is readily refuted by evidence. For example, Asian Americans earn more advanced degrees and have higher incomes than do White Americans.[114] The notion that all inequality reflects systemic racism leads to the absurd conclusion that the U.S. is an Asian supremacist country. Many more examples of this kind can be found in *Discrimination and Disparities*.[115]

Articles accusing science of racism often support their claims by historical examples of scientists who held racist beliefs—like those in Darwin's day who, while they may have been abolitionists (like Darwin himself), still believed in a racial hierarchy of intelligence with White people on top. But one would be hard-pressed to give examples of institutional features today that foster discrimination and are responsible for the dearth of minority scientists in STEM. For example, the authors of the *Nature* editorial[116] support their claim of current systemic racism by asserting that people like J. D. Watson, C. Murray, and R. Herrnstein are racist. Even if true, three anecdotal cases do not indict science itself as rife with systemic racism. Several contributions to the topical issue on racism published by *Nature*[117] also support claims of current systemic racism by personal anecdotes. A paper in *Nature Geoscience* titled "Scientists from Historically Excluded Groups Face a Hostile Obstacle Course"[118] supports the title thesis by citing a tweet and a peer-reviewed paper based on "an interpretation of the dream of an African American woman."[119]

The proposed solutions—to a problem that has not been shown to exist—endanger the integrity of the scientific enterprise. Scientific positions, grants, and article acceptances should be awarded on the basis of their quality rather than treated as commodities to be distributed based on identity categories. The telos of science is the search for provisional truth and the production of knowledge, not the redistribution of rewards to achieve activists' visions of equity or reparative justice.

Claims of systemic racism in academic research have spilled over into applied domains, notably medicine.[120] An article, "An Antiracist Agenda for Medicine," characterizes the handling of the COVID19 crisis as "ongoing genocide, shamefully, if quietly, embedded in a centuries-old legacy of structural, scientific and medical racism."[121] That the absurd comparison of the COVID19 crisis to genocide made it into print is consistent with a growing body of evidence suggesting that, in the "right" circles, one can make almost any ridiculous claim, as long as one frames it as advancing "Social Justice."[122]

The American Medical Association has produced a guide to language, asking practitioners to avoid using adjectives such as "vulnerable" and "high-risk" and to avoid saying "target," "combat," or other "terms with violent connotation" because they reinforce "narratives that constantly shift and adapt as conditions change and serve to rationalize the privileges of racism that sustain white supremacy."[123] These recommendations and similar DEI guidelines issued by the

American Association of Medical Colleges[124] are set to be implemented in medical schools' curricula.

The American Psychological Association makes a lengthy apology to people of color for the association's supposed role in "promoting, perpetuating, and failing to challenge racism, racial discrimination and human hierarchy in the U.S."[125] They promote a radical, non evidence-based, untested psychotherapy that encourages patients to see their problems through a lens of power and race, a recommendation flagrantly abandoning known best practices, such as centering therapy on the concerns of the patient, rather than those of the therapist,[126] and cognitive behavioral therapy. This is not science; it is ideology and, arguably, malpractice.

Theme 3: Merit-Based Policies Should Be Replaced by Identity-Based Policies

Many scientific fields are now under pressure to rethink how research is conducted. The forms of pressure range from injunctions to increase the diversity of researchers to calls to eliminate merit-based metrics of the performance of students, postdocs, and faculty.[127] The existing standards are purported to be "White," "colonial," "sexist," and insufficiently inclusive. Traditional success and impact metrics (e.g., citations and impact factors) are claimed to be "flawed and biased against already marginalized groups" and to perpetuate "sexist and racist 'rewards.'"[128]

Major scientific journals such as *Nature, Science,* and their sister publications regularly publish opinions, editorials, and letters to the editor calling for increasing the number of women and selected minorities among tenure-track faculty, graduate students, award recipients, conference speakers, and editorial boards. In response, scientific institutions have begun implementing identity-based practices and social engineering.[129] Some faculty hiring committees are prioritizing diversity over merit or even using ideology as a filter by, for example, eliminating candidates solely based on DEI statements.[130]

Many scientific societies now encourage or require identity-based quotas for speakers and award recipients.[131] NAS now penalizes its nominating committees if their nominations are insufficiently diverse.[132] If one has any doubt that CSJ ideology is replacing merit-based science, this quote from McNutt (president of the NAS) and Castillo-Page (its Chief Diversity and Inclusion Officer) is the smoking gun:

> Not so long ago, the NAS might have naively argued that its membership could not reflect the diversity of the American public it serves until universities fixed the 'leaky pipeline' of too many women opting out of careers in scientific research almost before they begin, or until elementary and secondary schools started motivating more students of color to study STEMM disciplines and prepared them for success in college and beyond. But in 2021, it is simply not acceptable to wait for 'bottom-up' solutions.[133]

This implies that membership in the Academy should reflect an aspirational dream of proportional representation, rather than the real demographics of the most meritorious scientists. The secretary of the NAS revealed how this will operate: "We assign slots [to different fields] based on the diversity of the lists of nominees that get forwarded" and "If they used [their slots] to pick a bunch of white guys from Harvard, they get penalized."[134]

In some ways, this is trivial concerning the production of science. Membership in NAS is not science; it is an honor in recognition of contributions to science. In that sense, it is a reward to be distributed, not a scientific discovery or invention of any import. But if we continue to subjugate meritocracy to CSJ by failing to reward the best performing individuals and recognize the most creative and influential work, we risk eroding scientific excellence. When NAS signals "this is the way we provide scientific rewards," other scientific institutions will follow their lead.

Race and gender-based selection for honors, conference presentations, and awards undermines the achievements of individuals from underrepresented groups by creating an impression that women and minorities cannot compete in an open marketplace of ideas and talent. It is also offensive to know that one's research was selected, not strictly for its merit, but at least partly due to one's ethnicity or gender. This is "the soft bigotry of low expectations"—the creation of different standards based on the perceived or real historical oppression of some individuals.[135]

Some form of affirmative action might be effective in college admissions, when students do not yet possess demonstrated credentials and many have lacked educational opportunities. However, when preferential selection goes overboard, e.g., when the mean scores on admission criteria of affirmative action students is a standard deviation (or more) below those of students admitted under conventional standards, the practice becomes counterproductive in helping underrepresented groups to advance.[136] This failure of affirmative action in the U.S. is well documented; despite being in place for more than half a century in U.S. colleges, race-conscious admissions have not led to proportional representation in STEMM.[137] The total number of Black students matriculating in U.S. medical schools has not changed in over three decades.[138] This is striking because, in the U.S., students from minority backgrounds indicate more interest in STEM than White students: a 1985 study of 27,065 incoming freshmen in 388 colleges found that the initial interest in STEM majors was 53%, 34–35%, and 17% for Asian American, Hispanic/African American, and White students, respectively.[139] Despite this initial interest, the rates of graduation with STEM majors vastly differ: 70% of Asian Americans persist in their ambition compared to 61% of Whites, 55% of Hispanics, and 34% of African Americans. The disparities are even more extreme at elite institutions.[140] The analysis attributes this attrition to academic mismatch—by admitting minority students to schools that do not match their academic preparation, these students are at a disadvantage and often drop out or change to non STEM majors, ironically, often to identity studies. In better matched schools, students do well and graduate in STEM fields. Paradoxically, strong affirmative action appears to lead to a decrease of African American and Hispanic American students entering STEM fields.[141]

CRT-informed social engineering is now present in every domain of science, including publishing, hiring, and research funding.[142] The Royal Society of Chemistry has issued a quota of 35% representation of women on editorial boards and in reviewer pools[143]—considerably greater than the current representation of women holding tenure and tenure-track positions in chemistry departments (~20%).[144] Australia's National Health and Medical Research Council will allocate half the funding for its largest research program to women and non-binary applicants.[145]

Some journal editorials have begun urging authors to preferentially cite "articles led by colleagues from different gender identities and geographical areas,"[146] in the spirit of "citation justice."[147] Tools to implement "citation justice" already exist.[148] The publisher Elsevier encourages authors to apply "citation justice" on a voluntary basis,[149] while other publishers have implemented policies, such as mandatory DEI statements,[150] to that end. The promoters of "citation justice" justify the practice by the assumption that differences in citation rates are due to racist or sexist biases in publishing.[151] This, however, is an unsubstantiated claim, as we discuss below.

Claims of bias in STEM, which now pervade the literature, are typically based on anecdotal evidence, superficial analyses, or ideologically based assumptions. A typical example is a paper that alleges the existence of gender bias in chemistry publishing based on a superficial analysis of publication statistics.[152] Although the authors found gender differences in various metrics of professional accomplishment, the differences were small—e.g., on the order of one percentage point in manuscript acceptance rates. Moreover, the authors failed to adequately control for potentially confounding factors (e.g., seniority of researchers) that could explain the observed gender discrepancies. Yet, despite this paper's poor scholarship, it has been cited as evidence of biases in chemistry and used to justify imposing gender quotas on editorial boards and in reviewer pools.[153]

When confounding factors are controlled, evidence of gender bias in STEM all but vanishes. Controlling for confounding variables, a recently completed quantitative synthesis of the literature on gender gaps in six academic science domains (manuscript acceptance rates, recommendation letters, tenure-track hiring, grant funding, salaries, and teaching ratings) found convincing evidence of bias only in teaching ratings, and the oft-cited gender pay gap of 18%[154] was reduced to 4%. In the other five domains, the authors concluded that there has been "no systematic gender bias in the last 10–20 years."[155] Similarly, a recent encyclopedic review of the literature on gender gaps in STEM found that "the evidence for endemic anti-female bias is inconclusive at best," and that, instead, "the main cause of the gender gaps in STEM appears to be average sex differences in people's vocational preferences."[156]

Furthermore, there is no evidence that introducing identity-based biases to the peer review process will do anything to improve science. Adding citational "representation" to redress grievances makes sense only if one views citations as rewards to be distributed rather than as acknowledgments of scientific contributions. Although the current peer-review system is not perfect and is sometimes affected by personal biases, these imperfections do not justify adding non-scientific considerations to review processes. Bias should be eliminated by procedures that cleave to truth and rigorous evidence, not by reversing the direction of the biases or adding irrelevant noise. Intentionally adding biases and imperfections erodes the integrity of the literature.

In a similar vein, institutions justify mandatory DEI training by alleged implicit biases, based mostly on the implicit association test (IAT), which is riddled with conceptual, theoretical, empirical, statistical, and methodological limitations, weaknesses, and artifacts.[157] Indeed, there is no evidence that receiving implicit bias training or reducing implicit bias as measured by the IAT reduces discriminatory behavior.[158]

In hiring at many universities, faculty applicants are now required to write DEI statements.[159] In recent faculty searches in the life sciences at UC Berkeley, three-quarters of the candidates were eliminated solely on the basis on their DEI statements.[160] Putting aside separate objections that the use of DEI statements to screen applicants constitutes a political litmus test and a form of (possibly illegal) compelled speech, by reducing the viable applicant pool, it likely undermines the quality of science.[161] Thus, a brilliant mathematician (or physicist or cognitive scientist) may be filtered out by virtue of having expressed insufficient enthusiasm or familiarity with the particular version of DEI that the institution supports.

DEI statements are often expected to embrace CSJ; statements that express support for the ideals of liberal social justice, such as Dr. Martin Luther King Jr.'s dream of a colorblind society, are rejected. As UC Berkeley's sample rubric for evaluating diversity statements states, candidates who intend to treat "all students the same regardless of their background" will be given the lowest score.[162] In 2021, job advertisements for STEMM faculty often devote more space to DEI requirements than to actual technical qualifications. As McWhorter notes, job advertisements for physicists now sound like advertisements for social workers or anthropologists.[163] Some universities have begun to incorporate DEI statements in tenure and promotion.[164] The process of evaluation needs to be reformed, according to a 2022 paper in the journal *eLife*, which provides "A Guide for Writing Anti-Racist Tenure and Promotion Letters."[165] The authors recommend that the letter writers include their positionality statements, invite the evaluation committee to reflect on "White supremacy culture" in academia, and redefine what is considered to be meritorious.

In research funding, some grant programs now require that applications include an explanation of how the proposed project will address the principles of

DEI.[166] Failure to adequately address DEI bears the risk of rejection. Should government funding advance science—fundamental research, energy solutions, health, and medicine—or social engineering? McWhorter notes:

> The notion seems to be that practitioners and scholars, across disciplines, must devote a considerable part of their time to putatively antiracist initiatives. It's a bold proposition, but given how shaky its actual justification is, it is reasonable to think that lately this devotion is being imposed by fiat, as opposed to being an organic outpouring. And if the price for questioning that notion is to be seen as sitting somewhere on a spectrum ranging from retrogressive to racist, it's a price few are willing to pay. One is, rather, to pretend.[167]

Europe, like the U.S., is susceptible to the ideology of identity.[168] One of the five pillars of the 2021–2027 agenda of the European Union is developing a "more social and inclusive" Europe.[169] To implement this noble vision, most European calls for STEMM funding (e.g., Horizon Europe) require plans demonstrating how proposed research will benefit underrepresented minorities. Venerable institutions with a history of promoting excellence and being merit-driven, such as the German Science Foundation, the Alexander von Humboldt Foundation, and the Max Planck Society, have issued generic pledges to advance diversity, formulated in CSJ terms. More than 200 institutions from around the globe signed the Alba Declaration on Equity and Inclusion, which asserts that bias against women and minorities in STEM is ubiquitous and calls for social engineering.[170]

The Way Forward

Science has been the driving force behind unprecedented improvements in the global quality of life—from advances in medical diagnostics and cancer treatment to the information technology revolution, from the growth of agricultural productivity to the development of sustainable energy. Science and technology are global and highly competitive. If dismantling the merit-based practices of the U.S. and other democratic countries continues unabated, the loss of leadership in developing cutting-edge technologies is likely to eventuate.

For science to succeed, it must strive for the non-ideological pursuit of objective truth. Scientists should feel free to pursue political projects in the public sphere as private citizens, but not to inject their personal politics and biases into the scientific endeavor. Maintaining institutional neutrality is also essential for cultivating public trust in science.[171] The rush to create systems institutionalizing racial, ethnic, and gender preferences in college admissions and hiring will further corrode public trust in academia and science (e.g., surveys from the U.S. show that most Americans, including most Americans of color, reject such preferences).[172] Although no system is guaranteed to eliminate all biases, merit-based systems are the best tool to mitigate it. Moreover, they promote social cohesion because they can be observed to maximize fairness.

Admittedly, meritocracy is imperfect. The best and brightest do not always win. But the idea that meritocracy is nothing but a myth is demonstrably false, indeed absurd. Were it but a myth, college admissions and hiring could be conducted without regard to applicants' qualifications, and students or employees could be selected at random.

The role of science in rectifying social inequalities goes beyond "trickle-down" effects of scientific progress. Science can help to develop programs addressing both the root causes of inequalities and the effectiveness of remedial policies. Recent works by Banerjee and Duflo illustrate how well-founded scientific methodology can narrow the gap between rich and poor countries.[173] Heckman's work quantifies the impact of preschool education on students' success.[174] In the field of artificial intelligence, one of the most active areas of research is concerned with discrimination,[175] fairness,[176] and social accountability.[177] The distinctive features of these examples, setting them apart from CSJ, are that they are based on scientific evidence and logic and they address the root causes of inequalities, rather than their symptomatic manifestations.

There is a large literature in the field of psychology on the role that demographic biases play in how we judge individuals.[178] Such biases are real and a justified concern, but fighting them with opposite biases and undermining merit is counterproductive. Two of the most robust findings in the literature are: (1) people massively judge others on their merits when their merits are clear and salient; and (2) in such situations, stereotypes and implicit biases[179] are minimized. Thus, a sharp focus on merit minimizes bias and maximizes the chances that those who best meet the relevant standards (for admissions, hiring, publication, or anything else) will be rewarded, thereby promoting inclusion. For example, standardized tests can help to fairly evaluate applicants from diverse backgrounds[180] and—if used properly—increase diversity.[181] A strict focus on merit, properly implemented, also reduces the influence of bias, department politics, nepotism, and favoritism, thus facilitating diversity, while maximizing scientific quality and the public's confidence and trust in the academy and science.

How do we begin the process of depoliticizing science and strengthening merit-based practices? We offer six concrete suggestions:

- Insist that government funding for research be distributed solely on the basis of merit.
- Ensure that academic departments and conferences select speakers based on scientific, rather than ideological, considerations.
- Ensure that admissions, hiring, and promotion are merit based and free from ideological tests.
- Publish and retract scientific papers on the basis of scientific, not ideological, arguments or due to public pressure.

- Require that universities enforce policies protecting academic freedom and freedom of expression, according to best practices promulgated by nonpartisan free speech and academic freedom organizations, such as the Foundation for Individual Rights and Expression.
- Insist that university departments and professional societies refrain from issuing statements on social and political issues not relevant to their functioning, as recommended in the University of Chicago's Kalven Report.[182]

Although much has been written about DEI, the arguments advocating it fall into familiar categories: reparative justice is needed to redress historical discrimination; DEI is necessary to fight current discrimination; and DEI is needed to level the playing field and achieve equal outcomes.

With respect to reparative justice, affirmative action policies are ineffective, arguably unfair, and counterproductive. Although we see no role in science for identity-based policies, we recognize that the playing field is not level. Outreach in admissions and hiring to candidates from less advantaged backgrounds is important, not only to promote fairness, but to enlarge the pool of promising candidates. Schools and universities have a role to play in leveling the playing field by uplifting students who have come from more difficult life circumstances, not by imposing quotas or lowering academic standards, but by providing students with opportunities to develop the rigorous skills they need to enter scientific fields, and the support to do so. In this way, merit and diversity become synergistic rather than antagonistic.

Advocates of CSJ approaches to DEI often present the options as if it is either CSJ or bigotry. We reject this false dichotomy. Dismantling or disrupting institutional practices that have produced science's achievements, and replacing them with untested methods opposed to the Mertonian norms is a dangerous experiment that jeopardizes the future of science.

Conclusion

Imbuing science with ideology harms the scientific enterprise and leads to a loss of public trust. If we continue to undermine merit, our universities will become institutions of mediocrity rather than places of creativity and accomplishment, leading to the loss of the competitive edge in technology. Thus, we need to restore our commitment to practices grounded in epistemic humility and the meritocratic, liberal tradition.

We need to be vigilant against the dilution of our merit evaluations by biases, ideology, and nepotism. Moreover, as a community, we should continue to invest in mentoring and education to help people develop their full potential. Adopting the guidelines we have suggested does not mean that we ignore the contributions of past racism and sexism to the inequalities we observe today. It means addressing these issues in a fundamentally positive way—not by introducing diversity metrics into funding or hiring decisions, nor by weakening the standards for university admissions and professional advancement, but by investing in the early pipeline, for example, by strengthening educational outreach and programs to increase access to sustained quality education and early exposure to STEMM.

Scientists must start standing up for the integrity of their fields despite the risk of bullying and verbal attacks; donors and funders should condition their support on nonpartisan and rational scientific pursuit. Science as a free pursuit of knowledge untainted by ideological orthodoxies maximally enhances the public good.

Afterword

Perhaps the grandest irony of them all, and the saddest commentary on the state of academia, is that this article, defending merit, could only be published in a journal devoted to airing "controversial" ideas.[183] As we were finalizing the manuscript for publication, the Office of Science and Technology Policy of the White House released a 14 page long vision statement outlining the priorities for the U.S. STEMM ecosystem.[184] The word "merit" appears nowhere in the document. In February, 2023, The National Academy of Sciences released a report titled "Advancing Antiracism, Diversity, Equity, and Inclusion in STEMM Organizations: Beyond Broadening Participation." The report describes merit as a non-objective, "culturally construed" concept used to hide bias and perpetuate privilege, refers to objectivity and meritocracy in STEMM as myths, and calls for merit-based metrics of evaluation to be dismantled.[185]

CHAPTER 44
The Importance of Facts and Expertise[1]

Featuring Tom Nichols and Lee McIntyre

Moderator: Could we begin with brief overviews of your most recent books, *Post-Truth* [by Lee McIntyre] and *The Death of Expertise* [by Tom Nichols], as well as whether anything has changed since their publication?

Lee McIntyre (LM): I defined post-truth in the first part of the book as the political subordination of reality. I started writing that book just after the Oxford Dictionary named post-truth as the 2016 Word of the Year. Some of the examples that I discussed in the book were: how many people were or were not at Trump's inauguration, whether it rained at the inauguration, the path of the hurricane, and a few things like that. The book actually came out in early 2018 and things just kept happening, there were just more and more examples.

When I saw the Capitol Riot on January 6th, 2021, I think that was the ultimate example of the political subordination of reality. It was not just a one-off, it was something that had been cultivated over many months, if not years, and it had enormous consequences for our democracy. Here somebody didn't like what reality was, and so they pretended it was otherwise. They then mobilized a crew of people to believe it and to assault Congress. I think that's kind of the ultimate example. I don't really feel like things changed other than to confirm the point that I was making early on.

Post-truth as a phenomenon did not just go away when Trump left office because I don't think that he was the cause of it, he was a symptom of it.

Tom Nichols (TN): I agree with Lee that Trump was not the motivator of this.

Trump rode this wave, he surfed it, but he didn't create it.

When I wrote *Death of Expertise* I think I was too optimistic. Toward the end of the book, although I didn't have a lot of solutions, I said that usually a disaster is what snaps people out of this—if there's a war or a recession or a pandemic. I said, well, you can't argue with a pandemic, you do what you can to get by it and we would all kind of pull together. I perhaps did not understand the depth to which the post-truth problem as a political problem had taken root. I thought of it primarily as a social problem, and I did not fully account for the fact that there would be a national leader and an entire political party that would actually continue to drive insane narratives about science. I didn't realize the degree to which that kind of political opposition to scientific reasoning, not fact, but just scientific reasoning—hypotheses, methods, evidence, logic, etc.—would simply go out the window so that people could feel better about their politics. I really underestimated the degree to which that was possible.

So I am more pessimistic about the problem now than I was when I wrote the book.

Moderator: We know that humans have hard-wired cognitive biases that can make it difficult for them to do a good job of finding reliable news sources and interpreting information accurately. Could you talk a little bit about this problem?

TN: The average person says, "A good source is one that agrees with me and the things I already think. And a bad source is one that presents me with uncomfortable cognitive dissonance. A bad source is one that challenges my tribal political affiliations with information that makes me uncomfortable about those affiliations."

LM: Cognitive biases have been with us throughout the evolution of our species, I'm sure. It's actually an interesting academic question, why we have them. I mean, what's the survival value for making a mistake in reasoning? But for whatever reason they're there—no matter what your political convictions are, liberals and conservatives both have them. They're wired in.

Some pushback that I get on the concept of post-truth is that politicians have always lied, or that people have always lied. I agree there's always been a certain amount of lying, it's not that this was born in 2016. What happened is it got worse. This predilection that people have to believe fake things when they hear them more than once or from multiple sources, these biases that we have are made much worse when they're amplified. And that's what social media has done.

Fringe conspiracy theories were always out there, but somebody had to mimeograph them and hand them out on the sidewalk, or if they could get into a tabloid at the grocery store then maybe the folks standing in line would buy it. Now it's on the internet, and people can get traction for just about anything that they think of.

TN: Physiologically it feels bad to be wrong. We literally have a physical reaction to being wrong because it feels good to be right. There is an evolutionary basis.

We're also hardwired to cooperate. So when enough people believe something, you want to believe it too, because being the truth teller is like being the uncomfortable skunk at the garden party.

People have always doubted experts. In *The Death of Expertise*, I talk about when I was a young brand-new assistant professor, I used to go down and hang out with my brother in his bar down in our very working-class neighborhood in Massachusetts. I'd go hang out with my brother and one time when I left, this guy turned to my brother and asked, "So your brother's a professor?" And my brother said, "Yeah." And the guy replied, "Seems like he's a good guy anyway." So that goes with the territory, you know. Nobody likes exclusion and expertise is exclusionary by its nature.

This predates social media. I date this from maybe the late 1960s or early 1970s. There is a tidal wave of narcissism that starts to overtake us in the late 1960s and early 1970s, where it's not just people doubting experts, but believing they are smarter than experts.

Somebody in the past might say to a doctor, "I don't trust your diagnosis, I'm gonna get another opinion." What's really different now is they walk in and say, "Here's what's wrong with me, and here's what you are going to do." Parents will say to doctors, "We're not here to argue with you. We've done our research, we know what we want."

People thinking that they know more about a subject than doctors or diplomats or arms control experts or neurosurgeons or whatever it is, it is really remarkable.

And you saw it in spades when Donald Trump became president. He goes to the CDC and he says, "I know more than the doctors. They're amazed at how much I know. Everyone tells me I should have been a doctor." And millions of Americans said, "I totally get that guy. I totally understand this."

My high school English teacher used to call it aggressive stupidity. There is this almost kind of feral stupidity. It's not just, "I believe what I believe and leave me alone." It's evangelical: "I believe this, and you must believe it, too."

LM: You talk about narcissism and people tend to think that that's just an individual thing, but it's heightened in the group, right? Through the amplification of disinformation on social media and elsewhere, if you can find other people who agree with you, then that makes it even more aggressive. That makes the person even more likely to say, not just "I know better than the experts," but "We know better than the experts" because they can find a bunch of other people who aren't experts either who agree with them.

TN: Yeah, this is where social media has become terrifying. Yevgeny Simkin says that every town has a guy shouting that "the end is near." In previous times, that guy had a sandwich board and everybody went, "That's just Billy. He does that." But when 10,000 of them reach out and form a union, then they're like, "Well, 10,000 of us can't be wrong."

Moderator: Yevgeny Simkin is great. He wrote the following in *The Bulwark*:

> Let's take a short walk down memory lane. It's 1995. A man stands on a busy street corner yelling vaguely incoherent things at the passersby. He's holding a placard that says 'THE END IS NIGH. REPENT.' You come upon this guy while out getting the paper. How do you feel about him? You might feel some flavor of annoyance. Most people would also feel compassion for him as he is clearly suffering from something. No reasonable person would think of convincing this man that his point of view is incorrect. This isn't an opportunity for an engaging debate. This guy doesn't kill at parties. This guy doesn't go to parties. He's only out here because he's not violent and there's no room for him at Bellevue. Now fast forward to 2020. In terms of who this guy is and who you are absolutely nothing has changed. And yet here you are—arguing with him on Twitter or Facebook. And you, yourself, are being brought to the brink of insanity. . . Back in 2011 Chamath Palihapitiya left Facebook and said of his former company, 'It literally is a point now where I think we have created tools that are ripping apart the social fabric of how society works'. . . [Social media] is single-handedly responsible for the tearing apart of our social fabric which Palihapitiya so presciently predicted. . . An insidious malware slowly corrupting our society in ways that are extremely difficult to quantify, but the effects of which are evident all around us. Anti-vaxxers, anti-maskers, QAnon, cancel-culture, Alex Jones, flat-earthers, racists, anti-racists, anti-anti-racists, and of course the Twitter stylings of our Dear Leader.[2]

That's a great quote. Can you talk a little bit about different media practices that have played a role in all of this?

The Importance of Facts and Expertise   315

<u>LM</u>: I think that the model here that everybody will understand is what the media used to do with science denial topics like anti-vax or climate change. You don't have to go back that many years to remember the split screen debates. They would have an expert from the National Academy of Sciences on one side and some guy with a website on the other side. They would give them equal time to talk and make their points. At the end the host would say, "It's a complicated issue. You decide."

Journalists are afraid of being accused of being biased and the easiest way to get around that is just to let both sides talk and give them equal time. But that leads to something called information bias, when you leave your audience less well in-formed than when they started watching your program. And I'm afraid that that's what happened with anti-vax and with climate change.

Now a number of the media outlets stopped doing that because things got real. There started to be measles outbreaks. They started to understand they were caus-ing real damage. The trouble is that that instinct is still there. You'll see it on political topics. You can have differences of opinion where it's perfectly legitimate to have a split screen debate and hear both sides. But when they're talking about matters of fact, it's not appropriate to do it that way.

The halfway point between the truth and a lie is still a lie. You can't just give both sides equal time and think, "Well, the truth is probably somewhere in the middle." It is the responsibility of media to tell the truth. You shouldn't give liars a micro-phone. They have to stop giving a platform to people with an agenda who are creating disinformation and lies and trying to amplify that out to their followers.

<u>TN</u>: As usual I sign on to everything Lee said. But a part of the problem is not with the media, it's with us. Why do we have these big gladiatorial arguments on television? Because that's what people want.

If you've ever been in a modern newsroom, they know exactly what you're read-ing all the time. They have these big electronic command centers. They know what page most people are on. They know how long they dwell on an article. They know all this stuff.

I was on a panel one time with somebody from *The Washington Post*. Somebody stood up and kind of pointed their finger and said, "Why don't you guys write more explainers and help us understand things?" And he said, "We do. You don't read them."

Capitalism has created news as a product, and so we get what we want. We have information poisoning for the same reason that we are all overweight and diabetic—because we like to eat junk food and so we do. That's what we want and so that's what the market provides to us.

The problem of "presenting both sides" is partly to service our narcissism. It's like, "Well, they didn't represent somebody who has my view on it. Are they saying that my view isn't good enough?" And instead of being courageous and saying, "Yes, that's right, your view is stupid, your view is crazy, the world is not flat," they say, "Well, all right, we'll have it as a debate because everybody loves a debate."

It's also our false sense of egalitarianism that we don't like to have anyone on who speaks authoritatively without being challenged. So somebody says that the world is round, we have to have one person who "speaks for the common person" saying the world isn't round, and that makes us feel good. We sit back in our chairs and we say, "See, somebody stuck it to that smarty pants."

We lost our nerve somewhere. There's a loss of virtue in all this.

I gave a talk awhile back to a committee at the National Academy of Sciences. I said, "Get out there and plant the flag. Stop arguing with people about the basic nature of reality. Say, 'Look, I'm a Nobel Prize-winning astrophysicist, and I promise you that the world is not flat and I'm not gonna argue about this.'"

I think the media is saying, "Well, we don't wanna offend anybody, so we have to have a variety of views." And in a market where eyeballs are money, you fight for every set of eyeballs.

Moderator: Lee, you have a great example involving Indiana Jones when talking about this flood of information that we have available to us today, and the need to be able to identify what is good information and what's bad information.

LM: People have said, "Look, the internet is wonderful because you can find truth. I mean, you don't need an encyclopedia anymore. It's all there, you can go out and find it." The problem is that it's cluttered with a lot of other stuff that you've gotta be able to find your way through.

There's this wonderful scene in *Indiana Jones and the Last Crusade* where Indiana Jones is looking for the Holy Grail. It's right in front of him with like 99 fakes, and he doesn't know which one it is. That's what the internet is like. We've got true information at our fingertips but we cannot always discern the difference.

Another metaphor I talk about is when I was a little boy, I would be standing in line talking to my mom as we were checking out at the grocery store. And there was the *National Enquirer* with this scandalous headline. I'd said, "Wow, mom, you know, look at that. Aliens have landed." And she'd say, "No, no. That's the *National Enquirer.*" And she explained to me what they were doing. But imagine if you took a copy of the *National Enquirer* and a copy of the *New York Times* and you made all the formatting and the fonts the same and presented all the articles side by side. That's what you see now on Facebook and Twitter. That's how people get their news.

Tom, your insight about expertise is spot on. And I think another problem is, not only do people not trust experts, they don't have the wherewithal sometimes to know who the experts are. It's not just that they challenge scientific facts but the process by which scientific facts are discovered. It's the Dunning-Kruger effect, right? Too stupid to know they're stupid.

TN: I think sometimes students think I'm a Luddite, but I'm a techno optimist. I'm 60, and the internet came of age when I did. I had my first email account in 1983, before people used that term. I was totally a nerd about everything related to computers and I still am. I mean I'm 60 years old and I'm still a computer gamer. I probably shouldn't admit that out loud, but I am.

Students say to me, "The internet, it's the Library of Alexandria online." And I say, "No, the internet is a giant dumpster." They think I hate the internet, but that's not true, I hate anything that doesn't have gatekeepers. I had a blog. I took it down because a student said to me, "Can I quote your blog?" And I said, "No, the editor's an idiot." You should never be your own editor, there is no quality control. If it doesn't have editors, if it doesn't have a corrections page, if it's not an established press, etc.

I think the other problem with the internet is that we have come to believe that information is always interesting. Tucker Carlson and Rachel Maddow both present information in the same way: I am letting you into something very cool. I am here to tell you secret stuff, I will make you one of the elect who understands. The internet plays to that all the time in a similar way. The internet is the worst of all worlds in that way. We've come to expect that information is this constant jolt of dopamine because we expect that everything in the 21st century has to be a constant jolt of dopamine.

I'm a huge fan of boring news and gatekeepers. Now the gatekeepers don't have to be all men or all White, but they have to be somebody. I don't know how we get back to that.

LM: There's some empirical research which shows that people are more prone to believe a conspiracy theory if they think that it's unpopular. It's sexier when you, one of the initiates, have taken the red pill and you're one of the few people who really know the truth.

TN: I watch all of the cable networks, and at least with the personality driven shows, they have a similar style of, "I am speaking directly to you. You are going to learn cool stuff that no one else really understands. And I'm gonna connect the dots for you."

We have to feel like we are being initiated into special knowledge. If you take the red pill, you see that we're really all just living in a big computer simulation. Whereas if you take the blue pill, you get to live in the fantasy. The red pill clears their eyes and they see reality for what it is. They suddenly realize that we're all living in the guts of this huge machine. It's a completely paranoid concept that came out of a science fiction movie that people now use unironically and without realizing how crazy it sounds,

The nightly news used to be 15 minutes long. That was it. You would just get a droning recitation of, "We signed an arms control treaty. Today inflation is 2%. The unemployment rate spiked." Fifteen minutes and that is it. The rest of the time you had to read a newspaper. That is inconceivable to the modern viewer.

LM: There's a difference between misinformation and disinformation. A lot of the mistakes that people come up with are fed to them by somebody who intentionally created them. I study science deniers, and in many cases they're victims. They're the audience, they're the pawns for people who are profiting either economically or politically or ideologically. Victims of people who have created an enormous disinformation campaign because it serves their interests. It's not just that people are stupid for believing—somebody is creating this who understands exactly how the human mind works and what people will go for and what they won't. It is information warfare.

Moderator: Could you speak to the role of higher education and academia in all of this?

LM: I teach philosophy and so I'll always make a plug for more critical thinking and logic courses. Finland has a wonderful program which teaches kids how to resist propaganda, disinformation, and fake news. I think it's too late by the time people get to college.

I tell the story in *Post-Truth* of a fifth grade teacher out in California who had a game called the "Fake News Game." He had a rubric and he would teach students how to identify good sources. They loved the game so much that they wouldn't go to recess. They'd say, "Give us another one!" We really need to be doing more of that—not just in higher education, but younger than that.

But I've got to say, I don't think that's going to solve it. We can't just educate our way out of this. We have to do something to keep the disinformation from getting as much reach as it does. There are so many platforms, unregulated and unedited. The Holy Grail surrounded by 99 fakes. How can any reasonable person tell the difference?

TN: I do think that an educated public can be the kind of antibodies for a lot of the fake stuff that comes across. We are not completely hopeless on this. Colleges can do a better job in returning to a much harder-edged form of education that gets away from what I call the therapeutic model of education. We do spend too much time asking students if they are happy, if they are enjoying themselves. Instead of saying, "College is uncomfortable, and it should be uncomfortable. It's where you learn to challenge things. It's where you go to take a class that makes you think about life in a different way." And nobody's asking you if you like it. Plato's *Republic* is not an easy read. It should make you uncomfortable.

We need to get away from the kind of Yelp restaurant review model and toward a more rigorous version of critical thinking and Socratic dialogue. We need to create people who then go out into the world and are intellectually fearless. We've bred that out of ourselves somehow.

A more confrontational, intellectually aggressive give-and-take with students about important topics. It would create better citizens who are more capable of confidently engaging with a lot of these adversarial sources of information that are just attacks on knowledge.

This is a virtue problem rather than a knowledge problem. This is a particular kind of decadence that makes people susceptible to this—that comes with affluence, high levels of technology, endless amounts of entertainment and calories.

Moderator: Lee, tell us about your experience going to flat Earth conventions. Do people really believe these things?

LM: I went to a flat Earth convention in November 2018. There were 650 flat Earthers there and some media. I will tell you, they either really believed it or I'm the biggest sucker that ever existed. I spent 48 hours with them talking about everything under the sun. They genuinely really believe it and they're growing.

I think to a certain extent it's about identity. It's about group identity. They're finding other people that agree with them who tell them that they're smart, that they're the elite. The flat Earthers happen to love *The Matrix*. They like the idea of the red pill because that's how they see themselves.

TN: I can't say it's a fully formed approach yet, but I have become a fan of stigma. I hate to say it, it seems very old fashioned, but I would like to make flat Earth like smoking. At some point you just simply are not taken seriously in the same way.

Think about how it was accepted in the United States, for years, that racial differences among people are moral and intellectual. That African Americans were stupid. Hispanics are just temperamental and violent. Instead of saying, "Now look, you know, we've done the research and that's just wrong." We say, "We're not going to argue. It's wrong and you're holding onto a belief that is scientifically unsustainable. We're not going to have these arguments with you."

LM: My concern is that if we don't take them seriously and engage with them, if we just stigmatize them and walk away, they're going to grow to the point where they choke out good information.

TN: When I was younger, every Sunday I had a little job where I went down to the drug store and I bought my neighbor, who was disabled and could not do it herself, I would buy her all of her tabloids for the week. She believed all the stuff in them, like the moon landing was fake and stuff like that. What kept people like her in check was that they were embedded in an entire society of people who shook their heads and said, "You know, that's not true. This is not gonna be a thing." What made it a thing now is the ability to reach out to people who believe these things. Now they create a union.

There are moments when you have to bring everything to a kind of record scratch halt and say, "I have to stop right here. That is wrong. That is simply not a factually true thing." I think we have to start doing that with our fellow citizens. I think the best thing a Nobel Prize winning scientist could do is come out and say, "The world is not flat. It's the last thing I can say about it. I can't have this discussion."

I've dealt with political conspiracy theorists myself. Every argument becomes proof that the conspiracy is true. The more you argue, the more you become identified as an agent of the conspiracy. The effort you put into it validates their belief. If you spend two hours arguing with a conspiracy theorist, they say, "You know what? Lee McIntyre spent two hours arguing with me. I am onto something."

I have finally gotten to the point with people where I've said, "You're not only wrong, but deep in your heart somewhere, you know you are wrong. I cannot get you to where you need to be. You think Donald Trump is fighting pedophiles? Deep down you know you're wrong." It seems to have an effect. I admit it's unscientific on my part, but I think engaging has been the way we have done it for 40 or 50 years, and it's not working.

LM: The empirical literature shows that if you confront somebody and insult them, it doesn't work. And by confronting them you are insulting them because their beliefs are based in their identity. So when you're challenged on your beliefs, you're being challenged as a person.

I took a guy who had just given a flat Earth presentation out to dinner. We had a two-hour debate, just the two of us. This kid was extremely intelligent and a great rhetorician. Everything I could say to him, he had already thought of a response. So I didn't argue facts because it wasn't about facts or information. Jonathan Swift said that you can't reason somebody out of something they didn't reason themself into. So I wasn't trying to present him with facts because he knew all the same facts that I did. Instead, I challenged his reasoning strategy. I said to him, "Okay, you say that this is about evidence. So what evidence could I present to you that would prove you wrong? Just in theory, what would I have to show you?" And he couldn't answer that question.

Now, I'm not gonna say that he then ripped off his lanyard and left with me and said, "What a fool I've been!" But I did stop him in his tracks to have to think of what he could possibly say and maybe plant a seed of doubt."

So I'm planning to go back to talk to science deniers, not just to try to convince them with the facts, but to build some trust so that they can see that there's room for them on the science team. There is a shockingly small amount of research literature on what works and what doesn't. But the anecdotal literature is quite clear; if someone is going to change their mind this is how they do it, after face-to-face conversation with someone they trust.

The real threat to our democracy is when facts and truth and reality don't matter anymore. And you're seeing this now, unfortunately, infiltrating Congress. They simply are unable to legislate to make any policy decisions based on facts. And it's not just for scientific facts, it's any sort of facts. I'm sort of afraid of exactly what Tom's afraid of, that we're gonna back ourselves into this corner where authoritarianism is the end result because we're not doing enough not only to protect facts, but the process by which we verify factual information.

I'm afraid for our future. I don't think we have that much time to push back. It's to the point where it's not just about beliefs anymore, it's about action. There's this moment when extremist beliefs become extremist actions. And I'm afraid that's where we might be headed.

CHAPTER 45
What Caused the Alt-Left and Alt-Right?[1]

By Kevin McCaffree

The rise of the political ideologies of the Alt-Left and Alt-Right—and their cynical prophesying of a radical, grievance-driven, reconstruction of society—is due to numerous factors. Among the most important are rising income and wealth inequality, declining religiosity, declining trust and civic engagement, and political polarization.

Further, the popularization of 24-hour cable advocacy-news channels (such as Fox News, MSNBC, and CNN) has facilitated the construction of echo chambers in peoples' living rooms. Until recently, people tended only to watch Fox News or CNN, for example, effectively shutting themselves inside of a closed off room of journalistic mirrors.[2] The things that matter on CNN (Republicans' role in perpetuating racism, sexism, homophobia, transphobia, islamophobia, police misconduct) don't matter on Fox News; and what matters on Fox News (Democrats' role in over-regulating business, raising taxes, the declining importance of the family, and misinterpreting the Founding Fathers and the Constitution) doesn't matter on CNN.

The moderate American in the middle, not an adherent of the Alt-Left or the Alt-Right, thus feels increasingly torn between two zealous contending worldviews. Occupying a moderate position becomes more and more difficult to justify to impatient peers as the shrill screams on each political end of the spectrum grow in dystopian prophecy.

What is metastasizing on both the political left and right has a common origin in anger, fear, and paranoid hopelessness. The crystalizing ideologies of the far Left and the far Right thus have a great deal in common:

- Our institutions are corrupt and abusive (Alt-Left: "the patriarchy," "system of White supremacy," or "heteronormativity"; Alt-Right: "the Cathedral," "stolen election," "abortion as murder").

- Equality is a pointless goal (Alt-Left: due to historical and present oppression; Alt-Right: due to biological differences between men and women and between races).
- Democracy is impossible (Alt-Left: the system is rigged by wealthy, cis-gender, White men; Alt-Right: the masses are too easily manipulated).
- People are defined and determined by the social or biological history of the groups they belong to (Alt-Left: women as a group, race/ethnic groups, and LGBTQIA people; Alt-Right: European and Western culture).
- People are fundamentally power hungry and manipulative (Alt-Left: White people are driven by a desire to racially oppress others and men are driven by a desire to dominate women; Alt-Right: women and minorities are driven by a desire for racial domination and cultural control).

It is unfortunate that these similarities are so hopeless in outlook. Saul Alinsky, a figurehead of the Alt-Left, remarked to William Buckley in a 1967 interview that, "People only do the right things for the wrong reasons," and even compares himself and his cause to Lucifer in an epigrammatic self-quotation for his book *Rules for Radicals*.[3]

Echoing a similar sentiment, Nick Land says:

> Where the progressive enlightenment sees political ideals, the dark enlightenment sees appetites. . . Setting its expectations as low as reasonably possible, [the dark enlightenment] seeks only to spare civilization from frenzied, ruinous, gluttonous debauch.[4]

Is America's future truly so hopeless? The best data analysis on the topic suggests otherwise.[5] Rather, it is likely that the extreme outlooks of Alt-Left and Alt-Right are being driven by the emergence of exemplars that embolden extremists on the other side.

Trump, for example, is the paradigmatic devil for the Alt-Left—a White, heterosexual male who supports police and military, and who can be heard boasting about grabbing women by their genitals. In the ideology of the Alt-Left, Donald Trump is an abomination, almost inhuman, and this magnitude of disgust confers the worried perception of a growing supporter base of abominable Trump followers.

There are consequences to the popularity of Alt-Left and Alt-Right ideology. Both, for example, have already slowed the progress of science. The Alt-Left regards as taboo any biological or evolutionary research exploring differences between men and women, really, groups of any kind. This is prima facie anti-intellectualism. The Alt-Right regards as unnecessary any sociological or social-psychological research on the intergenerational transmission of poverty, inequality, and stigma. This too is prima facie anti-intellectualism. Both oppose any scientific inquiry that would challenge their existing assumptions (for the left that all people are the same, and for the right, that there is a natural hierarchy). When you're already sure you know the truth, science isn't necessary.

What of the idea that the Alt-Left are wimpy and fearful, talk of "safe spaces" and all of that? They certainly are sensitive to words or actions that they regard as evidence of sinister intent to oppress. But this expression of vulnerability and fear of victimization exists on the Alt-Right too: if one looks closely at 4chan message boards and other places where self-professed Alt-Right trolls hang out, it is easy to find a lot of self-deprecation about how trolls are slovenly unemployed losers in their mother's basement changing the world in a "meme war."

The late psychologist Fred Rothbaum and his colleagues argued that self-attributions of weakness, sensitivity, fear, or "severely limited ability" could serve the function of lowering expectations for achievement.[6] Considering the rising cost of higher education, and the tough job market—think about the large number of people in their 20s and 30s still living at home—I suspect anyone taking a close look at both the Alt-Left and the Alt-Right will find a tendency toward fear-induced self-deprecation.

In the end, these American swan songs fall under the allure of two stubborn illusions.

The Alt-Left's illusion is to see abuses of power as being intrinsically or necessarily Western, White, and male. Even the briefest glance at world history reveals enslavement, mass murder, and subjugation occurring at some level in every large society for which there are historical records. The problem of abuses of power is a human problem, not a Western one exclusively, and one we should be wrestling with even if White men had disappeared years ago (no doubt one of many fever dreams of the Alt-Left).

The Alt-Right's illusion is to see sex and race only as statistical abstractions. Thinking that men, on average, are more competitive than women on average, tells you nothing about whether or not any given woman walking by you on the street is a competitive person. Similarly, pointing to average IQ or standardized test differences between Whites and non-Whites tells you nothing about how smart the African American next to you on the commute to work is. Statistics about populations cannot be used to accurately predict attributes of specific individuals. Generalized abstractions and stereotypes are not people—people are people.

Yet, despite these illusions, the Alt-Left and the Alt-Right pose some deep questions that threaten to eat away like acid at the columns supporting American democracy. At what point are historical abuses of power large enough to require significant institutionalized redress? Is any human group truly innocent of the desire for and abuse of power? Are differences or tragedies ever truly insurmountable?

Each question is a different reflection of the core concern: the difficulty of understanding disappointments in ourselves and in one another.

CHAPTER 46
Disinformation, Democracy, and the Rule of Law[1]

By Asha Rangappa

Much of the public discussion on Russia's disinformation operations in the U.S. has focused on their impact on the 2016 election and how they might affect elections in the future. But the damage that Russia seeks to inflict through its disinformation campaign is not limited to electoral contests. Rather, its long-term strategy has been to erode faith in the primary pillars upon which our democracy is based—including the rule of law and the institutions that support it. For now, its efforts seem to be working, and the legal profession may be both the first and last line of defense. Let me explain why.

Although Russia utilized relatively recent technology like social media platforms in its assault on the 2016 election, its overarching tactics and goals were not new. "Active measures"—as the full panoply of Russia's subversive measures, including disinformation and propaganda, are known—were a central component of the KGB's intelligence operations in the U.S. during the Cold War. Yuri Bezmenov, a KGB officer who defected to the United States, explained in 1984 that the central focus of the KGB's active measures were to "subvert anything of value in [its] enemy's country," and to do so by pitting groups against each other and creating internal chaos within the enemy state.[2] The idea is to destroy your enemy without ever having to fire a shot.

In the United States, of course, a central value established by the Constitution is the rule of law. The idea that any individual can have their voice heard, and be treated as an equal in a court of law, is a building block of a democratic society: Courts are the guardians of individual rights, and having faith in their legitimacy is a necessary prerequisite for having faith in fundamental democratic ideals like equality, due process, and freedom. Not surprisingly, Bezmenov notes that fostering mistrust in the justice system was one of the primary objectives for the KGB's active measures, since undermining the legitimacy of courts and law enforcement would ultimately undermine Americans' belief in the rights they protect.[3]

Fortunately for America, the KGB had limited success in its attempts to subvert the rule of law during the Cold War. In 1982, the House Select Committee on Intelligence held hearings to examine the Soviet's use of active measures (Yes, this isn't Congress's first rodeo on the topic, believe it or not). It found that the Soviet Union's operations suffered from several weaknesses, the most notable one of which was its ideology.[4] The House Committee determined that the KGB had the most success with groups in which it could find a common cause with marginalized groups—in that era, that was mostly individuals and organizations on the political left, who were already challenging the political and legal status quo in the realm of civil rights, racial justice, and Vietnam. But as a nation-state that was, ultimately, seeking to spread communism—and notably, had a political philosophy that was explicitly atheistic—the Soviet Union made little headway in recruiting agents in the political mainstream, particularly on the right.

Fast forward almost three decades and the same does not hold true. Russia is no longer constrained by a political ideology, giving it more flexibility to appeal to a broader swath of the political spectrum. Indeed, not having to offer an alternative to the U.S. capitalist model has left Russia free to focus simply on division. As a result, Russia, for the first time, has made headway in undermining the rule of law from both sides of the political spectrum, particularly through politicians who amplify this message: calls to "abolish ICE" from the left, or attacking the FBI, Justice Department, and "so called judges" from the right, has "mainstreamed" an objective that was once only on the political fringe.

In the 21st century, Russia also no longer suffers from another shortcoming the House Committee identified in 1982: Technological weakness.[5] A disinformation campaign would have once taken two years of methodical planning, using human sources, to enter into mainstream media, as the Soviet Union's planting of a rumor that the United States military created the AIDS virus did. Through cheap, accessible, and viral social media platforms, Russia has the capacity to artificially amplify divisive messages it wants to spread—including those that color the U.S. legal system as biased and corrupt—within hours, and to hundreds of millions of people.[6] The old adage that "a lie can get halfway around the world before the truth can get its boots on," has never been more true than today.

Partly because social media has been the big game-changer in terms of the effectiveness of Russia's disinformation efforts, it's tempting to believe that the answer lies purely in changing, or at least tweaking, the social media platforms themselves and strengthening our cyber defenses. But this approach standing alone doesn't address the core vulnerabilities which allowed Russian disinformation to take root.

For that purpose, social capital theory provides a useful framework. Social capital, as defined by Harvard Professor Robert Putnam in his book *Bowling Alone*, refers to the way we create value from social relationships.[7] According to Putnam, social capital is an important indicator of a society's health, because it reflects, in part, the level of social trust among individuals. In a society with high social capital, there will also be a high level of "generalized" social trust. That trust is expressed as a willingness to believe in the goodwill of fellow citizens, even those we do not know, and give them the benefit of the doubt. High levels of social trust, in turn, are related to civic values. Putnam notes that:

> [P]eople who trust their fellow citizens volunteer more often, contribute more to charity, participate more often in politics and community organizations, serve more readily on juries, give blood more frequently, comply more fully with their tax obligations, are more tolerant of minority views, and display many other forms of civic virtue.[8]

That's not all. Putnam writes that social capital is formed in one of two ways: Through bonding, and through bridging.[9] Bonding is when individuals create relationships with others based on shared characteristics—race, or religion, for example. Bridging, by contrast, is when relationships are formed across social cleavages, among diverse groups of people. Both are necessary for a healthy society: bonding offers a social safety net and can leverage shared strengths (think of ethnic enclaves that provide communities for newly arrived immigrants), and bridging allows new ideas to travel, fostering innovation (universities aspire to do this).

Importantly, however, Putnam observes that there are more negative externalities associated with bonding than with bridging: Specifically, too much bonding can lead to factionalism, exclusive groups, and policies based on mistrust.[10] In a word, it can lead to tribalism.

Alarmingly, however, social capital, and its accompanying levels of civic engagement, has dropped precipitously since World War II in the U.S. Putnam notes that compared with Americans born before 1945, each successive generation has been less likely to participate in civic life. Relatedly, levels of social trust are at an all-time low. The last poll from the General Social Survey, which asks Americans whether they believe "most people can be trusted," is at its lowest point since they began asking the question.[11]

Putnam found that technology contributed significantly to the decline in social capital and social trust over the last half century. Putnam was writing in 2000, after the dotcom boom but before the explosion of wireless broadband Internet and the smartphone era. But there's reason to believe that social media has continued this trend, and perhaps even made it worse. This is because of the intersection between social capital theory and how social media operates.

Social media, which emphasizes connectivity based on people who share our preferences, encourages bonding, at the expense of bridging—studies of "red feeds" and "blue feeds" on social media illustrate how ideas can ricochet within a political social media "bubble" without ever crossing over into another, separate bubble.[12] Further, Putnam underscores that virtual media doesn't allow for the exchange of important social cues—like facial expressions, emotions, and other nonverbal behavior—which are indispensable for creating trust among individuals who interact in person. We now have tribes: political tribes.

How does all of this relate to the rule of law? With Americans spending an average of six and a half hours a day online—about a third on social media—virtual bubbles, rather than real relationships formed with real people, can become their factual reality.[13] This tribalism can impact how individuals perceive our civic institutions, which include those that uphold the rule of law. As noted previously, decreased civic engagement is associated with low social trust—which offers a fertile mindset for believing that public servants, judges, and law enforcement are untrustworthy, biased, and even corrupt.

In fact, recent statistics suggest that Americans' commitment to rule of law values has in fact eroded significantly. Professor Austin Sarat at Amherst College notes that 38% of people surveyed in 2017 trust the president, more than judges, to make the right decision for the United States.[14] The statistics are even more alarming when broken down by generation: Another study found that less than 33% of millennials agreed with the idea that it "is essential to live in a democracy," compared with 72% of Americans born before World War II.[15]And only 19% of millennials believe that a military takeover of the government would be illegitimate, compared with 43% of older generations.[16]

In short, as Americans have become less civically engaged over the last five decades, they have essentially made Russia's job to foment division among Americans and sow mistrust in our institutions that much easier. We are, in effect, all primed to become unwitting Russian assets.

The challenge we face as we regroup from the Russia's disinformation campaign in 2016 is how to revitalize civic engagement in a digital world.

At one point in time, voluntary associations like the Scouts, Rotary Clubs, local PTAs, and churches were essentially "schools for democracy" and inculcated their members with civic skills such as "how to run meetings, speak in public, write letters, organize projects, and debate public issues with civility."[17] In the face of waning membership in such organizations, our schools have unfortunately not picked up the slack: Only nine states and the District of Columbia currently require a minimum of one year of education in U.S. government or civics, and ten states have no civics requirement at all (Connecticut requires only half a year of civics education).[18]

One type of organization that can fill the gap is local, state, and national bar associations. Members of the legal profession are ideally suited to be educators and disseminators of civic values for two reasons. First, as a profession, they have remained strong, particularly in an organizational form—unlike many other types of voluntary organizations, associations like the American Bar Association have actually increased their membership over the last several decades. Second, and more importantly, lawyers are trained to put higher principles above emotional, personal, and political beliefs. Defense lawyers, for instance, are proud to uphold and zealously defend their clients' rights to due process and a fair trial, regardless of whether they personally believe in their innocence or guilt. Supreme Court Justice John Roberts embodied this recently in pushing back against President Trump's attacks on the judiciary, declaring, "We do not have Obama judges or Trump judges, Bush judges or Clinton judges. What we have is an extraordinary group of dedicated judges doing their level best to do equal right to those appearing before them."[19]

Being able to articulate and appeal to these higher values is critical in today's tribal politics. Political scientists have found that appealing to civic values can help loosen and even transcend tribal ties: "When such civic-minded motivations are primed. . . people [are] more willing to adjust important attitudes (including partisan identification) in response to new information."[20] Members of the legal profession have the skills to utilize a variety of avenues to pass on these values: lectures on important court cases, conferences on topics like the free press or the presidential power, sponsoring civic and community debates on public issues, and hosting mock trial and moot court programs in schools.

The intense public coverage of the investigation into Russian election interference and the politicization of the same has framed countering disinformation as a partisan issue. In fact, this very framing is what has encouraged U.S. pundits and politicians to attack law enforcement, the courts, and public servants—which only furthers Russia's interests. Underscoring that defending against disinformation is about preserving our democratic norms and principles, not about any particular political candidate or party, is a major obstacle to overcome.

The legal profession has both the training and responsibility to take the lead in this effort. Unless we reclaim democratic principles that transcend political differences, we are likely to see a dismantling of the values we as lawyers hold so dear. That dismantling need not involve anything more than instilling apathy, cynicism, and mistrust when it comes to Americans' beliefs in the institutions and individuals who uphold the rule of law. Russia's attack on our democracy is an invitation for us to examine our relationship with fellow citizens, and how technology has affected the way we engage with them online and in real life. We still have time to promote and connect over our democratic principles, including the rule of law, and generate a long-term immunity against efforts to fragment our democratic social fabric from within.

CHAPTER 47
Strengthening Information Ecosystems[1]

By Claire Wardle

In the fall of 2017, Collins Dictionary named *fake news* word of the year. It was hard to argue with the decision. Journalists were using the phrase to raise awareness of false and misleading information online. Academics had started publishing copiously on the subject and even named conferences after it. And of course, U.S. president Donald Trump regularly used the epithet from the podium to discredit nearly anything he disliked.

By spring of that year, I had already become exasperated by how this term was being used to attack the news media. Worse, it had never captured the problem: most content wasn't actually fake, but genuine content used out of context—and only rarely did it look like news. I made a rallying cry to stop using *fake news* and instead use *misinformation, disinformation*, and *malinformation* under the umbrella term *information disorder*. These terms, especially the first two, have caught on, but they represent an overly simple, tidy framework I no longer find useful.

Both *disinformation* and *misinformation* describe false or misleading claims, but disinformation is distributed with the intent to cause harm, whereas misinformation is the mistaken sharing of the same content. Analyses of both generally focus on whether a post is accurate and whether it is intended to mislead. The result? We researchers become so obsessed with labeling the dots that we can't see the larger pattern they show.

By focusing narrowly on problematic content, researchers are failing to understand the increasingly sizable number of people who create and share this content, and are also overlooking the larger context of what information people actually need. Academics are not going to effectively strengthen the information ecosystem until we shift our perspective from classifying every post to understanding the social contexts of this information, how it fits into narratives and identities, and its short-term impacts and long-term harms.

What's Getting Left Out

To understand what these terms leave out, consider "Lynda," a fictional person based on many I track online. Lynda fervently believes vaccines are dangerous. She scours databases for newly published scientific research, watches regulatory hearings for vaccine approvals, reads vaccine inserts to analyze ingredients and warnings. Then she shares what she learns with her community online.

Is she a misinformer? No. She's not mistakenly sharing information that she didn't bother to verify. She takes the time to seek out information.

Nor is she a disinformation agent as commonly defined. She isn't trying to cause harm or get rich. My sense is that Lynda is driven to post because she feels an overwhelming need to warn people about a health system she sincerely believes has harmed her or a loved one. She is strategically choosing information to connect with people and promote a worldview. Her criteria for choosing what to post depends less on whether it makes sense rationally and more about her social identities and affinities.

Dismissing Lynda for her selective interpretation and lack of research credentials risks failing to see what she's accomplishing overall: taking snippets or clips that support her belief systems from information published by authoritative institutions (maybe an admission by a scientist that more research is needed, or a disclaimer about known side effects) and sharing that without any wider context or explanation. This "accurate" information that she has uncovered via her own research is used to support inaccurate narratives—perhaps that governments are rolling out vaccines for population control, or doctors are dupes or pharmaceutical company shills.

To understand the contemporary information ecosystem, researchers need to move away from our fixation on accuracy and zoom out to understand the characteristics of some of these online spaces that are powered by people's need for connection, community, and affirmation. As communications scholar Alice Marwick has written, "Within social environments, people are not necessarily looking to inform others: they share stories (and pictures and videos) to express themselves and broadcast their identity, affiliations, values, and norms."[2] This motivation can apply to Beatles fans as well as to cat lovers, activists for social justice, or promoters of various conspiracy theories.

Siloed Research

Lynda's online world points to something else that the labels misinformation and disinformation cannot capture: connections. While Lynda might post primarily in anti-vaccine Facebook groups, if I follow her activities, it's very likely I'll also find her posting in #stopthesteal or similar groups and sharing climate denial memes or conspiracy theories about the latest mass shooting on Instagram. But that's a big if; no one expects me as a researcher to ask questions so broadly.

One of the challenges of studying this arena is that its narrow focus means that the role of the world's Lynda's is barely understood. A growing body of research points to the volume of problematic content online that can be traced back to a surprisingly small number of so-called superspreaders, but so far even that work studies those who amplify content within a particular topic rather than create it—leaving the impacts of devoted true believers like Lynda still understudied.

This reflects a larger issue. Those of us who are funded to track harmful information online too often work in silos. I'm based in a school of public health, so people assume I should just study health misinformation. My colleagues in political science departments are funded to investigate speech that might erode democracy. I suspect that people like Lynda drive an outsize amount of wide-ranging problematic content, but they do not operate the way we academics are set up to think about our broken information systems.

Every month there are academic and policy conferences focused on health misinformation, political disinformation, climate communication, or Russian disinformation in Ukraine. Often each has very different experts talking about identical problems with little awareness of other disciplines' scholarship. Funding agencies and policymakers inadvertently create even more siloes by concentrating on nation states or distinct regions such as the European Union.

Events and incidents also become silos. Funders fixate on high-profile, scheduled events like an election, the rollout of a new vaccine, or the next United Nations climate change conference. But those trying to manipulate, monetize, recruit, or inspire people excel at exploiting moments of tension or outrage, whether it's the latest British royals documentary, a celebrity divorce trial, or the World Cup. No one funds investigations into the online activity *those* moments generate, although doing so could yield crucial insights.

Authorities' responses are siloed as well. In November 2020, my team published a report on 20 million posts we had gathered from Instagram, Twitter, and Facebook that included conversations about COVID-19 vaccines (Note that we didn't set out to collect posts containing misinformation; we simply wanted to know how people were talking about the vaccines). From this large data set, the team identified several key narratives, including the *safety, efficacy, and necessity* of getting vaccinated and the *political and economic motives* for producing the vaccine. But the most frequent conversation about vaccines on all three platforms was a narrative we labeled *liberty and freedom*. People were less likely to discuss the safety of the vaccines than whether they would be forced to get vaccinated or carry vaccine verification. Yet agencies like the Centers for Disease Control and Prevention are only equipped to engage the single narrative about safety, efficacy, and necessity.

Not "Atoms," but Narratives and Networks

Unfortunately, most scholars who study and respond to polluted information still think in terms of what I call *atoms of content*, rather than in terms of narratives. Social media platforms have teams making decisions about whether an individual post should be fact-checked, labeled, down-ranked, or removed. The platforms have become increasingly deft at playing whack-a-mole with posts that may not even violate their guidelines. But by focusing on individual posts, researchers are failing to see the larger picture: people aren't influenced by one post so much as they're influenced by the narratives that these posts fit into.

In this sense, individual posts are not atoms, but something like drops of water. One drop of water is unlikely to persuade or do harm, but over time, the repetition starts to fit into overarching narratives—often, narratives that are already aligned with people's thinking. What happens to public trust when people repeatedly see, over months and months, posts that are "just asking questions" about government institutions or public health organizations? Like drops of water on stone, one drop will do no harm, but over time, grooves are cut deep.

What Is To Be Done?

Over the past few years, it's been much easier to blame Russian trolls on Facebook or teenage boys on 4chan than to recognize how those tasked with providing clear, actionable information to meet communities' needs have regularly failed to do so. Bad actors who are trying to manipulate, divide, and sow chaos have taken advantage of these vacuums. In this confusing space, trusted institutions have not kept up.

To really move forward, proponents of healthy information ecosystems need a broader, integrated view of how and why information circulates.

Organize and Fund Cross-Cutting Research

Those hoping to foster healthy information ecosystems must learn to assess multilingual, networked flows of content that span conventional boundaries of disciplines and regions. I chaired a taskforce that proposed a permanent, global institution to monitor and study information that would be centrally funded and thus independent of both nations and tech companies. Right now, efforts to monitor disinformation often do overlapping work but fail to share data and classification mechanisms and have limited ability to respond in a crisis.

Learn to Participate

The polluted information ecosystem is participatory—a site of constant experimentation as participants drive engagement and better connect with their audiences' concerns. Although news outlets and government agencies appear to embrace social media, they rarely engage the two-way, interactive features that characterize web 2.0. Traditional science communication is still top down, based on the paternalistic deficit model, which assumes that experts know what information to supply and that audiences will passively consume information and respond as intended. These systems have much to learn from people like Lynda about how to connect with, rather than present to, audiences. An essential first step is to train government communications staff, community organizations, librarians, and journalists to seek out and listen to the public's questions and concerns.

Support Community-Led Resilience

Today, global and national funders have an outsized focus on platforms, filters, and regulation—that is, how to expunge the "bad stuff" rather than how to expand the "good stuff." Instead of pursuing such whack-a-mole efforts, major funders should find a way to support specific place-based responses for what communities need. For example, health researcher Stephen Thomas created the Health Advocates In-Reach and Research (HAIR) campaign that trains local barber shop and beauty salon owners to listen to their customers about health concerns and then to provide advice and direct people to appropriate resources for follow-up care. And after assessing information needs of the local Spanish-speaking community in Oakland, California, and finding it woefully underserved, journalist Madeleine Bair founded the participatory online news site *El Tímpano* in 2018.

Targeted "cradle to grave" educational campaigns can also help people learn to navigate polluted information systems. Teaching people techniques such as the SIFT method (which outlines steps to assess sources and trace claims to their original context) and lateral reading (which teaches how to verify information while consuming it) have been proven effective, as have programs to equip people with skills to understand how their emotions are targeted and other techniques used by manipulators.

* * * * *

For each of these tasks, people and entities hoping to foster healthy information ecosystems must commit to the long game. Real improvement will be a decades-long process, and much of it will be spent playing catchup in a technological landscape that evolves every few months, with disruptions such as ChatGPT emerging seemingly overnight. The only way to make inroads is to look beyond the neat diagrams and tidy typologies of misinformation to see what is really going on, and craft a response not for the information system itself but the humans operating within it.

CHAPTER 48
We Need a Shared Reality

Featuring Lee McIntyre and Lawrence M. Eppard

The United States finds itself in a "post-truth" age, where millions of Americans rely on poor sources of information, have lost faith in experts, and cannot distinguish between what is factual and what is not. A variety of factors have helped bring us to this place, including extreme partisanship, the dawn of the internet, a decline in trust in institutions which create and disseminate information, the decline of traditional news outlets and rise of partisan ones (including cable news, talk radio, and partisan websites), and the advent of social media.

Lee McIntyre has written an excellent book on this topic titled *Post-Truth*.[1] The following is a conversation between McIntyre and Lawrence Eppard about post-truth trends in the U.S.

* * * * *

<u>Lawrence M. Eppard (LE)</u>: Let's start our conversation by defining how you use the term "post-truth."

<u>Lee McIntyre (LM)</u>: Post-truth is a term of regret for those who think truth is under assault. It refers to the political subordination of reality. It is using your desired political outcomes to decide which things you are going to say are true and which things you are going to bury.

<u>LE</u>: What would you consider to be the major take-home message from your book, *Post-Truth*?

LM: I wrote *Post-Truth* because I was alarmed. I think people need to be aware of the erosion of the norms and values of truth-telling and what that can lead to. I don't talk a lot about authoritarianism in the book, but that is the worry that is hanging over it, which is why I quote George Orwell and Hannah Arendt.

It is so dangerous because people are not lying for no purpose. If somebody has control over our stream of information, or they have so demoralized the population with lies that people think it isn't even possible to know the truth anymore, that is an easier population to rule.

Early in the book I quote an exchange between CNN's Alisyn Camerota and Trump surrogate Newt Gingrich. They go back and forth—she quotes FBI data showing the crime rate is going down, but Gingrich replies that he "feels" the crime rate is going up, even though that isn't factual:

> Alisyn Camerota (AC): Violent crime is down. The economy is picking up—
>
> Newt Gingrich (NG): It is not down in the biggest cities.
>
> AC: Violent crime, murder rate is down. It is down.
>
> NG: Then how come it's up in Chicago, up in Baltimore, and up in—
>
> AC: There are pockets where certainly we—
>
> NG: Your national capital, your third biggest city—
>
> AC: But violent crime across the country is down. We're not under siege in the way that we were in say, the 80s.
>
> NG: ... The average American, I will bet you this morning, does not think crime is down, does not think they are safer.
>
> AC: But we are safer, and it is down.
>
> NG: No, that's your view.
>
> AC: It's a fact.
>
> NG: ... But what I said is also a fact. . . I understand your view. The current view is that liberals have a whole set of statistics which

theoretically may be right, but it's not where human beings are. People are frightened. People feel that their government has abandoned them. . .

AC: . . . but hold on, Mr. Speaker, because you're saying liberals use these numbers, they use this sort of magic math. This is the FBI statistics. They're not a liberal organization.

NG: No, but what I said is equally true. People feel it.

AC: They feel it, yes, but the facts don't support it.

NG: As a political candidate, I'll go with how people feel and I'll let you go with the theoreticians.

That's dangerous. Policy shouldn't be based on how we feel, that will not make good and effective policy. Policy is built on a shared understanding of facts. If you aren't dealing with facts, you aren't dealing with reality, and you will have no way to deal with problems. If we decide to build a prison, it should be because it is needed. We shouldn't build it because we think the crime rate is going up when it is going down.

LE: You mention the subordination of truth for political purposes. An example that comes to mind is unauthorized immigration and crime in the U.S. Studies consistently show that unauthorized immigrants are not more likely to commit violent or property crimes compared with legal immigrants and native-born Americans, and yet it can be darn near impossible to convince somebody of this who does not want to believe it. They've been told a different story for a political purpose.

LM: We could have a normative debate about a number of topics. So we could have a normative debate about whether we want more immigration, which isn't about facts but about values and who we think we are as a country. But we need to know what the facts are in order to have those debates. What distresses me is when facts are spun to back up what is essentially a normative position. If Trump doesn't want immigrants in the U.S., he should just say it. He shouldn't pretend they have higher rates of criminality when they don't. He's lying, and that's the problem. He's claiming something is true that isn't for a desired political outcome.

LE: You mention natural human tendencies in your book like motivated reasoning and confirmation bias. So many people today have what are perceived to be gatekeeper credentials that in the past would have signified they were disseminating reliable information, but those credentials are not what they used to be—working at Fox News or MSNBC gives you the symbolic authority of a journalist, for instance, when it really shouldn't. There are so many places today on television and the internet where one can get a wide variety of false or misleading claims validated by people who they believe have the authority to do so. This seems to let motivated reasoning and confirmation bias out of the box to do more damage.

LM: Yeah, conservatives and liberals both use motivated reasoning. We all want certain things to be true and look for information that confirms it. It is so cognitively wired we don't even think about it. But what thirty years ago were fringe beliefs are now capable of being validated on partisan television and the internet. You can find somebody to tell you, "No, you really *are* right, we *didn't* land on the Moon!"

I write about science denial, and the really radicalizing thing for science denial has been the internet. All of these fringe beliefs and conspiracy theories are finding validation on the internet. Maybe you've heard something about vaccines and autism, but you didn't really know the facts. But now you go on the internet and there are many anti-vaxxer websites, and they lead you down a rabbit hole. The brain is wired for motivated reasoning and cognitive bias, but the internet enables them and feeds them. So we end up feeling validated for believing something that isn't true.

LE: Let's talk about ideological silos in general. There seem to be whole infrastructures on both the left and the right that allow you to believe what you want to believe and not be confronted with many pieces of information which might change your mind. The brain is not impenetrable, but it has to be presented with facts that contradict your beliefs, they have to be presented more than once, and they really need to come from sources that you trust.

LM: That's right—it's not just hearing facts, but as you say, hearing them from a source that you trust. If you "otherize" certain media and are told not to believe anything that they say, the facts are there but they are not going to get through.

Silos are a real problem. It is the repetition effect. You hear the same false information over and over again from people you trust and you begin to believe it. I mean I have talked to science deniers, and so many just absolutely cannot be moved by evidence. It is heart breaking.

On the left, when I am out talking to people about this stuff, they will be nodding along in agreement. Then I mention GMO denial, and they stop me, "No! GMOs are dangerous. *That's* real! What are you talking about?!?" I get myself into trouble.

LE: So what has changed so much in the U.S. to lead us to this post-truth moment?

LM: The decline of traditional media, the rise of the internet, and the rise of social media. The cognitive bias has always been there. The internet was the accelerant which democratized all of the disinformation and misinformation and diminished the experts. Democratization has led to the abandonment of standards for testing beliefs. It leads people to think they are just as good at reasoning about something as anybody else. But they're not. At the doctor's office, I don't ask for the data and reason through it myself and decide on the course of treatment. It takes expertise and experience to make that judgement. Just like I can't fly my own plane.

There is a scene in one of the *Indiana Jones* movies where he is in the room with all of these goblets and chalices and doesn't know which one is the Holy Grail. That's where we are right now. We have the truth right in front of us, but we don't know which one it is.

There is a slogan that science deniers use, "Do your own research." If science is about facts, why can't I just go out and find my facts? But you need guidance to know what is factual, you need experts. Many Americans have an enormous misunderstanding about science generally. They misunderstand the term "theory," for instance, thinking that any theory is as good as any other, rather than realizing that some theories are more credible than others because they are warranted by the evidence.

What's funny is many science deniers accept most science, just not the things they care about personally, whether it is evolution or vaccines or something else. Then they don't trust the experts.

LE: Let's talk about climate change as an example. In some places in the world, it is much less likely to be denied because people are seeing it tangibly with their own eyes, not hearing about it as an abstract thing from a partisan media outlet.

LM: I've been to the Maldives and snorkeled in open water in the Indian Ocean. I saw coral death. I worked with a marine biologist who talked to me about how coral reefs protect the islands and about the problem of elevation of the islands. They will be overrun by rising sea levels, they won't be here much longer. I mean you could see it with your own eyes. I spoke to the driver of my boat, he said that everybody in the Maldives knows about climate change because they live it.

LE: From your perspective, what has Donald Trump's contribution been to post-truth?

LM: Trump is not the cause of post-truth, but he has accelerated it. He's made it worse. He has perfected the tactic of making people cynical about whether it is possible to know what is true outside a political context. That's his goal, to make people cynical, make them think they can't know truth. Trump says, "Don't believe what you see in the media, I alone am the one giving you the truth." He's using it in exactly the way that a wannabe authoritarian would, to get people to distrust other sources of information and only trust him so he can get them to do what he wants. I think his goal has always been authoritarianism.

LE: How do we fix the problem of post-truth on a large scale?

LM: I think that there's a strong analogy between post-truth and science denial. In my book, I talk about how 60 years of science denial is what led us to the post-truth era. If we could help scientists to communicate better, we might have a shot. It can't just be about sharing facts and walking away. We need an army of good communicators.

Media is doing a better job with science denial. You are seeing less of that side-by-side split screen debate style on issues like climate change, for instance, where you give somebody from the National Academy of Sciences and some guy with a website equal time.

They need to do a better job with other issues. They need to call out a lie when it is a lie. They need to help people understand the stakes. They also need to treat many issues as not just problems of information but of values. Do you care about other people? Does it matter if some people are oppressed as long as you're not? What kind of world do you want to leave your grandchildren?

Facebook and Twitter will have to be regulated, their self-regulation has been a joke. They're capable of it. They have a room full of people who are able to keep pornography and terrorism and violent videos off of Facebook. They find it and they squash it. They could do it with political lies.

But we are also going to have to find a way to get information out in front of people who wouldn't normally encounter it. I'm not sure the most effective way to do that.

CHAPTER 49
The Epistemological Conditions of a Liberal Democratic Republic

By Jacob L. Mackey

This book is, in a sense, about how we form beliefs, what can go wrong to distort the process, and modern epistemic methods that protect against such distortions. There are five sources from which we derive our beliefs: sensory perception, memory, inference, intuition, and testimony.[1] Testimony—that is, the claims and other representations made by those in our social and media environments—is most relevant here. Overwhelmingly, most of what we believe about social, political, religious, historical, and scientific issues comes from the testimony of trusted others. None of us is in a position to perceive with our senses, recall from personal memory, infer, or intuit all the relevant facts about our enormously complex social, political, religious, historical, and scientific world. Instead, we rely on the media, politicians, academics, religious leaders, experts of various sorts, other public figures, and our family and friends, to acquaint us with such facts by way of the testimony they offer.

As a rule, testimony is reliable and our trust in it is warranted. We are complex social animals who come into the world with none of the substantive knowledge we need to survive in either our physical or social environments. We must learn everything we need to know. Some of what we learn is done strictly on our own by exploring our environment. The vast majority of what we learn, however, from earliest infancy until our last day of life, we learn socially—that is, from other people. We do this by observing, imitating, and cooperating with others, by encountering the artifacts others have created, and most importantly through the communications of others, that is, in contexts of testimony, of listening and dialogue.

Most of what we learn in this way gives us valuable information that is crucial to our social and material thriving. We learn, for example, how to interact appropriately with prestigious individuals in our group as well as how to prepare food so as to detoxify and extract maximum nutrients from it. This is not to say, however, that everything we learn is *true*. Every society inculcates its own myths and inaccurate beliefs about human nature, the natural world, and a putative world of superhuman beings. These inaccurate beliefs are typically not detrimental to a society's flourishing. Egyptian civilization, after all, persisted for 3,000 years with the Egyptians believing a creation myth according to which the sun god Ra separated the Earth, Geb, from Sky, Nut, when he became angry at them for having children together against his decree.

Indeed, myths such as this one can serve as markers of in-group identity and create in-group solidarity and cohesion. *We* are the people who believe in Nut and Geb. *They* are the people who believe in Ouranos and Gaia. This may be fitness-producing in homogenous societies, helping to bind the in-group together in the face of threats from out-groups and to produce pro-social behavior among in-group members. The problem comes in pluralistic modern societies.

Earlier pluralistic societies tended to reside within the boundaries of large empires, such as the Roman, Mongol, Ottoman, or British empires. These empires tended to be relativistic with respect to local laws and customs, which they often permitted to flourish relatively unmolested. The pluralism of these empires was manageable not only because diversity was a matter of minimally-overlapping regional differences but also because imperial rule was authoritarian. Insofar as imperial subjects had no hand in determining imperial (as opposed to local) policy, it did not matter whether everyone agreed about matters of facts and values. Conflicting or incommensurable local belief networks could sit contiguously within the empire and coexist coterminously in imperial metropolises as long as everyone obeyed the imperial authorities and paid their taxes. When strife over conflicting beliefs arose, the imperial authorities crushed it.

In contrast to this ancient pluralism, distributed in distinct regions and subsumed under an autocratic regime, the United States represents an experiment in pluralism unparalleled in human history. We endorse norms both of tolerance for ideological diversity and of cooperation in processes of democratic self-determination. Moreover, while it is true that ideological diversity is to some extent regionally distributed in the United States (Red versus Blue states, progressive versus conservative cities, and so on), nonetheless, people of every imaginable ethnic, religious, and political persuasion are also intermingled inextricably in our most populous states and cities.

These circumstances create unique demands with respect to our belief ecosystem. To put it simply, while ideological diversity *per se* is a strength in a democracy, because, among other things, it allows for innovative solutions to pressing problems, *too much* ideological diversity makes the *cooperation* upon which democracy, or more precisely, competition within a democratic framework, difficult.

Here is one way to conceptualize this latter point.[2] We may distinguish the beliefs and values subsisting within a political community as primary, secondary, and tertiary. A political community's primary beliefs and values determine its regime type. One package of beliefs and values sustains, say, an absolute monarchy while an incommensurable package, including a concern with equality, individual rights, and a commitment to collective self-governance sustains republics like the United States and the countries of Western Europe. The secondary beliefs and values of a political community determine its national culture and identity, its conception of the shared duties and privileges of citizenship, and its healthy nationalism, or sense of "usness." These secondary beliefs and values distinguish the United States from the countries of Western Europe and the countries of Western Europe from one another. Tertiary beliefs and values, finally, determine the "discrete subnational cultural communities" that exist within the nation-state. These subnational cultural communities include everything from small, exclusive groups like the Amish to internally diverse larger groups, such as Chicanos, Midwestern Protestants of Scandinavian descent, or African Americans, as well as ideology-based communities, such as the Seventh Day Adventists.

The belief ecosystem of the United States must accommodate the broadest possible—and indeed increasing—doxastic diversity at the level of tertiary beliefs and values, yet at the same time it must find a way to maintain enough shared primary and secondary beliefs and values to promote a common sense of "Americanness" and to maintain buy-in and faith with respect to our system and the functioning of its electoral, legislative, executive, and judicial processes. Only thus, that is, only if enough of us regard ourselves as fellow citizens pursuing a common civic project whose basic civic institutions are legitimate, can we Americans cooperate in the project of democratic self-governance.

Note that the cooperation of which I speak here is not a matter of linking arms and singing Kumbaya. Rather, it is the condition of the possibility of channeling the inevitable competition that arises in a pluralistic society in productive rather than destructive ways. That is, our *cooperation* with respect to the higher-level primary and secondary norms that define our American system of government and its institutions is precisely what allows us to *compete* with respect to our diverse lower-level tertiary norms within the field demarcated and the rules of play determined by those institutions—for example, in elections, referenda, legal challenges to legislation, and other channels of cooperative competition. To indulge in a simile: to win a tennis match, opponents must cooperate in abiding by the rules of the game.

This cooperation that is the condition of the possibility of democratic contestation and competition is what has been most deeply at stake in this book. It is even more deeply at stake than a concern with drawing attention to the characteristic epistemic vices afflicting the right or the left, or with arguing that modern knowledge-production practices such as the scientific method produce results that are reliably asymptotic to objective truth. That is, what has been most at stake is the question of how the profusion of testimony in the age of social media, the internet, cable news, and an increasingly ideologically monolithic academia not only radically expands the diversity of tertiary beliefs and values, which is often to the good, but also, in the process, risks poisoning the American mind by undermining the secondary beliefs and values that maintain our sense of American "unity-in-diversity," as Ralph Ellison put it,[3] as well as the primary beliefs and values upon which the continued functioning and even existence of the institutions of our republic depend.

This poisoning of the mind is clearly underway, as the preceding chapters have demonstrated. Today, White nationalists and some conservatives lament the imposition of a holiday like Juneteenth, which they perceive as being a special dispensation for Black people, and thus un-American and exclusionary, rather than, as I believe Juneteenth to be, a celebration of the full flowering of the American promise of freedom for everyone. Such perceptions, along with racialized paranoia about "replacement," are corrosive to the secondary beliefs and values that contribute to a sense of American "usness." For its part, the left is prone to cultivating a sense of alienation from America, her founding, and her institutions—all of which it is fashionable to denounce as White supremacist in its very DNA—that seems calculated to fracture a broad, transracial embrace of American identity and thereby to undermine any stable sense of national belonging and any faith in American institutions.

Even the primary values that define our liberal republican regime are no longer secure. Beginning with the presidential election of 2000, the Democrats and their accomplices in the media began a campaign of undermining the institutions and procedures by which we conduct national elections and even, arguably, the indispensable norm that a president should be democratically elected. It is not that there were no irregularities and causes for concern in the 2000 election, which was decided for George W. Bush by the Supreme Court. There were. However, Democratic outrage over the Supreme Court's decision in 2000 yielded four years later to a full-blown conspiracy theory according to which Bush was reelected only because the Diebold voting machines in Ohio had been rigged to systematically tilt the vote in his favor. By the time Trump began his assault on American electoral institutions by declaring the 2020 results a fraud, promulgating a conspiracy theory about Dominion voting machines (history rhymes!), filing dozens of spurious suits in support of these contentions, and cajoling election officials in Georgia to reverse their state's results, Hillary Clinton had already joined several other Democrats in denouncing Donald Trump's 2016 win as illegitimate.[4]

This elite assault on the legitimacy of our institutions of electoral democracy is paralleled by an abandonment on the part of voters of a central tenet in the package of primary beliefs and values that determine our regime type—that is, the principle that our presidents should be chosen through a democratic process (however imperfect). Thus, in 2016, electors in Arizona, Idaho, Michigan, and Texas received harassing communications, and some received death threats, from people who wanted them to disregard the will of the voters and switch their votes from Trump to Hillary.[5] What might have encouraged this behavior? Perhaps it was a *Washington Post* opinion piece that appeared in November by Lawrence Lessig, the Roy L. Furman Professor of Law and Leadership at Harvard Law School, titled "The Constitution Lets the Electoral College Choose the Winner. They Should Choose Clinton."[6] Or maybe it was an opinion piece that appeared in the same paper in December titled "The Electoral College Should Be Unfaithful."[7] Then again, perhaps it was a December *New York Times* op-ed by David Pozan, the Charles Keller Beekman Professor of Law at Columbia, titled "Why G.O.P. Electoral College Members Can Vote Against Trump."[8] These sober rationalizations by scholars of the Constitution for overturning the 2016 election appeared around the same time that the *New York Times* devoted op-ed space to an elector in Texas who promised to behave "faithlessly" in order to deny Trump the presidency.[9]

Similarly, but much more systematically, state-level Republicans in 2022 floated a slew of legislative proposals and candidates, all dedicated to disenfranchising Democratic voters and delivering their states to Trump in 2024. These candidates and proposals were largely rejected by voters in 2022. However, it is hard to miss an encroachment of authoritarian beliefs and values upon the primary beliefs and values that have defined our republican regime, with its procedures for collectively choosing a chief executive, for over two centuries.

What could explain the bipartisan abandonment, sketched in the preceding paragraphs, of secondary American and even primary democratic republican beliefs and values? One dynamic that emerges as a likely explanation—and it is hardly original with me—is that voters are becoming increasingly mutually fearful of their counterparts on the other side. As mutual fear increases, voters on each side become more likely to countenance "any means necessary" tactics to deprive their opponents of victory, even if it entails betraying beliefs and values central to our regime. What are they afraid of? Precisely the beliefs and values that they see evinced on the other side, beliefs and values that appear to grow ever scarier. Thus, Trump represented so grave a threat that it was acceptable to some Democrats to contemplate disregarding the will of his voters. For their part, some Republicans see Democrats as so subversive of our social order that installing provisions to override their voters' will is acceptable if it keeps them out of office.

Here's the rub. Each side perceives the other side's most distorted beliefs clearly and accurately. A frightening majority of Republicans persist in thinking that Biden did not win the 2020 election legitimately, and Democrats easily recognize this for the delusion that it is. Republicans recognize that Democrats, including President Biden himself, are caught in an ideological fantasy about human biological sex that leads them to support medicating children with puberty blockers and hormones to potentially irreversible effect and surgically altering their bodies, despite the lack of good science to support such practices. Of course each side is scared of the other! They are both frightening. However, each side can only see the mote in its neighbor's eye and is blind to the log in its own.

We are thus coming dangerously close to being hermetically sealed off from one another, isolated inside airtight terrariums defined by the circulation and recirculation of incommensurate belief systems. Our first task, as fellow citizens of the American polity, is to claw our way back to a place where we can all agree upon a minimal set of primary and secondary beliefs and values that define not only our liberal republican regime type as such but also the unique Americanness of its instantiation as the United States. Beyond this, however, we should strive to reclaim the highest aspiration of our enlightenment heritage and take full advantage of the hard-won epistemological methodologies at our disposal to foster a set of beliefs that are both commonly agreed-upon and evermore asymptotic to the truth.

That we are failing in this project at the moment is a result of a variety of factors, including the ones we've discussed in this book: a left-wing academy which promulgates virtuous lies and a right-wing subset of the media which promotes misleading information and conspiracy theories.

Both of these problems could be significantly improved by diversifying both academia and the mainstream media. With a broader spectrum of views represented among the professoriate, our higher education institutions will be less likely to act as factories for the production of self-serving "Professional Managerial Class" ideology. If truth is, to paraphrase the philosopher Richard Rorty, whatever your colleagues will let you get away with saying, then the presence of heterodox colleagues, not only in the faculty lounge but on the editorial boards of journals and involved in the peer-review process, will act as a salutary check on the claims that academics can pass off as truths.

The same goes for the mainstream media. An important factor in the rise of Fox News was the obvious leftward bias of the mainstream media. It's not enough for the *New York Times* to have a Ross Douthat and a Brett Stephens on its staff. These institutions must train themselves to hold off reflexively labeling every adverse news story or Republican victory a manifestation of White supremacy. They must learn to represent not only conservative perspectives but also the spectrum of views that predominate in the country but whose existence the liberal arts college graduates that populate newsrooms are not even aware of. If our most important media organizations remade themselves into institutions in which all Americans could see their concerns and perspectives reflected, and which all Americans could therefore trust, this would go a long way to deflating Fox News and other purveyors of right-wing counternarratives.

What I have tried to do in this chapter is to frame the book as a whole as a plea for self-reflection on the part of those on both sides of our political divide. This includes the actors in the institutions that promulgate left-wing virtuous lies and right-wing conspiracy theories as well as those who receive these testimonies.

Jonathan Haidt warns that "American democracy is now operating outside the bounds of sustainability. If we do not make major changes soon, then our institutions, our political system, and our society may collapse."[10] As my colleague Lawrence Eppard notes, none of us—left, right, or center—want to live in a world where this situation continues to spin out of control. We *must* solve this epistemic crisis, and *both* Red *and* Blue America must look deep inside themselves, be honest about the ways in which they have contributed, and work in good faith toward solutions.

Perhaps we can restore our sense of American "usness" by solving these problems *together.*

CHAPTER 50
Searching for Answers[1]

By Lawrence M. Eppard

I do not pretend to know how to solve the epistemic crisis we are mired in. I feel as lost as anybody else.

At the macro-level, organizations that promote themselves as "news organizations" should not be allowed to spread obvious misinformation and disinformation. I am hoping that somebody much smarter than me will find a reasonable way to regulate these organizations without running afoul of the law, the Constitution, or the wishes of the general public (whether such regulation comes in the form of mandatory public retraction of misleading stories, heavy fines, suspension of a news organization's ability to operate, and/or something else).

I realize that, in our current highly polarized political environment, such an idea might be dead on arrival. I am also well aware of how such power could be abused by partisans who choose to incorrectly label legitimate information as misinformation/disinformation simply because it is unfavorable to their side. Developing meaningful regulation of news organizations would take a considerable amount of time and very careful deliberation—and even then, it may not be feasible. But I believe we should make a good faith effort.

I have one possible idea. For organizations who market themselves as news organizations, the government could require them to display their trustworthiness rating—such as the ratings produced by NewsGuard (newsguardtech.com)—prominently in their content (much like television shows carry ratings like "TV-MA"). Whether it's a Fox News television broadcast or CNN website article or some other news content, the rating could appear prominently in one of the corners of the screen/page.

Social media platforms have made efforts to stop the spread of misleading information—we should encourage the continuation and strengthening of these efforts.

While segments of academia have done a poor job of regulating themselves, it is not clear to me that outside actors would do a better job. In fact, I suspect that people like Ron DeSantis and Christopher Rufo would not only simply reverse the ideological bias in the other direction, they would probably do considerable damage to the large areas of our epistemic system (constituting a majority of that system) that are not in crisis and in fact are working very well. But if academia does not fix itself, the Rufos and DeSantises of the world will step in with a sledge-hammer and begin indiscriminately smashing away. As Jonathan Rauch writes: "[I]t's reasonable to worry about. . . bias in traditional media and a replication crisis in establishment science. The answer, however, is to remediate the defects, not to trash the institutions."[2] And as Michael Jindra and Arthur Sakamoto argue:

> 'Progressive activists,' only 8 percent of the population, now dominate much of the social sciences and humanities. There should be a way to check institutions whose groupthink produces flawed research, though that of course has its dangers. The activists' enemies on the hard right control many state legislatures and, as in Florida, are attempting to legislate speech in higher ed. This is a recipe for continued polarization and conflict, not for truth.[3]

To avoid incompetent, irresponsible, and/or bad faith actors from coming in and destroying the epistemic system because of the sins of a minority of its members, we must fix ourselves.

We need to make peer review more rigorous. We need to find a way to systematically attempt replications of major research findings. It is vitally important that we increase intellectual diversity in terms of who is teaching in the classroom, who is conducting research, and who is making decisions about knowledge production (such as who we select as journal editors and anonymous peer reviewers). We can also create new university centers and institutes specifically designed to foster intellectual diversity and open scholarly debate.[4]

* * * *

At the individual level, I have a few suggestions that each of us might find useful. First and foremost, consume information from credible sources. There are a variety of online news literacy courses available from reputable places like the Poynter Institute and Stony Brook University. There are also several fact-checking websites, including *Snopes, PolitiFact, FactCheck.org, AP Fact Check,* and the *Washington Post Fact Checker.*

While all of this is valuable, it is unreasonable to expect most people to have the time, skills, and desire to fact check every piece of information they see or hear. Therefore, I believe the most important strategy is to only consume information from sources whose content has recently been scrutinized by independent, professional analysts using rigorous, objective, and rule-based methodologies—and been deemed high-quality. At the Connors Forum (ConnorsForum.org) we have identified several trustworthy news and information sources that have been shown to provide accurate information with limited bias.

Here is our rubric for classifying news and information outlets as trustworthy. We disqualify an outlet from receiving our trustworthy classification if it fails in *any* of the following areas:

- All outlets must receive high scores from NewsGuard (newsguardtech. com) on all five of their credibility measures:
    ◊ Not publishing false content
    ◊ Demonstrating responsible news gathering/presentation
    ◊ Making corrections/clarifications
    ◊ Demonstrating responsible news/opinion differentiation
    ◊ Avoiding deceptive headlines
- Outlets cannot fall outside of Ad Fontes Media's (adfontesmedia.com) most reliable zone.
- Outlets cannot be rated lower than high quality by The Factual (thefactual.com).
- Outlets cannot be rated as hyperpartisan by either Ad Fontes Media or AllSides (allsides.com/media-bias).

Using all four of these tools (NewsGuard, Ad Fontes Media, The Factual, and AllSides) in conjunction is akin to a "Swiss cheese defense."[5] While it is possible that one of these organizations could make a mistake in their analysis of a particular outlet, it is highly unlikely that *all four* would give an unreliable outlet high marks (see Figure 50.1).

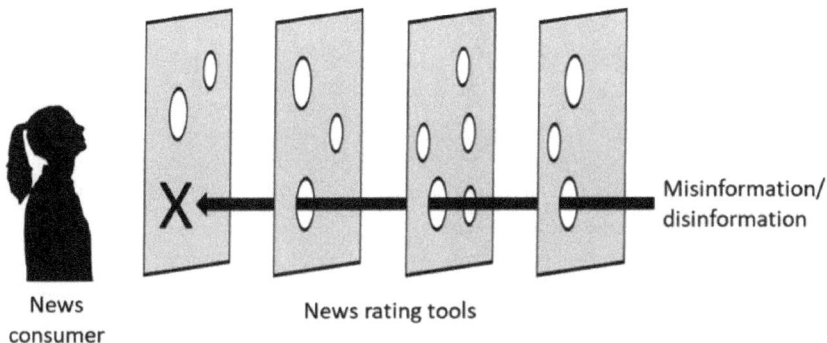

News consumer

News rating tools

Misinformation/ disinformation

Figure 50.1. The Connors "Swiss Cheese" Defense Against Misleading Information.
Adapted by the author from Ian Mackay's Swiss cheese virology infographic. Female silhouette from pexels.com. Ian M. Mackay, "The Swiss Cheese Infographic That Went Viral," *Virology Down Under,* December 26, 2020, https://virologydownunder.com/the-swiss-cheese-infographic-that-went-viral/.

You can read about the methodologies of these organizations at their websites. But in a nutshell, these organizations employ multiple analysts to rate the content that individual outlets produce. These ratings are rigorous, objective, and rule-based.

As one example, NewsGuard employs analysts like James Warren, who amassed a wealth of journalistic experience and knowledge in his five decades in the news industry. This experience included working as managing editor at the *Chicago Tribune*, chief media writer at the Poynter Institute, and Washington bureau chief for the *New York Daily News*.

When NewsGuard analysts rate an outlet, they first rigorously assess the outlet's content against nine objective criteria related to credibility and transparency. During this process, they draft a "Nutrition Label" for the outlet consisting of a grid showing its performance on each of the nine criteria and a written explanation of the rating. If it is believed that the outlet fell short of NewsGuard's credibility or transparency standards, then the analyst will call the outlet for comment.

The analyst's work is then reviewed and fact-checked by at least one senior editor, and then reviewed and fact-checked *again* by both of NewsGuard's CEOs to ensure that the rating is as fair and accurate as possible. The outlet is then given a rating and the analysis is posted online for transparency purposes.

* * * * *

Beyond relying on sources that have been rigorously evaluated for their trustworthiness, individuals can guard against consuming misleading information in a variety of other ways:[6]

- Be curious.
- Value getting to the truth more highly than winning the argument or affirming your beliefs.
- Know what you don't know and the limits of your understanding.
- Avoid being tribal—no side has a monopoly on truth. Commit yourself to being aggressively nonpartisan and objective.
- Value changing your mind when the evidence warrants it. Constantly check your beliefs against evidence and update your views/pivot to a new understanding when new information is available.
- Practice intellectual humility.
- The best writing goes through many drafts, each time getting better. Even after a piece is published, writers know they could keep making it better with endless subsequent drafts. Treat your opinions, assumptions, and beliefs like drafts—keep revising them, over and over and over again, throughout your life. They will only get better and better with each try.
- All of your ideas and beliefs at any given moment should be provisional—simply a reflection of where you stand at a given moment with the

information you have available to you at that point—because you know with time and more information your view of the world will inevitably change for the better.

- Refuse to let your beliefs become ideologies.
- When you find yourself about to respond emotionally to new informa- tion—pause, deliberate, and reflect.
- Try to be emotionally invested in the smallest number of beliefs as pos- sible (we should of course be emotionally invested in *some* beliefs, but ask yourself which ones deserve it). It is hard to change beliefs that we've become emotionally attached to and/or incorporated into our identity, even when we find out they are flawed.
- Always ask yourself: What new information would be necessary to make me change this deeply held belief? If I *were* to be wrong about this, what would the most likely reason be? Then be on the lookout for such discon- firming evidence.[7]
- Do as my colleague and former *Chicago Tribune* editor Michael A. Deas does: Try to cross-examine the information you are consuming like a prosecuting attorney by actively and rigorously *trying* to discredit it. Only when information can stand up to such scrutiny should it be considered reliable.
- Don't overconsume the news.
- Build a media diet that includes a center-left source (like the *Washing- ton Post*), a center-right source (like the *Wall Street Journal*), and a centrist source (like the Associated Press or Reuters).
- Don't lock yourself in an ideological silo, surrounded only by people and sources of information you agree with. Everybody has blind spots in their knowledge (none of us are perfect!) and we are most likely to find flaws in our beliefs when they are challenged.
- Practice viewpoint diversity everywhere (in your personal life, profession- al life, media diet, and beyond). Being confronted with opposing views won't necessarily change all of your beliefs—it shouldn't, many of them are correct—but it will help you identify weaknesses in your preexisting assumptions.
- Jonathan Rauch argues that, "[W]hen we encounter an unwelcome and even repugnant new idea, the right question to ask is 'What can I learn from this?' rather than 'How can I get rid of this?'"[8] When confronted with a different point of view, *listen*, and find at least some kernel of truth in what is being claimed—and then identify which *strong evidence* tells you the rest of the claim is wrong.
- Always play devil's advocate and try your hardest to find information that contradicts your beliefs. Don't avoid opposing arguments—seek out the strongest and most reasonable counterarguments (not the weakest straw men). If you end up revising your beliefs *that's a good thing*—you've

just grown smarter. As Ray Dalio argues, "If you don't look back at your-self and think, 'Wow, how stupid I was a year ago,' then you must not have learned much in the last year."[9] Growing smarter is awesome, I try to do it every day if I can. If you test your beliefs and they remain un-changed *you're also better off* because you're more confident in the strength of your position.

- One way to understand flaws in your beliefs and gaps in your knowledge is to practice explaining a firmly held belief in great detail as if you were talking to an expert on the subject. If you cannot do so thoroughly and without your argument breaking down, more knowledge is necessary.
- Avoid cable news, partisan websites, and personality- or pundit-driven shows (whether on television, radio, or online).
- Be wary of news that comes via social media unless you click on the story and it brings you to a known credible news outlet.
- Compare any piece of news or information you consume to other sourc-es reporting the same thing—what does the weight of the evidence say *together*, not simply the one piece of evidence that you most agree with?
- When you see a particularly important news story, a controversial story, and/or a hard-to-believe story, see if it is being covered by multiple cred-ible outlets and covered in the same manner. If not, ask why.
- Always identify whether you are reading a story that is labeled as news or as opinion/commentary. This is an extremely important distinction, and trustworthy news outlets will label stories appropriately for you.
- When you notice opinion statements, attempts at persuasion, language meant to trigger an emotional reaction, and/or selective or misleading info in a hard news story, this should alert you that the news source is of poor quality.
- Headlines meant to trigger strong emotions should raise a red flag.
- If a story makes you feel particularly good or particularly angry, you should ask yourself why. Be particularly skeptical of stories that make you feel this way.
- Don't let lies go unchallenged—but challenge them gently, with respect, and with questions instead of certainty.
- Challenge the message, not the messenger.
- Don't assume people you disagree with are lying—assume they believe what they are saying until clearly proven otherwise.
- Debate in good faith.
- Do not paint those you disagree with as monsters (unless of course they undeniably are). Assume they have at least a somewhat valid (if flawed) and good faith reason to believe what they believe, not that they have dark motivations or that they are brainwashed or stupid. If you are ar-guing in good faith about something you believe to be true, assume the same of other people until clearly proven otherwise.

- Identify the *many* areas you are *not* an expert in and be able to identify who the appropriate experts are in these areas.
- Avoid beginning to read a news story or seeking information with the answers or solutions already in your mind.
- Constantly doubt what you know, rethink your beliefs, and remain curious about what you don't know.
- Evolve rather than affirm your beliefs.
- Test your hypotheses and then test alternative hypotheses.
- Support trustworthy news sources (financially if you are able) so they continue to exist.

* * * * *

There are no "right" or "wrong" answers to many of the biggest challenges facing our country. There are facts and data that support a variety of positions, but how this information should be prioritized is subjective. But whatever we decide to do, we should insist that the information we use to make our decisions is factual and of the highest possible quality.

Ideology presented as fact, misinformation, disinformation, and malinformation are demonstrably dangerous and are poisoning the American mind. They help diseases once thought to be a thing of the past to rear their ugly heads again. They destabilize our democracy:

> Americans like to think our country is immune to authoritarianism. We have a culture of freedom, a tradition of elected government, and a Bill of Rights. We're not like those European countries that fell into fascism. We'd never willingly abandon democracy, liberty, or the rule of law. But that's not how authoritarianism would come to America. In fact, it's not how authoritarianism has come to America. The movement to dismantle our democracy is thriving and growing, even after the failure of the Jan. 6th coup attempt, because it isn't spreading through overt rejection of our system of government. It's spreading through lies.[10]

The Bulwark's Will Saletan goes on to argue that, "We're in a battle to save democracy, but the battleground isn't values. It's facts." He would write in another piece:

> In a traditional anti-democratic coup, the military or the armed opposition seizes power in overt defiance of a previous election. But that isn't what happened in the United States two years ago. Donald Trump summoned a mob to Washington and unleashed it on the U.S. Capitol not by calling for the overthrow of the government but by claiming, falsely, that he was the duly elected head of the govern-

ment. He used fictitious allegations of election fraud to manipulate his followers. They stormed the Capitol believing that they were defending, not deposing, the winner of the election. . . [W]e don't need to persuade most people that democracy should be respected. They already understand that. What we need to do is persuade them that the person who was certified as the winner of the election actually won it. This isn't a fight over ideology. It's a fight over information.[11]

Jonathan Haidt warns that: "American democracy is now operating outside the bounds of sustainability. If we do not make major changes soon, then our institutions, our political system, and our society may collapse."[12] Yochai Benkler and his colleagues explain that, "Rebuilding a basis on which Americans can form a shared belief about what is going on is a precondition of democracy."[13] *How Democracies Die* authors Stephen Levitsky and Daniel Ziblatt note that:

> Blatant dictatorship—in the form of fascism, communism, or military rule—has disappeared across much of the world. . . Democracies still die, but by different means. Since the end of the Cold War, most democratic breakdowns have been caused not by generals and soldiers but by elected governments themselves. . . Democratic backsliding today begins at the ballot box.[14]

On Tyranny author Timothy Snyder writes that:

> [A] belief in truth is what makes trust in authority possible. Without trust, without respect for journalists or doctors or politicians, a society can't hang together. Nobody trusts anyone, which leaves society open to resentment and propaganda, and of course to demagogues.[15]

And as Tom Nichols cautions:

> The citizens of the world's democracies now must live with the undeniable knowledge that they are capable of embracing illiberal movements and attacking their own liberties as a matter of their own free will rather than as the result of disaster or foreign conquest. Worse, the budding authoritarians who live among us now know it too. They have seen a demonstrated market for what they are selling.[16]

He goes on to note that, in America, people involved in illiberal movements:

> see their own actions not as a problem but as a solution. Illiberal cit-

izens do not think of themselves as illiberal; they think of themselves as populist or ultra-democratic (at least where their own preferred groups are concerned). When the rest of us are vigilantly scanning the horizon for the 'man on horseback' or for the shock troops of a mass movement, it is easy to underestimate the impact of millions of people exchanging paranoid memes on Facebook who are already immune both to reason and to the basic requirements of anything like informed participation in democratic politics.[17]

None of us—left, right, or center—want to live in a world where this situation continues to spin out of control. We *must* solve this epistemic crisis.

Notes

Chapter 1

1. Originally published and adapted here with permission by Lawrence M. Eppard, "The Poisoning of the American Mind," *Connors Newsletter*, June 15, 2023, https://connorsforum.substack.com/p/the-poisoning-of-the-american-mind.

2. Tom Nichols, *The Death of Expertise: The Campaign Against Established Knowledge and Why It Matters* (New York: Oxford University Press, 2017), 2-3.

3. Adrienne LaFrance, "The New Anarchy," *The Atlantic*, April 2023, 37.

4. Jonathan Haidt, "Why the Past 10 Years of American Life Have Been Uniquely Stupid," *The Atlantic*, April 11, 2022, https://www.theatlantic.com/magazine/archive/2022/05/social-media-democracy-trust-babel/629369/.

5. Anne Applebaum, *Twilight of Democracy: The Seductive Lure of Authoritarianism* (New York: Anchor Books, 2020), 113.

6. Tom Nichols, *Our Own Worst Enemy: The Assault from Within on Modern Democracy* (New York: Oxford University Press, 2021), 87.

7. Martin Gurri, *The Revolt of the Public and the Crisis of Authority in the New Millennium* (San Francisco, CA: Stripe Press, 2018), 328.

8. Naomi Oreskes and Erik M. Conway, *Merchants of Doubt: How a Handful of Scientists Obscured the Truth on Issues from Tobacco Smoke to Global Warming* (New York: Bloomsbury Press, 2010), 240-241.

9. Jonathan Rauch, "The Constitution of Knowledge," *National Affairs*, Fall 2018, https://www.nationalaffairs.com/publications/detail/the-constitution-of-knowledge.

10. Alison Durkee, "Republicans Increasingly Realize There's No Evidence Of Election Fraud—But Most Still Think 2020 Election Was Stolen Anyway, Poll Finds," *Forbes*, March 14, 2023, https://www.forbes.com/sites/alisondurkee/2023/03/14/republicans-increasingly-realize-theres-no-evidence-of-election-fraud-but-most-still-think-2020-election-was-stolen-anyway-poll-finds/?sh=113c205628ec.

11. Isaac Saul, "Not Rigged! How We Know Recent Elections Are Not Fraudulent," *Skeptic Magazine*, November 1, 2022, https://www.skeptic.com/reading_room/not-rigged-how-we-know-recent-elections-not-fraudulent/.

12. Morgan Chalfant, "Trump: 'The Only Way We're Going to Lose This Election Is If the Election Is Rigged,'" *The Hill*, August 17, 2020, https://thehill.com/homenews/administration/512424-trump-the-only-way-we-are-going-to-lose-this-election-is-if-the/.

13. Aja Romano, "J.K. Rowling's Transphobia: A History," *Vox*, March 3, 2023, https://www.vox.com/culture/23622610/jk-rowling-transphobic-statements-timeline-history-controversy.

14. Robert Lynch, "From Sex To Gender: The Modern Dismissal of Biology," *Skeptic*

Magazine, April 7, 2023, https://www.skeptic.com/reading_room/from-sex-to-gender-modern-dismissal-of-biology/.

15. Jonathan Rauch, *The Constitution of Knowledge: A Defense of Truth* (Washington, D.C.: Brookings Institution Press, 2021), 162.

16. Yes, yes, I understand, the phone would not work—no cell towers in that time, no internet, etc. etc. etc. Humor me and play along.

17. As naïve as it may sound now, many thought the internet and social media would *reduce* misinformation and disinformation, not unleash it. As Jonathan Haidt explains: "In the first decade of the new century, social media was widely believed to be a boon to democracy. What dictator could impose his will on an interconnected citizenry? What regime could build a wall to keep out the internet?" And as Tom Nichols writes: "Years of better education, increased access to data, the explosion of social media, and lowered barriers of entry into the public arena were supposed to improve our abilities to deliberate and decide. Instead, these advances seem to have made all of this worse rather than better." Jonathan Haidt, "Why the Past 10 Years of American Life Have Been Uniquely Stupid," *The Atlantic,* April 11, 2022, https://www.theatlantic.com/magazine/archive/2022/05/social-media-democracy-trust-babel/629369/; Nichols, *The Death of Expertise,* 40.

18. Frum posted this on *Twitter* on February 13, 2020: https://twitter.com/davidfrum/status/1228009917682012160.

19. Haidt, "Why the Past 10 Years of American Life Have Been Uniquely Stupid."

20. "We need an elite consensus, and hopefully also something approaching a public consensus, on the *method* of validating propositions. We needn't and can't all agree that the same things are true, but a critical mass needs to agree on what it is we *do* that distinguishes truth from falsehood, and more important, on who does it" (Rauch, "The Constitution of Knowledge").

21. "What is often called the marketplace of ideas would be more accurately described as a marketplace of *persuasion,* because the only way to establish knowledge is to convince others you are right" (Rauch, "The Constitution of Knowledge").

22. "Who can be trusted to resolve questions about objective truth? The best answer turns out to be no one in particular. The greatest of human social networks was born centuries ago...a decentralized, globe-spanning community of critical testers who hunt for each other's errors. In other words, they outsourced objectivity to a social network... Though nowhere encoded in law, the constitution of knowledge has its own equivalents of checks and balances (peer review and replication), separation of powers (specialization), governing institutions (scientific societies and professional bodies), voting (citations and confirmations), and civic virtues (submit your beliefs for checking if you want to be taken seriously)" (Rauch, "The Constitution of Knowledge").

23. Rauch, "The Constitution of Knowledge.

24. Rauch, "The Constitution of Knowledge.

25. Jonathan Rauch, The Constitution of Knowledge, 87.

26. Rauch, "The Constitution of Knowledge."

27. Steven Sloman and Philip Fernbach, *The Knowledge Illusion: Why We Never Think Alone* (New York: Riverhead Books, 2017).

28. Sloman and Fernbach, *The Knowledge Illusion*.

29. Nichols, *The Death of Expertise*, 14.

30. Elizabeth Kolbert, "Why Facts Don't Change Our Minds," *The New Yorker*, February 19, 2017, https://www.newyorker.com/magazine/2017/02/27/why-facts-dont-change-our-minds.

31. "The great advantage of scientific investigation is not that it frames hypotheses and then tries to confirm them (everyone does that), but that it floats and falsifies hypotheses on an industrial scale, something no other system can do" (Rauch, *The Constitution of Knowledge*, 58).

32. Rauch, *The Constitution of Knowledge*, 15.

33. Rauch, *The Constitution of Knowledge*, 87.

34. In the current environment not everybody in the epistemic system is acting honorably: "It is especially important to remember: politicizing an academic discipline like sociology or literary criticism, or spreading propaganda to discredit and drown out fact-based journalism, or shading an intelligence assessment to please a president, or lying to a judge: each of those is every bit as much an attack on the Constitution of Knowledge as is, say, banning the teaching of evolution or propagating fake science about vaccines. The reality-based community is defined not by its particular disciplines or findings but by its rules and values, and an attack on those rules and values in any one part of the community is an attack on them in every part" (Rauch, *The Constitution of Knowledge*, 99–100).

35. Rauch, *The Constitution of Knowledge*, 15–16.

36. Guy Elgat, "'Prove that I am Wrong!' What QAnon, Descartes, and Brains in Vats Have in Common," *Skeptic Magazine*, https://pocketmags.com/skeptic-magazine/244.

37. "You can keep accumulating evidence to confirm a hypothesis, and it will never prove it to be absolutely true. This is because you can't rule out the possibility of another similar hypothesis being correct, or of making some new observation that shows your hypothesis to be false....So while you can never prove a hypothesis true simply by making more confirmatory observations, you only need one solid contrary observation to prove a hypothesis false. This notion is at the core of the hypothetico-deductive model of science. This is why a great deal of science is focused on testing hypotheses, pushing them to their limits, and attempting to break them through experimentation. If the hypothesis survives repeated testing, our confidence in it grows." See Tim Dean, "How We Edit Science [Parts 1 through 5]," *The Conversation*, March 17, 2017, https://theconversation.com/how-we-edit-science-part-1-the-scientific-method-74521.

38. John Wright, "Why Should We Trust Science? Because It Doesn't Trust Itself," *The Conversation*, September 18, 2022, https://theconversation.com/why-should-we-trust-science-because-it-doesnt-trust-itself-188988.

39. D. Abbot et. al., "In Defense of Merit in Science," *Journal of Controversial Ideas* 3, no. 1 (2023): 3.

40. Dean, "How We Edit Science [Parts 1 through 5]."

41. Gurri, *The Revolt of the Public and the Crisis of Authority in the New Millennium*, 266.

42. "Creating knowledge is inherently a professionalized and structured affair. Whether you are engaged in bench chemistry, daily journalism, or intelligence analysis, testing hypotheses requires time, money, skill, expertise, and intricate social interaction. . . . At the core of the constitution of knowledge, by its very nature, are professional networks" (Rauch, "The Constitution of Knowledge").

43. Helen E. Longino argued, "The greater the number of different points of view included in a given community, the more likely it is that [the community's] scientific practice will be objective." Jonathan Rauch argues, "When we encounter an unwelcome and even repugnant new idea, the right question to ask is 'What can I learn from this?' rather than 'How can I get rid of this?'" (Rauch, *The Constitution of Knowledge*, 194, 198).

44. And ideally a civil manner, critiquing the proposition, not its proponent.

45. Kolbert, "Why Facts Don't Change Our Minds."

46. Greg Lukianoff and Jonathan Haidt, *The Coddling of the American Mind: How Good Intentions and Bad Ideas Are Setting Up a Generation for Failure* (London: Penguin Books, 2018), 109.

47. "Once scientists have conducted their experiment and found some interesting results, they move on to publishing them. Science is somewhat unique in that the norm is towards full transparency, where scientists effectively give away their discoveries to the rest of the scientific community and society at large. This is not only out of a magnanimous spirit, but because it also turns out to be a highly effective way of scrutinizing scientific discoveries and helping others to build upon them" (Dean, "How We Edit Science [Parts 1 through 5]").

48. Rauch, *The Constitution of Knowledge*, 93.

49. William Feather wrote that being educated means "being able to differentiate between what you know and what you don't." From David Dunning, "We Are All Confident Idiots," *Pacific Standard*, October 27, 2014, https://psmag.com/social-justice/confident-idiots-92793.

50. Rauch, *The Constitution of Knowledge*, 263.

51. Rauch, *The Constitution of Knowledge*, 95.

52. "It is important that we recognize the fallibility of science and the scientific method. But within this fallibility lies its greatest strength: self-correction. Whether mistakes are made honestly or dishonestly, whether a fraud is unknowingly or knowingly perpetrated, in time it will be flushed out of the system through the lack of external verification." See Michael Shermer, "A Skeptical Manifesto," https://www.skeptic.com/about_us/manifesto/#0.

53. "Think of the constitution of knowledge as a funnel. At the wide end, millions of people float millions of hypotheses every day. Only an infinitesimal fraction of new ideas will be proven true. To find them, we run the hypotheses through a massive, socially distributed error-finding process. Only a tiny few make it to the narrow end of the funnel. There, often years later, a kind of social valve—call it prestige and recog-

nition—admits the surviving propositions into the canon of knowledge" (Rauch, "The Constitution of Knowledge").

54. "Science helps us avoid dogmatism: the basing of conclusions on authority rather than science" (Shermer, "A Skeptical Manifesto").

55. Lukianoff and Haidt, *The Coddling of the American Mind*, 39–40.

56. Rauch, *The Constitution of Knowledge*, 87.

57. Rauch, *The Constitution of Knowledge*, 75.

58. Tom Nichols notes, "Experts being wrong on occasion about certain issues is not the same thing as experts being wrong consistently on everything. The fact of the matter is that experts are more often right than wrong, especially on essential matters of fact. And yet the public constantly searches for the loopholes in expert knowledge that will allow them to disregard all expert advice they don't like....No one is arguing...that experts can't be wrong...the point is that they are less likely to be wrong than nonexperts" (Nichols, *The Death of Expertise*, 23–24).

Chapter 2

1. Originally published and adapted here with permission by Lawrence M. Eppard, "The Poisoning of the American Mind," *Connors Newsletter,* June 15, 2023, https://connorsforum.substack.com/p/the-poisoning-of-the-american-mind.

2. Jonathan Rauch, "The Constitution of Knowledge," *National Affairs,* Fall 2018, https://www.nationalaffairs.com/publications/detail/the-constitution-of-knowledge.

3. Martin Gurri, *The Revolt of the Public and the Crisis of Authority in the New Millennium* (San Francisco, CA: Stripe Press, 2018), 20.

4. Nichols, *The Death of Expertise: The Campaign Against Established Knowledge and Why It Matters* (New York: Oxford University Press, 2017), 16.

5. Nichols, *The Death of Expertise*, 16.

6. As Jonathan Rauch explains: "Accurate reportage is orders of magnitude more expensive to produce than disinformation," and "social media created a distribution platform for disinformation. Putting stuff out there costs effectively nothing" (Rauch, "The Constitution of Knowledge").

7. For an example of the massive damage that Fox News has done to American society, see Amanda Carpenter, "Exposed: Fox's Pander-for-Profit Business Model," *The Bulwark,* February 28, 2023, https://www.thebulwark.com/exposed-foxs-pander-for-profit-business-model/.

8. For a critique of fad psychology see Jesse Singal, *The Quick Fix: Why Fad Psychology Can't Cure Our Social Ills* (New York: Farrar, Straus and Giroux, 2021).

9. "Unlike ordinary lies and propaganda, which try to make you believe *something,* disinformation tries to make you disbelieve *everything.* It scatters so much bad information, and casts so many aspersions on so many sources of information, that people throw up their hands and say, 'They're all a pack of liars.' As Steve Bannon, a former Trump aide

and former leader of *Breitbart News*, succinctly put it in an interview with *Bloomberg*, "[T]he way to deal with [the media] is to flood the zone with shit.'" (Rauch, "The Constitution of Knowledge.")

10. Lee McIntyre, *Post-Truth* (Cambridge, MA: The MIT Press, 2018), 10.

11. Hannah Arendt, *The Origins of Totalitarianism* (Boston, MA: Houghton Mifflin, 1951), 474.

12. Humans likely developed many cognitive biases "to make certain guesses or predictions. Those cognitive shortcuts save time, energy, and potentially lives. On the savanna, where underreacting to a danger can be deadly and statistical risk analyses are hard to come by, it makes sense to be guided by emotional responses to stimuli or threats." Rauch goes on to say that, "No one with a real-world time budget could process all of the information" in most circumstances. "Relying on shortcuts...is a necessary part of navigating daily life in a complicated world." See Jonathan Rauch, *The Constitution of Knowledge: A Defense of Truth* (Washington, D.C.: Brookings Institution Press, 2021), 27.

13. Tom Nichols, *Our Own Worst Enemy: The Assault From Within on Modern Democracy* (New York: Oxford University Press, 2021), 192.

14. Rauch, *The Constitution of Knowledge*, 30, 32.

15. David Dunning, "We Are All Confident Idiots," *Pacific Standard*, October 27, 2014, https://psmag.com/social-justice/confident-idiots-92793.

16. Dunning, "We Are All Confident Idiots."

17. Chris Mooney, "Liberals Deny Science, Too," *The Washington Post*, October 28, 2014, https://www.washingtonpost.com/news/wonk/wp/2014/10/28/liberals-deny-science-too/.

18. And as Jonathan Rauch notes, "As demagogues have demonstrated time and again, the tendency to react emotionally to emotionally charged issues is easy to exploit and manipulate." He also notes that, "When forming political loyalties, we rationalize backward from our emotions and intuitions." (Rauch, *The Constitution of Knowledge*, 24-25, 27).

19. Rauch, *The Constitution of Knowledge*, 32.

20. Justin Kruger and David Dunning explain: "We argue that the skills that engender competence in a particular domain are often the very same skills necessary to evaluate competence in that domain—one's own or anyone else's....For example, consider the ability to write grammatical English. The skills that enable one to construct a grammatical sentence are the same skills necessary to recognize a grammatical sentence, and thus are the same skills necessary to determine if a grammatical mistake has been made. In short, the same knowledge that underlies the ability to produce correct judgment is also the knowledge that underlies the ability to recognize correct judgment. To lack the former is to be deficient in the latter." See Justin Kruger and David Dunning, "Unskilled and Unaware of It: How Difficulties in Recognizing One's Own Incompetence Lead to Inflated Self-Assessments," *Psychology 77*, no. 6 (1999): 1121-1122.

21. Steven Sloman and Philip Fernbach, *The Knowledge Illusion: Why We Never Think Alone* (New York: Riverhead Books, 2017).

22. List of cognitive biases developed based on the writings of a variety of people, including Jonathan Rauch, Tom Nichols, Lee McIntyre, Steven Sloman, Philip Fernbach, Elizabeth Kolbert, Justin Kruger, and David Dunning, among others.

23. Rauch, *The Constitution of Knowledge*, 27.

24. Ian Bogost, "The Internet is Kmart Now," *The Atlantic*, December 19, 2022, https://www.theatlantic.com/technology/archive/2022/12/kmart-yahoo-partnership-gen-x-e-business/672506/.

25. Bogost, "The Internet is Kmart Now."

26. Erica Pandey, "America's Kids Get an Internet Librarian," *Axios*, January 25, 2022, https://www.axios.com/2022/01/25/schools-misinformation-internet-newsguard.

27. Gurri, *The Revolt of the Public and the Crisis of Authority in the New Millennium*, 20.

28. As Jeffrey Rosen explains, "Today, all congressional Republicans fall to the right of the most conservative Democrat, and all congressional Democrats fall to the left of the most liberal Republican. In the 1960s, at times, 50 percent of the lawmakers overlapped ideologically." See Jeffrey Rosen, "America Is Living James Madison's Nightmare," *The Atlantic*, October 2018, https://www.theatlantic.com/magazine/archive/2018/10/james-madison-mob-rule/568351/.

29. Yoni Appelbaum, "How America Ends," *The Atlantic*, December 2019, https://www.theatlantic.com/magazine/archive/2019/12/how-america-ends/600757/.

30. Greg Lukianoff and Jonathan Haidt, *The Coddling of the American Mind: How Good Intentions and Bad Ideas Are Setting Up a Generation for Failure* (London: Penguin Books, 2018), 129.

31. "From the 1940s to around 1980, American politics were about as centrist and bipartisan as it has ever been." (Lukianoff and Haidt, *The Coddling of the American Mind*, 130).

32. As David French argues, "America's most partisan citizens view their political opponents as deeply reprehensible. Overwhelming majorities of Republicans and Democrats view the other side as 'hateful,' 'racist,' 'brainwashed' and 'arrogant.' That's why they seek to squelch opposing views. They see no value in the speech of people they despise. Instead, they see only bad people expressing bad ideas in bad faith. We're losing the capacity for empathy. We simply can't place ourselves in the other person's shoes. Yet it takes a certain degree of arrogance to presume that we're so obviously correct that disagreement isn't just a sign of error but of moral defect." David French, "Two Different Versions of 'Cancel Culture,'" *The New York Times*, March 2, 2023, https://www.nytimes.com/2023/03/02/opinion/lab-leak-dilbert-cancel-culture.html.

33. Alan Abramowitz and Steven Webster, "'Negative Partisanship' Explains Everything," *Politico*, September/October 2017, https://www.politico.com/magazine/story/2017/09/05/negative-partisanship-explains-everything-215534/. For more, see also Alan I. Abramowitz and Steven Webster, "The Rise of Negative Partisanship and the Nationalization of U.S. Elections in the 21st Century," *Electoral Studies* 41, (March 2016): 12-22.

34. Rauch, *The Constitution of Knowledge*, 41.

35. As Lee McIntyre notes, "With fact and opinion now presented side by side on the Internet, who knows what to believe anymore? With no filters and no vetting, readers and viewers these days are readily exposed to a steady stream of pure partisanship." See Lee McIntyre, *Post-Truth* (Cambridge, MA: MIT Press, 2018), 87.

36. "Information may want to be free, but knowledge wants to be expensive—very expensive. Just one investigative reporting project or academic study requires work by multiple full-time professionals and budgets in the tens of thousands and often much, much more. Whereas making stuff up is cheap." (Rauch, *The Constitution of Knowledge*, 135-36).

37. Tom Nichols argues that, "The death of expertise is...like a national bout of ill temper, a childish rejection of authority in all its forms coupled to an insistence that strongly held opinions are indistinguishable from facts." (Nichols, *The Death of Expertise*, 28).

38. Rauch, *The Constitution of Knowledge*, 10.

39. As Jonathan Rauch notes, "Trump and his media echo chambers [normalized] lying in order to obliterate the distinction, in the public realm, between truth and untruth. They were practicing the hallowed (if infamous) art of disinformation....Their goal was to denude the public's capacity to make any distinctions at all" (Rauch, *The Constitution of Knowledge*, 8).

40. Which treats news like entertainment to keep people's interest, requires the elevation of non-news to the forefront to fill time, and requires networks to have analysis all day long, meaning many non-experts are opining about things about which they have little knowledge.

41. Jonathan Haidt argues that, "In the 21st century, America's tech companies have rewired the world and created products that now appear to be corrosive to democracy, obstacles to shared understanding, and destroyers of the modern tower....Social scientists have identified at least three major forces that collectively bind together successful democracies: social capital (extensive social networks with high levels of trust), strong institutions, and shared stories. Social media has weakened all three." See Jonathan Haidt, "Why the Past 10 Years of American Life Have Been Uniquely Stupid," *The Atlantic*, April 11, 2022, https://www.theatlantic.com/magazine/archive/2022/05/social-media-democracy-trust-babel/629369/.

42. A former Facebook executive was quoted saying: "It literally is a point now where I think we have created tools that are ripping apart the social fabric of how society works." And a worker at Facebook was quoted as saying: "I am convinced the devil lives in our phones and is wreaking havoc on our children." (Nichols, *Our Own Worst Enemy*, 172-73).

43. Research shows that "posts that trigger emotions—especially anger at out-groups—are the most likely to be shared." Jonathan Haidt explains that, "One of the engineers at Twitter who had worked on the 'Retweet' button later revealed that he regretted his contribution because it had made Twitter a nastier place. As he watched Twitter mobs forming through the use of the new tool, he thought to himself, 'We might have just handed a 4-year-old a loaded weapon.'" (Haidt, "Why the Past 10 Years of American Life Have Been Uniquely Stupid,").

44. Rauch, *The Constitution of Knowledge*, 125.

45. "What has caused such rancor? The stresses of a globalizing, postindustrial economy. Growing economic inequality. The hyperbolizing force of social media. Geographic sorting. The demagogic provocations of the president himself. As in *Murder on the Orient Express,* every suspect has had a hand in the crime." (Appelbaum, "How America Ends").

46. Narcissism meaning: "The unhealthy preoccupation with the self to the exclusion of all else." Entitlement meaning: "The selfish and self-absorbed conviction that our own importance merits constant reward." Tom Nichols argues, "By definition, democracy is a community. By definition, a narcissist is incapable holding or granting membership in a community." He discusses the work of Christopher Lasch in *The Culture of Narcissism,* who "raged against the arrival of the 'new narcissist,' a hedonist questing for personal fulfillment while fending off the onset of adulthood and its responsibilities." He wrote that the average American was an "overgrown child who 'extols cooperation and teamwork' while 'harboring deeply antisocial impulses,' who 'praises respect for rules and regulations in the secret belief that they do not apply to himself,' whose 'cravings have no limits,' and whose constant demands for immediate gratification create a 'state of restless, perpetually unsatisfied desire.'" (Nichols, *Our Own Worst Enemy,* 91-92).

47. In the United States, "Americans no longer distinguish the phrase 'you're wrong' from the phrase 'you're stupid.' To disagree is to disrespect. To correct another is to insult. And to refuse to acknowledge all views as worthy of consideration, no matter how fantastic or inane they are, is to be closed minded." (Nichols, *The Death of Expertise,* 25).

48. While criticizing emotional safetyism, Jonathan Rauch argues that, "If subjectively hurtful expressions are violence, then criticism is violence, and then science is a human rights violation." (Rauch, *The Constitution of Knowledge,* 202).

49. Jacob Soll, "The Long and Brutal History of Fake News," *Politico Magazine,* December 18, 2016, https://www.politico.com/magazine/story/2016/12/fake-news-history-long-violent-214535/.

50. Soll, "The Long and Brutal History of Fake News."

51. Soll, "The Long and Brutal History of Fake News."

52. Lukianoff and Haidt, *The Coddling of the American Mind,* 130-31.

53. Fox, "Standards of Business Conduct," As of June 2022, https://www.foxcorporation.com/corporate-governance/sobc/guiding-principles/.

54. Adam Serwer, "Why Fox News Lied to Its Viewers," *The Atlantic,* February 19, 2023, https://www.theatlantic.com/ideas/archive/2023/02/fox-news-dominion-lawsuit-trump/673132/.

55. Kimberly Nordyke, "'Fox & Friends' Slam SpongeBob SquarePants' 'Global Warming Agenda' (Video)," *The Hollywood Reporter,* August 8, 2011, https://www.hollywoodreporter.com/tv/tv-news/fox-friends-hosts-slam-spongebob-220459/.

56. Philip Bump, "Why Tucker Carlson's Recent Embrace of 'Great Replacement' Is Different," *The Washington Post,* July 20, 2022, https://www.washingtonpost.com/politics/2022/07/20/why-tucker-carlsons-recent-embrace-great-replacement-is-different/.

57. Isaac Saul, "Not Rigged! How We Know Recent Elections Are Not Fraudulent," *Skeptic Magazine*, November 1, 2022, https://www.skeptic.com/reading_room/not-rigged-how-we-know-recent-elections-not-fraudulent/.

58. Claims made in Tucker Carlson's *Patriot Purge* documentary: https://nation.fox-news.com/watch/d6eecfabb4cb2572324269885cf21114/.

59. Mona Charen, "Please Lie to Me, Tucker," *The Bulwark*, March 2, 2023, https://www.thebulwark.com/please-lie-to-me-tucker/.

60. Saul, "Not Rigged! How We Know Recent Elections Are Not Fraudulent."

61. Alex Woodward, "'Insane, Lying, Complete Nut': How Fox News Stars Rejected Trump's Election Conspiracies While Network Pushed Them," *Independent*, February 28, 2023, https://www.independent.co.uk/news/world/americas/us-politics/fox-news-trump-election-lies-dominion-lawsuit-b2291010.html.

62. Serwer, "Why Fox News Lied to Its Viewers."

63. McIntyre, *Post-Truth*.

64. Lawrence Eppard, Erik Nelson, Cynthia Cox, and Eduardo Bonilla-Silva, "Obligations to the Future," *Journal of Working-Class Studies* 5, no. 2 (October 2020): 52.

65. The Editors of Goop, "Earthing: The Art of Walking Barefoot," *Goop*, July 26, 2021, https://goop.com/wellness/health/earthing-how-walking-barefoot-could-cure-your-insomnia-more/.

66. Dave Collins, "Alex Jones Ordered To Pay $473M More to Sandy Hook Families," *Associated Press*, November 10, 2022, https://apnews.com/article/entertainment-shootings-business-connecticut-alex-jones-c6d0563dc17e7bfa83a881b44e7b9eec.

67. Nichols, *The Death of Expertise*, 108.

68. Nichols, *The Death of Expertise*, 109.

69. Estimate from InternetLiveStats.com.

70. Ted Koppel, "Viewpoint: Olbermann, O'Reilly and the Death of Real News," *MLive*, November 21, 2010, https://www.mlive.com/opinion/kalamazoo/2010/11/viewpoint_olbermann_oreilly_an.html.

71. McIntyre, *Post-Truth*, 72.

72. Yevgeny Simkin, "Social Media is the Problem," *The Bulwark*, July 31, 2020, https://www.thebulwark.com/social-media-is-the-problem/.

Chapter 3

1. Originally published and adapted here with permission by Lawrence M. Eppard, "The Poisoning of the American Mind," *Connors Newsletter*, June 15, 2023, https://connorsforum.substack.com/p/the-poisoning-of-the-american-mind.

2. How many readers have unfriended or unfollowed somebody on social media because of their opposing political views? I would bet a significant number—I'm embarrassed to say I have!

3. Jonathan Haidt, "Why the Past 10 Years of American Life Have Been Uniquely Stupid," *The Atlantic*, April 11, 2022, https://www.theatlantic.com/magazine/archive/2022/05/social-media-democracy-trust-babel/629369/.

4. "Software learned to hack our brains. Sophisticated algorithms and granular data allowed messages and images to be minutely tuned and targeted. These are powerful new tools that humans are not designed to encounter or resist." See Jonathan Rauch, "The Constitution of Knowledge," *National Affairs*, Fall 2018, https://www.nationalaffairs.com/publications/detail/the-constitution-of-knowledge.

5. Greg Lukianoff and Jonathan Haidt, *The Coddling of the American Mind: How Good Intentions and Bad Ideas Are Setting Up a Generation for Failure* (London: Penguin Books, 2018), 10.

6. Jonathan Rauch, *The Constitution of Knowledge: A Defense of Truth* (Washington, D.C.: Brookings Institution Press, 2021), 174.

7. As an example, Marjorie Taylor Greene stated: "We need a national divorce. We need to separate by red states and blue states and shrink the federal government. Everyone I talk to says this." She posted this on *Twitter* on February 20, 2023: https://twitter.com/mtgreenee/status/1627665203398688768.

8. Haidt, "Why the Past 10 Years of American Life Have Been Uniquely Stupid."

9. Anne Applebaum, *Twilight of Democracy: The Seductive Lure of Authoritarianism* (New York: Anchor Books, 2020), 113.

10. Rauch, *The Constitution of Knowledge*, 9.

11. Rauch, *The Constitution of Knowledge*, 17.

12. Mona Charen, "Please Lie to Me, Tucker," *The Bulwark*, March 2, 2023, https://www.thebulwark.com/please-lie-to-me-tucker/.

13. David Roberts, "Donald Trump and the Rise of Tribal Epistemology," *Vox*, May 19, 2017, https://www.vox.com/policy-and-politics/2017/3/22/14762030/donald-trump-tribal-epistemology.

14. Charen, "Please Lie To Me, Tucker."

15. Yoni Appelbaum, "How America Ends," *The Atlantic*, December 2019, https://www.theatlantic.com/magazine/archive/2019/12/how-america-ends/600757/.

16. Tom Nichols, *Our Own Worst Enemy: The Assault From Within on Modern Democracy* (New York: Oxford University Press, 2021), 168.

17. Nichols, *Our Own Worst Enemy*, 189.

18. Roberts, "Donald Trump and the Rise of Tribal Epistemology."

19. Yochai Benkler, Robert Faris, Hal Roberts, and Ethan Zuckerman, "Study: Breitbart-Led Right-Wing Media Ecosystem Altered Broader Media Agenda," *Columbia Journalism Review*, March 3, 2017, https://www.cjr.org/analysis/breitbart-media-trump-harvard-study.php.

20. Roberts, "Donald Trump and the Rise of Tribal Epistemology."

21. Roberts, "Donald Trump and the Rise of Tribal Epistemology."

22. Benkler, Faris, Roberts, and Zuckerman, "Study: Breitbart-Led Right-Wing Media Ecosystem Altered Broader Media Agenda."

23. As Lee McIntyre explains: "If we are already motivated to *want* to believe certain things, it doesn't take much to tip us over to believing them, especially if others we care about already do so. Our inherent cognitive biases make us ripe for manipulation and exploitation by those who have an agenda to push, especially if they can discredit all other sources of information. But we are especially vulnerable when they tell us exactly what we want to hear." See Lee McIntyre, "How Cognitive Bias Can Explain Post-Truth," *Salon.com*, January 23, 2021, https://www.salon.com/2021/01/23/how-cogni-tive-bias-can-explain-post-truth_partner/.

24. American Association for the Advancement of Science (AAAS), "What We Know," https://whatweknow.aaas.org/.

25. Isaac Saul, "Not Rigged! How We Know Recent Elections Are Not Fraudulent," *Skeptic Magazine*, November 1, 2022, https://www.skeptic.com/reading_room/not-rigged-how-we-know-recent-elections-are-not-fraudulent/.

26. Lawrence M. Eppard, "Do Unauthorized Immigrants Commit a Lot of Crime?", *Connors Newsletter*, March 6, 2022, https://connorsforum.substack.com/p/do-unautho-rized-immigrants-commit.

27. Michael Anton, "The Flight 93 Election," *Claremont Review of Books*, September 5, 2016, https://claremontreviewofbooks.com/digital/the-flight-93-election/.

28. Peter Wehner, "Christian Doomsayers Have Lost It," *The New York Times*, December 6, 2019, https://www.nytimes.com/2019/12/06/opinion/sunday/trump-chris-tian-conservatives.html.

29. Applebaum, *Twilight of Democracy*, 166.

30. At CPAC in March 2023, for instance, former President Donald Trump stated: "The greatest in our history, most important battle in our lives is taking place right now as we speak. For seven years, you and I have been engaged in an epic struggle to rescue our country from the people who hate it and want to absolutely destroy it. The sinister forces trying to kill America have done everything they can to stop me, to silence you, and to turn this nation into a socialist dumping ground for criminals, junkies, Marxists, thugs, radicals, and dangerous refugees that no other country wants. No other country wants them. If those opposing us succeed, our once beautiful USA will be a failed country that no one will even recognize. A lawless, open borders, crime-ridden, filthy, communist nightmare." He went on to say that: "We have no choice. If we don't do this, our country will be lost forever....This is the final battle. They know it, I know it, you know it, everybody knows it. This is it. Either they win or we win. And if they win, we no longer have a country." See "Trump Speaks at CPAC 2023 Transcript," March 6, 2023, https://www.rev.com/blog/transcripts/trump-speaks-at-cpac-2023-transcript.

31. Jamie Gangel, Jeremy Herb, and Elizabeth Stuart, "CNN Exclusive: Mark Mead-ows' 2,319 Text Messages Reveal Trump's Inner Circle Communications Before and After January 6," CNN, April 25, 2022, https://www.cnn.com/2022/04/25/politics/mark-meadows-texts-2319/index.html.

32. *Talking Points Memo*, "The Meadows Texts," December 12-13, 2022, https://talking-

pointsmemo.com/meadows-texts.

33. Tom Nichols notes, "When a layperson's riposte to an expert consists of 'I read it in the paper' or 'I saw it on the news,' it may not mean very much. Indeed, the information may not have come from the 'news' or 'the paper' at all, but from something that only looks like a news source. More likely, such an answer means 'I saw something from a source I happen to like and it told me something I wanted to hear.' At that point, the discussion has nowhere to go; the original issue is submerged or lost in the effort to untangle which piece of misinformation is driving the conversation in the first place." See Nichols, *The Death of Expertise: The Campaign Against Established Knowledge and Why It Matters* (New York: Oxford University Press, 2017), 138.

34. *Talking Points Memo*, "The Meadows Texts."

35. Jonathan V. Last, "Elaina Plott Calabro: MTG Is More Cunning than You Think," *The Bulwark Podcast*, December 13, 2022, https://www.thebulwark.com/podcast-episode/elaina-plott-calabro-mtg-is-more-cunning-than-you-think/.

36. Eugene Scott, "White House Condemns Greene Over Claim She Would Have 'Won' Jan. 6 Insurrection," *The Washington Post*, December 12, 2022, https://www.washingtonpost.com/politics/2022/12/12/greene-jan6-white-house-armed-insurrection/.

37. Yoni Appelbaum, "How America Ends," *The Atlantic*, December 2019, https://www.theatlantic.com/magazine/archive/2019/12/how-america-ends/600757/.

38. Appelbaum, "How America Ends."

39. David Michaels, *Doubt Is Their Product: How Industry's Assault on Science Threatens Your Health* (New York: Oxford University Press, 2008), x.

40. Michaels, *Doubt Is Their Product*, xiii.

41. Erik M. Conway and Naomi Oreskes, *Merchants of Doubt: How a Handful of Scientists Obscured the Truth on Issues from Tobacco Smoke to Climate Change* (New York: Bloomsbury, 2010), 241. As an example: "[Researchers] examined newspaper and magazine coverage of research on passive smoking and found that 62 percent of all articles published between 1992 and 1994 concluded that the research was 'controversial.' Yet…the scientific community had by that point reached consensus, and the tobacco industry had known the degree of danger even before that" (p. 242).

42. Rob Moodie, "The Seven Tactics Unhealthy Industries Use To Undermine Public Health Policies," *The Conversation*, August 17, 2017, https://theconversation.com/the-seven-tactics-unhealthy-industries-use-to-undermine-public-health-policies-81137.

43. Philip Bump, "The Unique, Damaging Role Fox News Plays in American Media," *The Washington Post*, April 4, 2022, https://www.washingtonpost.com/politics/2022/04/04/unique-damaging-role-fox-news-plays-american-media/.

44. Rauch, "The Constitution of Knowledge."

45. American Association for the Advancement of Science (AAAS), "What We Know."

46. Lydia Saad, "Global Warming Attitudes Frozen Since 2016," *Gallup*, April 5, 2021, https://news.gallup.com/poll/343025/global-warming-attitudes-frozen-2016.aspx.

47. Chris Mooney, "Liberals Deny Science, Too," *The Washington Post*, October 28,

2014, https://www.washingtonpost.com/news/wonk/wp/2014/10/28/liberals-deny-science-too/.

48. From May 19, 2023: https://twitter.com/glaad/status/1659552178720178179.

49. Mooney, "Liberals Deny Science, Too."

50. This concept comes from my colleague Jacob Mackey at Occidental College.

51. D. Abbot et. al. "In Defense of Merit in Science," *Journal of Controversial Ideas* 3, no. 1 (2023): 14.

52. Michael Jindra and Arthur Sakamoto, "When Ideology Drives Social Science: Statistical Malfeasance and Cherry-Picking Are Rife," *The Chronicle of Higher Education*, March 6, 2023, https://www.chronicle.com/article/when-ideology-drives-social-science.

53. D. Abbot et. al. "In Defense of Merit in Science," 12.

54. Rauch, *The Constitution of Knowledge*, 224.

55. Greg Lukianoff and Jonathan Haidt, *The Coddling of the American Mind: How Good Intentions and Bad Ideas Are Setting Up a Generation for Failure* (London: Penguin Books, 2018), 111.

56. Rauch, *The Constitution of Knowledge*, 224.

57. Jonathan Rauch, "The Constitution of Knowledge."

58. Rauch, *The Constitution of Knowledge*, 227.

59. Lukianoff and Haidt, *The Coddling of the American Mind*, 112.

60. Lukianoff and Haidt, *The Coddling of the American Mind*, 113.

61. Ramesh Ponnuru, "How To Restore Intellectual Diversity on College Campuses," *The Washington Post*, February 27, 2023, https://www.washingtonpost.com/opinions/2023/02/27/nurturing-conservative-ideas-on-campus/.

62. Jonathan Haidt, "Why Universities Must Choose One Telos: Truth or Social Justice," Heterodox Academy, October 21, 2016, https://heterodoxacademy.org/blog/one-telos-truth-or-social-justice-2/.

63. "Many professors now say that they are 'teaching on tenterhooks' or 'walking on eggshells,' which means that fewer of them are willing to try anything provocative in the classroom—or cover important but difficult course material." (Lukianoff and Haidt, *The Coddling of the American Mind*, 205).

64. To voice a good faith and reasonable critique of somebody's argument about race or gender identity, for instance, may get you labeled as somebody who is committing "violence" against marginalized groups, who "denies their right to exist."

65. Thomas Chatterton Williams, "The French Are In a Panic Over *Le Wokisme*," *The Atlantic*, February 4, 2023, https://www.theatlantic.com/magazine/archive/2023/03/france-tocqueville-democracy-race-le-wokisme/672775/.

66. He posted this on Twitter on July 12, 2020: https://web.archive.org/web/20230310124335/https://twitter.com/NAChristakis/

status/1282143257309450240?s=20.

67. David French, "Two Different Versions of 'Cancel Culture,'" *The New York Times*, March 2, 2023, https://www.nytimes.com/2023/03/02/opinion/lab-leak-dilbert-cancel-culture.html..

68. Lukianoff and Haidt, *The Coddling of the American Mind*, 138.

69. French, "Two Different Versions of 'Cancel Culture.'"

70. Lee McIntyre, *Respecting Truth: Willful Ignorance in the Internet Age* (New York: Routledge), 135.

71. DEI stands for diversity, equity, and inclusion.

72. Tuvel had published a journal article defending transracialism. Her article was claimed to have "enact[ed] violence" by critics, hundreds of academics called for her article to be retracted, and in a resulting social media pile-on some of her critics advocated that she be fired. (Rauch, *The Constitution of Knowledge*, 211-12).

73. For the article in question, see: Laura Kipnis, "Sexual Paranoia Strikes Academe," *The Chronicle of Higher Education*, February 27, 2015, https://www.chronicle.com/article/sexual-paranoia-strikes-academe/.

74. Elliot Ackerman et. al., "A Letter on Justice and Open Debate," *Harper's Magazine*, July 7, 2020, https://harpers.org/a-letter-on-justice-and-open-debate/.

Chapter 4

1. Originally published by *National Affairs* and adapted here with permission: Jonathan Rauch, "The Constitution of Knowledge," *National Affairs*, Fall 2018, https://www.nationalaffairs.com/publications/detail/the-constitution-of-knowledge. Note: This book is intended for a general audience, and thus throughout we have tried to minimize footnotes in some chapters for purposes of readability—for the full set of footnotes/citations/hyperlinks for each chapter, see the original source.

Chapter 5

1. Originally published by *The Conversation* and adapted here with permission: John Wright, "Why Should We Trust Science? Because It Doesn't Trust Itself," *The Conversation*, September 18, 2022, https://theconversation.com/why-should-we-trust-science-because-it-doesnt-trust-itself-188988. Note: This book is intended for a general audience and thus throughout we have tried to minimize footnotes in some chapters for purposes of readability—for the full set of footnotes/citations/hyperlinks for each chapter, see the original source.

2. Szu Shen Wong, "Syphilis and the Use of Mercury," *The Pharmaceutical Journal*, September 8, 2016, https://pharmaceutical-journal.com/article/opinion/syphilis-and-the-use-of-mercury.

3. The Editors of Encyclopedia Britannica, "Phrenology," *Encyclopedia Britannica*, https://www.britannica.com/topic/phrenology.

4. LIGO, "Gravitational Waves Detected 100 Years After Einstein's Prediction," February 11, 2016, https://www.ligo.caltech.edu/news/ligo20160211.

5. Naomi Oreskes, *Why Trust Science?* (Princeton, NJ: Princeton University Press, 2019).

6. Svante Arrhenius, "On the Influence of Carbonic Acid in the Air Upon the Temperature of the Ground," *Philosophical Magazine and Journal of Science* 41, (April 1896): 237-276.

7. Mark Lynas, Benjamin Z. Houlton, and Simon Perry, "Greater Than 99% Consensus on Human Caused Climate Change in the Peer-reviewed Scientific Literature," *Environmental Research Letters* 16, no. 11 (October 2021), https://iopscience.iop.org/article/10.1088/1748-9326/ac2966.

Chapter 6

1. Originally published by *The Conversation* and adapted here with permission: Tim Dean, "How We Edit Science [Parts 1 through 5]," *The Conversation*, March 17, 2017, https://theconversation.com/how-we-edit-science-part-1-the-scientific-method-74521. Note: This book is intended for a general audience and thus throughout we have tried to minimize footnotes in some chapters for purposes of readability—for the full set of footnotes/citations/hyperlinks for each chapter, see the original source.

2. Thomas Nagel, *The View From Nowhere* (New York: Oxford University Press, 1989).

3. The Editors of *Encyclopedia Britannica*, "Hypothetico-Deductive Method," https://www.britannica.com/science/hypothetico-deductive-method.

4. Will J. Grant, "Trolling Our Confirmation Bias: One Bite and We're Easily Sucked In," *The Conversation*, June 2, 2015, https://theconversation.com/trolling-our-confirmation-bias-one-bite-and-were-easily-sucked-in-42621.

5. You can visit their site at https://retractionwatch.com/.

6. Eric Michael Johnson, "The WEIRD Evolution of Human Psychology," *Scientific American*, December 7, 2011, https://blogs.scientificamerican.com/primate-diaries/the-weird-evolution-of-human-psychology/.

7. Shashwath A. Meda et. al., "Longitudinal Influence of Alcohol and Marijuana Use on Academic Performance in College Students," *PLoS One*, (March 2017), https://journals.plos.org/plosone/article?id=10.1371/journal.pone.0172213.

Chapter 7

1. Originally published by the Australian Academy of Science and adapted here with permission. See their website for the original source: https://www.science.org.au/curious/policy-features/how-does-science-work#:~:text=Although%20different%20scientific%20disciplines%20may,then%20analysis%20of%20experimental%20data. Note: This book is intended for a general audience and thus throughout we have tried to minimize footnotes in some chapters for purposes of readability—for the full set of footnotes/citations/hyperlinks for each chapter, see the original source.

2. To check out the IceCube Neutrino Observatory, visit their website: https://icecube.wisc.edu/.

Chapter 8

1. Published on *Skeptic Magazine's* website and adapted here with permission. See their website for more: https://www.skeptic.com/about_us/manifesto/#0. Note: This book is intended for a general audience, and thus for purposes of readability, we have tried to minimize footnotes in some chapters—for the full set of footnotes/citations/hyperlinks for each chapter, see the original source.

2. Vincent Dethier, *To Know a Fly* (San Francisco, CA: Holden-Day), 2.

3. See original source for citation: https://www.skeptic.com/about_us/manifesto/#0.

4. See original source for citation.

5. See original source for citation.

6. See original source for citation.

7. See original source for citation.

8. See original source for citation.

9. See original source for citation.

10. See original source for citation.

11. See original source for citation.

12. See original source for citation.

13. See original source for citation.

14. See original source for citation.

15. See original source for citation.

16. See original source for citation.

17. See original source for citation.

18. See original source for citation.

19. See original source for citation.

20. See original source for citation.

21. See original source for citation.

Chapter 9

1. This piece was originally published by *The Conversation* and is adapted here with permission: Lee McIntyre, "5 Ways Trump and His Supporters Are Using the Same Strategies as Science Deniers," *The Conversation*, November 27, 2019, https://theconversation.com/5-ways-trump-and-his-supporters-are-using-the-same-strategies-as-science-deniers-127076. Note: This book is intended for a general audience and thus throughout

we have tried to minimize footnotes in some chapters for purposes of readability—for the full set of footnotes/citations/hyperlinks for each chapter, see the original source.

2. Mark Hoofnagle and Chris Hoofnagle, "Hello Scienceblogs," ScienceBlogs, April 30, 2007, https://scienceblogs.com/denialism/about.

3. Pascal Diethelm and Martin McKee, "What Is It, and How Should Scientists Respond?", *European Journal of Public Health* 19, no. 1 (January 2009): 2-4.

4. John Cook, "The 5 Characteristics of Science Denialism," Skeptical Science, March 17, 2020, https://skepticalscience.com/5-characteristics-of-scientific-denialism.html.

5. Stephan Lewandowsky et. al., *The Debunking Handbook 2020* (Fairfax, VA: George Mason Center for Climate Change Communication, 2020).

6. Chris Mooney, "Ted Cruz Says Satellite Data Show the Globe Isn't Warming. This Satellite Scientist Feels Otherwise," *The Washington Post*, March 24, 2015, https://www.washingtonpost.com/news/energy-environment/wp/2015/03/24/ted-cruz-says-satellite-data-show-the-globe-isnt-warming-this-satellite-scientist-feels-otherwise/.

Chapter 10

1. This chapter is adapted from the article "Reflections on Journalism," which originally appeared in the *Connors Newsletter* on February 21, 2022. Adapted and printed here with permission. Newsletter website: ConnorsForum.substack.com. Note: This book is intended for a general audience and thus throughout we have tried to minimize footnotes in some chapters for purposes of readability—for the full set of footnotes/citations/hyperlinks for each chapter, see the original source.

2. Lee Enterprises is a national provider of local news and information in the United States serving 77 markets across 26 states.

3. Please visit our website, ConnorsForum.org, to see our trustworthy news guide, the numerous news and information outlets that we have graded as trustworthy, and our comprehensive rubric (involving analyses from organizations such as NewsGuard, Ad Fontes Media, The Factual, and AllSides) we use to assess outlets.

Chapter 11

1. Originally published by The Lorem Ipsum and adapted here with permission: Alison Dagnes and Daniel Herndon, "Breaking Bad News," The Lorem Ipsum, February 21, 2023, https://www.danielkherndon.com/breaking-bad-news/. Note: This book is intended for a general audience and thus throughout we have tried to minimize footnotes in some chapters for purposes of readability—for the full set of footnotes/citations/hyperlinks for each chapter, see the original source.

2. *New York Times*, "Fact Checking Day 1 of the Republican National Convention," August 24, 2020, https://www.nytimes.com/live/2020/08/24/us/rnc-fact-check.

3. Cristian G. Rodriguez, Jake P. Moskowitz, Rammy M. Salem, and Peter H. Ditto, "Partisan Selective Exposure: The Role of Party, Ideology and Ideological Extremity

Over Time," *Translational Issues in Psychological Research* 3, no. 3 (2017): 254-271.

4. David Broockman and Joshua Kalla, "The Impacts of Selective Partisan Media Exposure: A Field Experiment with Fox News Viewers," OSF Preprints, September 1, 2022, https://osf.io/jrw26/.

5. Rachel E. Greenspan, "The Bizarre Origins of the Lizard-People Conspiracy Theory Embraced by the Nashville Bomber, and How It's Related to Qanon," *Insider*, January 7, 2021, https://www.insider.com/lizard-people-conspiracy-theory-origin-nashville-bomber-qanon-2021-1.

Chapter 12

1. This material was created by NewsGuard and is housed on their website: https://www.newsguardtech.com/ratings/rating-process-criteria/. Adapted here with permission. Note: This book is intended for a general audience and thus throughout we have tried to minimize footnotes in some chapters for purposes of readability—for the full set of footnotes/citations/hyperlinks for each chapter, see the original source.

Chapter 13

1. Originally published by Ad Fontes Media and adapted here with permission: Vanessa Otero, "Ad Fontes Media's Multi-Analyst Content Analysis White Paper," Ad Fontes Media, September 2021, https://adfontesmedia.com/white-paper-2021/. Note: This book is intended for a general audience and thus throughout we have tried to minimize footnotes in some chapters for purposes of readability—for the full set of footnotes/citations/hyperlinks for each chapter, see the original source.

2. Tom Rosenstiel, Marion Just, Todd L. Belt, Atiba Pertilla, Walter Dean, and Dante Chinni, *We Interrupt This Newscast: How to Improve Local News and Win Ratings, Too* (New York: Cambridge University Press, 2007).

3. Ad Fontes Media, "News Literacy Training, Lesson 5, Thursday, 5/20/21," https://www.youtube.com/watch?v=jZXEBXm2Dg8.

4. Ad Fontes Media, "News Literacy Training, Lesson 3, Thursday, 5/6/21," https://www.youtube.com/watch?v=RHkT1tlbI7s.

Chapter 14

1. This open letter was originally published by *Harper's Magazine* on July 7, 2020: https://harpers.org/a-letter-on-justice-and-open-debate/. Reprinted here with permission. Visit their website to see the full list of signatories. Note: This book is intended for a general audience and thus throughout we have tried to minimize footnotes in some chapters for purposes of readability—for the full set of footnotes/citations/hyperlinks for each chapter, see the original source.

Chapter 15

1. Originally published by *The Bulwark* and adapted here with permission: William Saletan, "Lies Are the Building Blocks of Trumpian Authoritarianism," *The Bulwark*, February 7, 2022, https://www.thebulwark.com/lies-are-the-building-blocks-of-trumpian-authoritarianism/. Note: This book is intended for a general audience and thus throughout we have tried to minimize footnotes in some chapters for purposes of readability—for the full set of footnotes/citations/hyperlinks for each chapter, see the original source.

2. Christina Zhao, "Trump Insists 'I'm Not the One Trying to Undermine American Democracy...I'm Trying to Save It,'" *Newsweek*, June 5, 2021, https://www.newsweek.com/trump-insists-im-not-one-trying-undermine-american-democracy-im-trying-save-it-1597930.

3. C-SPAN, "Former President Trump Speaks at Arizona Republican Party Political Rally," January 15, 2022, https://www.c-span.org/video/?517043-1/president-trump-speaks-arizona-gop-political-rally.

4. C-SPAN, "Former President Trump Texas Rally," January 29, 2022, https://www.c-span.org/video/?517404-1/president-trump-texas-rally.

5. DonaldJTrump.com, "News," https://www.donaldjtrump.com/news.

6. *The New York Times*, "Read the Republican Censure of Cheney and Kinzinger," February 4, 2022, https://www.nytimes.com/interactive/2022/02/04/us/rnc-resolution-censure-cheney-kinziger.html.

7. Brandon Mulder, "The Voting Rights Bill 'Would Register Millions of Illegal Aliens to Vote. It is Intended to Do That,'" *PolitiFact*, May 14, 2021, https://www.politifact.com/factchecks/2021/may/14/ted-cruz/ted-cruz-repeats-false-claim-voting-bill-would-reg/.

8. Fox News, "Newt Gingrich: Democrats Are 'Running Over People's Civil Liberties,'" January 23, 2022, https://www.foxnews.com/video/6293237706001.

9. Fox News, "McCarthy: Election Bill About 'Gaming the System,'" January 13, 2022, https://www.foxnews.com/video/6291608232001. .

10. Jim Jordan, "Jim Jordan UNLEASHES on the Democrats," YouTube, December 14, 2021, https://www.youtube.com/watch?v=HAj0dhhuzKs..

11. Grinnell College, "National Poll October 2021," October 13-17, 2021, https://www.grinnell.edu/sites/default/files/docs/2021-10/GCNP%20Oct21%20Toplines%20Methodology%20Crosstabs%20v2.pdf..

12. NPR/PBS Newshour/Marist Poll, October 18-22, 2021, https://maristpoll.marist.edu/wp-content/uploads/2021/10/NPR_PBS-NewsHour_Marist-Poll_USA-NOS-and-Tables_B_202110251104.pdf.

13. Quinnipiac University Poll, January 12, 2022, https://poll.qu.edu/images/polling/us/us01122022_ubjw88.pdf.

14. Quinnipiac University, "78% Of Republicans Want To See Trump Run For President In 2024, Quinnipiac University National Poll Finds; Americans Now Split On

Border Wall As Opposition Softens," October 19, 2021, https://poll.qu.edu/poll-release?releaseid=3825.

15. The Economist/YouGov Poll, January 22-25, 2022, https://docs.cdn.yougov.com/idsbkknia1/econTabReport.pdf.

16. Tatishe Nteta, "Toplines and Crosstabs December 2021 National Poll: Presidential Election & Jan 6th Insurrection at the US Capitol," December 28, 2021, https://polsci.umass.edu/toplines-and-crosstabs-december-2021-national-poll-presidential-election-jan-6th-insurrection-us.

17. Morning Consult/Politico Poll, January 8-9, 2022, https://assets.morningconsult.com/wp-uploads/2022/01/11193212/2201029_crosstabs_POLITICO_RVs_v1_SH.pdf.

18. Anthony Salvanto, Kabir Khanna, Fred Backus, and Jennifer Depinto, "CBS News Poll: A Year After Jan. 6, Violence Still Seen Threatening U.S. Democracy, and Some Say Force Can Be Justified," CBS News, January 2, 2022, https://www.cbsnews.com/news/january-6-opinion-poll-2022/.

19. ABC News/Ipsos Poll, December 27-29, 2021, https://www.ipsos.com/sites/default/files/ct/news/documents/2021-12/Topline%20ABC_Ipsos%20Poll%20January%202%202022%20for%201.2.pdf.

20. See original article for surveys.

21. Quinnipiac University, "Political Instability Not U.S. Adversaries, Seen As Bigger Threat, Quinnipiac University National Poll Finds; Nearly 6 In 10 Think Nation's Democracy Is In Danger Of Collapse," January 12, 2022, https://poll.qu.edu/poll-release?releaseid=3831.

22. Harvard CAPS/Harris Poll, January 19-20, 2022, https://harvardharrispoll.com/wp-content/uploads/2022/01/January-2022_HHP_Crosstab.pdf.

23. NPR/PBS Newshour/Marist Poll, October 18-22, 2021, https://maristpoll.marist.edu/wp-content/uploads/2021/10/NPR_PBS-NewsHour_Marist-Poll_USA-NOS-and-Tables_B_202110251104.pdf.

24. Fox News Poll, January 16-19, 2022, https://static.foxnews.com/foxnews.com/content/uploads/2022/01/January-16-19-2022_Topline-Tables_January-23-Release.pdf.

Chapter 16

1. Originally published by The Lorem Ipsum and adapted here with permission: Alison Dagnes and Daniel Herndon, "Fox and The Backlash of Right-Wing Media," The Lorem Ipsum, April 18, 2023, https://www.danielkherndon.com/overcompensation-the-backlash-of-right-wing-media/. Note: This book is intended for a general audience and thus throughout we have tried to minimize footnotes in some chapters for purposes of readability—for the full set of footnotes/citations/hyperlinks for each chapter, see the original source.

2. Sarah Ellison, Paul Farhi, and Jeremy Barr, "Fox News Feared Losing Viewers by

Airing Truth About Election, Documents Show," *Washington Post*, February 17, 2023, https://www.washingtonpost.com/media/2023/02/17/fox-news-dominion-ratings-fear/.

3. Adan Serwer, "Why Fox News Lied to Its Viewers," *The Atlantic*, February 19, 2023, https://www.theatlantic.com/ideas/archive/2023/02/fox-news-dominion-lawsuit-trump/673132/.

4. Andy Meek, "Fox News Channel Has Now Spent 20 Years In The #1 Spot On The Cable News Rankings," *Forbes*, February 1, 2022, https://www.forbes.com/sites/andymeek/2022/02/01/fox-news-channel-has-now-spent-20-years-in-the-1-spot-on-the-cable-news-rankings/?sh=2e186c8072f2..

5. Semrush Blog, "Top 100: The Most Visited Websites in the US [2023 Top Websites Edition]," https://www.semrush.com/blog/most-visited-websites/.

6. Nicholas Reimann, "Murdoch Admits Fox News Hosts Pushed False Election Fraud Claims," *Forbes*, March 6, 2023, https://www.forbes.com/sites/nicholasreimann/2023/02/27/murdoch-admits-fox-news-hosts-pushed-false-election-fraud-claims/?sh=36fed97b494b..

7. Valerie Wirtschafter, "Audible Reckoning: How Top Political Podcasters Spread Unsubstantiated and False Claims," Brookings Institution, February 2023, https://www.brookings.edu/essay/audible-reckoning-how-top-political-podcasters-spread-unsubstantiated-and-false-claims/.

8. Carolyn E. Schmitt, "Political Discourse and the 2020 U.S. Election," Harvard Law Today, November 24, 2020, https://hls.harvard.edu/today/political-discourse-and-the-2020-u-s-election/.

9. Clare Malone, "The Fallout of Fox News' Public Shaming," *The New Yorker*, March 15, 2023, https://www.newyorker.com/news/annals-of-communications/the-fallout-of-fox-news-public-shaming.

Chapter 17

1. Originally published by *The Bulwark* and adapted here with permission: Amanda Carpenter, "Exposed: Fox's Pander-for-Profit Business Model," *The Bulwark*, February 28, 2023, https://www.thebulwark.com/exposed-foxs-pander-for-profit-business-model/. Note: This book is intended for a general audience and thus throughout we have tried to minimize footnotes in some chapters for purposes of readability—for the full set of footnotes/citations/hyperlinks for each chapter, see the original source.

2. See https://int.nyt.com/data/documenttools/dominion-fox-news/54e33f20f7fb6e8d/full.pdf, and here: https://int.nyt.com/data/documenttools/redacted-documents-in-dominion-fox-news-case/dca5e3880422426f/full.pdf.

3. Cybersecurity & Infrastructure Security Agency, "Joint Statement from Elections Infrastructure Government Coordinating Council & the Election Infrastructure Sector Coordinating Executive Committees," November 12, 2020, https://www.cisa.gov/news-events/news/joint-statement-elections-infrastructure-government-coordinating-council-election.

4. Ken Meyer, "Fox Reporter Kristin Fisher Fact Checks Giuliani's 'Bold and Baseless' Presser: 'So Much Of What He Said Was Simply Not True,'" *Mediate*, November 19, 2020, https://www.mediaite.com/tv/foxs-kristen-fisher-torches-giulianis-bold-and-baseless-team-trump-presser-never-credibly-explained-a-single-path-to-victory/.

5. Anne Applebaum, "Tucker Carlson's Sinister New Documentary," *The Atlantic*, November 2, 2021, https://www.theatlantic.com/ideas/archive/2021/11/patriot-purge-tucker-carlson-documentary/620589/.

Chapter 18

1. Originally published by *The Bulwark* and adapted here with permission: Mona Charen, "Please Lie to Me, Tucker," *The Bulwark*, March 2, 2023, https://www.thebulwark.com/please-lie-to-me-tucker/. Note: This book is intended for a general audience and thus throughout we have tried to minimize footnotes in some chapters for purposes of readability—for the full set of footnotes/citations/hyperlinks for each chapter, see the original source.

2. Hadas Gold, "Survey: 7 Percent of Reporters Identify as Republican," *Politico*, May 6, 2014, https://www.politico.com/blogs/media/2014/05/survey-7-percent-of-reporters-identify-as-republican-188053.

3. Ed Pilkington and Nina Lakhani, "'You're Not Forgotten': How the Right Racialized the Ohio Train Disaster," *The Guardian*, February 26, 2023, https://www.theguardian.com/us-news/2023/feb/26/trump-fox-news-east-palestine-ohio-right-wing-race-baiting.

4. Justin Baragona, "Charlie Kirk Claims Ohio Derailment Is Proof of 'War on White People,'" *The Daily Beast*, February 14, 2023, https://www.thedailybeast.com/charlie-kirk-claims-ohio-derailment-is-proof-of-war-on-white-people.

5. Jeff Jacoby, "Katrina's Colorblind Relief," *The Boston Globe*, September 14, 2005, https://www.laits.utexas.edu/africa/ads/1134.html.

6. Michael Kelly, "Playing With Fire," *The New Yorker*, July 7, 1996, https://www.newyorker.com/magazine/1996/07/15/playing-with-fire.

7. David Bauder, "Center of Debate: An 'SNL' Skit," CBS News, February 28, 2008, https://www.cbsnews.com/news/center-of-debate-an-snl-skit/.

8. David Folkenflik, "By Attacking The Media, Gingrich Built A Following," NPR, November 17, 2011, https://www.npr.org/2011/11/17/142421000/by-attacking-the-media-gingrich-built-a-following.

9. Folkenflik, "By Attacking The Media, Gingrich Built A Following."

10. See https://int.nyt.com/data/documenttools/redacted-documents-in-dominion-fox-news-case/dca5e3880422426f/full.pdf. And here: https://int.nyt.com/data/documenttools/dominion-fox-news/54e33f20f7fb6e8d/full.pdf.

Chapter 19

1. Originally published by *Skeptic Magazine* and adapted here with permission: Isaac Saul, "Not Rigged! How We Know Recent Elections Are Not Fraudulent," *Skeptic Magazine*, November 1, 2022, https://www.skeptic.com/reading_room/not-rigged-how-we-know-recent-elections-not-fraudulent/. Note: This book is intended for a general audience and thus throughout we have tried to minimize footnotes in some chapters for purposes of readability—for the full set of footnotes/citations/hyperlinks for each chapter, see the original source.

2. Colby Itkowitz, "Hillary Clinton: Trump Is an 'Illegitimate President,'" *The Washington Post*, September 26, 2019, https://wapo.st/3Ct2jUs.

3. Glenn Greenwald, "Biden Appointee Neera Tanden Spread the Conspiracy That Russian Hackers Changed Hillary's 2016 Votes to Trump," *Glenn Greenwald*, November 30, 2020, https://bit.ly/3VwMF3p.

4. John H. Fund, *Stealing Elections: How Voter Fraud Threatens Our Democracy* (Encounter Books, 2008).

5. Isaac Saul, "The Real Fraud Is 'Election Fraud,'" *Tangle*, November 13, 2020, https://bit.ly/3VmWHDO.

6. John C. Danforth et al., *Lost, Not Stolen: The Conservative Case That Trump Lost and Biden Won the 2020 Presidential Election*, 2022.

7. Special Counsel's Office, "Report on the Investigation into Russian Interference in the 2016 Presidential Election," n.d., accessed May 5, 2023.

8. Ellen Nakashima and Shane Harris, "How the Russians Hacked the DNC and Passed Its Emails to WikiLeaks," *The Washington Post*, July 13, 2018, https://www.washingtonpost.com/world/national-security/how-the-russians-hacked-the-dnc-and-passed-its-emails-to-wikileaks/2018/07/13/af19a828-86c3-11e8-8553-a3ce89036c78_story.html.

9. Greenwald, "Biden Appointee Neera Tanden Spread the Conspiracy That Russian Hackers Changed Hillary's 2016 Votes to Trump."

10. Special Counsel's Office, "Report on the Investigation into Russian Interference in the 2016 Presidential Election."

11. Miles Parks, "Florida Governor Says Russian Hackers Breached 2 Counties In 2016," NPR, May 14, 2019, https://n.pr/3Cqstar.

12. Saul, "Not Rigged! How We Know Recent Elections Are Not Fraudulent."

13. Twitter, accessed May 5, 2023, https://bit.ly/3euuNVT.

14. Aaron Gordon, "Why the Post Office's Last-Minute Ballot Crisis Isn't as Dire as It Seems," November 3, 2020, https://bit.ly/3ywKtyK.

15. Twitter, accessed May 5, 2023, https://bit.ly/3Vl3huQ.

16. "Was McConnell's Re-Election a Fraud? (And Graham's and Collins's.)," Daily Kos, accessed May 5, 2023, https://bit.ly/3RT1UQU.

17. "Was McConnell's Re-Election a Fraud? (And Graham's and Collins's.)."

18. Alison Greene, "Why The Numbers Behind Mitch McConnell's Re-Election Don't Add Up," *DCReport.org*, December 19, 2020, https://bit.ly/3T6zzYE.

19. Glenn Kessler and Salvador Rizzo, "President Trump's False Claims of Vote Fraud: A Chronology," *The Washington Post*, November 5, 2020, https://wapo.st/3yxwqJt.

20. BBC News, "US Election 2020: What to Look out for on Election Night," BBC News, October 28, 2020, https://bbc.in/3yxn68o.

21. Cynthia Fernandez and Jonathan Lai, "Talks Collapse on a Deal to Let Pennsylvania Counties Open Mail Ballots before Election Day," *The Philadelphia Inquirer*, October 22, 2020, https://bit.ly/3EzaPUM.

22. Martin Pengelly, "Trump Claims 5,000 Dead People Voted in Georgia—but the Real Number Is Four," *The Guardian*, December 28, 2021, https://bit.ly/3MrNgPK.

23. Ali Swenson, "Officials Debunk Multiple Claims of Dead Georgia Residents Voting," *Associated Press*, accessed May 5, 2023, https://bit.ly/3fOPc8s.

24. Swenson, "Officials Debunk Multiple Claims of Dead Georgia Residents Voting."

25. Fact Check, "Team Trump's Dead Voters in Georgia: 3 Falsehoods, 1 Truth," Fact Check, November 16, 2020, https://bit.ly/3Mmfhbf.

26. FOX 5 Atlanta, "January 6 Hearing: Full Testimony of Brad Raffensperger, Gabriel Sterling on Georgia 2020 Election," Video, YouTube, June 21, 2022, https://bit.ly/3MonnA8.

27. Mark Niesse, "Alleged 'Dead' Georgia Voters Found Alive and Well after 2020 Election," *The Atlanta Journal-Constitution*, December 27, 2021, https://bit.ly/3fSQX4t.

28. "Voter Registration List Maintenance," accessed May 5, 2023, https://bit.ly/3Eztm32.

29. "Elections Portal," accessed May 5, 2023, https://bit.ly/3yzEIQO.

30. *The Georgia Risk-Limiting Audit/Hand Tally: A Carter Center Observation Report*, 2020, The Carter Center.

31. Mark Niesse, "No Fraud: Georgia Audit Confirms Authenticity of Absentee Ballots," *The Atlanta Journal-Constitution*, December 30, 2020, https://bit.ly/3SS960Y.

32. Gabriel Sterling, n.d., accessed May 5, 2023.

33. "Los Angeles Goes All Out to Process Millions of Mail-In Ballots," *Bloomberg*, November 3, 2020, https://bloom.bg/3TcCVcl..

34. "Los Angeles Goes All Out to Process Millions of Mail-In Ballots."

35. Kate Brumback, "Georgia Poll Worker in Hiding after False Claims Online," Associated Press, April 20, 2021, https://bit.ly/3ffZC0U.

36. Twitter, accessed May 5, 2023, https://twitter.com/realDonaldTrump/status/1326926226888544256?lang=en.

37. Alec Dent, "Did Edison Research Find That Dominion Deleted Trump Votes or Switched Votes to Biden?," *The Dispatch*, November 12, 2020, https://bit.ly/3g25bQR.

38. Hayes Brown, "Mike Lee's Texts Dinged Sidney Powell but He Still Backed Trump,"

MSNBC, April 15, 2022, https://on.msnbc.com/3rNOR8J.

39. Isaac Saul, "An Honest Look at 2,000 Mules, the New Stolen Election Story," Tangle, May 13, 2022, https://bit.ly/3TiCGwF.

40. Saul, "An Honest Look at 2,000 Mules, the New Stolen Election Story."

41. V. Saxe, "Junk Evidence: A Call to Scrutinize Historical Cell Site Location Evidence," 2020, *The University of New Hampshire Law Review*, 133.

42. Danforth et al., *Lost, Not Stolen*.

43. Danforth et al., *Lost, Not Stolen*.

44. Danforth et al., *Lost, Not Stolen*.

45. "Read the Third Circuit Court of Appeals Ruling in Pennsylvania Election," *The Washington Post*, accessed May 5, 2023, https://wapo.st/3yyGx0w.

46. Alison Durkee, "Trump-Appointed Judge In Wisconsin Shuts Down Campaign's Legal Argument For Why Election Was Rigged," *Forbes*, December 12, 2020, https://bit.ly/3CN8yUu.

47. Callie Patteson, "Ex-AG Barr: Trump Was 'detached from Reality' over Election Fraud Claims," *New York Post*, June 13, 2022, https://bit.ly/3CKsPJp.

Chapter 20

1. Originally published by *The Bulwark* and adapted here with permission: Jonathan V. Last, "Fox Paid a Parking Ticket; Mike Lindell Is Going To Get Wrecked," *The Bulwark*, April 20, 2023, https://thetriad.thebulwark.com/p/fox-paid-a-parking-ticket-mike-lindell. Note: This book is intended for a general audience and thus throughout we have tried to minimize footnotes in some chapters for purposes of readability—for the full set of footnotes/citations/hyperlinks for each chapter, see the original source.

2. Chris Dehghanpoor, Emma Brown, and Jon Swaine, "Mike Lindell's Firm Told To Pay $5 Million in 'Prove Mike Wrong' Election-fraud Challenge," *The Washington Post*, April 20, 2023, https://www.washingtonpost.com/investigations/2023/04/20/mike-lindell-prove-wrong-contest.

3. Jack Holmes, "Fox News Will Pay Dominion Voting Systems $787 Million to Settle. What Does That Mean for Fox?", *Esquire*, April 18, 2023, https://www.esquire.com/news-politics/a43636240/fox-news-dominion-defamation-settlement.

4. Fox Corporation, the parent company, does about $14 billion in revenue annually. Fox News is a fairly important (and profitable) division.

5. Dominion Voting, "Dominion Files Defamation Suit Against Mike Lindell and MyPillow," February 22, 2021, https://www.dominionvoting.com/latest-news-dominion-files-defamation-suit-against-mike-lindell-and-mypillow.

6. And also by the people who declined to go along with Trump. Those people got wrecked, too.

Chapter 21

1. Originally published by *The Bulwark* and adapted here with permission: Theodore R. Johnson, "The Tangle of Trumpian Conspiracy Theories," *The Bulwark*, May 26, 2022, https://www.thebulwark.com/the-tangle-of-trumpian-conspiracy-theories/. Note: This book is intended for a general audience and thus throughout we have tried to minimize footnotes in some chapters for purposes of readability—for the full set of footnotes/citations/hyperlinks for each chapter, see the original source.

2. Nick Corasaniti, Karen Yourish, and Keith Collins, "How Trump's 2020 Election Lies Have Gripped State Legislatures," *The New York Times*, May 22, 2022, https://www.nytimes.com/interactive/2022/05/22/us/politics/state-legislators-election-denial.html.

3. Kristine Phillips, "'Damaging to Our Democracy': Trump Election Lawsuits Targeted Areas With Large Black, Latino Populations," *USA Today*, December 1, 2020, https://www.usatoday.com/story/news/politics/2020/12/01/trump-voter-fraud-claims-target-counties-more-black-latino-votes/6391908002/.

4. NBC10 Philadelphia, "'Bad Things Happen in Philadelphia,' Trump Says During Debate," YouTube, September 30, 2020, https://www.youtube.com/watch?v=QSQXg-BUcIE4.

5. Jessica Calefati, "Trump Says Philly Democrats Stole an Election in the '90s. Is That True?", *The Philadelphia Inquirer*, November 18, 2020, https://www.inquirer.com/politics/trump-philadelphia-pennsylvania-voter-fraud-20201118.html.

6. Tucker Carlson, "Tucker Carlson: The Truth About Demographic Change and Why Democrats Want It," Fox News, April 12, 2021, https://www.foxnews.com/opinion/tucker-carlson-immigration-demographic-change-democrats-elections.

7. John Wagner, "Rep. Stefanik Claims in Ads That Democrats Seek a 'Permanent Election Insurrection' by Providing Pathways to Citizenship," *The Washington Post*, September 16, 2021, https://www.washingtonpost.com/powerpost/rep-stefanik-claims-in-ads-that-democrats-are-seeking-a-permanent-election-insurrection-by-providing-pathways-to-citizenship/2021/09/16/7372011a-16eb-11ec-a5e5-ceecb895922f_story.html.

8. Founders Online, "Robert Yates's Version, [18 June 1787]," https://founders.archives.gov/documents/Hamilton/01-04-02-0098-0004.

9. Katie Nodjimbadem, "Why Is Pennsylvania Ave D.C.'s Main Thoroughfare and More Questions From Our Readers," *Smithsonian Magazine*, March 2017, https://www.smithsonianmag.com/smithsonian-institution/pennsylvania-ave-dc-main-thoroughfare-180962122/.

10. Kate Ly Johnston, "Doug Mastriano Said for Months He Has His Secretary of State Pick. He Still Hasn't Said Who It Is," WCPT820 Radio, May 17, 2022, https://heartlandsignal.com/2022/05/17/doug-mastriano-said-for-months-he-he-has-his-secretary-of-state-pick-he-still-hasnt-said-who-it-is/.

11. Mike Wereschagin, "Pa. Republicans' Hedged Language May Have Saved Them From Prosecution Over Electoral Vote Scheme," LancasterOnline, January 17, 2022,

https://lancasteronline.com/news/politics/pa-republicans-hedged-language-may-have-saved-them-from-prosecution-over-electoral-vote-scheme/article_849d4f7e-7589-11ec-8881-6383a823557d.html.

Chapter 22

1. Originally published by *The Bulwark* and adapted here with permission: Jim Swift, "The 'Ground Zero Mosque' Fight That Presaged Today's GOP," *The Bulwark*, September 9, 2021, https://www.thebulwark.com/the-ground-zero-mosque-fight-that-presaged-todays-gop/. Note: This book is intended for a general audience and thus throughout we have tried to minimize footnotes in some chapters for purposes of readability—for the full set of footnotes/citations/hyperlinks for each chapter, see the original source.

2. Ralph Blumenthal and Sharaf Mowjood, "Muslim Prayers and Renewal Near Ground Zero," *The New York Times*, December 8, 2009, https://web.archive.org/web/20121125062214/http://www.nytimes.com/2009/12/09/nyregion/09mosque.html?_r=1&sq=mosque%20ground%20zero&st=nyt&scp=1&pagewanted=all.

3. Brendan O'Connor, "The Sad, True Story of the Ground Zero Mosque," The Awl, October 1, 2015, https://www.theawl.com/2015/10/the-sad-true-story-of-the-ground-zero-mosque/.

4. Center for American Progress, "Fear, Inc.", August 26, 2011, https://www.americanprogress.org/article/fear-inc/.

5. Abby Phillip, "King Flips on Mosques," *Politico*, August 15, 2010, https://www.politico.com/story/2010/08/king-flips-on-mosques-041093.

6. https://www.thebulwark.com/the-ground-zero-mosque-fight-that-presaged-todays-gop/.

7. Camille Caldera, "Fact Check: In 2010, Donald Trump Offered $6M To Try To Stop a Mosque Near Ground Zero," *USA Today*, September 15, 2020, https://www.usatoday.com/story/news/factcheck/2020/09/15/fact-check-donald-trump-offered-6-m-stop-mosque-near-ground-zero/5791809002/.

8. Mark Abadi, "Trump Had an Unusual Reaction to 9/11 Just Hours After the Attacks," Insider, September 11, 2020, https://www.businessinsider.com/trump-september-11-interview-tallest-building-manhattan-2017-9.

9. Glenn Kessler, "Trump's Outrageous Claim That 'Thousands' of New Jersey Muslims Celebrated the 9/11 Attacks," *The Washington Post*, November 22, 2015, https://www.washingtonpost.com/news/fact-checker/wp/2015/11/22/donald-trumps-outrageous-claim-that-thousands-of-new-jersey-muslims-celebrated-the-911-attacks/.

10. Jenna Johnson and Abigail Hauslohner, "'I Think Islam Hates Us': A Timeline of Trump's Comments About Islam and Muslims," *The Washington Post*, May 20, 2017, https://www.washingtonpost.com/news/post-politics/wp/2017/05/20/i-think-islam-hates-us-a-timeline-of-trumps-comments-about-islam-and-muslims/.

11. Bianca Quilantan and David Cohen, "Trump Tells Dem Congresswomen: Go

Back Where You Came From," *Politico*, July 14, 2019, https://www.politico.com/story/2019/07/14/trump-congress-go-back-where-they-came-from-1415692.

12. George W. Bush, "'Islam Is Peace' Says President," The White House, September 17, 2001, https://georgewbush-whitehouse.archives.gov/news/releases/2001/09/20010917-11.html.

13. Ryan Teague Beckwith, Mark Niquette, and Gregory Korte, "GOP Candidates Want Refugees Out of Afghanistan But Not in U.S.," Bloomberg, September 4, 2021, https://www.bloomberg.com/news/articles/2021-09-04/gop-candidates-want-refugees-out-of-afghanistan-but-not-in-u-s?leadSource=uverify%20wall.

Chapter 23

1. Originally published by the *Connors Newsletter* and adapted here with permission: Lawrence M. Eppard, "Do Unauthorized Immigrants Commit a Lot of Crime?", March 6, 2022, https://connorsforum.substack.com/p/do-unauthorized-immigrants-commit.

2. John B. Bellinger III, "How Russia's Invasion of Ukraine Violates International Law," Council on Foreign Relations, February 28, 2022, https://www.cfr.org/article/how-russias-invasion-of-ukraine-violates-international-law.

3. Dan Sabbagh, "Researchers Gather Evidence of Possible Russian War Crimes in Ukraine," *The Guardian*, March 2, 2022, https://www.theguardian.com/world/2022/mar/02/researchers-gather-evidence-of-possible-russian-war-crimes-in-ukraine.

4. Fox News, "Tucker: How Will This Conflict Affect You?", February 22, 2022, https://video.foxnews.com/v/6298540966001#sp=show-clips.

5. Fox News, "Tulsi Gabbard: 'Sanctions Don't Work,' They Only Punish the American People," February 22, 2022, https://video.foxnews.com/v/6298542058001#sp=show-clips.

6. Fox News, "Tucker: Why Would Biden Do This to His Own Country?", YouTube, September 22, 2021, https://www.youtube.com/watch?v=Z_0iFBJPWoY.

7. Phillip Bump, "Tucker Carlson's Rhetoric on Immigrants and Crime is Wildly Misleading," *The Washington Post*, August 24, 2018, https://www.washingtonpost.com/news/politics/wp/2018/08/24/tucker-carlsons-rhetoric-on-immigrants-and-crime-is-wildly-misleading/.

8. CSPAN, "Donald Trump Presidential Campaign Announcement Full Speech," June 16, 2015, https://www.youtube.com/watch?v=apjNfkysjbM&t=208s.

9. Eugene Scott, "Trump Defends Inflammatory Comments, Asks 'Who Is Doing the Raping?'" CNN. July 2, 2015, https://www.cnn.com/2015/07/01/politics/donald-trump-immigrants-raping-comments/index.html.

10. Philip Bump, "Within an Hour, Tucker Carlson and President Trump Embrace Broad Disparagements of Immigrants," *The Washington Post*, December 11, 2019, https://www.washingtonpost.com/politics/2019/12/11/carlson-ocasio-cortez-is-phony-environmentalist-since-her-constituents-are-littering-immigrants/.

11. Michael T. Light, Jingying He, and Jason P. Robey, "Comparing Crime Rates Be-

tween Undocumented Immigrants, Legal Immigrants, and Native-born U.S. Citizens in Texas," *PNAS* 117, no. 51 (2020): 32340-32347.

12. Light, He, and Robey, "Comparing Crime Rates Between Undocumented Immigrants, Legal Immigrants, and Native-born U.S. Citizens in Texas."

13. Light, He, and Robey, "Comparing Crime Rates Between Undocumented Immigrants, Legal Immigrants, and Native-born U.S. Citizens in Texas."

14. Michael T. Light and Ty Miller, "Does Undocumented Immigration Increase Violent Crime?", *Criminology* 56, no. 2 (2018): 370-401.

15. ABC News, "Immigration Debate Rages On After San Francisco Pier Shooting," July 7, 2015, https://abcnews.go.com/US/immigration-debate-rages-san-francisco-pier-shooting/story?id=32263093.

16. Alex Nowrasteh, "Terrorists by Immigration Status and Nationality: A Risk Analysis, 1975–2017," CATO Institute, May 7, 2019, https://www.cato.org/publications/policy-analysis/terrorists-immigration-status-nationality-risk-analysis-1975-2017.

Chapter 24

1. Mike Rothschild, *The Storm Is Upon Us: How QAnon Became a Movement, Cult, and Conspiracy Theory of Everything* (Melville House Books, 2021).

2. CNN, "Filmmaker Says He Potentially Uncovered Man behind QAnon," Video, YouTube, April 6, 2021, https://www.youtube.com/watch?v=evqRMVW7lvc.

3. "Understanding QAnon's Connection to American Politics, Religion, and Media Consumption," PRRI, May 27, 2021, https://www.prri.org/research/qanon-conspiracy-american-politics-report/.

4. Dareh Gregorian, "With Drastically Different Tones, Biden and Trump Appear in Dueling Town Halls," NBC News, October 15, 2020, https://www.nbcnews.com/politics/2020-election/biden-trump-appear-dueling-town-halls-n1243480.

5. Claire Sanford, "Donald Trump NBC Town Hall Transcript October 15," Rev, October 15, 2020, https://www.rev.com/blog/transcripts/donald-trump-nbc-town-hall-transcript-october-15.

6. "Trump Isn't Secretly Winking at QAnon. He's Retweeting Its Followers.," *Politico*, accessed May 5, 2023, https://www.politico.com/news/2020/07/12/trump-tweeting-qanon-followers-357238.

7. Magda Teter, *Blood Libel: On the Trail of an Antisemitic Myth* (Cambridge, MA: Harvard University Press, 2020).

8. Richard J. Goodrich - The Peripatetic Historian, "Cannibals at an Orgy - Lessons from History - Medium," *Lessons from History*, May 5, 2022, https://medium.com/lessons-from-history/cannibals-at-an-orgy-45f478e760ba.

9. *Modest Enquiry Into the Nature of Witchcraft*, accessed May 5, 2023, https://books.google.com/books?id=opvczTeULKwC&lpg=PA24&vq=bitten&pg=PA24#v=onepage&q&f=false.

10. Mary Beth Norton, *In the Devil's Snare: The Salem Witchcraft Crisis of 1692* (Alfred A. Knopf, 2002).

11. Michelle Smith and Lawrence Pazder, *Michelle Remembers* (Condon & Lattes Inc., 1980).

12. "Exoneration Detail List," accessed May 5, 2023, https://www.law.umich.edu/special/exoneration/Pages/detaillist.aspx?View=%7b-FAF6EDDB-5A68-4F8F-8A52-2C61F5BF9EA7%7d&FilterField1=Group&FilterValue1=CSH&FilterField2=ST&FilterValue2=CA.

13. "West Memphis Three Trial: Testimony of Dale Griffis," accessed May 5, 2023, http://law2.umkc.edu/faculty/projects/ftrials/memphis3/WestMemphis3EBGriffis.html.

14. "Investigator's Guide to Allegations of 'Ritual' Child Abuse," National Center for the Analysis of Violent Crime, January 1992, https://www.ojp.gov/pdffiles1/Digitization/136592NCJRS.pdf.

15. Rob Brotherton, *Suspicious Minds: Why We Believe Conspiracy Theories* (Bloomsbury, 2017).

16. Chauncey DeVega, "Trump and the Christians: Evangelical Historian John Fea on Decoding the Great Paradox," Salon.com, February 19, 2020, https://www.salon.com/2020/02/19/trump-and-the-christians-evangelical-historian-john-fea-on-decoding-the-great-paradox/.

17. Kaleigh Rogers, "Why QAnon Has Attracted So Many White Evangelicals," FiveThirtyEight, March 4, 2021, https://fivethirtyeight.com/features/why-qanon-has-attracted-so-many-white-evangelicals/.

18. Timothy Pettipiece, "History Repeats Itself: From the New Testament to QAnon," The Conversation, March 21, 2021, https://theconversation.com/history-repeats-itself-from-the-new-testament-to-qanon-156915.

19. EJ Dickson, "The Birth of QAmom," *Rolling Stone*, September 2, 2020, https://www.rollingstone.com/culture/culture-features/qanon-mom-conspiracy-theory-parents-sex-trafficking-qamom-1048921/.

Chapter 25

1. Originally published by *The Conversation* and adapted here with permission: Rob Moodie, "The Seven Tactics Unhealthy Industries Use To Undermine Public Health Policies," *The Conversation*, August 17, 2017, https://theconversation.com/the-seven-tactics-unhealthy-industries-use-to-undermine-public-health-policies-81137. Note: This book is intended for a general audience and thus throughout we have tried to minimize footnotes in some chapters for purposes of readability—for the full set of footnotes/citations/hyperlinks for each chapter, see the original source.

2. Naomi Oreskes and Erik M. Conway, *Merchants of Doubt: How a Handful of Scientists Obscured the Truth on Issues From Tobacco Smoke to Climate Change* (London, England: Bloomsburg Press, 2011).

3. Bill Wiist, "The Corporate Playbook, Health, and Democracy: The Snack Food and Beverage Industry's Tactics in Context," ResearchGate, January 2011, https://www.researchgate.net/publication/285481340_The_corporate_play_book_health_and_democracy_The_snack_food_and_beverage_industry's_tactics_in_context.

4. Nicholas Freudenberg, *Lethal But Legal: Corporations, Consumption, and Protecting Public Health* (New York: Oxford University Press, 2014).

Chapter 26

1. Originally published by *The Conversation* and adapted here with permission: Katharine Hayhoe, "I Was an Exxon-funded Climate Scientist," The Conversation, August 24, 2017, https://theconversation.com/i-was-an-exxon-funded-climate-scientist-49855. Note: This book is intended for a general audience and thus throughout we have tried to minimize footnotes in some chapters for purposes of readability—for the full set of footnotes/citations/hyperlinks for each chapter, see the original source.

2. Geoffrey Supran and Naomi Oreskes, "Assessing ExxonMobil's Climate Change Communications (1977–2014)," *Environmental Research Letters* 12, no. 8 (August 2017), https://iopscience.iop.org/article/10.1088/1748-9326/aa815f.

3. Union of Concerned Scientists, "Smoke, Mirrors & Hot Air: How ExxonMobil Uses Big Tobacco's Tactics to 'Manufacture Uncertainty' on Climate Change," July 16, 2007, https://www.ucsusa.org/resources/smoke-mirrors-hot-air#.WZ8syZOGM6h.

4. See Sara Jerving, Katie Jennings, Masako Melissa Hirsch, and Susanne Rust, "What Exxon Knew About the Earth's Melting Arctic," *Los Angeles Times*, October 9, 2015, https://graphics.latimes.com/exxon-arctic/. See also Neela Banerjee, John H. Cushman Jr., David Hasemyer, and Lisa Song, "Exxon: The Road Not Taken," Inside Climate News, https://insideclimatenews.org/book/exxon-the-road-not-taken/.

5. Geoffrey Supran and Naomi Oreskes, "Assessing ExxonMobil's Climate Change Communications (1977–2014)," *Environmental Research Letters* 12, no. 8 (August 2017), https://iopscience.iop.org/article/10.1088/1748-9326/aa815f.

6. You can visit their website here: https://energy.stanford.edu/research/gcep.

7. Colby Itkowitz, "Scientists to Smithsonian: Cut Ties With Koch Brothers," *Washington Post*, March 24, 2015, https://www.washingtonpost.com/blogs/in-the-loop/wp/2015/03/24/scientists-to-smithsonian-cut-ties-with-koch-brothers/.

8. Jeff Nesbit, "Shell and the London Science Museum," *U.S. News & World Report*, June 1, 2015, https://www.usnews.com/news/blogs/at-the-edge/2015/06/01/science-museum-exhibit-funded-by-shell-under-fire.

Chapter 27

1. Originally published by *Skeptic Magazine* and adapted here with permission: Kevin McCaffree, "When Secularism Becomes a Religion: The Alt-Left, the Alt-Right, and Moral Righteousness," *Skeptic Magazine*, Fall 2017, https://go.gale.

com/ps/i.do?id=GALE%7CA520714005&sid=googleScholar&v=2.1&it=r&link-access=abs&issn=10639330&p=AONE&sw=w&userGroupName=anon%7E-2beb6548. Note: This book is intended for a general audience and thus throughout we have tried to minimize footnotes in some chapters for purposes of readability—for the full set of footnotes/citations/hyperlinks for each chapter, see the original source.

2. Michael Schaub, "Happy Birthday, Aldous Huxley!," *Los Angeles Times*, July 26, 2016, https://www.latimes.com/books/jacketcopy/la-et-jc-aldous-huxley-20160726-snap-story.html.

3. See, for example, S. Kanazawa, "The Evolution of General Intelligence," *Personality and Individual Differences* 53: 90–93. See also J. M. Kaplan, "Race, IQ, and the search for statistical signals associated with so-called 'X'-factors: environments, racism, and the 'hereditarian hypothesis,'" *Biology & Philosophy* 30: 1–17.

4. Bryan Caplan, *The Myth of the Rational Voter: Why Democracies Choose Bad Policies* (NJ: Princeton University Press, 2011).

Chapter 28

1. The author, Jacob L. Mackey, owns the copyright to this chapter. It is reprinted here with his permission.

2. Alan L. Olmstead and Paul W. Rhode, "Cotton, Slavery, and the New History of Capitalism," *Explorations in Economic History* 67 (January 2018): 1-17, https://doi.org/10.1016/j.eeh.2017.12.002. Cf. Gavin Wright, "Slavery and the Rise of the Nineteenth-Century American Economy," *Journal of Economic Perspectives* 36, no. 2, (Spring 2022): 123-48, https://www.aeaweb.org/articles?id=10.1257/jep.36.2.123.

3. Kimberlé Williams Crenshaw, "The Unmattering of Black Lives," *The New Republic*, May 21, 2020, https://newrepublic.com/article/157769/unmattering-black-lives.

4. Derecka Purnell, "The George Floyd Act Wouldn't Have Saved George Floyd's Life. That Says It All," *The Guardian*, March 4, 2021, https://www.theguardian.com/commentisfree/2021/mar/04/the-george-floyd-act-wouldnt-have-saved-george-floyds-life-thats-says-it-all.

5. Roland G. Fryer, Jr., "What the Data Say About Police," *Wall Street Journal*, June 22, 2020, https://www.wsj.com/articles/what-the-data-say-about-police-11592845959.

6. Sendhil Mullainathan, "Police Killings of Blacks: Here Is What the Data Say," *New York Times*, October 18, 2015, https://www.nytimes.com/2015/10/18/upshot/police-killings-of-blacks-what-the-data-says.html.

7. Ted R Miller, et al. "Perils of Police Action: A Cautionary Tale from US Data Sets," *Injury Prevention* 23 (2017): 27-32, https://injuryprevention.bmj.com/content/injuryp-rev/23/1/27.full.pdf.

8. Roland G. Fryer, Jr. "An Empirical Analysis of Racial Differences in Police Use of Force," *Journal of Political Economy* 127, no. 3 (June 2019): 1210-1261, https://scholar.harvard.edu/files/fryer/files/empirical_analysis_tables_figures.pdf.

9. Roland G. Fryer, "Reconciling Results on Racial Differences in Police Shootings,"

AEA Papers and Proceedings 108: 228-33, https://scholar.harvard.edu/files/fryer/files/fryer_police_aer.pdf.

10. Phillip Atiba Goff, et al. *The Science of Justice: Race, Arrests, and Police Use of Force* (Los Angeles: Center for Policing Equity, University of California, 2016), https://policingequity.org/images/pdfs-doc/CPE_SoJ_Race-Arrests-UoF_2016-07-08-1130.pdf.

11. Shea Streeter, "Lethal Force in Black and White: Assessing Racial Disparities in the Circumstances of Police Killings," *The Journal of Politics* 81, no. 3: 1124-1132, https://www.journals.uchicago.edu/doi/10.1086/703541.

12. Charles Menifield, et al., "Do White Law Enforcement Officers Target Minority Suspects?" *Public Administration Review* 79, no. 1 (January/February 2019): 56-68, https://onlinelibrary.wiley.com/doi/10.1111/puar.12956.

13. "Herstory," Black Lives Matter, accessed at https://blacklivesmatter.com/herstory/ on June 29, 2023.

14. Zac Kriegman, "The post that led to my termination," *Zac Kriegman*, December 7, 2021, https://kriegman.substack.com/p/post-leading-to-termination-blm-falsehoods.

15. David J. Johnson, et al., "Officer Characteristics and Racial Disparities in Fatal Officer-Involved Shootings," *PNAS* 116, no. 32 (July 22, 2019): 15877-882, https://www.pnas.org/doi/full/10.1073/pnas.1903856116 (retracted July 10, 2020).

16. For an account of this episode, see Jukka Savolainen, "Unequal Treatment Under the Flaw: Race, Crime & Retractions," *Current Psychology* (2023): https://link.springer.com/article/10.1007/s12144-023-04739-2.

17. "AB-241 Implicit bias: continuing education: requirements," https://leginfo.legislature.ca.gov/faces/billTextClient.xhtml?bill_id=201920200AB241.

18. See Olivier Corneille and Mandy Hütter, "Implicit? What Do You Mean? A Comprehensive Review of the Delusive Implicitness Construct in Attitude Research," *Personality and Social Psychology Review* 24, no. 3 (2020): 212-32, https://journals.sagepub.com/doi/full/10.1177/1088868320911325; Lee Jussim et al. "Do IAT Scores Explain Racial Inequality?," in *Applications of Social Psychology*, eds. Joseph P. Forgas et al. (New York: Routledge, 2020): 312-33, https://sites.rutgers.edu/lee-jussim/wp-content/uploads/sites/135/2019/09/Do-IAT-Scores-Explain-Racial-Inequalities.docx.

19. Lee Jussim et al. "IAT Scores, Racial Gaps, and Scientific Gaps," in *The Cambridge Handbook of Implicit Bias and Racism*, eds. Jon A. Krosnick et al. (Cambridge: Cambridge University Press, 2023). A draft is available here: https://osf.io/mpdx5.

20. Musa al-Gharbi, "Diversity Is Important. Diversity-Related Training Is Terrible," originally published by *Heterodox Academy*, November 16, 2020, https://musaalgharbi.com/2020/09/16/diversity-important-related-training-terrible/.

21. Lee Jussim, "12 Reasons to Be Skeptical of Common Claims About Implicit Bias," *Psychology Today*, March 28, 2022, https://www.psychologytoday.com/us/blog/rabble-rouser/202203/12-reasons-be-skeptical-common-claims-about-implicit-bias.

22. Keith C. Norris, et al., "Removal of Race From Estimates of Kidney Function: First, Do No Harm," *JAMA* 325, no. 2 (2021):135-37, https://jamanetwork.com/journals/jama/article-abstract/2773807.

23. Kelly M. Hoffman et al., "Racial Bias in Pain Assessment and Treatment Recommendations, and False Beliefs about Biological Differences between Blacks and Whites," *PNAS* 113, no. 16 (April 4, 2016): 4296-301, https://www.pnas.org/doi/abs/10.1073/pnas.1516047113. Kevin Drum offers reasons to be skeptical of this study on his website: https://jabberwocking.com/pain/.

24. al-Gharbi, "Diversity is Important. Diversity-Related Training is Terrible."

25. There is a large literature attesting to the problems with the implicit bias construct: in addition to the items in my footnotes, see the overviews in Jesse Singal, "Psychology's Favorite Tool for Measuring Racism Isn't Up to the Job," *The Cut* (January 2017), https://www.thecut.com/2017/01/psychologys-racism-measuring-tool-isnt-up-to-the-job.html; and Justin Weinberg, "Reconsidering Implicit Bias," *Daily Nous* (January 12, 2017), https://dailynous.com/2017/01/12/reconsidering-implicit-bias/.

26. Rodrigo Pérez Ortega, "Do No Unconscious Harm," *Science*, March 2, 2023, https://www.science.org/content/article/do-no-unconscious-harm-can-hidden-prejudices-medicine-stamped.

27. Jerry Coyne, "An Article in *Science* Takes Implicit Bias (and Its Measurement) for Granted Despite the Problems, and Suggests Interventions That Haven't Been Shown to Work," Why Evolution Is True, March 25, 2023, https://whyevolutionistrue.com/2023/03/25/an-article-in-science-takes-implicit-bias-and-its-measurement-for-granted-despite-the-problems-and-suggests-interventions-that-havent-been-shown-to-work/.

28. "Herstory," Black Lives Matter.

29. Heather Mac Donald, "The Corruption of Medicine," *City Journal* (Summer 2022), https://www.city-journal.org/article/the-corruption-of-medicine-2.

30. "Structural Racism for Doctors—What Is It?," *JAMA Clinical Reviews* (February 2021), https://static1.squarespace.com/static/5d7d985bfc6bb40f1d-fae872/t/6061d1425689961a044a3ac0/1617023298545/Transcript+-+Structural+Racism+for+Doctors.pdf.

31. Katie Herzog, "What Happens When Doctors Can't Tell the Truth?," *The Free Press*, June 3, 2021, https://www.thefp.com/p/what-happens-when-doctors-cant-speak.

32. Wesley J. Smith, "Why We Can't Have 'An Honest Conversation about Race,'" *National Review*, March 9, 2021, https://www.nationalreview.com/corner/why-we-cant-have-an-honest-conversation-about-race/.

33. Amanda Heidt, "Howard Bauchner Leaves JAMA Following Podcast Fallout," *The Scientist*, June 2, 2021, https://www.the-scientist.com/news-opinion/howard-bauchner-leaves-jama-following-podcast-fallout-68839.

34. Rob Henderson, "Luxury Beliefs are Status Symbols: The Struggle for Distinction," *Rob Henderson's Newsletter*, June 12, 2022, https://robkhenderson.substack.com/p/status-symbols-and-the-struggle-for.

35. Steven W Thrasher, "Police Hunt and Kill Black People Like Philando Castile. There's No Justice," *The Guardian*, June 19, 2017, https://www.theguardian.com/commentisfree/2017/jun/19/philando-castile-police-violence-black-americans.

36. "Herstory," Black Lives Matter.

37. CNN poll (March 2023), https://s3.documentcloud.org/documents/23706881/cnn-poll-most-republicans-care-more-about-picking-a-2024-gop-nominee-who-agrees-with-them-on-issues-than-one-who-can-beat-biden.pdf.

38. Musa al-Gharbi, "How to Understand the Well-Being Gap between Liberals and Conservatives," *American Affairs*, March 21, 2023, https://americanaffairsjournal.org/2023/03/how-to-understand-the-well-being-gap-between-liberals-and-conservatives/.

39. Gallup Poll, "Race Relations," https://news.gallup.com/poll/1687/race-relations.aspx.

40. Zach Goldberg, "How the Media Led the Great Racial Awakening," *Tablet*, August 4, 2020, https://www.tabletmag.com/sections/news/articles/media-great-racial-awakening.

41. David Rozado, "Prevalence of Prejudice-Denoting Words in News Media Discourse: A Chronological Analysis," *Social Science Computer Review* 41, no. 1: 99-122, https://journals.sagepub.com/doi/full/10.1177/08944393211031452.

42. Matt Yglesias, "Defund Police Is a Bad Idea, Not a Bad Slogan," *Slow Boring*, December 7, 2020, https://www.slowboring.com/p/defund-police-is-a-bad-idea-not-a.

43. See, for example, Steven Mello, "More COPS, Less Crime," *Journal of Public Economics* 17, issue C (2019): 174–200, https://doi.org/10.1016/j.jpubeco.2018.12.003; Tanaya Devi and Roland G. Fryer, Jr., "Policing the Police: The Impact of 'Pattern-or-Practice' Investigations on Crime," NBER Working Paper no. 27324 (June 2020), https://www.nber.org/papers/w27324; Justin Nix et al., "When Police Pull Back: Neighborhood-Level Effects of De-Policing on Violent and Property Crime," March 3, 2023, https://osf.io/preprints/socarxiv/54dyh/.

44. Jennifer A. Kingson, "Exclusive: $1 Billion-Plus Riot Damage Is Most Expensive in Insurance History," *Axios*, September 16, 2020, https://www.axios.com/2020/09/16/riots-cost-property-damage.

45. Demographic data on fatal police shootings are available in the *Washington Post*'s "Fatal Force" database: https://www.washingtonpost.com/graphics/investigations/police-shootings-database/.

46. Bodycam video of the shooting of Dylan Noble, https://youtu.be/_nFYueyf-EM; witness cell phone video: https://www.theguardian.com/us-news/video/2016/jul/07/dylan-noble-fresno-fatal-police-shooting-witness-video.

47. Sam Levin, "How 'White Lives Matter' Protests Over a Police Shooting Were Misunderstood," *The Guardian*, June 30, 2016, https://www.theguardian.com/us-news/2016/jun/30/white-lives-matter-protest-dylan-noble-shooting-fresno.

48. Krysta Scripter, "Music, Activism Go Hand in Hand for Protest Organizer Justice Medina," *Fresno Bee*, August 6, 2016, https://www.fresnobee.com/article94088077.html.

49. Adam Rothman and Barbara J. Fields, "The Death of Hannah Fizer," *Dissent*, July 24, 2020, https://www.dissentmagazine.org/online_articles/the-death-of-hannah-fizer.

Chapter 29

1. Originally published by the Heterodox Academy and adapted here with permission: Jonathan Haidt, "Why Universities Must Choose One Telos: Truth or Social Justice," Heterodox Academy, October 21, 2016, https://heterodoxacademy.org/blog/one-telos-truth-or-social-justice-2/. Note: This book is intended for a general audience and thus throughout we have tried to minimize footnotes in some chapters for purposes of readability—for the full set of footnotes/citations/hyperlinks for each chapter, see the original source.

2. Jonathan Haidt and Lee Jussim, "Hard Truths About Race On Campus," *Wall Street Journal,* May 6, 2016, https://www.wsj.com/articles/hard-truths-about-race-on-campus-1462544543.

3. You can watch the talk here at https://heterodoxacademy.org/blog/one-telos-truth-or-social-justice-2/. You can also see the PowerPoint slides at https://www.dropbox.com/s/9bq5fuml4fotsn5/haidt.slides%20from%20duke%20lecture%20on%20truth%20vs%20social%20justice.for%20posting.pptx?dl=0.

4. Mitchell Langbert, Anthony J. Quain, and Daniel B. Klein, "Faculty Voter Registration in Economics, History, Journalism, Law, and Psychology," *Econ Journal Watch* 13, no. 3 (September 2016): 422-51.

5. You can check out the Heterodox Academy at https://heterodoxacademy.org/.

6. Nassim Nicholas Taleb, *Antifragile: Things That Gain from Disorder* (New York: Random House, 2012).

7. Sean Stevens, "The Heterodox Academy Guide to Colleges: Starting A Methodological Discussion," Heterodox Academy, October 27, 2016, https://heterodoxacademy.org/blog/the-heterodox-academy-guide-to-colleges-starting-a-methodological-discussion/.

8. Jonathan Haidt, "Which Will Be America's First Heterodox University?", Heterodox Academy, August 23, 2016, https://heterodoxacademy.org/blog/which-will-be-americas-first-heterodox-university/.

Chapter 30

1. Originally published by Arc Digital and adapted here with permission: Cathy Young, "Defining 'Wokeness,'" Arc Digital, October 2, 2021, https://www.arcdigital.media/p/defining-wokeness. Note: This book is intended for a general audience and thus throughout we have tried to minimize footnotes in some chapters for purposes of readability—for the full set of footnotes/citations/hyperlinks for each chapter, see the original source.

2. Posted on Twitter on September 21, 2021. Tweet since deleted. See screenshot here: https://www.arcdigital.media/p/defining-wokeness.

3. Ross Douthat, Coleman Hughes, Wesley Yang, and Reihan Salam, "The Success

Ideology," The Manhattan Institute, August 6, 2020, https://www.manhattan-institute. org/the-successor-ideology.

4. Marc Lamont Hill, Twitter, July 11, 2021, https://twitter.com/marclamonthill/status/1414266804730351617.

5. Isobel Lewis, "George Floyd Protests: JK Rowling Says 'White People Have to Change' as She Shows Support for Black Lives Matter," *Independent*, June 1, 2020, https://www.independent.co.uk/arts-entertainment/books/news/jk-rowling-twitter-black-lives-matter-george-floyd-ickabog-a9542741.html.

6. J.K. Rowling, "J.K. Rowling Writes about Her Reasons for Speaking Out on Sex and Gender Issues," JKRowling.com, June 10, 2020, https://www.jkrowling.com/opinions/j-k-rowling-writes-about-her-reasons-for-speaking-out-on-sex-and-gender-issues/.

7. David Frum, "Why Garry Trudeau Is Wrong About Charlie Hebdo," *The Atlantic*, April 13, 2015, https://www.theatlantic.com/politics/archive/2015/04/why-garry-trudeau-is-wrong-about-charlie-hebdo/390336/.

8. Jill Lepore, "The Invention of the Police," *The New Yorker*, July 13, 2020, https://www.newyorker.com/magazine/2020/07/20/the-invention-of-the-police.

9. Cathy Young, "The Real Dr. Seuss Scandal," March 12, 2021, https://medium.com/arc-digital/the-real-dr-seuss-scandal-95467822898a.

10. Jamie Palmer, "The Shame and the Disgrace of the Pro-Islamist Left," Quillette, December 6, 2015, https://quillette.com/2015/12/06/the-shame-and-the-disgrace-of-the-pro-islamist-left/.

11. Kat Rosenfield, "The Toxic Drama on YA Twitter," Vulture, https://www.vulture.com/2017/08/the-toxic-drama-of-ya-twitter.html.

12. Emily Yoffe, "The Question of Race in Campus Sexual-Assault Cases," *The Atlantic*, September 11, 2017, https://www.theatlantic.com/education/archive/2017/09/the-question-of-race-in-campus-sexual-assault-cases/539361/.

13. Robby Soave, "Survey: Only 2% of Hispanics Prefer the Politically Correct Term 'Latinx'", *Reason*, November 4, 2019, https://reason.com/2019/11/04/latinx-poll-think-now-hispanics-2020-woke/.

14. Roni Molla, Twitter, August 1, 2018, https://imgur.com/a/dCIoLY6.

15. Tom Jacobs, "Talking About White Privilege Can Reduce Liberals' Sympathy for Poor White People," *Pacific Standard*, May 30, 2019, https://psmag.com/news/talking-about-white-privilege-can-reduce-liberal-sympathy-for-poor-white-people.

16. Various Signatories, "A Letter on Justice and Open Debate," *Harper's Magazine*, July 7, 2020, https://harpers.org/a-letter-on-justice-and-open-debate/.

17. Zack Beauchamp, "The 'Free Speech Debate' Isn't Really About Free Speech," *Vox*, July 22, 2020, https://www.vox.com/policy-and-politics/2020/7/22/21325942/free-speech-harpers-letter-bari-weiss-andrew-sullivan.

18. Rowling, "J.K. Rowling Writes about Her Reasons for Speaking out on Sex and Gender Issues.".

19. The statement can be found at https://twitter.com/CHSommers/sta-

tus/970506084472336384.

20. Brian Boucher, "Social Media Erupts as the Art World Splits in Two Over Dana Schutz Controversy," Artnet, March 24, 2017, https://news.artnet.com/art-world/art-world-split-dana-schutz-controversy-902423.

21. Chad Sanders, "I Don't Need 'Love' Texts From My White Friends," *New York Times,* June 5, 2020, https://www.nytimes.com/2020/06/05/opinion/whites-anti-blackness-protests.html.

22. George Orwell, "The Prevention of Literature," https://www.orwell.ru/library/essays/prevention/english/e_plit.

23. Christopher F. Rufo, "Cult Programming in Seattle," *City Journal,* July 8, 2020, https://www.city-journal.org/seattle-interrupting-whiteness-training.

24. Goldman Sachs, "Bringing Your Authentic Self to Work: Pronouns," November 22, 2019, https://www.goldmansachs.com/careers/blog/posts/bring-your-authentic-self-to-work-pronouns.html.

25. Ibram X. Kendi, "Pass an Anti-Racist Constitutional Amendment," *Politico,* https://www.politico.com/interactives/2019/how-to-fix-politics-in-america/inequality/pass-an-anti-racist-constitutional-amendment/.

26. Democracy Now!, "Ibram X. Kendi on Trump, Obama & Why 'Internalized Racism Is the Real Black-on-Black Crime,'" August 13, 2019, https://www.democracynow.org/2019/8/13/ibram_x_kendi_interview_racism_antiracism.

27. Politico Staff, "Text of Obama's Fatherhood Speech," *Politico,* June 15, 2008, https://www.politico.com/story/2008/06/text-of-obamas-fatherhood-speech-011094..

28. Shree Paradkar, "Radical Changes Show How Fast the State Can Act When It Cares About the Lives at Risk," *Toronto Star,* March 18, 2020, https://www.thestar.com/opinion/star columnists/2020/03/18/radical-changes-show-how-fast-the-state-can-act-when-it-cares-about-the-lives-at-risk.html.

Chapter 31

1 Originally published by the Heterodox Academy and adapted here with permission: Carl Bankston III, "The Institutionalization of Ideology in Sociology," Heterodox Academy, January 12, 2017, https://heterodoxacademy.org/blog/the-institutionalization-of-ideology-in-sociology/. Note: This book is intended for a general audience and thus throughout we have tried to minimize footnotes in some chapters for purposes of readability—for the full set of footnotes/citations/hyperlinks for each chapter, see the original source.

2 See Christian Smith, *The Sacred Project of American Sociology* (New York: Oxford University Press, 2014).

3 See Irving Louis Horowitz, *The Decomposition of Sociology* (New York: Oxford University Press, 1994).

4 See Stephen Cole, ed., *What's Wrong with Sociology?* (New Brunswick, NJ: Transaction Publishers, 2001).

5 Mathieu Deflem, "The Structural Transformation of Sociology," *Society* 50, no. 2 (2013): 156-66..

6 Jonathan Haidt, "Why Universities Must Choose One Telos: Truth or Social Justice," Heterodox Academy, October 21, 2016, https://heterodoxacademy.org/blog/one-telos-truth-or-social-justice-2/.

Chapter 33

1 Originally published by *Skeptic Magazine* and adapted here with permission: Terence Hines, "Bad Behavioral Science Exposed: Review of *The Quick Fix: Why Fad Psychology Can't Cure Our Social Ills* by Jesse Singal," *Skeptic Magazine*, February 25, 2023, https://www.skeptic.com/reading_room/review-quick-fix-why-fad-psychology-cant-cure-social-ills/. Note: This book is intended for a general audience and thus throughout we have tried to minimize footnotes in some chapters for purposes of readability—for the full set of footnotes/citations/hyperlinks for each chapter, see the original source.

2 Jesse Singal, *The Quick Fix: Why Fad Psychology Can't Cure Our Social Ills* (New York: Picador, 2021).

3 Alan Carr et. al., "Effectiveness of Positive Psychology Interventions: A Systematic Review and Meta-Analysis," *The Journal of Positive Psychology* 16, no. 6 (2021): 766.

Chapter 34

1 This chapter adapted from two of my previous articles: (1) Edward Cantu and Lee Jussim, "Microaggressions, Questionable Science, and Free Speech," *Texas Review of Law & Politics* 26, no. 1 (2021): 217–67, and (2) Lee Jussim, "The Dubious Science of Microaggressions," *Unsafe Science*, June 12, 2022, https://unsafescience.substack.com/p/the-dubious-science-of-microaggressions.

2 Monnica T. Williams, "Microaggressions: Misconceptions, Politics, and New Science," *Psychology Today*, August 31, 2021, https://www.psychologytoday.com/us/blog/culturally-speaking/202108/microaggressions-misconceptions-politics-and-new-science.

3 Cantu and Jussim, "Microaggressions, Questionable Science, and Free Speech," 248.

4 Cantu and Jussim, "Microaggressions, Questionable Science, and Free Speech," 226.

5 Scott O. Lilienfeld, "Microaggressions: Strong Claims, Inadequate Evidence," *Perspectives on Psychological Science* 12, no. 1 (January 2017): 163.

6 Derald Wing Sue, Christina M. Capodilupo, Gina C. Torino, Jennifer M. Bucceri et al., "Racial Microaggressions in Everyday Life: Implications for Clinical Practice," *American Psychologist* 62, no. 4 (May-June 2007): 275.

7 Kevin L. Nadal, "The Racial and Ethnic Microaggressions Scale (REMS): Construction, Reliability, and Validity" *Journal of Counseling Psychology* 58, no. 4 (2011): 470.

8 Sue, Capodilupo, Torino, Bucceri, et al., "Racial Microaggressions in Everyday Life: Implications for Clinical Practice," 271.

9 Derald Wing Sue, Christina M. Capodilupo, and Kevin L. Nadal, "Racial Microaggressions and the Power to Define Reality," *American Psychologist* 63, no. 4 (2008): 277-78.

10 Monnica T. Williams, "Microaggressions: Clarification, Evidence, and Impact," *Perspectives on Psychological Science* 15, no. 1 (2020), https://journals.sagepub.com/doi/full/10.1177/1745691619827499.

11 You can find the survey results at: https://www.skeptic.com/research-center/reports/Research-Report-CUPES-007.pdf.

12 Lilienfeld, "Microaggressions: Strong Claims, Inadequate Evidence," 138-69.

13 Williams, "Microaggressions: Clarification, Evidence, and Impact."

14 Jonathan W. Kanter, Monnica T. Williams, Adam M. Kuczynski, Katherine E. Manbeck et al., "A Preliminary Report on the Relationship Between Microaggressions Against Black People and Racism Among White College Students," *Race and Social Problems* 9, (2017): 291, 294.

15 Cantu and Jussim, "Microaggressions, Questionable Science, and Free Speech," 217-67.

16 Williams, "Microaggressions: Clarification, Evidence, and Impact."

17 For the scale, see Kevin L. Nadal, "The Racial and Ethnic Microaggressions Scale (REMS): Construction, Reliability, and Validity," *Journal of Counseling Psychology* 58, no. 4 (2011): 470–80.

18 Cantu and Jussim, "Microaggressions, Questionable Science, and Free Speech," 217–67.

19 Williams, "Microaggressions: Misconceptions, Politics, and New Science."

20 Nientara Anderson, Elle Lett, Emmanuella Ngozi Asabor, Amanda Lynn Hernandez et al., "The Association of Microaggressions with Depressive Symptoms and Institutional Satisfaction Among a National Cohort of Medical Students," *Journal of General Internal Medicine* 37, no. 2 (February 2022): 298–307.

21 Anderson, Lett, Asabor, Hernandez et al., "The Association of Microaggressions with Depressive Symptoms and Institutional Satisfaction Among a National Cohort of Medical Students," 303.

22 Cantu and Jussim, "Microaggressions, Questionable Science, and Free Speech," 217–67.

23 From the Foundation for Individual Rights and Expression (FIRE): "The inherent subjectivity and elasticity of the concept of microaggressions make a clear, objective definition all but impossible in practice. And without a shared understanding of what speech or action may constitute a microaggression, students and faculty run the risk of being reported for speech protected by the First Amendment that nevertheless crosses an invisible line, drawn by and known only to the offended party." See FIRE, "What Are Microaggressions?" https://www.thefire.org/research-learn/what-are-microaggressions#:~:text=%E2%80%9CMicroaggressions%E2%80%9D%20are%20subtle%20slights%20against,slights%20made%20unconsciously%20or%20unintentionally.

24 "It should be sufficiently clear that researchers have not come close to substantiating

their central premise about embedded racist meanings. Researchers rather assume the validity of the premise, and this assumption is the thread that holds the CMC together. Without it, the CMC would reduce to simply lists of items that people do or say that *could* be inspired by racism or interpreted as racist. But such a construct would be next to useless for obvious reasons" (Cantu and Jussim, "Microaggressions, Questionable Science, and Free Speech," 245).

25 "The inclusion of a small number of more likely problematic statements that actually do correlate with measures of racism, when summed together with the weaker items, misleadingly produces a scale with a substantial overall correlation with racism....The more ambiguous and facially non-racist items ride on the correlative coattails of the more blatant, weaseling their way into seeming conceptual legitimacy as microaggressions when they don't belong. This is damning" (Cantu and Jussim, "Microaggressions, Questionable Science, and Free Speech," 240–41).

26 Microaggression researchers make claims about supposedly "hidden, embedded 'metacommunications' that exist independent of how either the speaker or the recipient experiences a given statement. Microaggression researchers simply have not provided a valid basis for concluding that alleged microaggressions are what researchers claim they are. And even a charitable reconstruction of methodology cannot hide the fact that the basis for the researchers' conclusions about embedded meanings appears to be an a priori belief in the existence of those embedded meanings" (Cantu and Jussim, "Microaggressions, Questionable Science, and Free Speech," 241).

27 Cantu and Jussim, "Microaggressions, Questionable Science, and Free Speech," 226.

28 Cantu and Jussim, "Microaggressions, Questionable Science, and Free Speech," 249.

29 As Robert Shibley, executive director of the Foundation for Individual Rights in Education (FIRE), noted, "Whoever is making the decisions about what constitutes a microaggression has been handed an enormous amount of power to put certain political beliefs off-limits. There are a lot of people out there that believe that America *is* a melting pot, or that the most qualified person *should* get the job. It has not escaped their notice that it is their beliefs and not others' that have been singled out as harmful" (Cantu and Jussim, "Microaggressions, Questionable Science, and Free Speech," 256).

30 "One could fairly suspect that the [prevailing microaggression research] represents an activism of sort, wherein the problem—widespread subtle racism—is assumed, such that reinforcement of an activist narrative is the pre-ordained conclusion" (Cantu and Jussim, "Microaggressions, Questionable Science, and Free Speech," 245).

31 Cantu and Jussim, "Microaggressions, Questionable Science, and Free Speech," 247–48.

32 Jonathan Haidt, "Why Concepts Creep to the Left," *Psychological Inquiry* 27, no. 1 (January 2016): 40-45.

33 Prevailing conceptualization of microaggressions "appears to be a product of idea laundering because it is currently ricocheting through psychology scholarship and the broader culture as if its validity has already been scientifically established. The problem is, discovery that the emperor has no clothes (at least not yet) requires a deep dive into

primary sources that most writers are not inclined to, or don't have the time to, undertake." (Cantu and Jussim, "Microaggressions, Questionable Science, and Free Speech," 242).

34 Cantu and Jussim, "Microaggressions, Questionable Science, and Free Speech," 250.

35 Cantu and Jussim, "Microaggressions, Questionable Science, and Free Speech," 251.

36 "For example, University of North Texas professor Nathaniel Heirs was recently fired for criticizing the concept of microaggressions and for failing to attend microaggression training that would set him straight. Apparently, the head of Heirs's department told Heirs that 'he fired him because he criticized…'microaggressions' fliers and didn't express 'honest regret' about his actions" (Cantu and Jussim, "Microaggressions, Questionable Science, and Free Speech," 260).

37 Cantu and Jussim, "Microaggressions, Questionable Science, and Free Speech," 250.

38 "In short, patterns…in researchers' accusations toward one another…combined with the scientific weaknesses of the [prevailing microaggression research] suggests that… [it] is little more than a mechanism to vindicate the intuitive hunches of those who see racism as more pervasive than others do, and to silence those whose worldviews are premised on different hunches" (Cantu and Jussim, "Microaggressions, Questionable Science, and Free Speech," 256).

39 Cantu and Jussim, "Microaggressions, Questionable Science, and Free Speech," 264.

Chapter 35

1 Originally published by *Skeptic Magazine* and adapted here with permission: Carol Tavris, "Are You an Unconscious Racist?" *Skeptic Magazine*, November 1, 2017, https://www.skeptic.com/reading_room/are-you-an-unconscious-racist/. Note: This book is intended for a general audience and thus throughout we have tried to minimize footnotes in some chapters for purposes of readability—for the full set of footnotes/citations/hyperlinks for each chapter, see the original source.

2 For example, see Alessandro Acquisti and Christina M. Fong, "An Experiment in Hiring Discrimination Via Online Social Networks," *Management Science* 66, no. 3 (November 2019): 1005-24.

3 One of the first published papers was Anthony G. Greenwald, Debbie E. McGhee, and Jordan L. K. Schwartz, "Measuring Individual Differences in Implicit Cognition: The Implicit Association Test," *Journal of Personality and Social Psychology* 74, (1998): 1464–480. Mahzarin Banaji and Greenwald went on to write a book for general audiences: *Blindspot: Hidden Biases of Good People* (New York: Delacorte, 2013).

4 Klaus Rothermund and Dirk Wentura, "Underlying Processes in the Implicit Association Test: Dissociating Salience from Associations," *Journal of Experimental Psychology: General* 133, (2004): 139-65.

5 You can check out the test for yourself here: https://implicit.harvard.edu/implicit/.

6 Banaji and Greenwald, *Blindspot: Hidden Biases of Good People*. Gladwell also tells this story in his book *Blink* (New York: Little, Brown and Co., 2007).

7 Banaji and Greenwald, *Blindspot: Hidden Biases of Good People*.

8 Project Implicit, "FAQs," https://app-prod-03.implicit.harvard.edu/implicit/faqs.jsp.

9 For three superb reviews of the research, with interviews with the IAT's proponents and its critics, see these articles by Jesse Singal (https://www.thecut.com/2017/01/psychologys-racism-measuring-tool-isnt-up-to-the-job.html), Tom Bartlett (https://www.chronicle.com/article/can-we-really-measure-implicit-bias-maybe-not/), and Gregory Mitchell and Philip E. Tetlock (https://psycnet.apa.org/record/2017-24429-011).

10 Frederick L. Oswald, Gregory Mitchell, Hart Blanton, James Jaccard et al., "Predicting Ethnic and Racial Discrimination: A Meta-Analysis of IAT Criterion Studies," *Journal of Personality and Social Psychology* 105, no. 2 (2013): 171-92.

11 Anthony G. Greenwald, Mahzarin R. Banaji, and Brian A. Nosek, "Statistically Small Effects of the Implicit Association Test Can Have Societally Large Effects," *Journal of Personality and Social Psychology* 108, no. 4 (2015): 553-61.

12 Jesse Singal, "Psychology's Favorite Tool for Measuring Racism Isn't Up to the Job," The Cut, https://www.thecut.com/2017/01/psychologys-racism-measuring-tool-isnt-up-to-the-job.html.

Chapter 36

1 Originally published by *Skeptic Magazine* and adapted here with permission: Lisa Selin Davis, "Trans Matters: An Overview of the Debate, Research, and Policies," *Skeptic Magazine*, May 25, 2022, https://www.skeptic.com/reading_room/trans-matters-overview-debate-research-policies/. Note: This book is intended for a general audience and thus throughout we have tried to minimize footnotes in some chapters for purposes of readability—for the full set of footnotes/citations/hyperlinks for each chapter, see the original source.

2 Gender Identity Development Services (GIDS), "Referrals to GIDS, Financial Years 2010-11 to 2021-22," https://gids.nhs.uk/about-us/number-of-referrals/.

3 Johanna Olson-Kennedy et. al., "Chest Reconstruction and Chest Dysphoria in Transmasculine Minors and Young Adults: Comparisons of Nonsurgical and Postsurgical Cohorts," *JAMA Pediatrics* 172, no. 5 (May 2018): 431-36.

4 Christine Milrod, "How Young Is Too Young: Ethical Concerns in Genital Surgery of the Transgender MTF Adolescent," *The Journal of Sexual Medicine* 11, no. 2 (February 1, 2014): 338-46.

5 Christine Milrod and Dan H. Karasic, "Age Is Just a Number: WPATH-Affiliated Surgeons' Experiences and Attitudes Toward Vaginoplasty in Transgender Females Under 18 Years of Age in the United States," *The Journal of Sexual Medicine* 14, no. 4 (April 2017): 624-34.

6 Annelou L C de Vries and Peggy T Cohen-Kettnis, "Clinical Management of Gender Dysphoria in Children and Adolescents: The Dutch Approach." *Journal of Homosexuality* 59, no. 3 (2012): 301-20.

7 See original article for citation: https://www.skeptic.com/reading_room/trans-matters-overview-debate-research-policies/.

8 Grand Review Research, "U.S. Sex Reassignment Surgery Market Size, Share & Trends Analysis Report by Gender Transition (Male to Female, Female to Male), and Segment Forecasts, 2020–2027," December 2020, https://www.grandviewresearch.com/industry-analysis/us-sex-reassignment-surgery-market.

9 Human Rights Campaign, "Interactive Map: Clinical Care Programs for Gender-Expansive Children and Adolescents," accessed January 6, 2022, https://www.hrc.org/resources/interactive-map-clinical-careprograms-for-gender-nonconforming-childr.

10 Marco A. Hidalgo et al., "The Gender Affirmative Model: What We Know and What We Aim to Learn," *Human Development*, 56, no. 5 (2013): 285-90.

11 Tim Fitzsimons, "Puberty Blockers Linked to Lower Suicide Risk for Transgender People," NBC News, January 24, 2020, https://www.nbcnews.com/feature/nbc-out/puberty-blockers-linked-lower-suicide-risk-transgender-people-n1122101.

12 Family Research Council, "State Policy Brief: Save Adolescents from Experimentation (SAFE) Act," June 24, 2021, https://www.frc.org/statepolicybrief/save-adolescents-from-experimentation-safe-act.

13 Movement Advancement Project, "LGBTQ Policy Spotlight: Efforts to Ban Health Care for Transgender Youth," April 2021, https://www.lgbtmap.org/2021-spotlight-health-care-bans.

14 Mark Angelo Cummings, "Transitioning is for Those Who Can Vote and Drink," *New York Times,* June 18, 2015, https://www.nytimes.com/roomfordebate/2015/06/18/is-there-a-right-age-to-change-ones-sex/transitioning-is-for-those-who-can-vote-and-drink.

15 Laura Edwards-Leeper and Erica Anderson, "The Mental Health Establishment is Failing Trans Kids," *Washington Post*, November 24, 2021, https://www.washingtonpost.com/outlook/2021/11/24/trans-kids-therapy-psychologist/.

16 Anna Martha Vaitses Fontanari et al., "Gender Affirmation Is Associated with Transgender and Gender Nonbinary Youth Mental Health Improvement," *LGBT Health* 7, no. 5 (July 2020): 237-47.

17 See the original article for citation: https://www.skeptic.com/reading_room/trans-matters-overview-debate-research-policies/.

18 https://docs.google.com/viewerng/viewer?url=https://transyouthcan.ca/wp-content/uploads/2021/02/Vancouver_Webinar_2021_01_26.pdf&hl=en.

19 Chantal M. Wiepjes et al., "The Amsterdam Cohort of Gender Dysphoria Study (1972–2015): Trends in Prevalence, Treatment, and Regrets," *The Journal of Sexual Medicine* 15, no. 4 (April 2018): 582-90.

20 The Tavistock and Portman, "Referrals to the Gender Identity Development Ser-

vice (GIDS) Level Off in 2018-19," June 28, 2019, https://tavistockandportman.nhs.uk/about-us/news/stories/referrals-gender-identity-development-service-gids-level-2018-19/.

21 James Barrett, "Written Evidence Submitted by British Association of Gender Identity Specialists to the Transgender Equality Inquiry," August 20, 2015, http://data.parliament.uk/writtenevidence/committeeevidence.svc/evidencedocument/women-and-equalities-committee/transgender-equality/written/19532.html.

22 Kasia Kozlowska et al., "Australian Children and Adolescents with Gender Dysphoria: Clinical Presentations and Challenges Experienced by a Multidisciplinary Team and Gender Service," *Human Systems: Therapy, Culture, and Attachments* 1, no. 1 (April 2021), https://journals.sagepub.com/doi/full/10.1177/26344041211010777.

23 Riittakerttu Kaltiala-Heino et al., "Gender Dysphoria in Adolescence: Current Perspectives," *Adolescent Health, Medicine and Therapeutics* 9, (March 2018): 31-41.

24 William J. Malone, Paul W. Hruz, Julia W. Mason, and Stephen Beck, "Letter to the Editor from William J. Malone et al.: 'Proper Care of Transgender and Gender-diverse Persons in the Setting of Proposed Discrimination: A Policy Perspective,'" *The Journal of Clinical Endocrinology & Metabolism* 106, no. 8 (August 2021): e3287-288.

25 Lisa Littman. "Parent Reports of Adolescents and Young Adults Perceived to Show Signs of a Rapid Onset of Gender Dysphoria," *PLoS One* 14, no. 3 (August 2018), https://journals.plos.org/plosone/article?id=10.1371/journal.pone.0202330.

26 Jennifer Finney Boylan, "Coming Out as Trans Isn't a Teenage Fad," *New York Times*. January 8, 2019, https://www.nytimes.com/2019/01/08/opinion/trans-teen-transition.html.

27 Greta R. Bauer, Margaret Lawson, and Daniel Metzger, "Do Clinical Data from Transgender Adolescents Support the Phenomenon of 'Rapid Onset Gender Dysphoria?", *The Journal of Pediatrics,* (November 2021): P224-27.

28 Michael J. Bailey and Kenneth J. Zucker, "Childhood Sex-Typed Behavior and Sexual Orientation: A Conceptual Analysis and Quantitative Review," *Developmental Psychology* 31, no. 1 (1995): 43-55.

29 Francisco R. Gomez, Scott W. Semenyna, Lucas Court, and Paul L. Vasey, "Familial Patterning and Prevalence of Male Androphilia Among Istmo Zapotec Men and Muxes," *PLoS One* 13, no. 2 (February 2021), https://pubmed.ncbi.nlm.nih.gov/29466410/.

30 Paul L. Vasey and Doug P. VanderLaan, "Birth Order and Male Androphilia in Samoan *fa'afafine,*" *Proceedings of the Royal Society* 274, no. 1616 (June 2007): 1437-442.

31 Ray Blanchard, "Typology of Male-to-Female Transsexualism," *Archives of Sexual Behavior* 14, (June 1985): 247-61.

32 Kaltiala-Heino et al., "Gender Dysphoria in Adolescence: Current Perspectives," 31–41.

33 Julia Serano, "Autogynephilia: A Scientific Review, Feminist Analysis, and Alternative 'Embodiment Fantasies' Model," *The Sociological Review* 68, no. 4 (August 2020), https://journals.sagepub.com/doi/10.1177/0038026120934690.

34 Anne A. Lawrence, "Autogynephilia and the Typology of Male-to-Female Transexualism: Concepts and Controversies," *European Psychologist* 22, (2017): 39-54.

35 Jiska Ristori and Thomas D. Steensma, "Gender Dysphoria in Childhood," *International Review of Psychiatry* 28, no. 1 (January 2016): 13-20.

36 Devita Singh, Susan J. Bradley, and Kenneth J. Zucker, "A Follow-Up Study of Boys with Gender Identity Disorder," *Frontiers in Psychiatry* 12, (March 2021), https://www.frontiersin.org/articles/10.3389/fpsyt.2021.632784/full.

37 Kenneth J. Zucker, "Debate: Different Strokes for Different Folks," *Child and Adolescent Mental Health*, (2019), https://www.researchgate.net/profile/Kenneth-Zucker/publication/333516085_Debate_Different_strokes_for_different_folks/links/5cf4d-4c2299bf1fb18531b86/Debate-Different-strokes-for-different-folks.pdf.

38 Thomas D. Steensma et al., "Factors Associated with Desistence and Persistence of Childhood Gender Dysphoria: A Quantitative Follow-up Study," *Journal of the American Academy of Child and Adolescent Psychiatry* 52, no. 6 (June 2013): 582-90.

39 See the original article for citation: https://www.skeptic.com/reading_room/trans-matters-overview-debate-research-policies/.

40 Andreas Kyriakou, Nicolas C. Nicolaides, and Nicos Skordis, "Current Approach to the Clinical Care of Adolescents with Gender Dysphoria," *Acta Bio Medica: Atenei Parmensis* 91, no. 1. (2020): 165-75.

41 https://www.wpath.org/media/cms/Documents/SOC%20v8/SOC8%20Chapters%20for%20Public%20Comment/SOC8%20Chapter%20Draft%20for%20Public%20Comment%20-%20Child%20V2.pdf?_t=1638886917/.

42 COHERE Finland, "Medical Treatments for Gender Dysphoria That Reduces Functional Capacity in Transgender People—Recommendation," June 16, 2020, https://palveluvalikoima.fi/documents/1237350/22895838/Summary+transgender.pdf/2cc3f053-2e34-39ce-4e21-becd685b3044/Summary+transgender.pdf.

43 Bernard Lane, "Judges to Oversee Transgender Teen Treatment," *The Australian*, July 20, 2021, https://archive.ph/gWxDo.

44 RANZCP, "Recognising and Addressing the Mental Health Needs of People Experiencing Gender Dysphoria/Gender Incongruence," August 2021, https://www.ranzcp.org/news-policy/policy-and-advocacy/position-statements/gender-dysphoria.

45 Lisa Nainggolan, "Hormonal Tx of Youth with Gender Dysphoria Stops in Sweden," *Medscape Medical News*, May 12, 2021, https://www.medscape.com/viewarticle/950964.

46 Keira Bell, "Keira Bell: My Story," *Persuasion*, April 7, 2021, https://www.persuasion.community/p/keira-bell-my-story.

47 Haroon Siddique, "Appeal Court Overturns UK Puberty Blockers Ruling for Under-16s," *The Guardian*, September 17, 2021, https://www.theguardian.com/society/2021/sep/17/appeal-court-overturns-uk-puberty-blockers-ruling-for-under-16s-tavistock-keira-bell.

48 Lieke Josephina Jeanne Johanna Vrouenraets et al., "Early Medical Treatment of

Children and Adolescents With Gender Dysphoria: An Empirical Ethical Study," *Journal of Adolescent Health* 57, no. 4 (October 1, 2015): 367-73.

49 Jack L. Turban, Dana King, Jeremi M. Carswell, and Alex S. Keuroghlian, "Pubertal Suppression for Transgender Youth and Risk of Suicidal Ideation," *Pediatrics* 145, no. 2 (February 2020), https://www.ncbi.nlm.nih.gov/pmc/articles/PMC7073269/.

50 Michael Biggs, "Puberty Blockers and Suicidality in Adolescents Suffering from Gender Dysphoria," *Archives of Sexual Behavior* 49, no. 7 (2020): 2227-229..

51 Amy E. Green, Jonah P. DeChants, Myeshia Price, and Carrie K. Davis, "Association of Gender-Affirming Hormone Therapy with Depression, Thoughts of Suicide, and Attempted Suicide Among Transgender and Nonbinary Youth," *Journal of Adolescent Health* 70, no. 4 (December 2021), https://www.jahonline.org/article/S1054-139X(21)00568-1/fulltext.

52 The Trevor Project, "National Survey on LGBTQ Youth Mental Health 2021," https://www.thetrevorproject.org/survey-2021/?section=Introduction&fbclid=IwAR1TfGLz2UREuTUBiflP62f6R3mLahm_NS3F8DpEago4zwHs7pAL_zvKLuc.

53 Russell B. Toomey, Amy K. Syvertsen, and Maura Shramko, "Transgender Adolescent Suicide Behavior," *Pediatrics* 142, no. 4 (October 2018), https://publications.aap.org/pediatrics/article/142/4/e20174218/76767/Transgender-Adolescent-Suicide-Behavior?autologincheck=redirected.

54 Madison Aitken, Doug P. Vanderlaan, Lori Wasserman, and Sonja Olivera Stojanovski, "Self-Harm and Suicidality in Children Referred for Gender Dysphoria," *Journal of the American Academy of Child and Adolescent Psychiatry* 55, no. 6 (April 2016).

55 Hannah R. Lawrence et al., "Prevalence and Correlates of Suicidal Ideation and Suicide Attempts in Preadolescent Children: A US Population-Based Study," *Translational Psychiatry*, (September 2021), https://www.nature.com/articles/s41398-021-01593-3.

56 https://www.socialstyrelsen.se/globalassets/sharepoint-dokument/artikelkatalog/ovrigt/2020-2-6600.pdf.

57 Gender Identity Development Service, "Evidence Base," https://gids.nhs.uk/professionals/evidence-base/.

58 Polly Carmichael et al., "Short-Term Outcomes of Pubertal Suppression in a Selected Cohort of 12 to 15 Year Old Young People With Persistent Gender Dysphoria in the UK," *PLoS One*, (February 2021), https://journals.plos.org/plosone/article?id=10.1371/journal.pone.0243894.

59 Cecilia Dhejne et al., "Long-Term Follow-Up of Transsexual Persons Undergoing Sex Reassignment Surgery: Cohort Study in Sweden," *PLoS One*, (February 2011), https://journals.plos.org/plosone/article?id=10.1371/journal.pone.0016885.

60 Annelou L C de Vries et al., "Young Adult Psychological Outcome After Puberty Suppression and Gender Reassignment," *Pediatrics* 134, no. 4 (October 2014), https://pubmed.ncbi.nlm.nih.gov/25201798/.

61 Daniela Danna, "Gender-Affirming Model Still Based on 2014 Faulty Dutch Study," *AG About Gender - International Journal of Gender Studies* 10, no. 19 (June 2021), https://riviste.unige.it/index.php/aboutgender/article/view/1169.

62   Annelou L.C. de Vries, "Challenges in Timing Puberty Suppression for Gender-Nonconforming Adolescents," *Pediatrics* 146, no. 4 (October 2020): e2020010611.

63   See the original article for citation: https://www.skeptic.com/reading_room/trans-matters-overview-debate-research-policies/.

64   Carmichael et al., "Short-Term Outcomes of Pubertal Suppression in a Selected Cohort of 12- to 15-Year-Old Young People with Persistent Gender Dysphoria in the UK."

65   Ahmed Elhakeem et al., "Association Between Age at Puberty and Bone Accrual From 10 to 25 Years of Age," *JAMA Netw Open* 2, no. 8 (August 2019), https://jamanetwork.com/journals/jamanetworkopen/fullarticle/2747698.

66   Philip J. Cheng et al., "Fertility Concerns of the Transgender Patient," *Transl Androl Urol* 8, no. 3 (June 2019): 209-18.

67   Roberto D'Angelo, "Psychiatry's Ethical Involvement in Gender-Affirming Care," *Australas Psychiatry* 26, no. 5 (October 2018): 460-63.

68   Claudia Haupt et al., "Antiandrogen or Estradiol Treatment or Both During Hormone Therapy in Transitioning Transgender Women," *Cochrane Database of Systematic Reviews* 11, no. 11 (November 2020), https://pubmed.ncbi.nlm.nih.gov/33251587/.

69   M.E. Kerckhof et al., "Prevalence of Sexual Dysfunctions in Transgender Persons: Results from the ENIGI Follow-Up Study," *J Sex Med* 16, no. 12 (December 2019): 2018-29.

70   Paulette Cutruzzula Dreher et al., "Complications of the Neovagina in Male-To-Female Transgender Surgery: A Systematic Review and Meta-Analysis with Discussion of Management," *Clin Anat* 31, no. 2 (March 2018): 191-99.

71   N. Nassiri et al., "Urethral Complications After Gender Reassignment Surgery: A Systematic Review," *Int J. Impot Res* 33, no. 8 (December 2020): 793-800..

72   Talal Alzahrani et al., "Cardiovascular Disease Risk Factors and Myocardial Infarction in the Transgender Population," *Circulation* 12, no. 4 (April 2019), https://www.ahajournals.org/doi/10.1161/CIRCOUTCOMES.119.005597.

73   Elahe Fallahtafti et al., "Happiness and Mental Health in Pre-Operative and Post-Operative Transsexual People," *Iran J Public Health* 48, no. 12 (December 2019): 2277-284.

74   Valeria P. Bustos et al., "Regret after Gender-Affirmation Surgery: A Systematic Review and Meta-Analysis of Prevalence," *Plastic and Reconstructive Surgery—Global Open* 9, no. 3 (March 2021): e3477.

75   Pablo Expósito-Campos and Roberto D'Angelo, "Letter to the Editor: Regret after Gender-Affirmation Surgery: A Systematic Review and Meta-Analysis of Prevalence," *Plastic and Reconstructive Surgery—Global Open* 9, no. 11 (November 2021): e3951.

76   Lisa Marchiano, "Gender Detransition: A Case Study," *J Anal Psychol* 66, no. 4 (September 2021), https://pubmed.ncbi.nlm.nih.gov/34758129/.

77   Lisa Littman, "Individuals Treated for Gender Dysphoria with Medical and/or Surgical Transition Who Subsequently Detransitioned: A Survey of 100 Detran-

sitioners," *Arch Sex Behav* 50, no. 8 (November 2021), https://pubmed.ncbi.nlm.nih.gov/34665380/.

78 Jack Drescher, Ariel Shidlo, and Michael Schroeder, *Sexual Conversion Therapy: Ethical, Clinical and Research Perspectives* 5, no. 3–4 (CRC Press, 2002).

79 Movement Advancement Project, "Conversion 'Therapy' Laws," https://www.lgbtmap.org/equality-maps/conversion_therapy.

80 Roberto D'Angelo et al., "One Size Does Not Fit All: In Support of Psychotherapy for Gender Dysphoria," *Archives of Sexual Behavior* 50, no. 1 (January 2021): 7-16.

81 Their website: https://www.genderexploratory.com/about/.

82 Jason J. Westwater, Elizabeth A. Riley, and Gregory M. Peterson, "What About the Family in Youth Gender Diversity? A Literature Review," *Int J Transgend* 20, no. 4 (2019): 351-70.

Chapter 37

1 Originally published by *Skeptic Magazine* and adapted here with permission: Kevin McCaffree, "When Secularism Becomes a Religion: The Alt-Left, the Alt-Right, and Moral Righteousness," *Skeptic Magazine*, Fall 2017, https://go.gale.com/ps/i.do?id=GALE%7CA520714005&sid=googleScholar&v=2.1&it=r&linkaccess=abs&issn=10639330&p=AONE&sw=w&userGroupName=anon%7E2beb6548. Note: This book is intended for a general audience and thus throughout we have tried to minimize footnotes in some chapters for purposes of readability—for the full set of footnotes/citations/hyperlinks for each chapter, see the original source.

2 Michael Schaub, "Happy Birthday, Aldous Huxley!," *Los Angeles Times*, July 26, 2016, https://www.latimes.com/books/jacketcopy/la-et-jc-aldous-huxley-20160726-snapstory.html.

3 T. W. Adorno, *The Culture Industry: Selected Essays on Mass Culture* (New York: Routledge, 2001); T. W. Adorno, E. Frenkel-Brunswick, D. J. Levinson, and R. N. Sanford, *The Authoritarian Personality* (New York: Harper & Brothers, 1950).

4 Herbert Marcuse, "Repressive Tolerance," in *A Critique of Pure Tolerance*, ed. R. P. Wolff, B. Moore, and H. Marcuse (Boston: Beacon Press, 1965), 81–123.

5 U.S. Census Bureau, "Census Bureau Statistics Measure Equity Gaps Across Demographic Groups," Census.gov, June 10, 2022, https://www.census.gov/library/stories/2021/09/understanding-equity-through-census-bureau-data.html.

6 U.S. Census Bureau, "Census Bureau Statistics Measure Equity Gaps Across Demographic Groups."

7 Kimberlé Williams Crenshaw, "Black Women Still in Defense of Ourselves," *The Nation*, October 5, 2011, https://www.thenation.com/article/archive/black-women-still-defense-ourselves/.

8 D. A. Bell, "Who's Afraid of Critical Race Theory?" *University of Illinois Law Review* 4 (1995): 893–910.

9 R. Delgado and J. Stefancic, *Critical Race Theory: An Introduction* (New York: New York University Press, 2001).

10 M. Alexander, *The New Jim Crow: Mass Incarceration in the Age of Colorblindness* (New York: The New Press, 2012).

11 P. H. Collins, "Intersectionality's Definitional Dilemmas," *Annual Review of Sociology* 41 (2105): 1–20.

12 P. McIntosh, "White Privilege: Unpacking the Invisible Knapsack," *Peace and Freedom* (July/August 1989): 10–12.

13 S. Sontag, "What's Happening to America?" *Partisan Review* 34 (1967): 57–58.

Chapter 38

1 Originally published by *The Conversation* and adapted here with permission: Joshua Hart, "Something's Going On Here: Building a Comprehensive Profile of Conspiracy Thinkers," September 24, 2018, https://theconversation.com/somethings-going-on-here-building-a-comprehensive-profile-of-conspiracy-thinkers-101287. Note: This book is intended for a general audience and thus throughout we have tried to minimize footnotes in some chapters for purposes of readability—for the full set of footnotes/citations/hyperlinks for each chapter, see the original source.

Chapter 39

1 Originally published by *The Conversation* and adapted here with permission: Carlos Diaz Ruiz, "I Watched Hundreds of Flat-Earth Videos to Learn How Conspiracy Theories Spread—And What It Could Mean for Fighting Disinformation," *The Conversation*, June 27, 2022, https://theconversation.com/i-watched-hundreds-of-flat-earth-videos-to-learn-how-conspiracy-theories-spread-and-what-it-could-mean-for-fighting-disinformation-184589. Note: This book is intended for a general audience and thus throughout we have tried to minimize footnotes in some chapters for purposes of readability—for the full set of footnotes/citations/hyperlinks for each chapter, see the original source.

2 Farleigh Dickinson University, "FDU Poll: 2020 Election Conspiracy Believers More Likely to Embrace Bigfoot, Flat Earth," May 5, 2022, https://www.fdu.edu/news/fdu-poll-2020-election-conspiracies-more-likely-to-embrace-bigfoot-flat-earth/.

3 Farleigh Dickinson University, "FDU Poll: 2020 Election Conspiracy Believers More Likely to Embrace Bigfoot, Flat Earth."

4 Carlos Diaz Ruiz and Tomas Nilsson, "Disinformation and Echo Chambers: How Disinformation Circulates on Social Media Through Identity-Driven Controversies," *Journal of Public Policy & Marketing* 42, no. 1 (May 2022).

5 Ruiz, "I Watched Hundreds of Flat-Earth Videos to Learn How Conspiracy Theories Spread—And What It Could Mean for Fighting Disinformation."

Chapter 40

1 Originally published by *Skeptic Magazine* and adapted here with permission: Guy Elgat, "'Prove that I am Wrong!' What QAnon, Descartes, and Brains in Vats Have in Common," *Skeptic Magazine*, https://pocketmags.com/skeptic-magazine/244. Note: This book is intended for a general audience and thus throughout we have tried to minimize footnotes in some chapters for purposes of readability—for the full set of footnotes/citations/hyperlinks for each chapter, see the original source.

2 See video at https://www.youtube.com/watch?v=3dGVXmuLmEM.

3 René Descartes, *Descartes: Philosophical Writings*, Translated and edited by Elizabeth Anscombe and Peter Thomas Geach (Indianapolis, IN: Bobbs-Merrill Educational Publishing, 1971).

4 Descartes, *Descartes: Philosophical Writings*, 65.

Chapter 41

1 Originally published by *The Bulwark* and adapted here with permission: Jim Swift, "The Bogus Protest, the House Race, and the MAGA Grocer," *The Bulwark*, February 2, 2022, https://www.thebulwark.com/the-bogus-protest-the-house-race-and-the-maga-grocer/. Note: This book is intended for a general audience and thus throughout we have tried to minimize footnotes in some chapters for purposes.

2 Anthony Sabatini wrote this on Twitter on February 1, 2022: https://twitter.com/AnthonySabatini/status/1488609322531708940.

3 Bob Hazen, "Claims About Migrant Workers Seen at Maitland Hotel Debunked," WESH 2, January 31, 2022, https://www.wesh.com/article/maitland-hotel-migrant-workers/38941416#.

4 On January 30, 2022, Anthony Sabatini shared the video with his own message: "BREAKING: Hundreds of illegals were just SHIPPED into my congressional district yesterday—dropped off in Maitland We MUST stop & DEPORT them immediately—state law enforcement must be activated by @GovRonDeSantis ASAP Florida should NOT ask the federal government for permission!": https://twitter.com/AnthonySabatini/status/1487793599551279104.

5 Sabatini posted this on Twitter on January 30, 2022: https://twitter.com/AnthonySabatini/status/1487817303165128711.

6 Sabatini posted this on Twitter on January 30, 2022: https://twitter.com/AnthonySabatini/status/1487834067571814406.

7 Liggett posted this on Facebook on January 30, 2022, https://www.facebook.com/LiggettforCongress/posts/386374943397757.

8 Heath posted this on Twitter on January 31, 2022: https://twitter.com/CHeathWFTV/status/1488208167553191942.

9 He did so on Twitter on January 30, 2022: https://twitter.com/AnthonySabatini/status/1487817303165128711.

10 USA Facts, "Temporary Agricultural Visas Increase in 2020, Despite Pandemic," April 23, 2021, https://usafacts.org/articles/temporary-h2a-agricultural-visas-increase-in-2020-despite-pandemic/.

11 "Best Worst Bus Trip to an Insurrection," *Naples Florida Weekly*, May 6, 2021, https://naples.floridaweekly.com/articles/best-worst-bus-trip-to-an-insurrection/.

12 Ines Novacic, "Undocumented Farmworker Families Face Uncertain Fate," CBS News, November 2, 2016, https://www.cbsnews.com/news/undocumented-farmworker-families-immigration-reform/.

Chapter 42

1 This piece was originally published by *The Conversation* and is adapted here with permission: Adam G. Klein, "How To Fight Holocaust Denial in Social Media—With the Evidence of What Really Happened," *The Conversation*, December 3, 2020, https://theconversation.com/how-to-fight-holocaust-denial-in-social-media-with-the-evidence-of-what-really-happened-150719. Note: This book is intended for a general audience and thus throughout we have tried to minimize footnotes in some chapters for purposes of readability—for the full set of footnotes/citations/hyperlinks for each chapter, see the original source.

2 Claims Conference, "First-Ever 50-State Survey on Holocaust Knowledge of American Millennials and Gen Z Reveals Shocking Results," https://www.claimscon.org/millennial-study/.

3 Jason Murdock, "Bill Gates Dismisses Parler App, Says It's 'Great' for People Who Want Holocaust Denial," *Newsweek*, November 19, 2020, https://www.newsweek.com/bill-gates-parler-app-social-media-holocaust-denial-crazy-content-1548645.

4 History Unfolded, "Eisenhower Asks Congress and Press to Witness Nazi Horrors," https://newspapers.ushmm.org/events/eisenhower-asks-congress-and-press-to-witness-nazi-horrors.

Chapter 43

1 Originally published by the *Journal of Controversial Ideas* and adapted here with permission: D. Abbot et al., "In Defense of Merit in Science," *Journal of Controversial Ideas* 3, no. 1 (April 2023): 1–26, https://journalofcontroversialideas.org/article/3/1/236.

2 Authors include: D. Abbot, A. Bikfalvi, A.L. Bleske-Rechek, W. Bodmer, P. Boghossian, C.M. Carvalho, J. Ciccolini, J.A. Coyne, J. Gauss, P.M.W. Gill, S. Jitomirskaya, L. Jussim, A.I. Krylov, G.C. Loury, L. Maroja, J.H. McWhorter, S. Moosavi, P. Nayna Schwerdtle, J. Pearl, M.A. Quintanilla-Tornel, H.F. Schaefer III, P.R. Schreiner, P. Schwerdtfeger, D. Shechtman, M. Shifman, J. Tanzman, B.L. Trout, A. Warshel, and J.D. West.

3 Y. N. Harari, *Homo Deus: A Brief History of Tomorrow* (New York: Harper, 2017); S. Pinker, *The Better Angels of Our Nature* (New York: Viking Books, 2011); and S. Pinker, *Enlightenment Now: The Case for Reason, Science, Humanism and Progress* (New York: Penguin

Books, 2018). .

4 Harari, *Homo Deus: A Brief History of Tomorrow.*

5 Harari, *Homo Deus: A Brief History of Tomorrow*; S. Pinker, *The Better Angels of Our Nature*; and Pinker, *Enlightenment Now.*

6 "Postmodernism," *Stanford Encyclopedia of Philosophy,* https://plato.stanford.edu/entries/postmodernism/; "Critical Theory," *Stanford Encyclopedia of Philosophy*, https://plato.stanford.edu/entries/critical-theory/; "Critical Race Theory," *Encyclopedia Britannica*, https://www.britannica.com/topic/critical-race-theory. See also file:///C:/Users/David/Downloads/In%20Defense%20of%20Merit%20in%20Science-Supplementary.pdf for a compilation of quotes from scholarly sources and academic advocates of postmodernism and critical theories; J.F. Lyotard, *The Postmodern Condition: A Report on Knowledge* (Minneapolis: University of Minnesota Press, 1984); R. Delgado and J. Stefancic, *Critical Race Theory. An Introduction* (New York: New York University Press, 2001); H. Pluckrose and J. A. Lindsay, *Cynical Theories: How Activist Scholarship Made Everything about Race, Gender, and Identity—and Why This Harms Everybody* (Durham, NC: Pitchstone Publishing, 2020); H. Pluckrose, "What Do We Mean by Critical Social Justice," *Counterweight* (2021); Postmodernism and CSJ are broad intellectual enterprises with a literature comprising thousands of books and millions of academic papers and essays. Thus, it is impossible to critique postmodernism or CSJ in toto, and accordingly, we do not attempt to do so in this paper. Indeed, we do not advocate for a wholesale rejection of the postmodern or CSJ perspective. Rather, the purpose of our commentary is to defend and advance the importance of merit in science.

7 We use the term "merit" to mean the rigor, importance, and validity of a scientific idea or proposition or the accomplishments of an individual.

8 Pluckrose and Lindsay, *Cynical Theories*; Pluckrose, *What Do We Mean by Critical Social Justice.*

9 Harari, *Homo Deus: A Brief History of Tomorrow*; Pinker, *The Better Angels of Our Nature*; Pinker, *Enlightenment Now: The Case for Reason, Science, Humanism and Progress.*

10 J. Rauch, *The Constitution of Knowledge* (Washington, DC: Brookings, 2021).

11 J. Savolainen, P.J. Casey, J. McBrayer, and P. Nayna Schwerdtle, "Positionality and Its Problems: Questioning the Value of Reflexivity Statements in Research," *Perspectives on Psychological Science* (2023), https://journals.sagepub.com/doi/10.1177/17456916221144988.

12 R.K. Merton, *The Sociology of Science: Theoretical and Empirical Investigations* (Chicago,IL: The University of Chicago Press, 1973).

13 Rauch, *The Constitution of Knowledge.*

14 H.E. Longino, *Science as Social Knowledge* (Princeton, NJ: Princeton University Press, 2020).

15 Rauch, *The Constitution of Knowledge.*

16 Longino, *Science as Social Knowledge.*

17 Rauch, *The Constitution of Knowledge*; Merton, *The Sociology of Science.*

18 Pluckrose and Lindsay, *Cynical Theories;* Rauch, *The Constitution of Knowledge*; and A. Sullivan, "Removing the Bedrock of Liberalism," *The Weekly Dish* (2021), https:// andrewsullivan.substack.com/p/removing-the-bedrock-of-liberalism-826.

19 "Postmodernism," *Stanford Encyclopedia of Philosophy*; "Critical Theory," *Stanford Encyclopedia of Philosophy*; "Critical Race Theory," *Encyclopedia Britannica*; Lyotard, *The Postmodern Condition: A Report on Knowledge.*

20 "Postmodernism," *Stanford Encyclopedia of Philosophy*; "Critical Theory," *Stanford Encyclopedia of Philosophy*; "Critical Race Theory," *Encyclopedia Britannica*; Pluckrose and Lindsay, *Cynical Theories*; Rauch, *The Constitution of Knowledge*; and Sullivan, "Removing the Bedrock of Liberalism."

21 "Postmodernism," *Stanford Encyclopedia of Philosophy*; "Critical Theory," *Stanford Encyclopedia of Philosophy*; "Critical Race Theory," *Encyclopedia Britannica.*

22 Merton, *The Sociology of Science.*

23 J. Mervis, "U.S. Science No Longer Leads the World. Here's How Top Advisers Say the Nation Should Respond," *Science* (2022), https://www.science.org/content/ article/u-s-science-no-longer-leads-world-here-s-how-top-advisers-say-nation-should-respond?utm_source=sfmc&utm_medium=email&utm_campaign=WeeklyLatest-News&utm_content=alert&et_cid=4083470; P.R. Josephson, *Totalitarian Science and Technology* (Amherst, NY: Humanity Books, 2005); L.R. Graham, *Science, Philosophy, and Human Behavior in the Soviet Union* (New York: Columbia University Press, 1991); S. Zatravkin and E. Vishlenkova, "Early Soviet Medicine: Statistical and Narrative Utopias," *Kwartalnik Historii Nauki i Techniki* 64: 83–106 (2019), https://ejournals.eu/czasopismo/ kwartalnik-historii-nauki-i-techniki/artykul/early-soviet-medicine-digital-and-narrative-utopias; and A.I. Krylov, "The Peril of Politicizing Science," *J. Phys. Chem. Lett.* 12: 5371–76 (2021), https://pubs.acs.org/doi/10.1021/acs.jpclett.1c01475.

24 A. Loeb, "Benefits of Diversity," *Nat. Phys.* 10: 616–17 (2014), https://www.nature. com/articles/nphys3089; M. Carey, M. Jackson, A. Antonello, and J. Rushing, "Glaciers, Gender, and Science: A Feminist Glaciology Framework for Global Environmental Change Research," *Progress in Human Geography*, 40: 770–93 (2016), https://journals. sagepub.com/doi/abs/10.1177/0309132515623368. As part of Grievance Studies Affair, the following paper was almost accepted ("revise and resubmit status") into the Women's Studies International Forum: M. Gonzalez (pseudonym), "Stars, Planets, and Gender: A Framework for a Feminist Astronomy."

25 A. Wooldridge, *The Aristocracy of Talent: How Meritocracy Made the Modern World* (UK: Penguin, 2021); D.N. McCloskey, "The Great Enrichment: A Humanistic and Social Scientific Account," *Social Science History* 40: 583–98 (2016), https://www.cambridge. org/core/journals/social-science-history/article/abs/great-enrichment-a-humanistic-and-social-scientific-account/0B1B61EB978AF48709A7A1CAC498389C.

26 K. Herzog, "What Happens When Doctors Can't Tell the Truth?" *Common Sense* (2021),   https://www.thefp.com/p/what-happens-when-doctors-cant-speak?utm_ source=url; S. Satel, "Race for the Vaccine," *Persuasion* (2020), https://www.persuasion. community/p/race-for-the-vaccine?utm_source=url; S. Satel, "When Therapists Become Activists," *Persuasion* (2021), https://www.persuasion.community/p/when-therapists-become-activists; and S. Satel, "What Is Happening to My Profession?" *Quillette*

(2021), https://quillette.com/2021/11/30/what-is-happening-to-my-profession/.

27 Digest of Education Statistics, National Center for Education Statistics (NCES), the U.S. Department of Education (2021), https://nces.ed.gov/programs/digest/d21/tables/dt21_318.10.asp.

28 San Francisco Declaration on Research Assessment, https://sfdora.org/read/.

29 Josephson *Totalitarian Science and Technology*; Graham, *Science, Philosophy, and Human Behavior in the Soviet Union*; and Krylov, "The Peril of Politicizing Science."

30 Graham, *Science, Philosophy, and Human Behavior in the Soviet Union.*

31 Graham, *Science, Philosophy, and Human Behavior in the Soviet Union.*

32 L. Maroja, "Self-Censorship on Campus is Bad for Science," *The Atlantic* (2019), https://www.theatlantic.com/ideas/archive/2019/05/self-censorship-campus-bad-science/589969/; K. Herzog, "Med Schools Are Now Denying Biological Sex," *Common Sense* (2021), https://www.thefp.com/p/med-schools-are-now-denying-biological.

33 Krylov, "The Peril of Politicizing Science."

34 Krylov, "The Peril of Politicizing Science."

35 S. Ritchie, "Science Is Political – and That's a Bad Thing," *Science Fictions* (2022), https://www.sciencefictions.org/p/science-is-political?s=r.

36 P. Deift, S. Jitomirskaya, and S. Klainerman, "As US Schools Prioritize Diversity Over Merit, China Is Becoming the World's STEM Leader," *Quillette* (2021), https://quillette.com/2021/08/19/as-us-schools-prioritize-diversity-over-merit-china-is-becoming-the-worlds-stem-leader/; L. Krauss, "Indigenous Myth and Science: From Egypt to New Zealand," *Critical Mass* (2022), https://lawrencekrauss.substack.com/p/indigenous-myth-and-science-from?s=r; Association of American Medical Colleges, *Diversity, Equity, and Inclusion Competencies Across the Learning Continuum* (Washington, DC: AAMC New and Emerging Areas in Medicine Series, 2022), https://store.aamc.org/downloadable/download/link/id/MC4zMzA1MTgwMCAxNjU3ODM1NTg-1MTQxNTg3NTkxNTU0OTE0NDI%2C.

37 Herzog, "What Happens When Doctors Can't Tell the Truth?"; Satel, Race for the Vaccine; Satel, "When Therapists Become Activists"; Satel, "What is Happening to My Profession?"; The American Medical Association, Advancing Health Equity: Guide to Language, Narratives, and Concepts, (2021), https://www.ama-assn.org/system/files/ama-aamc-equity-guide.pdf; American Psychological Association, "Apology to People of Color for APA's Role in Promoting, Perpetuating, and Failing to Challenge Racism, Racial Discrimination, and Human Hierarchy in U.S.," Resolution adopted by the APA Council of Representative (2021), https://www.apa.org/about/policy/racism-apology; M. Hellowell and P. Nayna Schwerdtle, "Powerful ideas? Decolonisation and the Future of Global Health," *BMJ Global Health* 7: e006924 (2022), https://gh.bmj.com/content/7/1/e006924.

38 Hellowell and Schwerdtle, "Powerful ideas? Decolonisation and the Future of Global Health."

39 L. Nordling, "How Decolonization Could Reshape South African Science," *Nature*

554: 159–62 (2018), https://www.nature.com/articles/d41586-018-01696-w.

40 J. Sun et al., "A Systematic Analysis of FDA-Approved Anticancer Drugs," *BMC Syst. Biol.* 11, art. 87 (2017), https://bmcsystbiol.biomedcentral.com/articles/10.1186/s12918-017-0464-7.

41 M.K. Parvez and V. Rishi, "Herb Drug Interactions and Hepatotoxicity," *Curr. Drug Metab.* 20: 275–82 (2019), Herb-Drug Interactions and Hepatotoxicity | Bentham Science (eurekaselect.com).

42 S.M. McFadden, J. Demeke, D. Dada, L. Wilton et al., "Confidence and Hesitancy During the Early Rollout of COVID19 Vaccines Among Black, Hispanic, and Undocumented Immigrant Communities: A Review," *J. Urban Health* 99: 3–14 (2022), https://link.springer.com/article/10.1007/s11524-021-00588-1.

43 Mervis, "U.S. Science No Longer Leads the World. Here's How Top Advisers Say the Nation Should Respond."

44 H. Mac Donald, "The NIH's Diversity Obsession Subverts Science," *Wall Street Journal* (2021), https://www.wsj.com/articles/the-nihs-diversity-obsession-subverts-science-11625090811; A. Cho, "At DOE, Efforts to Address Climate and Diversity Dovetail," *Science* 372: 1379 (2021), https://www.science.org/doi/10.1126/science.372.6549.1379; "Promoting Inclusive and Equitable Research (PIER) Plans," Department of Energy Office of Science (2022), https://science.osti.gov/grants/Applicant-and-Awardee-Resources/PIER-Plans; M. Higgins, "Minority Professor Denied Grants Because he Hires on Merit: 'People are Afraid to Think,'" *National Post* (2021), https://nationalpost.com/news/canada/minority-professor-denied-grants-because-he-hires-on-merit-people-are-afraid-to-think."

45 A. Thompson, "The University's New Loyalty Oath," *Wall Street Journal* (2019), https://www.wsj.com/articles/the-universitys-new-loyalty-oath-11576799749; J. Coyne, "When Commitment to Diversity Outweighs Teaching and Research in a Biology Job" (2021), https://whyevolutionistrue.com/2021/09/28/an-ad-for-a-biology-professor-in-which-commitment-to-diversity-far-outweighs-commitment-to-teaching-and-research/; "Life Science Jobs at Berkeley Give Precedence to Candidates' Diversity and Inclusion Statements" (2019), https://whyevolutionistrue.com/2019/12/31/life-science-jobs-at-berkeley-with-hiring-giving-precedence-to-diversity-and-inclusion-statements/; "A Thread about University DEI Statements" (2023), Why Evolution Is True, https://whyevolutionistrue.com/2023/01/24/a-thread-about-universty-dei-statements/; J. Poff, "UC Santa Cruz Prescreens Faculty Job Applications Based on Mandatory Diversity Statements," *Washington Examiner* (2021), https://www.washingtonexaminer.com/news/1373763/uc-santa-cruz-prescreens-faculty-job-applications-based-on-mandatory-diversity-statements/; C. Flaherty, "The DEI Pathway to Promotion," *Inside Higher Ed.* (2021), https://www.insidehighered.com/news/2021/05/14/iupui-creates-path-promotion-and-tenure-based-dei-work; C. Flaherty, "Where DEI Work Is Faculty Work," *Inside Higher Ed.* (2022), https://www.insidehighered.com/news/2022/04/01/u-illinois-require-diversity-statements-tenure; and M. Wente, "At Canadian Universities, Race and Gender Quotas Have Become a Way of Life," *Quillette* (2022), https://quillette.com/2022/12/02/at-canadian-universities-race-and-gender-quotas-have-become-a-way-of-life/.

46   B. Leiter, "Diversity Statements Are Still in Legal Peril," *The Chronicle of Higher Ed.* (2022), https://www.chronicle.com/article/diversity-statements-are-still-in-legal-peril?cid2=gen_login_refresh&cid=gen_sign_in; Gail Heriot and Maimon Schwarzchild, eds., *A Dubious Expediency: How Race Preferences Damage Higher Education* (New York: Encounter Books, 2021); J.L. Riley, "A Chance to Remove Race from College Admissions," *Wall Street Journal* (2022), https://www.wsj.com/articles/chance-to-remove-race-college-admissions-supreme-court-racial-preference-test-score-affirmative-action-11643151400.

47   Q&A: Stuart Schmill on MIT's decision to reinstate the SAT/ACT requirement, *MIT News* (2022), https://news.mit.edu/2022/stuart-schmill-sat-act-requirement-0328; N.R. Kuncel and S.A. Hezlett, "Standardized Tests Predict Graduate Students' Success," *Science* 315: 1080–81 (2007), https://www.science.org/doi/10.1126/science.1136618; R. Henderson, "Don't End Aptitude Tests," *Persuasion* (2021), https://www.persuasion.community/p/dont-end-aptitude-tests; and L.M. Leslie, "Diversity Initiative Effectiveness: A Typological Theory of Unintended Consequences," *Academy of Management Review* 44: 538 (2019), https://journals.aom.org/doi/abs/10.5465/amr.2017.0087.

48   Deift, Jitomirskaya, and Klainerman, "As US Schools Prioritize Diversity Over Merit, China Is Becoming the World's STEM Leader"; Heriot and Schwarzchild, *A Dubious Expediency;* Riley, "A Chance to Remove Race from College Admissions"; R. Henderson, "Don't End Aptitude Tests"; L.M. Leslie, "Diversity Initiative Effectiveness: A Typological Theory of Unintended Consequences," *Academy of Management Review* 44: 538 (2019), https://journals.aom.org/doi/abs/10.5465/amr.2017.0087; P. Arcidiacono, E.M. Aucejo, and K. Spenner, "What Happens After Enrollment? An Analysis of the Time Path of Racial Differences in GPA and Major Choice," *IZA J. of Labor Econ. 1,* art. 5 (2012), https://link.springer.com/article/10.1186/2193-8997-1-5; A. Chung and L. Hurley, "U.S. Supreme Court to Hear Challenge to Race Conscious College Admissions," Reuters (2022), https://www.reuters.com/legal/government/us-supreme-court-hear-challenge-race-conscious-college-admissions-2022-01-24/; P. S. Arcidiacono, *Students for Fair Admissions, Inc. v. Harvard,* No. 14cv14176ADB (D. Mass), https://lawyerscommittee.org/wp-content/uploads/2020/07/Docket-413_SFFA-Memo-in-Sppt-of-SJ.pdf.

49   Thompson, "The University's New Loyalty Oath"; S.T. Stevens, L. Jussim, and N. Honeycutt, "Scholarship Suppression: Theoretical Perspectives and Emerging Trends," *Societies* 10: 82 (2020), https://www.mdpi.com/2075-4698/10/4/82; A.I. Krylov, J.S. Tanzman, G. Frenking, and P.M.W. Gill, "Scientists Must Resist Cancel Culture," *Nachrichten aus der Chemie* 70: 12–14 (2022), https://onlinelibrary.wiley.com/doi/10.1002/nadc.20224120702; L. Krauss, "The New Scientific Method: Identity Politics," *Wall Street Journal* (2021), https://www.wsj.com/articles/the-new-scientific-method-identity-politics-11620581262; E. Kaufman, "Academic Freedom in Crisis: Punishment, Political Discrimination, and Self-Censorship": CSPI Report No. 2, The Center for the Study of Partisanship and Ideology (2021), https://cspicenter.org/reports/academicfreedom.

50 Stevens, Jussim, and Honeycutt, "Scholarship Suppression: Theoretical Perspectives and Merging Trends"; Krylov, Tanzman, Frenking, and Gill, "Scientists Must Resist Cancel Culture"; and Kaufman, "Academic Freedom in Crisis: Punishment, Political

Discrimination, and Self-Censorship."

51 Krylov, "The Peril of Politicizing Science"; Ritchie, "Science Is Political – and That's a Bad Thing"; The degree of capture varies among institutions. Examples of essentially complete capture include the University of San Diego (see "The Woke Takeover at the University of San Diego," https://princetoniansforfreespeech.org/) and Evergreen State University (see "How Activists Took Control of a University: The Case Study of Evergreen State," https://quillette.com/2017/12/18/activists-took-control-university-case-study-evergreen-state/).

52 Hellowell and Schwerdtle, "Powerful ideas? Decolonisation and the Future of Global Health."

53 D.M. Kahan, "Fixing the Communications Failure," *Nature* 463: 296–97 (2010), https://www.nature.com/articles/463296a; D.M. Kahan, "What is the 'Science of Science Communication?'" *J. Sci. Comm.* 14: 1–10 (2015), https://papers.ssrn.com/sol3/papers.cfm?abstract_id=2562025.

54 J.M. Horowitz, "Americans See Advantages and Challenges in Country's Growing Racial and Ethnic Diversity," Pew Research Center (2019), https://www.pewresearch.org/social-trends/2019/05/08/americans-see-advantages-and-challenges-in-countrys-growing-racial-and-ethnic-diversity/; N. Graf, "Most Americans Say Colleges Should Not Consider Race or Ethnicity in Admissions," Pew Research Center (2019), https://www.pewresearch.org/short-reads/2019/02/25/most-americans-say-colleges-should-not-consider-race-or-ethnicity-in-admissions/.

55 J. Coyne, "Pinker vs. the AAAS on the Politicization of Climate Change—and Science in General," Why Evolution Is True (2022), https://whyevolutionistrue.com/2022/05/03/pinker-vs-the-aaas-on-the-politicization-of-climate-change/.

56 "Postmodernism," *Stanford Encyclopedia of Philosophy*; "Critical Theory," *Stanford Encyclopedia of Philosophy*; "Critical Race Theory," *Encyclopedia Britannica*. See supplemental material for a compilation of quotes from scholarly sources and academic advocates of postmodernism and critical theories; Lyotard, *The Postmodern Condition: A Report on Knowledge*; J. Stefancic, *Critical Race Theory: An Introduction*; Pluckrose and Lindsay, *Cynical Theories*; and A. Sullivan, "Removing the Bedrock of Liberalism."

57 Mervis, "U.S. Science No Longer Leads the World"; Herzog, "What Happens When Doctors Can't Tell the Truth?"; Satel, "Race for the Vaccine"; Satel, "When Therapists Become Activists"; Satel, "What is Happening to My Profession?"; Association of American Medical Colleges, *Diversity, Equity, and Inclusion Competencies Across the Learning Continuum*; and Hellowell and Schwerdtle, "Powerful ideas? Decolonisation and the Future of Global Health."

58 Stevens, Jussim, and Honeycutt, "Scholarship Suppression: Theoretical Perspectives and Merging Trends"; Kaufman, "Academic Freedom in Crisis: Punishment, Political Discrimination, and Self-Censorship"; and P. Boghossian, *Truth Must be the Highest Priority of a University*, in *Ben Ik Wel Woke Genoeg?* ed. M. Harlaar (Gompel & Svacina, 2022).

59 R. Delgado and J. Stefancic, *Critical Race Theory: An Introduction*.

60 R. DiAngelo, *White Fragility: Why It's So Hard for White People to Talk About Racism* (Boston, MA: Beacon Press, 2018); I.X. Kendi, *How to Be an Antiracist* (New York: One

World, 2019).

61 Rauch, *The Constitution of Knowledge;* Sullivan, "Removing the Bedrock of Liberalism."

62 "Postmodernism," *Stanford Encyclopedia of Philosophy*; "Critical Theory," *Stanford Encyclopedia of Philosophy*; "Critical Race Theory," *Encyclopedia Britannica*. See supplemental material for a compilation of quotes from scholarly sources and academic advocates of postmodernism and critical theories; Pluckrose and Lindsay, *Cynical Theories*; Pluckrose, "What Do We Mean by Critical Social Justice"; Rauch, *The Constitution of Knowledge*; and Sullivan, "Removing the Bedrock of Liberalism."

63 R.E. Nisbett and T.D. Wilson, Telling More Than We Can Know: Verbal Reports on Mental Processes," *Psych. Rev.* 84: 231–59 (1977), https://psycnet.apa.org/record/1978-00295-001.

64 Krylov, "The Peril of Politicizing Science."

65 R. Samra and O. Hankivsky, "Adopting an Intersectionality Framework to Address Power and Equity in Medicine," *The Lancet* 397: 857–59 (2020), https://www.thelancet.com/journals/lancet/article/PIIS0140-6736(20)32513-7/fulltext.

66 Josephson, *Totalitarian Science and Technology*; Graham, *Science, Philosophy, and Human Behavior in the Soviet Union*; Krylov, "The Peril of Politicizing Science."

67 Zatravkin and Vishlenkova, "Early Soviet Medicine: Statistical and Narrative Utopias."

68 Zatravkin and Vishlenkova, "Early Soviet Medicine: Statistical and Narrative Utopias."

69 J. Kaiser, "NIH Apologizes for 'Structural Racism,' Pledges Change," *Science* 371 (6533) (2021), https://www.science.org/doi/10.1126/science.371.6533.977.

70 E.O. McGee, "Dismantle Racism in Science," *Science* 375: 937 (2022), https://www.science.org/doi/10.1126/science.abo7849.

71 J. McWhorter, *Woke Racism: How a New Religion Has Betrayed Black America* (New York: Penguin Random House, 2021).

72 T. Sowell, *Discrimination and Disparities* (New York: Basic Books, 2019).

73 Sowell, *Discrimination and Disparities.*

74 M.J. Sandel, *The Tyranny of Merit* (New York: Picador, 2020).

75 D. Markovitz, *The Meritocracy Trap: How America's Foundational Myth Feeds Inequality, Dismantles the Middle Class, and Devours the Elite* (New York: Penguin Press, 2019).

76 Sandel, *The Tyranny of Merit.*

77 Sandel, *The Tyranny of Merit.*

78 R.T. Karcher, "The Chances of a Drafted Baseball Player Making the Major Leagues: A Quantitative Study," *Baseball Research J.* (2017), https://sabr.org/journal/article/the-chances-of-a-drafted-baseball-player-making-the-major-leagues-a-quantitative-study/.

79 E.R. Eide, M.J. Hilmer, and M.H. Showalter, "Is it Where You Go or What You Study? The Relative Influence of College Selectivity and College Major on Earnings," *Contemp. Econ. Policy* 34: 37–46 (2016), https://onlinelibrary.wiley.com/doi/abs/10.1111/coep.12115.

80 Loeb, Benefits of Diversity; Carey, Jackson, Antonello, and Rushing, "Glaciers, Gender, and Science"; Association of American Medical Colleges. *Diversity, Equity, and Inclusion Competencies Across the Learning Continuum*; American Medical Association, *Advancing Health Equity: Guide to Language, Narratives, and Concepts*; Cho, "At DOE, Efforts to Address Climate and Diversity Dovetail"; Samra and Hankivsky, "Adopting an Intersectionality Framework to Address Power and Equity in Medicine"; Kaiser, "NIH Apologizes for 'Structural Racism,' Pledges Change"; McGee, "Dismantle Racism in Science"; J. Mervis, "Can U.S. Physics Overcome its Record of Exclusion? *Science* 375: 950 (2022), https://www.science.org/content/article/why-are-efforts-to-boost-small-number-of-black-us-physicists-failing; J. Mervis, "The Toll of White Privilege," *Science* 375: 952 (2022), https://www.science.org/content/article/how-culture-of-white-privilege-discourages-black-students-from-becoming-physicists; J. Mervis, "Fix the System, not the Students," *Science*: 375: 956 (2022), https://www.science.org/content/article/diversity-researchers-say-fix-system-physics-not-students; Z.S. Wilson-Kennedy et al., "Introducing the Journal of Chemical Education's Special Issue on Diversity, Equity, Inclusion, and Respect in Chemistry Education Research and Practice," *Chem. Ed.* 99: 1–4 (2022), https://pubs.acs.org/doi/10.1021/acs.jchemed.1c01219; A. Ghosh and W.B. Tolman, "Out in Inorganic Chemistry: A Celebration of LGBTQIAPN+ Inorganic Chemists," *Inorg. Chem.* 61: 5435 (2022), https://pubs.acs.org/doi/10.1021/acs.inorgchem.2c00729; "Porphyrin Science by Women," ed. F. Dumoulin, T. Nyokong, and P.J. Brothers, *World Scientific* (2022), https://www.worldscientific.com/worldsci-books/10.1142/11917; M. Nobles, C. Womack, A. Wonkham, and E. Wathuti, "Science Must Overcome Its Racist Legacy: Nature's Guest Editors Speak," *Nature* 606: 225–27 (2022), https://www.nature.com/articles/d41586-022-01527-z?WT.ec_id=-NATURE-20220609&utm_source=nature_etoc&utm_medium=email&utm_campaign=20220609&sap-outbound-id=820336A29B04116A9C175560E-00CFF64FB196F03; *Racism*, a special issue of *Nature* 610 (7932) (2022); Decolonizing Science Toolkit, *Nature* (2022), https://www.nature.com/collections/giaahdbacj: "This collection of resources provides examples of how institutions and scientific departments are recasting curricula and addressing racism's influence"; V. Gewin, "Institutions Must Acknowledge the Racist Roots in Science," *Nature* 612: 178–179 (2022), https://www.nature.com/articles/d41586-022-04123-3; V. Gewin, "Decolonization Should Extend to Collaborations, Authorship and Co-Creation of Knowledge," *Nature* 612: 178 (2022), https://www.nature.com/articles/d41586-022-03822-1; L. Nordling, "Seeding an Anti-Racist Culture at Scotland's Botanical Gardens," *Nature* 611: 835 (2022), https://www.nature.com/articles/d41586-022-03797-z; T. Naidu, "Says Who? Northern Ventriloquism, or Epistemic Disobedience in Global Health Scholarship," *The Lancet* 9: e1332–e1335 (2021), https://www.thelancet.com/journals/langlo/article/PI-IS2214-109X(21)00198-4/fulltext; Statement by the President of the National Academy of Sciences (2020), https://www.nasonline.org/about-nas/leadership/president/diversity-equity-and-inclusion-statement.html; President's Statement on NAE's Commitment to Diversity, Equity, and Inclusion (2020), https://www.nac.edu/234339/Presidents-Statement-on-NAEs-Commitment-to-Diversity-Equity-and-Inclusion;   State-

ment on Racial Equity and the Adverse Effects of Racism by NAM President (2020), https://nam.edu/statement-on-racial-equity-and-the-adverse-effects-of-racism-by-nam-president-victor-j-dzau/; H. Holden Thorp, "Time to Look in the Mirror," *Science* 368: 1161 (2020), https://www.science.org/doi/full/10.1126/science.abd1896?versioned=true; "Systemic Racism: Science Must Listen, Learn and Change. Nature Commits to Working to End Anti-Black Practices in Research," *Nature* 582: 147 (2020), https://www.nature.com/articles/d41586-020-01678-x; "Confronting Racism in Chemistry Journals": An editorial published simultaneously in several ACS journals (JACS, JCTC, ACS Appl. Mater, etc.) (2020), https://pubs.acs.org/doi/10.1021/acs.jctc.0c00614; "Tackling Systemic Racism Requires the System of Science to Change," *Nature* 593: 313 (2021), https://www.nature.com/articles/d41586-021-01312-4; T. McAllister, "50 Reasons Why There Are No Māori in Your Science Department," *J. Global Indigeneity* 6: 1–10 (2022), https://www.journalofglobalindigeneity.com/article/55788-50-reasons-why-there-are-no-maori-in-your-science-department; "Gender Equality, Diversity, Inclusion Post-Corona: Quo Vadis?" Humboldt Foundation Conference (2021), https://www.humboldt-foundation.de/en/explore/newsroom/news/conference-gender-equality-diversity-inclusion-post-corona-quo-vadis; A.A. Berhe et al., "Scientists from Historically Excluded Groups Face a Hostile Obstacle Course," *Nature Geoscience* 15: 2–4 (2022), https://www.nature.com/articles/s41561-021-00868-0; L.K.G. Ackerman-Biegasiewicz et al., "Organic Chemistry: A Retrosynthetic Approach to a Diverse Field," *ACS Cent. Sci.* 6: 1845–850 (2020), https://pubs.acs.org/doi/10.1021/acscentsci.0c01138; S. Davies et al., "Promoting Inclusive Metrics of Success and Impact to Dismantle a Discriminatory Reward System in Science," *PLOS Biol.* 19: e3001282 (2021), https://journals.plos.org/plosbiology/article?id=10.1371/journal.pbio.3001282; L.M. Diele-Viegas, "Potential Solutions for Discrimination in STEM," *Nat. Hum. Behavior* 5: 672–74 (2021), https://www.nature.com/articles/s41562-021-01104-w; M. McNutt and L. Castilllo-Page, "Promoting Diversity and Inclusion in STEMM Starts at the Top," *Nat. Med.* 27: 1864–865 (2021), https://www.nature.com/articles/s41591-021-01496-2?utm_source=NASEM+News+and+Publications&utm_campaign=440581546a-NAP_mail_new_2021_11_15&utm_medium=email&utm_term=0_96101de015-440581546a-101923685&goal=0_96101de015-440581546a-101923685&mc_cid=440581546a; Royal Society of Chemistry, "A Framework for Action in Scientific Publishing," https://www.rsc.org/policy-evidence-campaigns/inclusion-diversity/framework-for-action/; B. Nogrady, "Game-changing Gender Quotas Introduced by Australian Research Agency," *Nature* (2022), https://www.nature.com/articles/d41586-022-03285-4; A.M. Valenzuela-Toro and M. Viglino, "How Latin American Researchers Suffer in Science," *Nature* 598: 374–75 (2021), https://www.nature.com/articles/d41586-021-02601-8; C. Mott and D. Cockayne, "Citation Matters: Mobilizing the Politics of Citation Toward a Practice of 'Conscientious Engagement,'" *Gender, Place, and Culture* 24: 954–73 (2017), https://www.tandfonline.com/doi/abs/10.1080/0966369X.2017.1339022?journalCode=cgpc20; P. Zurn, E.G. Teich, S.C. Simon, J.Z. Kim, and D.S. Bassett, "Supporting Academic Equity in Physics through Citation Diversity," *Comm. Phys.* 5: 240 (2022), https://www.nature.com/articles/s42005-022-00999-9; J.D. Dworkin, K.A. Linn, E.G. Teich, P. Zurn, R.T. Shinohara, and D.S. Bassett, "The Extent and Drivers of Gender Imbalance in Neuroscience Reference Lists," *Nature Neuroscience* 23: 918–26 (2020), https://www.nature.com/articles/s41593-020-0658-y; P.

Zurn, D.S. Bassett, and N.C. Rust, "The Citation Diversity Statement: A Practice of Transparency, A Way of Life," *Trends Cogn. Sci.* 24: 669–72 (2020), https://www.cell.com/trends/cognitive-sciences/abstract/S1364-6613(20)30164-9?_return-nURL=https%3A%2F%2Flinkinghub.elsevier.com%2Fretrieve%2F-pii%2FS1364661320301649%3Fshowall%3Dtrue; S. Else and J.M. Perkel, "The Giant Plan to Track Diversity in Research Journals," *Nature* 602: 566 (2022), https://www.nature.com/articles/d41586-022-00426-7; R. Luna, "The MPI Diversity & Inclusion Committee: Sparking Change" (2020), https://www.mpi.org/blog/article/the-mpi-diversity-inclusion-committee-sparking-change; "#ProgressDiversity: More Diversity for Science," Humboldt Kosmos (2021), https://www.humboldt-foundation.de/en/explore/newsroom/news/progressdiversity-more-diversity-for-science; Alba Declaration on Equity and Inclusion; H. Shen, "Inequality Quantified: Mind the Gender Gap," *Nature* 495: 22–24 (2013), https://www.nature.com/news/inequality-quantified-mind-the-gender-gap-1.12550; S.J. Ceci, S. Kahn, and W.M. Williams, "Stewart-Williams and Halsey Argue Persuasively That Gender Bias Is Just One of Many Causes of Women's Underrepresentation in Science," *Eur. J. Personality* 35: 40–44 (2021), https://journals.sagepub.com/doi/full/10.1177/0890207020976778; S. Stewart-Williams and L.G. Halsey, "Men, Women and STEM: Why the Differences and What Should Be Done?" *Eur. J. Personality* 35: 3–39 (2020), https://journals.sagepub.com/doi/full/10.1177/0890207020962326; The A4BL Antiracist Tenure Letter Working Group, "Equity, Diversity and Inclusion: A Guide for Writing Anti-Racist Tenure and Promotion Letters," *eLife* (2022), https://elifesciences.org/articles/79892; Gender Innovations 2, "How Inclusive Analysis Contributes to Research and Innovation," Luxembourg: Publications Office of the European Union (2020), https://op.europa.eu/en/publication-detail/-/publication/33b4c99f-2e66-11eb-b27b-01aa75ed71a1/language-enhttps://op.europa.eu/en/publication-detail/-/publication/33b-4c99f-2e66-11eb-b27b-01aa75ed71a1/language-en; and European Commission, "Priorities for 2021–2027," https://ec.europa.eu/regional_policy/policy/how/priorities_en.

81 McGee, "Dismantle Racism in Science"; Mervis, "Can U.S. Physics Overcome its Record of Exclusion?"; Mervis, "The Toll of White Privilege"; Mervis, "Fix the System, Not the Students."

82 Wilson-Kennedy et al., "Introducing the Journal of Chemical Education's Special Issue on Diversity, Equity, Inclusion, and Respect in Chemistry Education Research and Practice."

83 Ghosh and Tolman, "Out in Inorganic Chemistry: A Celebration of LGBTQIAPN+ Inorganic Chemists."

84 Dumoulin, Nyokong, and Brothers, "Porphyrin Science by Women."

85 Nobles, Womack, Wonkham, and Wathuti, "Science Must Overcome Its Racist Legacy."

86 *Racism*, a special issue of *Nature*.

87 Lyotard, *The Postmodern Condition*; Pluckrose, *Cynical Theories*.

88 Harari, *Homo Deus: A Brief History of Tomorrow*; Pinker, *The Better Angels of Our Nature*; Digest of Education Statistics, National Center for Education Statistics; Sowell, *Discrim-*

ination and Disparities.

89 Sowell, *Discrimination and Disparities.*

90 Pluckrose, *Cynical Theories*; Sullivan, "Removing the Bedrock of Liberalism."

91 Decolonizing Science Toolkit, *Nature.*

92 V. Gewin, "Institutions Must Acknowledge the Racist Roots in Science."

93 Gewin, "Decolonization Should Extend to Collaborations, Authorship and Co-Creation Of Knowledge.".

94 Nordling, "Seeding an Anti-Racist Culture at Scotland's Botanical Gardens."

95 Krauss, "Indigenous Myth and Science."

96 McAllister, "50 Reasons Why There Are no Māori in Your Science Department."

97 Nordling, "How Decolonization Could Reshape South African Science."

98 Naidu, "Says Who? Northern Ventriloquism, or Epistemic Disobedience in Global Health Scholarship."

99 Hellowell and Schwerdtle, "Powerful ideas? Decolonisation and the Future of Global Health."

100 Statement by the President of the National Academy of Sciences.

101 President's Statement on NAE's Commitment to Diversity, Equity, and Inclusion.

102 Statement on Racial Equity and the Adverse Effects of Racism by NAM President.

103 Kaiser, "NIH Apologizes for 'Structural Racism,' Pledges Change."

104 Thorp, "Time to Look in the Mirror."

105 "Systemic Racism: Science Must Listen, Learn and Change."

106 "Confronting Racism in Chemistry Journals."

107 "Tackling Systemic Racism Requires the System of Science to Change."

108 *Racism*, a special issue of *Nature.*

109 McGee, "Dismantle Racism in Science."

110 Mervis, "Can U.S. Physics Overcome its Record of Exclusion?"

111 Mervis, "The Toll of White Privilege."

112 Mervis, "Fix the System, Not the Students."

113 Sowell, *Discrimination and Disparities.*

114 G.G. Guzman, "Household Income: 2016," U.S. Department of Commerce, Economics and Statistics Administration, U.S. Census Bureau (2017), https://www.census.gov/library/publications/2017/acs/acsbr16-02.html.

115 Sowell, *Discrimination and Disparities.*

116 Nobles, Womack, Wonkham, and Wathuti, "Science Must Overcome Its Racist Legacy: Nature's Guest Editors Speak."

117 *Racism*, a special issue of *Nature*.

118 Berhe et al., "Scientists from Historically Excluded Groups Face a Hostile Obstacle Course."

119 See original article for citation.

120 Herzog, "What Happens When Doctors Can't Tell the Truth?"

121 B. Wispelwey and M. Morse, "An Antiracist Agenda for Medicine," *Boston Review* (2021), https://www.bostonreview.net/articles/michelle-morsebram-wispelwey-what-we-owe-patients-case-medical-reparations.

122 L. Jussim, N. Honeycutt, P. Paresky, A. Careem, D. Finkelstein, and J. Finkelstein, *The Radicalization of the American Academy*, in *The Palgrave Handbook of Left-Wing Extremism*, ed. J.P. Zúquete (New York: Palgrave MacMillan, 2023).

123 The American Medical Association, "Advancing Health Equity."

124 Association of American Medical Colleges, *Diversity, Equity, and Inclusion Competencies Across the Learning Continuum*.

125 American Psychological Association, "Apology to People of Color."

126 Satel, "Race for the Vaccine."

127 McGee, "Dismantle Racism in Science"; Mervis, "Can U.S. Physics Overcome its Record of Exclusion?"; Mervis, "The Toll of White Privilege"; Mervis, "Fix the System, Not the Students"; Wilson-Kennedy et al., "Introducing the Journal of Chemical Education's Special Issue on Diversity, Equity, Inclusion, and Respect in Chemistry Education Research and Practice"; Ghosh and Tolman, "Out in Inorganic Chemistry"; Ackerman Biegasiewicz et al., "Organic Chemistry: A Retrosynthetic Approach to a Diverse Field."; Davies et al., "Promoting Inclusive Metrics of Success and Impact to Dismantle a Discriminatory Reward System in Science"; Diele-Viegas, "Potential Solutions for Discrimination in STEM.".

128 Davies et al., "Promoting Inclusive Metrics of Success and Impact to Dismantle a Discriminatory Reward System in Science."

129 Heriot and Schwarzchild, *A Dubious Expediency;* Krauss, "The New Scientific Method: Identity Politics"; McNutt and Castilllo-Page, "Promoting Diversity and Inclusion in STEMM Starts at the Top"; and "A Framework for Action in Scientific Publishing," Royal Society of Chemistry.

130 Coyne, "When Commitment to Diversity Outweighs Teaching and Research in a Biology Job"; Poff, "UC Santa Cruz Prescreens Faculty Job Applications Based on Mandatory Diversity Statements"; and Leiter, "Diversity Statements Are Still in Legal Peril."

131 "A Framework for Action in Scientific Publishing," Royal Society of Chemistry.

132 Krauss, "The New Scientific Method: Identity Politics"; McNutt and Castilllo-Page, "Promoting Diversity and Inclusion in STEMM Starts at the Top."

133 McNutt and Castilllo-Page, "Promoting Diversity and Inclusion in STEMM Starts at the Top."

134 Krauss, "The New Scientific Method: Identity Politics."

135 McWhorter, *Woke Racism*.

136 C.T. Laurencin and M. Murray, "An American Crisis: The Lack of Black Men in Medicine," *J. Racial and Ethn. Health Disparities* 4: 317–21 (2017), https://link.springer.com/article/10.1007/s40615-017-0380-y.

137 Heriot and Schwarzchild, *A Dubious Expediency.*

138 Laurencin and Murray, "An American Crisis: The Lack of Black Men in Medicine."

139 Heriot and Schwarzchild, *A Dubious Expediency.*

140 Heriot and Schwarzchild, *A Dubious Expediency*.

141 Heriot and Schwarzchild, *A Dubious Expediency.*

142 Mac Donald, "The NIH's Diversity Obsession Subverts Science"; Cho, "At DOE, Efforts to Address Climate and Diversity Dovetail"; "Promoting Inclusive and Equitable Research (PIER) Plans," Department of Energy Office of Science (2022); Higgins, "Minority Professor Denied Grants Because He Hires on Merit: 'People are Afraid to Think'"; Thompson, "The University's New Loyalty Oath"; Coyne, "When Commitment to Diversity Outweighs Teaching and Research in a Biology Job"; "Life Science Jobs at Berkeley Give Precedence to Candidates' Diversity and Inclusion Statements"; A Thread about University DEI Statements, Why Evolution Is True; Poff, "UC Santa Cruz Prescreens Faculty Job Applications Based on Mandatory Diversity Statements"; Flaherty, "The DEI Pathway to Promotion"; Flaherty, "Where DEI Work Is Faculty Work"; Wente, "At Canadian Universities, Race and Gender Quotas Have Become a Way of Life"; Leiter, *Diversity Statements Are Still in Legal Peril*; Heriot and Schwarzchild, *A Dubious Expediency*; Riley, A Chance to Remove Race from College Admissions; Krauss, "The New Scientific Method: Identity Politics"; Kaiser, "NIH Apologizes for 'Structural Racism,' Pledges Change"; Mervis, "Fix the System, not the Students"; Confronting Racism in Chemistry Journals"; "Tackling Systemic Racism Requires the System of Science to Change"; Davies et al., Promoting Inclusive Metrics of Success and Impact to Dismantle a Discriminatory Reward System in Science"; Diele-Viegas, "Potential Solutions for Discrimination in STEM; McNutt and Castilllo-Page, "Promoting Diversity and Inclusion in STEMM Starts at the Top"; "A Framework for Action in Scientific Publishing, Royal Society of Chemistry; Nogrady, "Game-Changing Gender Quotas Introduced by Australian Research Agency"; Mott and Cockayne, "Citation Matters: Mobilizing the Politics of Citation Toward a Practice of 'Conscientious Engagement'"; Zurn, Teich, Simon, Kim, and Bassett, "Supporting Academic Equity in Physics through Citation Diversity"; Dworkin, Linn, Teich, Zurn, Shinohara, and Bassett, "The Extent and Drivers of Gender Imbalance in Neuroscience Reference Lists; Zurn, Bassett, and Rust, "The Citation Diversity Statement: A Practice of Transparency, A Way of Life"; Else and Perkel, "The Giant Plan to Track Diversity in Research Journals"; Stewart-Williams and Halsey, "Men, Women and STEM: Why the Differences and What Should Be Done?"; The A4BL Antiracist Tenure Letter Working Group, "Equity, Diversity and Inclusion; "Rubric for Assessing Candidate Contributions to Diversity, Equity, Inclusion, and Belonging," UC Berkeley; *Working Toward Racial and Social Equity: Research and Commentary*, Elsevier (2020), https://www.elsevier.com/connect; Sweet, *The*

Inclusion and Diversity Statement – One Year On.

143 "A Framework for Action in Scientific Publishing," Royal Society of Chemistry.

144 L. Wang and A. Widener, The Struggle to Keep Women in Academia, CE&N 97 (2019), https://cen.acs.org/careers/diversity/struggle-keep-women-academia/97/i19.

145 B. Nogrady, "Game-Changing Gender Quotas Introduced by Australian Research Agency."

146 Valenzuela-Toro and Viglino, "How Latin American Researchers Suffer in Science."

147 Mott and Cockayne, "Citation Matters: Mobilizing the Politics of Citation Toward a Practice of Conscientious Engagement"; Zurn, Teich, Simon, Kim, and Bassett, "Supporting Academic Equity in Physics through Citation Diversity; Dworkin, Linn, Teich, Zurn, Shinohara, and Bassett, "The Extent and Drivers of Gender Imbalance in Neuroscience Reference Lists"; Zurn, Bassett, and Rust, "The Citation Diversity Statement: A Practice of Transparency, A Way of Life."

148 A Gender Citation Balance Indexer Online Tools, https://postlab.psych.wisc.edu/gcbialyzer; Citation Transparency Chrome Extension.

149 *Working Toward Racial and Social Equity: Research and Commentary,* Elsevier.

150 Else and Perkel, "The Giant Plan to Track Diversity in Research Journals"; Sweet, *The Inclusion and Diversity Statement – One Year On.*

151 See original article for citation.

152 A. E. Day, P. Corbett, and J. Boyle, "Is there a Gender Gap in Chemical Sciences Scholarly Communication?" *Chem. Sci.* 11: 2277–301 (2020), https://postlab.psych.wisc.edu/gcbialyzer. See references 3–16 citing similar studies carried by Elsevier, Nature Publishing, Institute of Physics, Functional Ecology, and American Geophysical Union.

153 "A Framework for Action in Scientific Publishing," Royal Society of Chemistry.

154 Shen, "Inequality Quantified: Mind the Gender Gap."

155 Ceci, Kahn, and Williams, "Stewart Williams and Halsey Argue Persuasively that Gender Bias Is Just One of Many Causes of Women's Underrepresentation in Science."

156 Stewart-Williams and Halsey, "Men, Women and STEM: Why the Differences and What Should Be Done?"

157 U. Schimmack, "Invalid Claims About the Validity of Implicit Association Tests by Prisoners of the Implicit Social Cognition–Paradigm," *Perspect. Psychol. Sci.* 16: 435–42 (2021), https://journals.sagepub.com/doi/full/10.1177/1745691621991860.

158 E.L. Paluck, R. Porat, C.S. Clark, and D.P. Green, "Prejudice Reduction: Progress and Challenges," *Ann. Rev. Psych.* 72: 533–60 (2021), https://www.annualreviews.org/content/journals/10.1146/annurev-psych-071620-030619.

159 Thompson, "The University's New Loyalty Oath"; Coyne, "When Commitment to Diversity Outweighs Teaching and Research in a Biology Job"; "Life Science Jobs at Berkeley Give Precedence to Candidates' Diversity and Inclusion Statements"; "A

Thread about University DEI Statements," Why Evolution Is True; Poff, "UC Santa Cruz Prescreens Faculty Job Applications Based on Mandatory Diversity Statements"; and B. Leiter, "Diversity Statements Are Still in Legal Peril."

160 Coyne, "When Commitment to Diversity Outweighs Teaching and Research in a Biology Job"; "Life Science Jobs at Berkeley Give Precedence to Candidates' Diversity and Inclusion Statements"; and "A Thread about University DEI Statements," Why Evolution Is True.

161 Jussim, Honeycutt, Paresky, Careem et al., *The Radicalization of the American Academy.*

162 "Rubric for Assessing Candidate Contributions to Diversity, Equity, Inclusion, and Belonging,"UC Berkeley.

163 McWhorter, "Here's a Fact: We're Routinely Asked to Use Leftist Fictions."

164 Flaherty, "The DEI Pathway to Promotion"; Flaherty, "Where DEI Work Is Faculty Work."

165 The A4BL Antiracist Tenure Letter Working Group, "Equity, Diversity and Inclusion."

166 Mac Donald, "The NIH's Diversity Obsession Subverts Science"; Cho, "At DOE, Efforts to Address Climate and Diversity Dovetail"; "Promoting Inclusive and Equitable Research (PIER) Plans," Department of Energy Office of Science; Higgins, "Minority Professor Denied Grants Because He Hires on Merit: 'People Are Afraid to Think,'" *National Post;* and McWhorter, "Here's a Fact: We're Routinely Asked to Use Leftist Fictions."

167 McWhorter, "Here's a Fact: We're Routinely Asked to Use Leftist Fictions."

168 "Gender Equality, Diversity, Inclusion Post-Corona: Quo Vadis?" Humboldt Foundation Conference; Luna, "The MPI Diversity & Inclusion Committee: Sparking Change"; "#ProgressDiversity: More Diversity for Science," Humboldt Kosmos; Alba Declaration on Equity and Inclusion; Gender Innovations 2, "How Inclusive Analysis Contributes to Research and Innovation"; and European Commission, "Priorities for 2021–2027."

169 European Commission, "Priorities for 2021–2027."

170 Alba Declaration on Equity and Inclusion.

171 Kahan, "Fixing the Communications Failure"; Kahan, "What Is the 'Science of Science Communication?'"

172 Horowitz, "Americans See Advantages and Challenges in Country's Growing Racial and Ethnic Diversity"; Graf, "Most Americans Say Colleges Should Not Consider Race or Ethnicity in Admissions."

173 Press release by the Royal Swedish Academy of Sciences; the Sveriges Riksbank Prize in Economic Sciences in Memory of Alfred Nobel 2019 was awarded to Abhijit Banerjee, Esther Duflo, and Michael Kremer "for their experimental approach to alleviating global poverty."

174 J. Heckman, G. Karpakula, "Intergenerational and Intragenerational Externalities of the Perry Preschool Project," NBER Working Paper No. 25889, JEL No. C4, 121

(2019).

175 J. Kleinberg, J. Ludwig, S. Millainathan, and C. Sunstein, "Algorithms as Discrimination Detectors," *PNAS* 117: 30096–100 (2020), https://www.pnas.org/doi/full/10.1073/pnas.1912790117.

176 J. Zhang and E. Bareinboim, "Fairness in Decision-Making—The Causal Explanation Formula," Proceedings of the 32nd AAAI Conference on Artificial Intelligence (2018), https://causalai.net/r30.pdf.

177 The Fifth Annual ACM FAccT Conference on Fairness, Accountability, and Transparency (ACM FAccT), https://causalai.net/r30.pdf.

178 L. Jussim, *Social Perception and Social Reality: Why Accuracy Dominates Bias and Self-Fulfilling Prophecy*, Oxford: Oxford University Press (2019).

179 R. Rubinstein, L. Jussim, and S. Stevens, "Reliance on Individuating Information and Stereotypes in Implicit and Explicit Person Perception," J. Exp. Soc. Psych. 75: 54–70 (2018), https://causalai.net/r30.pdf.

180 Kuncel and Hezlett, "Standardized Tests Predict Graduate Students' Success."

181 "Q&A: Stuart Schmill on MIT's decision to reinstate the SAT/ACT requirement."

182 Kalven Committee: Report on the University's Role in Political and Social Action.

183 We first approached a prominent interdisciplinary science journal with our manuscript, which we thought would be an appropriate venue for our commentary because it had published several perspectives on the topic from the CSJ point of view. We were given approval to submit our manuscript as a perspective but advised to remove the word "merit" from the title by the editorial board, who wrote, "Most readers will immediately associate the term 'merit' with the ongoing . . . debate about merit in college admissions, and the whole concept of meritocracy in education. The problem is that this concept of merit, as the authors surely know, has been widely *and legitimately* attacked as hollow. . . . If the authors could use a different term, I would encourage that [emphasis ours]." Thus, not only is meritocracy in science a controversial idea, in some circles the very existence of merit as a concept is questioned. So it appeared right from the start that publishing our manuscript was going to be an uphill battle. Indeed, our paper was reviewed and rejected largely on ideological grounds, citing, among other reasons, its "hurtfulness." We then approached several other scientific journals with informal inquiries about the suitability of the manuscript for publication and the outcome was not encouraging. Therefore, the paper was submitted to the *Journal of Controversial Ideas*, where we believe it will add balance to viewpoints appearing in academic journals on this important topic.

184 OSTP, White House, "Equity and Excellence: A Vision to Transform and Enhance the U.S. STEMM Ecosystem," (2022), https://www.whitehouse.gov/ostp/news-updates/2022/12/12/equity-and-excellence-a-vision-to-transform-and-enhance-the-u-s-stemm-ecosystem/.

185 National Academies of Sciences, Engineering, and Medicine, "Advancing Antiracism, Diversity, Equity, and Inclusion in STEMM Organizations."

Chapter 44

1 This is an edited transcript of a conversation that happened on *The Utterly Moderate Podcast* on April 5, 2021. Adapted here with permission. See ConnorsForum.org for more information about this episode.

2 Yevgeny Simkin, "Social Media Is the Problem," *The Bulwark*, July 31, 2020, https://www.thebulwark.com/social-media-is-the-problem/.

Chapter 45

1 Originally published by *Skeptic Magazine* and adapted here with permission: Kevin McCaffree, "When Secularism: Becomes a Religion: The Alt-Left, the Alt-Right, and Moral Righteousness," *Skeptic Magazine*, Fall 2017, https://go.gale.com/ps/i.do?id=GALE%7CA520714005&sid=googleScholar&v=2.1&it=r&linkaccess=abs&issn=10639330&p=AONE&sw=w&userGroupName=anon%7E-2beb6548. Note: This book is intended for a general audience and thus throughout we have tried to minimize footnotes in some chapters for purposes of readability—for the full set of footnotes/citations/hyperlinks for each chapter, see the original source.

2 Lydia Saad, "TV Is Americans' Main Source of News," *Gallup*, July 8, 2013, http://bit.ly/1mLnRMl.

3 "Firing Line with William F. Buckley Jr.: Mobilizing the Poor," YouTube, January 25, 2017, http://bit.ly/2uA5wht.

4 "The Dark Enlightenment, by Nick Land," The Dark Enlightenment, December 25, 2012, http://bit.ly/1d405tG.

5 S. Pinker, *The Better Angels of Our Nature: Why Violence Has Declined* (New York: Viking, 2011); M. Shermer, *The Moral Arc: How Science and Reason Lead Humanity Toward Truth, Justice, and Freedom* (New York: Henry Holt, 2015).

6 F. Rothbaum, J.R. Weisz, and S.S. Snyder, "Changing the World and Changing the Self: A Two-Process Model of Perceived Control," *Journal of Personality and Social Psychology* 42 (1982): 5–37.

Chapter 46

1 This chapter based on remarks delivered by Asha Rangappa at the Connecticut Legal Conference in June 2019. Reprinted here with permission: Asha Rangappa, "Disinformation, Democracy, and the Rule of Law," Luncheon Keynote Address, Connecticut Legal Conference, June 10, 2019, https://www.ctbar.org/docs/default-source/connecticut-legal-conferences/2019-connecticut-legal-conference/asha-rangappa-keynote-address.pdf?sfvrsn=3c35d354_2. Note: This book is intended for a general audience and thus throughout we have tried to minimize footnotes in some chapters for purposes of readability—for the full set of footnotes/citations/hyperlinks for each chapter, see the original source.

2 Awakening 3648, "Yuri Bezmanov Explains the Communist 'Smart War' 'ACTIVE

MEASURES,'" YouTube, https://www.youtube.com/watch?v=YM2YqYGUPTc.

3 Tomas D. Schuman, "Love Letter to America," https://www.economicsvoodoo.com/wp-content/uploads/Yuri-Bezmenov-Love-Letter-To-America.pdf.

4 House of Representatives Permanent Select Committee on Intelligence, "Soviet Active Measures," July 13, 1982, https://play.google.com/books/reader?id=yWDHh-vlvNZoC&pg=GBS.PA12&printsec=frontcover&output=reader&hl=en.

5 House of Representatives Permanent Select Committee on Intelligence, "Soviet Active Measures."

6 Molly K. McKew, "How Twitter Bots and Trump Fans Made #ReleaseTheMemo Go Viral," Politico, February 4, 2018, https://www.politico.com/magazine/story/2018/02/04/trump-twitter-russians-release-the-memo-216935.

7 Robert Putnam, *Bowling Alone: The Collapse and Revival of American Community* (New York: Simon and Schuster, 2000).

8 Putnam, *Bowling Alone*, 136–37.

9 Putnam, *Bowling Alone*, 22–24. .

10 Putnam, *Bowling Alone*, 23, 358. See also Sabina Panth, "Bonding vs. Bridging," World Bank, June 2, 2010, https://blogs.worldbank.org/publicsphere/bonding-and-bridging.

11 Chris Cillizza, "Watch Americans' Trust in Each Other Erode Over the Last Four Decades," *Washington Post*, May 31, 2014, https://www.washingtonpost.com/news/the-fix/wp/2014/05/31/watch-americans-trust-in-each-other-erodeover-the-last-three-decades/.

12 Jon Keegan, "Blue Feed, Red Feed: See Liberal Facebook and Conservative Facebook, Side by Side," *Wall Street Journal*, May 18, 2016, http://graphics.wsj.com/blue-feed-red-feed/.

13 Jason Mander, "Daily Time Spent on Social Networks Rises to Over 2 Hours," Global Web Index, May 16, 2017, https://blog.globalwebindex.com/chart-of-the-day/daily-time-spent-on-social-networks/.

14 Austin Sarat, "Americans Aren't as Attached to Democracy as You Might Think," *The Guardian*, February 11, 2017, https://www.theguardian.com/commentisfree/2017/feb/11/americans-arent-attached-democracy-rule-law.

15 Roberto Stephan Foa and Yascha Mounk, "The Democratic Disconnect," *Journal of Democracy* 27, no. 3 (July 2016): 7–8.

16 Amanda Taub, "How Stable Are Democracies? 'Warning Signs Are Flashing Red,'" *New York Times*, November 29, 2016, https://www.nytimes.com/2016/11/29/world/americas/western-liberal-democracy.html.

17 Putnam, *Bowling Alone*, 338.

18 Sarah Shapiro and Catherine Brown, "The State of Civics Education," Center for American Progress, February 21, 2018, https://www.americanprogress.org/issues/education-k-12/reports/2018/02/21/446857/state-civics-education/.

19 Mark Sherman, "Roberts, Trump Spar in Extraordinary Scrap Over Judges," As-

sociated Press, November 21, 2018, https://www.apnews.com/c4b34f9639e141069c-08cf1e3deb6b84.

20 D.J. Flynn, Brendan Nyhan, and Jason Reifler, "The Nature and Origins of Misperceptions: Understanding False and Unsupported Beliefs About Politics," *Advances in Political Psychology* 38, no. 51 (February 2017): 127, 137.

Chapter 47

1 Originally published by *Issues in Science and Technology* and adapted here with permission: Claire Wardle, "Misunderstanding Misinformation," *Issues in Science and Technology* 39, no. 3 (Spring 2023): 38–40. Note: This book is intended for a general audience and thus throughout we have tried to minimize footnotes in some chapters for purposes of readability—for the full set of footnotes/citations/hyperlinks for each chapter, see the original source.

2 Alice E. Marwick, "Why Do People Share Fake News? A Sociotechnical Model of Media Effects," *The Georgetown Law Technology Review* 2, no. 2 (Spring 2018), https://go.gale.com/ps/i.do?p=AONE&sw=w&issn=&v=2.1&it=r&id=GALE%7CA560926928&sid=-googleScholar&linkaccess=abs&userGroupName=anon%7Eb24d1f88.

Chapter 48

1 Lee McIntyre, *Post-Truth* (Cambridge, MA: MIT Press, 2018).

Chapter 49

1 Jacob L. Mackey, *Belief and Cult* (Princeton, NJ: Princeton University Press, 2022).)

2 What follows is drawn from Michael Lusztig, *The Culturalist Challenge to Liberal Republicanism* (Montreal: McGill-Queens University Press, 2017).

3 Ralph Ellison, "The Little Man at Chehaw Station: The American Artist and His Audience," *The American Scholar* 47, no. 1 (1978).

4 Jessica Taylor, "Is Hillary Clinton Trying to Question the Legitimacy of Donald Trump Winning?" NPR, December 12, 2016, https://www.npr.org/2016/12/12/505286051/is-hillary-clinton-trying-to-question-the-legitimacy-of-donald-trump-winning; Colby Itkowitz, "Hillary Clinton: Trump Is an 'Illegitimate President,'" *Washington Post*, September 26, 2019, https://www.washingtonpost.com/politics/hillary-clinton-trump-is-an-illegitimate-president/2019/09/26/29195d5a-e099-11e9-b199-f638bf2c340f_story.html.

5 Alexandra King, "Electoral College Voter: I'm Getting Death Threats," CNN, November 30, 2016, https://www.cnn.com/2016/11/30/politics/banerian-death-threats-cnntv/index.html; Fox News, "Arizona's Presidential Electors Being Harassed, Urged Not to Cast Vote for Trump," November 18, 2016, https://www.foxnews.com/politics/arizonas-presidential-electors-being-harassed-urged-not-to-cast-vote-for-trump; and Valerie Richardson, "GOP Electors Harassed, Threatened as Foes Maneuver to Block

Donald Trump in Electoral College," *Washington Times*, November 22, 2016, https://www.washingtontimes.com/news/2016/nov/22/gop-electors-harassed-threatened-foes-maneuver-blo/..

6 Lawrence Lessig, "The Constitution Lets the Electoral College Choose the Winner. They Should Choose Clinton," *Washington Post*, November 24, 2016, https://www.washingtonpost.com/opinions/the-constitution-lets-the-electoral-college-choose-the-winner-they-should-choose-clinton/2016/11/24/0f431828-b0f7-11e6-8616-52b15787add0_story.html.

7 Kathleen Parker, "The Electoral College Should Be Unfaithful," *Washington Post*, December 6, 2016, https://www.washingtonpost.com/opinions/the-electoral-college-should-be-unfaithful/2016/12/06/360f8f2c-bbfb-11e6-ac85-094a21c44abc_story.html.

8 David Pozen, "Why G.O.P. Electoral College Members Can Vote Against Trump," *New York Times*, December 16, 2016, https://www.nytimes.com/2016/12/15/opinion/why-gop-electoral-college-members-can-vote-against-trump.html.

9 Christopher Suprun, "Why I Will Not Cast My Electoral Vote for Donald Trump," *New York Times*, December 5, 2016, https://www.nytimes.com/2016/12/05/opinion/why-i-will-not-cast-my-electoral-vote-for-donald-trump.html.

10 Jonathan Haidt, "Why the Past 10 Years of American Life Have Been Uniquely Stupid," *The Atlantic*, April 11, 2022, https://www.theatlantic.com/magazine/archive/2022/05/social-media-democracy-trust-babel/629369/.

Chapter 50

1 Originally published by the *Connors Newsletter* and adapted here with permission: Lawrence M. Eppard, "The Poisoning of the American Mind," *Connors Newsletter*, June 15, 2023, https://connorsforum.substack.com/p/the-poisoning-of-the-american-mind.

2 Jonathan Rauch, "The Constitution of Knowledge," *National Affairs*, Fall 2018, https://www.nationalaffairs.com/publications/detail/the-constitution-of-knowledge.

3 Michael Jindra and Arthur Sakamoto, "When Ideology Drives Social Science: Statistical Malfeasance and Cherry-Picking Are Rife," *The Chronicle of Higher Education*, March 6, 2023, https://www.chronicle.com/article/when-ideology-drives-social-science.

4 Ramesh Ponnuru, "How to Restore Intellectual Diversity on College Campuses," *Washington Post*, February 27, 2023, https://www.washingtonpost.com/opinions/2023/02/27/nurturing-conservative-ideas-on-campus/.

5 Adapted from Ian M. Mackay, "The Swiss Cheese Infographic That Went Viral," *Virology Down Under*, December 26, 2020, https://virologydownunder.com/the-swiss-cheese-infographic-that-went-viral/.

6 These suggestions are based on the work of many scholars, including Ali Dagnes, Michael A. Deas, Adam Grant, Tom Nichols, Lee McIntyre, Jonathan Rauch, Jonathan Haidt, Steven Sloman, Philip Fernbach, and Bruce Bartlett, among others.

7 "It is the hallmark of science that beliefs should be based on evidence, and that people

should be willing to change their beliefs based on new evidence. This means that people should be able to specify in advance what evidence, if it existed, would be sufficient to get them to change their minds." See Lee McIntyre, "5 Ways Trump and His Supporters Are Using the Same Strategies as Science Deniers," *The Conversation*, November 27, 2019, https://theconversation.com/5-ways-trump-and-his-supporters-are-using-the-same-strategies-as-science-deniers-127076.

8 Jonathan Rauch, *The Constitution of Knowledge: A Defense of Truth* (Washington, D.C.: Brookings Institution Press, 2021), 198.

9 Adam Grant, *Think Again: The Power of Knowing What You Don't Know* (New York: Viking, 2021), 63.

10 William Saletan, "Lies Are the Building Blocks of Trumpian Authoritarianism," *The Bulwark*, February 7, 2020, https://www.thebulwark.com/lies-are-the-building-blocks-of-trumpian-authoritarianism/.

11 William Saletan, "Don't Call the Brazil Insurrection 'Anti-Democratic,'" *The Bulwark*, January 12, 2023, https://www.thebulwark.com/dont-call-the-brazil-insurrection-anti-democratic/.

12 Jonathan Haidt, "Why the Past 10 Years of American Life Have Been Uniquely Stupid," *The Atlantic*, April 11, 2022, https://www.theatlantic.com/magazine/archive/2022/05/social-media-democracy-trust-babel/629369/.

13 Yochai Benkler, Robert Faris, Hal Roberts, and Ethan Zuckerman, "Study: Breitbart-Led Right-Wing Media Ecosystem Altered Broader Media Agenda," *Columbia Journalism Review*, March 3, 2017, https://www.cjr.org/analysis/breitbart-media-trump-harvard-study.php.

14 Stephen Levitsky and Daniel Ziblatt, *How Democracies Die* (New York: Broadway Books, 2018), 5.

15 Sean Illing, "Post-truth Is Pre-fascism": A Holocaust Historian on the Trump Era," *Vox*, March 8, 2017, https://www.vox.com/conversations/2017/3/9/14838088/donald-trump-fascism-europe-history-totalitarianism-post-truth.

16 Tom Nichols, *Our Own Worst Enemy: The Assault from Within on Modern Democracy* (New York: Oxford University Press, 2021), xxiii.

17 Nichols, *Our Own Worst Enemy*, 19. He goes on to argue: "The threat to democracy now in America and elsewhere comes from the working and middle classes...whose rage come overwhelmingly from cultural insecurity, inflated expectations, tribal partisan alliances, obsessions about ethnicity and identity, blunted ambition, and a childlike understanding of the limits of government" (21).